Corporate planning
Selected concepts

Corporate planning
Selected concepts

Editor: **Basil W. Denning** *(comp.)*
Senior Consultant,
Harbridge House, Europe

McGRAW-HILL · LONDON

New York · St Louis · San Francisco · Dusseldorf · Johannesburg
Kuala Lumpur · Mexico · Montreal · New Delhi · Panama · Rio de Janeiro
Singapore · Sydney · Toronto

658.4
D 41/

Published by

McGRAW-HILL Book Company (UK) Limited

MAIDENHEAD · BERKSHIRE · ENGLAND

07 094230 7

PRINTED AND BOUND IN GREAT BRITAIN

Preface

Any writer or editor of another book on the currently popular theme of corporate or long-range planning has some obligation to explain why he should feel justified in adding to this growing volume of literature. As one who has taught in this field for seven years; has been involved in strategy formulation in three companies, two educational institutions, and one London club; has been actively involved in the movement to encourage a greater degree of corporate planning in the United Kingdom through the Society for Long-Range Planning; and, more recently, has researched in the area, I have become increasingly concerned at various problem areas in the literature.

These seem to me to be fivefold. The first problem centres round confusion in definition arising partly from semantic differences and partly from unstated assumptions. The most obvious of these confusions stems from the failure to distinguish between the value of plans and the value of planning; and the most obvious mistaken assumption stems from the proposition that the sole important output of planning is a plan or set of plans. This assumption leads some to concentrate attention on the technical aspects of planning particular activities, and ignores the fact that planning any important activity in any real organization is as much a political activity between individuals and groups acting as centres of power as a technical activity. One finds, therefore, that many of the articulate protagonists of more and better planning assume that the major value will be a better technical solution to a measurable problem. Yet the practitioner of planning, whether in industry, government, or education, will usually argue that the process of planning in itself provides the major value, since the uncertainty of any plan over a period of time greater than one year must inevitably lead to scepticism about the plan itself. A corporate planner of distinction in a highly successful company has underlined this in a comment that 'the one thing of which I can be absolutely certain when I have obtained final approval of the company's five year plan is that that won't happen'.

A second confusion centres round the extent to which corporate planning, strategic planning, strategic formulation, long-range planning, top management planning, and several other terms, are used, interchangeably, with little distinction of meaning. In particular, with the almost synonymous use of long-range planning and corporate planning, there arises a frequent assumption that the essence of defining different types of planning lies in the time dimension. Such a view, in my opinion, ignores far more relevant factors in distinctive types of planning, and sometimes creates an unnecessary attitudinal barrier to more systematic planning by allowing resistance to focus on the single parameter of time rather than on the genuine differences of concept. This confusion, in my experience, tends to create barriers between many thoughtful writers and many enthusiastic but more hard-pressed practitioners.

A third difficulty arises from the natural and proper desire of the theorists to reach a level of generality that embraces effective concepts for all forms of organization, large and small, domestic and international, private and public. Such a level of generality certainly exists. But to many executives, contemplating or practising planning and faced with specific problems, the gulf between their problems and the written level of generality leads, and not always inappropriately, to the dismissal of the valuable elements of the general approach as too theoretical and academic, the latter term being used in its presentday connotation of irrelevance, rather than its historical meaning of high intellectual character. Rejection of a general approach can lead too swiftly into the mere exchange of experience, an exercise frequently of limited value unless the relevance of the conditions surrounding the experience are clearly understood.

Fourth, it is a truism that no organization can or does exist without planning. Strategies have been developed, projects have been planned and executed, operations have been worked out in detail, tactics have been employed in all human organizations since the first hunting expedition of primeval man. It is not unreasonable, therefore, to counter the enthusiasm of the would-be planner with the comment that 'this is what we do anyway'.

The problem of negativism to which this gives rise can usually be traced back to an excess of jargon by the protagonist and a lack of understanding by the protester about the important current developments. The more important developments in the present enthusiasm for corporate planning are centred on the creation of more systematic managerial processes; the use of improved analytical concepts and techniques to improve the quality of planning; and the coordination of the work of existing planning centres. All these developments are designed to help the top management of an institution to concentrate on its special task of managing the whole, rather than to consume its time in the overseeing of the planning and execution of the parts.

A more appropriate argument, in my view, is that effective corporate planning leads towards the better organization of more fully studied and analysed alternatives into a framework which is more mutually consistent than is likely to be achieved by chance, by natural growth in response to short-term opportunities or problems, or by the natural proclivities of individuals.

Finally, there are several interweaving factors, many of them based on the fear which arises from ignorance or a lack of understanding, which give rise to false expectations about corporate planning. These expectations range on a spectrum from an unjustified optimism that by introducing a new 'management technique' with one or more highly skilled and experienced planners the task of top management will miraculously become simplified, to a pessimistic reluctance about any more planners on the grounds that top management will somehow be deprived of freedom of action if sophisticated planners are introduced. Such false expectations must lead to disappointment or rejection, since the first is incapable of fulfilment and, given the second, any moves towards better planning are likely to be strangled at birth.

Against this background, then, what contribution can another book on corporate planning make? It will probably be clear that my aim is to help the practitioner by providing in a form which is moderately readable, some elements of the theory, but with emphasis on application. Hopefully, the book will be useful to managers of many different kinds of enterprise, and, by drawing on a collection of theoretical and practical writings, help them to develop a needed bridge between theory and practice.

To this end, the book is structured to offer first a broad introduction to the subject. The first part raises critical problems of definition and role and deliberately attempts to place a planning system in an explicit political framework. While some effort will be needed to translate the political model in the article into terms suitable for a private business, there are clear parallels, and the nature of the model may be helpful to planners across a broader spectrum of institutions.

The second part concentrates on the strategic appraisal and formulation area, with some practical articles of the 'How to' variety. It is followed by three articles on critical and, at times, neglected functional areas of planning, with a further article which discusses a technique which seems to require appreciation on a broader basis.

In the fourth part, some of the considerations relating to the organization of the corporate planning funtion are covered in a general and a practical way with a method of approach outlined.

The final two parts of the book are primarily designed to explore some of the different critical aspects of planning in quite different types of business. To refer again to the gulf arising between the general theory applicable to all organizations and the different needs of individual companies, it is hoped that the fifth part, with concentration on different key requirements in different types of company, including family owned companies, may be helpful to the existing or would-be practitioner. Finally, three case studies of quite different types of company in different businesses with different needs and different organizations, are offered as a set of practical examples of planning systems which have been evolved by managements to meet their individual needs.

On at least one point the indulgence of the reader must explicitly be sought. Each of the selected articles was initially written to stand alone in a journal. Inevitably, therefore, each article has its own introduction rather than continuing in immediate sequence from the previous chapter. This problem seems endemic in a book of this nature, since it is impractical, and would be improper as editor, to make the necessary changes to these self-contained pieces of work.

One emphasis must be made explicit. The concept of corporate planning is of a set of intellectual activities which, when taken together, comprise a managerial system. The introduction of improved systems will not improve an existing situation unless they lead to better, more informed decisions by men capable of executing them. The requirements for effective management have always called, and, in my view, always will call, for imagination, creativity, courage, and a high level of interpersonal skill. The merit of any corporate planning system should be judged by the extent to which it contributes to the effective liberation of these qualities at many levels in the organization. No system can be effective with inadequate people, but an intelligently designed system to meet specific managerial needs can augment the capacity of an organization by multiplying the effectiveness of a high-quality executive group, and thus increase the probability of wise decisions being reached and effectively implemented. If this book makes some small contribution to the needs of those faced with the difficult responsibilities of presentday management in our rapidly changing world, it will have achieved its modest objectives.

The recognition of specific intellectual debts in a diverse field is clearly enormous, and I see no way of selecting any one person or group for special mention. I am, however, very grateful to the authors of the individual articles who have allowed their contributions to be reproduced and to the editors of the journals concerned for their encouragement of the project. Finally, I am deeply indebted to the library of the London Business School, especially Mrs Claire Hansford, whose diligent searching over a very diverse field of literature gives me some confidence that the articles chosen represent a quality sample of the total literature on the subject.

Basil W. Denning

Contents

Preface

Biographies

The contributors

Robert G. Murdick
Professor of Management, State University of New York at Albany.

William H. Newman
Samuel Bronfman Professor of Democratic Business Enterprise at the Graduate School of Business, Columbia University.

David Novick
Head of the Cost Analysis Department of the RAND Corporation, California.

L. B. Pinnell
Group Planning Co-ordinator of Pilkington Brothers Limited, Lancashire, UK.

Millard H. Pryor Jnr
Director of Corporate Planning for the Singer Company, having formerly administered Singer's acquisition programme.

Melvin E. Salveson
With the Center for Advanced Management Inc, Connecticut, USA.

Walter B. Schaffir
Director of Corporate Planning, Continental Copper and Steel Industries, New York City.

W. W. Simmons
Director of Planning Systems, IBM New York.

Donald J. Smalter
Director of Planning, International Minerals and Chemical Corporation, Illinois, U.S.A.

George A. Steiner
Professor of Management and Public Policy, and Director of the Division of Research, in the Graduate School of Business, University of California, Los Angeles.

Charles E. Summer Jnr
Professor in the Graduate School of Business at the University of Washington, Seattle.

Seymour Tilles
Officer of The Boston Consulting Group, which is active in the area of corporate strategy.

Norman Berg
Assistant Professor of Business Administration, Harvard Business School.

Marvin J. Cetron
Head of the Technological Forecasting Group, US Navy Material Command.

Arthur P. Contas
President, Kane Financial Corporation, Boston, Massachusetts.

B. W. Denning
Editor of this volume, a Senior Consultant with Harbridge House, Europe.

Donald N. Dick
Member of the Advanced Planning Staff, US Navy Ordnance Laboratory

John Friedmann
Professor of Planning and Head, Urban Planning Program, School of Architecture and Urban Planning, University of California at Los Angeles.

William F. Glueck
Associate Professor of Management and Faculty Research Associate in Research Center, School of Business and Public Administration and Faculty Research Associate, Space Services Research Center, University of Missouri-Columbia.

C. P. Johnston
With Air Canada at their Head Office at Montreal, engaged in manpower planning and personnel research.

William G. Livingstone
Director of Program Evaluation, the Chemstrand Corporation, New York City.

Arthur W. Lucas
Vice president-finance, The Chemstrand Corporation, New York City.

H. A. Meredith
With P. S. Ross and Partners, carries out a wide variety of organization and personnel studies.

Henry Mintzberg
Associate Professor in the Faculty of Management at McGill University, Montreal.

1. Introduction

Basil W. Denning

Definitions

The late Professor C. E. M. Joad is famous on many counts, but it is probable
that he is most widely known among British people over the age of 45 for his
appearance in a regular series of radio programmes entitled. 'The Brains Trust'
which were a broadcasting feature during the Second World War. The reason
for this particular brand of fame centred not only on his entertaining replies
to a wide range of questions from listeners all over the country, but from his
almost inevitable triggering of a highly stimulating discussion with the
question 'it all depends on what you mean by . . .'.

Increasingly, my sympathies are with Professor Joad; and increasingly I
find that the major problems of beginning a discussion of corporate planning,
long-range planning, comprehensive planning, strategic planning, or any other
of the names ascribed to the activity, is to determine, 'What do you mean by
corporate planning?' Some give the term a specific connotation, the
determination of strategy; some consider it a process which extends and
enlarges the annual budgeting cycle; some consider it essentially a matter of
deciding 'what business you are in'; some consider that a major programme,
such as the conversion of the coal-based gas industry, represents a corporate
plan. Then, over and above the difficulty of definition of these terms, there
are classifications of planning, such as information planning, indicative
planning, and directive planning. And, finally, as if this were not enough,
there is a variety of individual words, objectives, strategy, purpose, aims,
targets, goals, policies, programmes, and even philosophies, all of which
appear in any comprehensive view of the literature.

Faced with this babel of semantic confusion, a good starting point for a
brief review of the essentials of corporate planning will be some definitions of
what is meant by various words. It probably matters less whether the reader
agrees with the definitions given than that he should understand—if only to

1

disagree with—what is being said, not on grounds of semantics, but on grounds of substance.*

I shall use the expression 'corporate planning' in the following sense: 'A formal, systematic, managerial process, organized by responsibility, time, and information, to ensure that operational planning, project planning, and strategic planning are carried out regularly to enable top management to direct and control the future of the enterprise.' This definition is of little value, however, unless the incorporated expressions concerning operational, project, and strategic planning are also defined.

In suggesting a definition of these three terms, I shall deliberately follow an order different from the majority of writing in this field which, in apparently logical fashion, starts with strategic planning. The reason for this reversal arises from close observation of the way in which corporate planning systems actually tend to develop in companies and the need, referred to later, for effective strategic planning to be based on a quantified forward view of the existing business and any developments to which commitments have been made. Thus, strategic planning is, in some ways, a step which follows the assessment of operational and project plans as well as giving rise to changes in operations and projects previously planned.

Operational planning—Despite the emphasis on change, it is still true for most corporations that what they will be doing in five years' time will contain a substantial element of their present activities. For example, there is every reason to believe that Shell will be extracting and transporting oil, refining it, and retailing it to large numbers of motorists in five years' time. Similarly, it seems probable that Marks and Spencer will be offering the majority of its present product range, but with differences in fashion, in most of its present locations, to most of its present customers in seven years' time. These continuing activities in fact form the operational heart of most businesses and have a substantial element of continuity, but are modified from time to time by strategic changes and new projects.

Thus, there is a continuing need for operational planning which is defined as 'the forward planning of existing operations in existing markets with existing customers and facilities'. It hardly seems necessary to offer examples of the need for operational planning which is so obviously a continuing feature of any organization's activity and a major preoccupation of middle management. Nevertheless, the timespan over which such planning can usefully be carried out depends on the nature of the business. For example, in the record business, with its need for quick response to changing taste,

* The reader is warned that, in the articles which follow, definitions made in this introduction will not necessarily be followed: other terms are sometimes employed by the different writers. This further demonstration of semantic confusion emphasizes the need for tighter definitions of different words in this area.

2

detailed operational planning for more than a year ahead is usually regarded as wasteful of management time and effort. On the other hand, in industries with a greater degree of stability, such as paper, it may be possible to develop effective detailed operational plans for five years or more.

Project planning—In addition to planned operations, any business will have, at any moment of time, a number of projects to which it is committed or on which appraisal has been started. A deliberately broad definition of project is intended and would include such diverse elements as a research and development project, the launching of a new product, the raising of a new debt issue, the entry into a new geographical market, the introduction of a new management accounting system, or the acquisition of a company. Some of these proposed actions may be closely related to the existing field of current operations; others may be designed to diversify out of existing operations.

Regardless of type, all projects require planning and control, and, thus, a useful definition of project planning is 'the generation and appraisal of, the commitment to, and the working out of the detailed execution of an action outside the scope of present operations, which is capable of separate analysis and control'.

Consider two different examples. With the discovery of natural gas in the North Sea, a strategic decision was taken by the Government to harness this new fuel resource over a timespan of about 15 years, and to provide the necessary finance to exploit this resource. This gave rise to an identifiable set of projects, the modification of users' equipment, the development of appropriate transmission lines, and the investment in plant to replace existing gas manufacturing installations throughout the country. To assist in finding an optimum programme for investment in manufacturing and transmission, the Gas Council developed a sophisticated model to deal with this identifiable problem. The action was capable of separate analysis, decision, and control, even though the phasing of the investment programme spanned 15 years.

In contrast, the Metal Box Company has steadily increased its manufacturing capacity at home and overseas over the last 30 years. A critical dimension of success in the supply of open top cans is the ability to meet rapidly varying demands from customers at very short notice. This factor in conjunction with the high costs of transporting empty cans leads to a highly diverse geographical pattern of comparatively small manufacturing units. The time between decision to erect a new plant and having the plant in operation is about two years. Nevertheless, the decision on each new factory is capable of separate analysis and the construction work is capable of separate control. Thus, each new factory represents a separate project.

These two contrasting situations have been chosen to illustrate different timespans over which project planning may be required, in the one case 15

3

years, in the other 3 years. But the nature of the planning task in these projects, assessment, analysis, decision, and progress control, has many common elements arising from the possibility and the need for separate analysis and control. The time dimension is of less importance than the nature of the task.

Strategic planning—Until recently, in many businesses, operational and project planning represented the sum of the planning activities. Both operations and projects were carried out in a framework of policy which was usually implicit rather than explicit. The advocates of systematic corporate planning base their case on the view that the determination of the future can be improved by a systematic, analytical approach which reviews the business as a whole in relation to its environment.

Thus 'strategic planning' is the determination of the future posture of the business with special reference to its product-market posture, its profitability, its size, its rate of innovation, and its relationships with its executives, its employees, and certain external institutions.

A classic example of the impact of a new strategy is the story of American Motors' struggle to survive after their creation from the merger of the Hudson Motor Car Company and the Nash, Kelvinator Corporation in 1954. At the time of the merger, the independent companies were showing severe declines in market share and were losing money. It seemed that the day of the independent was numbered and Nash and Hudson dealers were falling away rapidly. A short-term survival operation was launched involving cost-cutting, rationalization of models, and a deintegration of operations, in contrast to the increasing integration of operations in the big three, General Motors, Ford, and Chrysler.

Of greater importance, however, was the decision to find a particular niche in the market, a niche of consumer needs which were not being met by the big three. This involved commitment to a particular model of smaller size and different construction and a concentration of all resources on this new model. However, given the gestation time for a new model and the risk associated with it, the company had to take a number of interrelated steps to maintain the opportunity, particularly in terms of preserving dealer strength. The risk had to be mitigated by further deintegration of operations, reducing fixed costs and the breakeven point, and a special deal worked out with the labour force which introduced profit-sharing, but which gave much smaller increases in basic wages than the big three offered in their new contracts. Banks and insurance companies had to be nursed to maintain a high level of lending and the market had to be prepared by a prolonged campaign which drew attention to the absurdity of ever larger cars and ridiculed them by comparing them with dinosaurs. Leading cartoonists were even brought into the act with advertisements featuring, 'Siegfried slays the dragon'.

4

In brief, and vastly to over-compress a fascinating story, American Motors completely changed their product market posture, their financial and economic characteristics, their pattern of operation, their relationship with both labour force and with finance houses, by a deliberate series of steps aimed at creating an entirely different concept of the company. The success of the policy change can partly be measured by the conversion of losses of $30 million in 1956, and of $11 million in 1957, to a profit of $26 million in 1958 and $105 million in 1959. By 1961, the company had repaid all its debts.

A second example of similar significance would be the strategic response of three of the leading British clearing banks to the announcement of a merger between two of the Big Five, the National Provincial Bank and the Westminster Bank in January 1968. Two weeks later came a proposal by Barclays and Lloyds to merge and to incorporate Martins Bank thus creating the largest single bank in the country, the historical position of Barclays.

In practice, this move was frustrated by government intervention, but the implications of the proposal were clearly strategic in the desire to maintain a relative position in terms of size against a change in the power balance of the competition. The time between the announcement of the National Provincial/Westminster merger and the Barclays proposal was fourteen days. It is possible that this was a contingency plan carefully worked out well before the event which triggered its announcement. But on the published evidence it seems more probable that this major strategic move was devised and carried through at very high speed in response to a significant competitive move. The decision by Barclays, Lloyds, and Martins was clearly strategic in the sense that it involved the partial sacrifice of autonomy to maintain a dominant position in combination. The timespan of the effects would clearly be very long, but the timespan of the decision process was less than one month.

One reason for selecting these two examples of major strategic decisions is to underline the argument that strategic planning can vary greatly in nature in the timespan in which decisions are taken. In the one case, a carefully reasoned decision, arising from an analysis of environmental change, led to a strategic plan stretching over 10 years. In the other, a quick strategic decision, which cannot have allowed time for effective planning of the combined enterprise, was reached in a few weeks. The critical similarity in these situations centres on changing the concept of the institutions as a result of strategic decisions rather than the timespan over which the decisions were reached or the consequences were planned.

It is, however, important to note that a strategy can only be made a reality by undertaking projects or operations. Essentially, a strategy is a set of ideas about a desirable future and a broad pattern of attainment. A strategy is conceptual, rather than tangible. To achieve that future requires action, and, in business terms, this action will be expressed in projects or in operations.

5

From these definitions, one can begin to see broadly the way in which these three types of planning combine to include all the planning required in the business, other than contingency planning. A business at one moment of time is conducting operations and will have a variety of projects in various stages of completion. The sum of the plans of all operations and all projects at some point in the future will represent a strategic posture explicit or implicit, and will enable top management to see what the shape, size, profitability, etc., of the business are likely to be at that point in the future. This will probably raise questions as to whether this is a desirable future. If the answer is no, a desire for improvement can trigger off a strategic rethinking which will lead to the generation of new projects or more efficient operations, both of which will need to be planned. Thus, corporate planning made up of these three types of planning is of its essence an iterative, rather than a once and for all, process.

Critical distinctions in types of planning

It has been suggested that concentration on the time dimension as the critical element in planning is inadequate and not necessarily useful. If this is so then there is some obligation to suggest a classification of the types of planning listed in a way which does define their key characteristics in a more relevant way.

One method of identifying differences is by considering the types of planning along five different dimensions which can themselves be grouped into two broad classes, technical and non-technical. The two important technical areas of difference between these types of planning centre on

	Degree of uncertainty	Importance of value of judgements	Penalties for error
Strategic planning	Very high	Very high	Possible corporate death
Project planning	Ranges from high to low depending on project	High-medium	Loss of capital or opportunity
Operational planning	Low in the short term, but increasing with time	Low	Short-term loss of profits

Figure 1.1

6

differences in the quality and nature of the information, including forecasts, and the appropriate techniques of appraisal for decision and control. These differences are discussed in more detail later in this chapter.

On the non-technical side, the important differences centre round the degree of uncertainty, the role of value judgements, and the penalties for error. Taken together, these would form the area of 'subjective judgement' which needs to be brought to bear on the decisions required. The three elements can be broadly classed in the matrix shown in Fig. 1.1

Strategic planning

These definitions of different types of planning enable one to develop a clearer focus about recent developments. Originating largely from the United States, there are three developments of major importance which are now sweeping through the remainder of the industrial world under the general guise of 'long-range planning'. These are:

1 Formal examination and analysis of the strategic problems and opportunities of a business on regular basis.

2 The development of systematic processes within companies to ensure that strategic planning, project planning, and operational planning are effectively and regularly carried out and coordinated.

3 The development of a wide variety of techniques of information-processing and analysis to assist in decision-taking.

This book is not primarily concerned with the last area. There is a very large number of 'techniques of management', with large variations of application within each technique; such matters are far more effectively described in the specialized literature on these subjects. It is the first two areas which form the principal focus of this book, where three articles are devoted to aspects of strategic planning and the remainder to aspects of the systematic process. Given the vital importance of strategic planning, however, it may be helpful to review briefly the more important steps, and the remainder of this chapter is devoted to that end.

Strategic planning consists of three basic activities, environmental appraisal, corporate appraisal, and strategic formulation. The task of the strategic planner is thus to make a relevant analysis of the relevant environment, to appraise his company with respect to that environment, to generate strategic alternatives, to obtain top management's decisions on a particular alternative, and to express and communicate the resulting strategic decisions in an operationally useful manner. This process is encapsulated in Fig. 1.2. In practice, of course, the environmental appraisal and the corporate appraisal interact with each other and the present or envisaged posture of the company will determine the relevant environment. Nevertheless, in the

7

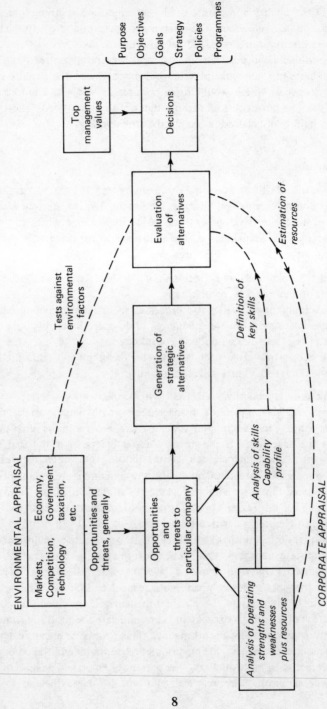

Figure 1.2   Strategic planning: Simple flowchart of key steps

interests of exposition and to develop the necessary breadth of thinking, it is helpful to start with environmental appraisal.

Strategic environmental appraisal–The relevant environment of any company is defined partly by its present activities and partly by its preparedness to consider new activities. Any one business will have a particular environment which may be quite limited, as with a local chain of supermarkets or a specialist producer of electronic components, or immensely broad, as in the case of multinational companies such as Shell, Unilever, or Philips. Nevertheless, a useful analysis of the environment can be partly structured and a suggested model is given in Fig. 1.3. This figure was prepared specifically to highlight a structured environmental appraisal relevant to companies operating in the British machine tool industry, but very similar structures can be developed for any area of business. Such structures allow the possibility of designing a more systematic external information system, an area in which too little work has been done either by business or by academics, but Joseph Aguilar offers one of the very few studies available.

There seem to be four key points on entry to such an analysis, the structure of an existing industry, demand (both nature and size), technology, and the role of government. Along these four points of entry, a first step is to gather information about the present position. From the present position one can develop, with varying degrees of precision, forecasts over relevant time periods of those changes over which the company and its executives will have little control. In the case of the British machine tool industry in 1967, for example, it was clear that substantial new supplies of machine tools would be entering world markets from Russia and Japan, and that there would be a sharp increase in world competition, that this competition would increasingly be a function of technical and control specification and delivery, rather than price, and that different market segments were emerging which would allow different possibilities of specialization both in manufacturing and in selling. Rapid developments in the technology of production as well as in the product were leading to increased automation possibilities, e.g., the design and use of unit building blocks for a range of machines and flowline production. Governments in the industrial countries, the major present markets, were generally moving towards freer trade through customs unions and the Kennedy Round, while less developed countries were exerting pressure to assemble machine tools in their own lands. The tendency for the Government in the United Kingdom to play an active role in the location, structure, and performance of this industry was leading to new policies with respect to investment grants, assistance for prototype development, directive government purchasing, and counter-cyclical action. These general statements of direction can, and in some cases should, be quantified at least within ranges by more sophisticated forecasting.

9

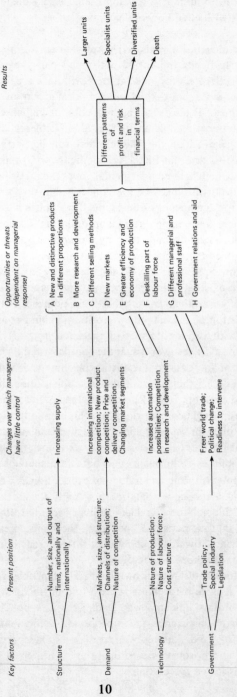

Figure 1.3 Strategic environmental appraisal

Key factors	Present position	Changes over which managers have little control	Opportunities or threats (dependent on managerial response)	Results
Structure	Number, size, and output of firms, nationally and internationally	Increasing supply	A New and distinctive products in different proportions	
Demand	Markets, size, and structure; Channels of distribution; Nature of competition	Increasing international competition; New product competition; Price and delivery competition; Changing market segments	B More research and development C Different selling methods D New markets E Greater efficiency and economy of production	Different patterns of profit and risk in financial terms
Technology	Nature of production; Nature of labour force; Cost structure	Increased automation possibilities; Competition in research and development	F Deskilling part of labour force G Different managerial and professional staff	Larger units Specialist units Diversified units Death
Government	Trade policy; Special industry Legislation	Freer world trade; Political change; Readiness to intervene	H Government relations and aid	

It is here that the analysis required by a businessman departs radically from that offered by an economist, a civil servant, or an academic, whose contribution may have been completed at the above point. To the businessman, the real work now starts. If these various trends are developing, how can they be viewed? Most of them are continuations of exising trends rather than dramatic discontinuities. But, taken together, they represent a drastic change in the total environment of any machine tool company. Are these changes opportunities or threats?

While the question of determining opportunities or threats is an extremely useful point of entry into consideration of a changing environment, it needs to be modified by the consideration that to a great extent the question of whether some factor is an opportunity or a threat is often as much a function of the perception and the attitude of the manager as it is of the factor itself. Consider two of the factors we have discussed, increased government intervention, and competition increasingly centred on technical specification of the control system as well as the machine. To the businessman, wedded to a philosophy of no government intervention of any type and to his existing well-proven product line, both factors are likely to be a threat. To a businessman with less rigid attitudes, a great opportunity is opened up in terms of a chance to break into an existing competitors' historical preserve by product innovation for which the Government may, for the first time, pay part of the cost and also to mitigate the risk through advance orders for prototypes for trial in ordnance factories. Opportunity or threat? Both words seem equally valid, and yet the same basic factors are merely viewed with different attitudes.

The useful approach, then, centres on the isolation and detailed examination of the key factors contributing to change in order to see what opportunities they present. To the enterprising businessman, all changes offer new opportunities, and the chance to generate new alternatives for an existing business. However, the implications of strategic change will probably alter not only the product-market posture of the business, but also the pattern of profit and risk. In our example above, to shift from batch manufacture of standard machine tools to flowline production of advanced, numerically controlled tools will probably require a different financial, personnel, and managerial structure, attachment to a larger unit to provide long-term development, or concentration through greater specialization.

Strategic changes to seize opportunities may then require rethinking the concept of the business in terms of its product market posture, its size, its capital structure, its personnel, and its external relations. Thus, an aspiring strategic planner must not only be an opportunity seeker, but also a man of broad insight into the full implications of change in its many dimensions, while the execution of such changes requires imagination and courage, but above all hard work and effective leadership on the part of top management to overcome the inevitable inertia of existing practices.

Corporate appraisal—The second major task in strategic planning is that of corporate appraisal. This is frequently an exceptionally difficult task for a company's own management to carry out, since perception of the relevant factors in one's own organization is often limited by familiarity and by experience, and the attempt to view an organization as a whole in relation to its environment is a demanding exercise in vision and breadth of understanding.

In the face of these difficulties, it is again helpful to structure one's thinking, even if this structure follows a checklist approach rather than a formal model. In considering a structure which is helpful and relevant, there are two different lines of approach, which partly overlap, but in general are complementary. These two approaches are basically to identify those things which are tangible and, in many cases measurable, and, quite separately, those things which are intangible, primary skills.

The first category is frequently referred to as strengths, weaknesses, and resources, and a short checklist of the elements which are usually of major importance is given in Fig. 1.4. The aim of an appraisal of this nature is to gather together in summary form the major parameters which define the company as it currently exists and to establish among those parameters where the company is strong, where it is weak, and what real resources it has to deploy in exploiting its strengths in the light of the environmental appraisal. For example, one well-established company in the beverage field, doing its first ever formal corporate appraisal, suddenly recognized the significance of the fact that 70 per cent of its profits came from one product, which was probably in a declining market. Other companies also have suddenly realized the extent to which there are badly used financial assets, due to the financing policy historically followed, and that large sums could be freed from their present unprofitable deployment and moved into more profitable areas. This, in turn, could lead to the development of a stronger borrowing capacity which would open up further possibilities for product diversification or a larger research and development effort.

Care needs to be exercised, however, in this type of appraisal since the allocation of an item to a strength or weakness depends not only on the facts, but on the question of strength or weakness for what? Consider the example of a company in a cyclical industry which has always retained a strong liquid position and, therefore, at first sight, is strong financially with ample scope to expand or diversify. Presumably a strength. Yet, unless this position is accompanied by an adequate record of profitability, this very strength may provide an attractive proposition for a takeover by a financial operation interested in asset stripping and dismemberment. Strength or weakness? No

12

Product/Market posture	Product range
	Quality position
	Share of markets
	Size of market
	Profitability of each product
	Dealer or sales organisation
	Service organisation
	Dependence on individual customers
	Nature of competition
	Numbers of competitors
Production	Number, size, capacity of plants
	Nature of production equipment
	Sources of supply of materials
	Extent of vertical integration
	Productivity
Finance	Nature of assets
	Profitability
	Unused cash resources
	Borrowing capacity
	Structure of costs
	Pattern of cash flows
Technology	Research and development capacity
Organization and management	Nature of organization
	Management capabilities
	Planning and control systems
	Succession arrangements
Labour force	Size of labour force
	State of training
	Pattern of union relations

Figure 1.4   Corporate strategic appraisal: Strengths, weaknesses, and resources

valid answer is possible unless the question is posed within the context of, 'Strengths or weaknesses for what?'

The second dimension of appraisal is frequently more difficult. The reasons for suggesting this second dimension centre on the argument that any organization which survives over a period of time develops within its personnel a particular set of skills. These skills will be of varying types, such as technical, marketing, managerial, entrepreneurial, or administrative. Collectively in any one organization they determine the continuing response of that organization to the activities in which it has been involved. They are the essence of the accumulated experience of an organization, and, as a result, the particular skills along these various dimensions may be very different in different organizations.

Consider an area such as promotional skills. Few would deny that organizations like Unilever or Procter and Gamble have developed an

13

incredibly high level of expertise in promotion. But would these skills be transferable to motor-cars, to the sale of building materials, to the sale of electric turbines or aircraft engines? A true answer is probably yes, in part, and in the sense of a conceptualization of the problem in marketing terms which would be relevant. But Unilever and Procter and Gamble would still face a learning situation where their performance would probably be inadequate in their early years.

It is suggested, then, that a more detailed and structured approach to the problem of analysing experience may be helpful in a genuine corporate appraisal, and a framework for such an analysis is presented in Fig. 1.5. Each company should be able to identify its own skills in each of the suggested areas and will be likely to show different profiles of their useful experience.

Such an analysis is of particular value if it is related to the concept of 'key skills'. This line of thought argues that in any business activity it is possible to identify quite a small number of skills which are critical to survival and profitability. Few organizations do everything well, but certain types of organization will be immensely skilled in certain activities because unless they are, they will perish. It has been suggested, for example,[2] that the ability of an automobile manufacturer to survive depends critically on five basic skills, the maintenance of a high quality dealer organization, efficient mass production with very tight cost control, which includes purchasing, and a highly developed ability to change models with minimum interruption to production. This would certainly seem true of the American manufacturers, although Volkswagen has deliberately opted out of the model-changing skill and substituted a servicing-skill which became a byword in the American market.

Contrast this set of key skills with those suggested as critical for survival in an international oil company. Here, a quite different set operates, namely, highly developed transportation skills, great skill in the choice of major investments, a remarkable ability to negotiate contracts, whether with the government of oil-rich lands or with major customers, and, finally, a curiously difficult skill to identify, the skill of international management.

The above suggestions do not imply that companies in these industries can afford to be totally incompetent outside the area of these key skills. Nevertheless, in a competitive world, the isolation of areas where very special competence exists can give a remarkable insight into a major competitive strength which can perhaps be exploited more fully. Additionally, if entry into some new field of activity is being considered, isolation of the critical skills needed to make a success of the new venture, and then ensuring that they either exist or are obtained, will probably do more to create success than any other single factor.

The second leg, then, of the corporate appraisal can usefully be a

14

Marketing | Customers | Channels | Servicing | Promotional skills | Export skills | Selling skills

Production | Process skills | Assembly skills | Batch / Mass / Process production skills | Quality control | Cost control skills | Transportation skills

Finance | Investment skills | Consumer financing | Credit control | Fund-raising skills | Working capital mgt. | International financial skills

Organization | Type of administrative skill | International Mgt skills | Mgt of new enterprises | Joint venture | Contract negotiation

Development | Types of research | e.g., process—new product—development skills— project teams work— | | | Model change skills

-------- = Key skills for an international oil company

———— = Key skills for an automobile manufacturer

Figure 1.5 Capability profile and key skills

structured critical analysis of the skills and capabilities of the existing organization and the establishment of a capability profile. This approach is a more explicit attempt to use the 'concept of synergy which, as a word, runs the risk of concealing more than it reveals.[3] Clearly, however, effective environmental or corporate appraisal must be based not on single snapshots of the environment and the enterprise as so far outlined, but on their probable development over some period of the future. The appropriate time period will vary from company to company but, in strategic terms, few organizations can afford not to look ahead five years on a broad front and rather further for specific aspects of the business with long lead times. This forward look is required both for the environment and for the company. Thus, there is the necessity to forecast in a variety of dimensions, both internally and externally.

It would be inappropriate to examine the wide variety of possible types of forecast which can be made, but it is fair to say that much of the detailed technical work in planning and many of the management techniques are primarily concerned with forecasting. Until recently, environmental variables have tended to be forecast largely on the basis of trend extrapolation, but, increasingly, useful quantitative models are being built which can be used in specific areas both to forecast and to examine the implications of different assumptions.

For example, a number of large companies commissioned the Battelle Institute in Geneva to develop a total environmental model incorporating economic, technological, and sociological variables, using input-output analysis techniques and forecasts of changing technological coefficients.* Such a model is usually beyond the scope of a single company and most have to rely on joint efforts, more limited models, or the critical appreciation of forecasts made by others. For example, a model for economic forecasting of key variables has been developed by Esso in the United Kingdom,[5] but this is of far more limited scope than the Battelle model.

Perhaps a more useful approach for the planner is systematically to consider the various sectors of the environmental appraisal task in terms of the information required and the techniques available for forecasting and analysis. Such a structure is presented in Fig. 1.6. Again, it does not attempt to be all inclusive, but offers a basis for systematic examination of information needs, their costs and the additional costs of developing special forecasts for particular environmental changes. Justification for the latter can frequently be found by analysing the company's sensitivity to individual variables in the environment.

Secondly, it is necessary to forecast the company's forward development as it can best be visualized over the next few years. This requires the

* This project is well described by A. P. Lien, P. Anton, and J. W. Duncan.[4]

	Information needed	Techniques
Economic forecasts 1. National economy 2. Sector forecasts	(a) Government and private forecasts (b) Industry association, government, private forecasts (c) Market research	(i) Critical appreciation of published forecasts (ii) Development of models or relationships for sector forecasts (iii) Input output analysis + wide variety of other forecasting techniques
Technological forecasts	(a) Technical intelligence service reports (b) Technical market research (c) Research into competitors' developments	(i) Demand and conditional demand analyses (ii) Opportunity identification techniques (iii) Theoretical limits testing (iv) Parameter analysis (v) Various systems analysis (vi) Discipline reviews
Sociological forecasts	Wide variety of sources of data, including government reports, educational forecasts, population forecasts, regional forecasts, skilled labour forecasts, institutional changes, etc.	(a) National models such as built by Battelle (unlikely to be done in any one corporation) (b) Expert opinion
Political forecasts	Political intelligence services and government reports	Expert opinion
Forecasting competitors' actions	Any intelligence about competitors	Any relevant technique to give information from intelligence

Figure 1.6 Environmental forecasting for planning assumptions

projection of existing operations and planned projects and a statement of their financial and other results. Normally, operating units, such as product divisions or subsidiaries, will be required to submit their forward proposals and budgets for three to five years. It needs to be stressed that these proposals serve two purposes. First, and obviously, they provide the major opportunity for top management to review the development, operation, and future performance of the unit. But equally important, they provide the essential information base on which a dynamic forward strategic appraisal can be made. Without such projections or proposals in reasonable detail, there will never exist an adequate information base for a dynamic analysis.

In order for operating units to make effective proposals, a great deal of detailed forecasting and planning work will be involved, and this will require both information and techniques. Figure 1.7 presents in summary form the more important aspects of the data requirements and analytical techniques required for formulating project proposals. The varied types of operational planning require so many different potential inputs of data, and there are such a large variety of techniques to assist in formulating plans, that is has not seemed possible to reduce them to a similar simple chart. It is, however, important to note that the quality of information for operational planning is usually of far greater reliability than that available for strategic and project planning and thus lends itself to more sophisticated techniques which can be used with greater confidence.

Armed with the external and internal information generated by relevant forecasts and internal proposals, the corporate planner is now in a position to make his appraisal on a forward basis. Strategic review and reformulation becomes a possibility, since he now has the information to view the company as a whole in relation to its environment over a reasonable period in the future. Thus, at this stage, the work of corporate appraisal can effectively be undertaken, and, in the interests of providing a structure within which to consider information needs and techniques, a diagrammatic structure of the work involved in corporate appraisal is set out in Fig. 1.8.

Even with this expansion of the initial static thinking into a forward projection, however, we have not fully moved away from the concept of static analysis. It could be implied that a strategic review was only required every three or five years. Yet the reality of the life of most planners in their especial world of uncertainty is that any plan expounded at one moment of time will not materialize in exactly the form in which it was planned. Reasons for this are many and varied and include inadequacies of the original plan in terms of information and assumptions, unexpected environmental changes, and the varying effectiveness of people in executing the part of the plan for which they are responsible. Thus, not only must strategic appraisal be based on projection as well as on the present, but it must also be a continuing activity. This is the pressure that has forced virtually every major organization

	Information needed	Techniques
New products	1. Technical specifications 2. Engineering estimates 3. Capital and unit cost estimates 4. Volume estimates 5. Price estimates 6. Servicing estimates 7. Profitability estimates	Techniques for the assessment and execution of projects are very varied and fall into three broad categories. 1. Assessment techniques. 2. Control techniques. 3. Capital budgeting techniques **1. Assessment techniques** Ultimately, most assessment techniques come down to a review of the relevant estimates with probability ratings, financial assessment with probability estimates and comparison with certain financial criteria. For large projects, simulation models can be useful.
New markets	1. Market intelligence re consumer habits, price, channels of distribution, discount structure, present shares of markets, servicing patterns, etc. 2. Estimates of setting up costs, e.g., initial promotion, establishment of selling force or agencies, stocking costs 3. Estimates of demand and share of market 4. Profitability estimates	In practice, projects are decided to a much greater extent on strategic criteria which are frequently less well defined and the financial criterion becomes one of several minimal criteria which have to be met. There is very little technique that I know of which explores this dimension of assessment systematically. **2. Control techniques** Virtually all identifiable projects are susceptible to network analysis, critical path techniques, and control through PERT. This will normally be complemented by budgetary control which, in the case of projects, is best suited to a budget based on PERT theory.
New processes	1. Technical specification 2. Success probability 3. Cost, time, and manpower estimates 4. Economic estimates of success 5. Capital costs of subsequent plant investment	The forward cost control of projects, as opposed to the establishment of overspending after the event, is achieved largely by managerial action on specific items ahead of events.
New facilities	1. Technical engineering estimates 2. Capital, time and operating cost estimates 3. Location analysis 4. Alternative sources of finance	**3. Capital budgeting** All aspects are relevant
Licensing, joint ventures, acquisition appraisal	1. Intelligence about possible licenses 2. Data on own patents, know-how, etc., available for licensing 3. Intelligence on intended moves by competitors 4. Intelligence about companies which could be purchased 5. Intelligence about potential acquirers 6. All relevant market, financial, product, R and D and organization data	1. Development of search criteria 2. Development of final criteria for decision 3. All forms of business analysis may be used in a merger or acquisition

Figure 1.7 Framework for corporate planning: Project planning

	Information needed	Techniques
Product analysis	1. Own and competitors' specifications, design, reliability, delivery, price 2. Intelligence about competitors' costs 3. Profitability data by product	1. Comparative technical/operating analyses 2. Comparative economic analyses 3. Variety of mixed economic/accounting analyses to establish profitability
Market analysis	1. Internal data about present and future markets, customers, volumes, transport costs 2. Market research data about competitors' markets, customers, volumes, transport costs, and promotion	1. Most of the well established analytical techniques relevant to using the marketing data 2. Market models in limited number of situations
Product and process development	1. Nature, size, and scope of technical resources 2. Nature, size, and scope of technical development facility 3. Development projects in hand	1. Technical appraisal by experts 2. R and D project evaluation techniques
Market development	Market research information about new markets, their design requirements, cost factors, and present competitive position	Most of the well-established analytical techniques relevant to assessment of a new product or a new market
Financial appraisal	Corporate financial statements of all types	1. Asset analysis 2. Profitability analysis 3. Project appraisal techniques

Facilities appraisal	1. Technical and cost information on present facilities 2. Technical and financial appraisal of projects to which committed 3. Information about competitors' technical state	1. Technical appraisal of processes, present and planned. 2. Comparison of own technical state with competitors
Executive organization appraisal	1. Organization structure 2. Planning and control systems 3. Management audit	1. Organization analysis 2. Systems analysis 3. Attitudinal appraisal
Manpower appraisal	1. Numbers, age, state of training of labour force 2. Union relationships and bargaining structure	Comparison with future requirements
Competitive appraisal	Any intelligence about competitors	Any relevant techniques to give information from intelligence
Evaluation of top management attitudes	Close knowledge of top management	A few attitudinal surveys of top management have been carried out in USA
Definition of capability profiles	Analysis of key characteristics of activities in which involved	Determination of key skills in present activities and comparison with needs of future activities

Figure 1.8 Framework for corporate planning: Strategic appraisal

which has undertaken systematic long-range planning into adopting a rolling plan, where appraisals of the type outlined are carried out on a regular time-cycle, usually every year. In these companies, a decision to maintain the present strategy is thus an explicit decision, rather than an implicit assumption.

To summarize, the comparatively simple concept of one-time static analysis has now elaborated into a regular activity based on a forward timespan of at least three years and frequently longer. But fortunately, while these additions modify substantially the internal processes by which a company determines its strategy, they do not undermine the essential structure of the analysis itself. Environmental appraisal and strategic appraisal remain the critical analytical steps in strategic planning.

Strategic formulation—With an environmental appraisal and corporate appraisal completed, one is in a position to move forward to the third and most exacting task, the formulation of strategy itself. If the appraisals have been effectively and imaginatively completed, a picture will have developed of the opportunities and threats to the particular company, an estimate of where presently conceived operations and projects will carry the company over the next few years, an estimate of the nature of any gap between such projection and desired results and a limited number of alternatives to fill the gap.

It is worth drawing attention at this point to this activity of generating alternatives. The devising of valid alternatives is an imaginative, creative act, quite different in character from the analytical work necessary for the earlier work. It may be that within the organization there exists a fund of imaginative ideas which merely require coordination, articulation, and analysis. But as often as not the generation of strategic alternatives which offer hope of meeting the company's needs will fall to the strategic planner and the top management team. These alternatives will require careful evaluation against the three critical factors: environmental change, corporate strengths, weaknesses, and resources, and the capability profile, and such evaluation will carry important non-quantifiable as well as quantifiable elements.

And, finally, decision. It would be comforting to think that after all this careful appraisal, all the evaluative work, and all the imaginative effort which has been carried out, an appropriate or optimum strategy would be so blindingly obvious that no real decision would be necessary. Alas, such a hope seems to bear little relation to the real world and perhaps a sounder line of argument would be that the more sophisticated and comprehensive the analysis and evaluation, the more difficult it frequently is to make a decision, since the full implications, risks and difficulties of any alternative are more likely to be understood.

22

The problem is simple to state and acutely difficult to solve in the real world. The problem is that of an absence of agreed criteria on which all those concerned with taking such decisions can agree. Decisions are being required on the future concept of the enterprise. These raise the necessity to apply complex criteria in many dimensions, profit, risk, relationships, future workloads, images, concepts of service, tradition, and many others. Difficult decisions are being asked of a group of people who will share some minimal common criteria, but hold widely divergent views on others. The criteria which individuals apply stem from their own subjective values with an inevitable interaction between the implications of such decisions for them personally as well as the effects for the organization. Volumes have been and will no doubt continue to be written on the role of values, their subjective nature, their influence in decision-making, and their complex nature. The one useful point which can be stressed in this introductory chapter is to note just how critical they are and what a determining role they play in strategic decisions. A senior executive who conceives of his activity in moving towards a strategic plan solely as a technical activity is wildly misinformed.

Is there an identifiable end product of all this analytical and creative effort, and if so, what is it? Again, when writing generally, it is possible to do little more than suggest a structure of thinking which may be helpful in reducing the abstract to more tangible terms. The problem is twofold: first, to formulate ideas in sufficiently concrete form to be communicable and, second, to move systematically in an operationally useful way from the broadest level of corporate aim to some directive or commitment which offers guidance to others charged with responsibility for execution. There are many mental structures of this type and most writers in this field offer their own version.[6] One of the more useful phrases to describe what a planner is attempting to produce is the expression 'A network of aims'.[7] This expression describes admirably the complex multidimensional nature and the interrelationship of corporate sets of aims.

At the risk of merely adding to the existing plethora of diagrams offering structure in this abstract area, a chart is presented as Fig. 1.9. It attempts to separate out means from ends and to offer definitions which ease the semantic difficulties outlined at the beginning of this chapter. The structure presented offers five levels.

The broadest level of aim is called a 'corporate purpose'. Without wishing to indulge in a prolonged dissertation about the purpose of business institutions in society, it is certain that any business organization is composed of human beings formed into varied groups. The top management of any business forms a group and as a group commands resources, exercises power, and has recognizable status. Membership frequently represents the major goal for which the individual has striven during his career. In addition, membership of the group provides interesting and stimulating work.

23

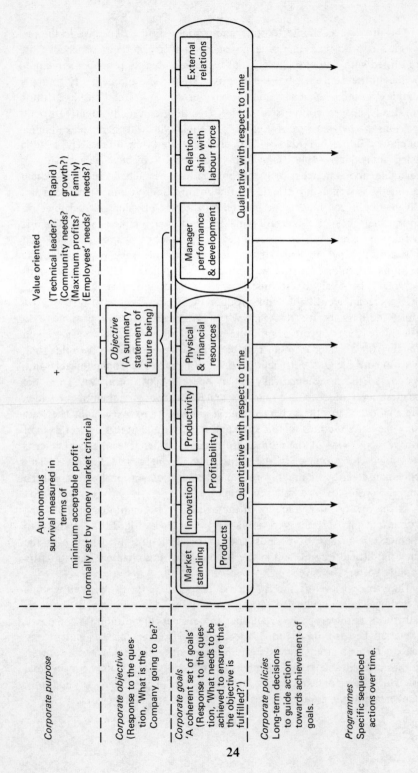

Figure 1.9 Strategic formulation: Corporate purpose, objective, goals, policy and programmes

24

One of the strongest factors operating in any group is the desire to survive, and this desire is enormously strengthened when membership of the group offers such substantial rewards to the individual. It seems more reasonable then in terms of finding a common denominator of corporate purpose to argue that the underlying purpose of most business organizations is to ensure autonomous survival.

But there is one fundamental condition for autonomous survival in the business world, namely the maintenance of some level of profitability. In a public company, this will be set primarily by stock market criteria; in a private company, by the expectations of the prime beneficiaries, the individual shareholders. Thus, it is suggested that, at the deepest level, autonomous survival, determined by some level of profitability, is a useful lowest common denominator of corporate purpose.

This concept can quite usefully be examined in terms of behaviour in a contested takeover battle. A classic example would be the pattern of opposition by the board of Associated Electrical Industries to a takeover by the General Electric Company in 1967. While the defence was centred on acceptable public statements, such as the best interests of shareholders, it is difficult to believe that the prime aim of the board of AEI was other than the autonomous survival of the company. They failed in this purpose because they had failed over a period of time to attain a level of profitability considered adequate by influential members of the financial markets.

Over and above this lowest common denominator, however, one finds a variety of additional corporate purposes. Virtually all of these will be value oriented. They may include such elements as the intention to become a technical leader, to maximize growth, to meet family needs, to make social experiments, or even assuming it can be defined, to maximize profits. At a philosophical level, if the concept of private enterprise is accepted in society it would seem eminently right that such freedom should not only be allowed but encouraged. At the same time, such freedom carries with it the requirement for responsible choice.

The autonomous survival of the entity is, then, being postulated as the prime purpose of most business organizations with the rider that once this is assured by an adequate level of profitability, other purposes develop. But survival of an entity implies some condition of 'being'. It implies that the entity is something and wishes to continue to be something. Thus it may be useful to think of the corporate objective as attaining a state of future being. This is a rather different and more sophisticated idea than that of future doing. It involves a reaching back into the fundamentals, not of action or activities, but of existence, and thus requires definition of the key parameters which determine the entity as an organism at present and in the future. A corporate objective then can usefully be thought of as an answer to the question 'What is this company going to be?'*

* An example of this thinking is given for a company in B. W. Denning.[8]

But 'being' in the real world will only be achieved by 'doing'. In order to be something, a company must do something. It is as this point that the concept of specific goals representing future achievements in particular dimensions becomes critical. The intellectual task is to determine a set of future achievements which collectively will allow the organization to be what it wishes to be. There are inevitably a variety of future achievements in different fields, all of which require simultaneous achievement. Many writers have attempted to set down areas in which goals need to be set and a version of these is presented in Fig. 1.9. It will be noted that all of them need to be expressed in specific form with respect to time.

Perhaps the important aspect of this presentation is the division into those which are predominantly quantitative in nature and those which are predominantly qualitative. At the present time, certainly in British industry, there is enormous scope for the increased use of quantitative analysis and goal-setting. However, in terms of the type of decisions on goals we are considering, the sophistication of the quantification is quite limited and simple figures are more helpful. For example, in 1963 Union Carbide Limited decided on a goal of increasing productivity by three per cent per annum over the next five years: not a very sophisticated goal and probably not arrived at by very sophisticated means. Nevertheless, in terms of providing both a measure of future achievement and a goal toward which action could be taken, its very simplicity had much to commend it.

Few today would argue the need for quantitative goals. But if we return to the concept of 'being' as an objective, it is inconceivable that a state of 'being' can be maintained without certain relationships, the nature of which may well be critical to achievement of the objective. Relationship goals are more difficult to define, but no less necessary on that account. It could certainly be argued, for example, that at the time of writing the British economy generally, with glaring examples in the motor industry, is as much threatened by failures to establish relevant, effective relationships with its labour force as by any other single factor. If a definable future state of being is to be achieved, goals in terms of certain desired relationships in key areas may well be as important as the goals of innovation or productivity. Perhaps one can add a personal view, that, in the rapidly changing educational and cultural climate of many industrial countries, relationship goals may need greater attention than has been historically attached to them and become ever more critical determinants of success.

Finally, if goals can be developed, at least in the key areas outlined, then it becomes possible to set policies and authorize programmes. A policy is possibly the most slippery word of those that have been discussed so far since in common usage it too frequently means any major decisions taken by a remote group at a high level in the hierarchy.

A policy is defined here as being a decision rule to guide others, usually those lower in the hierarchy, on desirable action. A set of policies taken collectively, then, largely define the boundaries within which decisions can be taken internally at lower levels and, externally, the area in which acceptable propositions can be made by outside bodies.

A programme, on the other hand, is a planned sequence of actions. To revert to Union Carbide, the goal of three per cent increase in productivity per annum required a programme of actions, which were expressed ultimately in individual projects which included capital investment, methods study, operational research, and computerization. The decision to embark on this programme required top management approval whereas few of the projects within the programme would require such authorization.

The attempt to evolve a structure such as has been described is difficult enough conceptually. Even greater practical difficulties usually exist in reaching agreement between the board and the top executives of a company. Indeed, it can be argued that as clear a structure as has been described is rarely achieved, and even when achieved still fails to solve many problems. The principal problem which it fails to solve, although it is helpful in approaching it, is the decision on trade-offs between different goals. Sir Geoffrey Vickers argues convincingly in his book *The Art of Judgement*[9] that the key role of the policy-maker is, in fact, to take decisions on these trade-offs, to estimate the balance of advantage in quantitative and qualitative terms of alternative policies and programmes. Nevertheless, in so far as goals are explicit, which is rare, a framework has been developed against which the probable effects of different policies and programmes can be tested. Explicit structures in general offer greater opportunity for rational choice than implicit structures and to this extent, despite the difficulties, it is suggested that the attempt to develop explicit structures deserves the substantial intellectual effort demanded.

Problems of the whole and the parts*

Implicit in the argument so far has been the assumption that top management has a special responsibility in its strategic planning to concentrate on the interests and future of the whole company rather than on any one of its parts. A clear strategic concept for the company is seen as a helpful device for enabling top management to set its sights more effectively.

In practice, however, it may be less easy to separate the whole from its parts, possibly because the parts contain strong groups with interests which do not totally coincide with the interests of the whole. The easiest example of this phenomenon is a company organized into several product groups deliberately granted a substantial degree of autonomy with a central staff

---

* I am much indebted to Professor Bailey and his book *Stratagems and Spoils* for an effective vocabulary in this section.[10]

structure built along specialist lines. It is the nature of those responsible for individual sectors to attach great importance to the goals for which they are responsible and on whose attainment they will largely be judged, and to subordinate the more remote goals of a larger entity for the achievement of which they probably feel less responsibility. In addition, and a very frequent source of conflict, the time horizons of people at different levels in the organization will tend to be different. This will mean different perceptions of relevance and importance when proposals are being discussed and will give rise to different weights being applied to different factors when decisions have to be made. Furthermore, as described earlier, an essential part of the information base for effective corporate appraisal requires projections and proposals from constituent units, proposals for continuation or demise of particular operations, and proposals for new projects. Finally, it has been pointed out that once autonomous survival has been assured at some level of profitability there are likely to develop a variety of purposes which are essentially value-oriented.

A final factor, and perhaps the most important, is that in any sizeable organization there is a form of competition between senior executives. This competition is of two types, competition as role-players for resources, and competition as individuals for rewards. The competition for resources can easily be seen in the context of capital allocations between activities when influences and pressures will be brought to bear on those responsible for the decision. The competition for rewards takes various forms since the rewards which individuals desire vary in kind, but the most obvious concerns rewards such as promotion. Within any hierarchical system, it is not unusual for several capable men to be competing internally for a top position.

These conditions form what can usefully be called a political arena in which there will be political competition. Under these circumstances, competition will take place under two sets of rules, normative rules and pragmatic rules. Normative rules in a business may include such acceptable justifications for conduct as 'maximizing profitability', 'increasing market share', 'developing younger men', 'participation'. The existence of normative rules means that for each and every proposed action there will be one of several acceptable reasons which can be publicly argued in the company and to which the action or plan may be related. Pragmatic rules, on the other hand, may be very different, and it usually requires a good deal of experience of a particular organization before they are fully understood. An acceptable pragmatic rule in some companies will be to conceal responsibility for a highly risky decision through some such device as a committee, but if the venture succeeds, to leave oneself in a position to claim the credit as originator of the idea. Another pragmatic rule may well centre round the amount of information which may be concealed by a division from the centre. To revert to the capital allocation example, it is not unknown for the assumptions used in a project appraisal to be shaded in a direction which makes the financial results appear more favourable. It may well be generally accepted that this is a fact of life in the company.

This concept of a political arena in which competition takes place according to two different sets of rules has direct relevance to top management's problem of coordinating the action of the parts into effective action for the whole, since, except in the case of totally autocratic behaviour, the procedure by which coordination is achieved contains a substantial element of bargaining and negotiation in the political arena.

Now an important aspect of the bargaining positions will be the information available to each party. A great deal of the information on which decisions will be reached will be submitted by subsidiary units in the form of budgetary proposals. These will conform to the required company format and will be likely to meet any standards or normative rules laid down by top management in terms of return on capital or increase in market share. But the information will suffer from the distortion in perception at each level which works on that information and the biases built in under acceptable pragmatic rules. Nevertheless, the proposals will concern the use of resources of great relevance to the company's strategic goals and they will be formally justified by reference to the normative rules of the company.

This situation raises two difficulties for top management. First, on the assumption that top management would prefer its decisions to be seen as being rationally guided, it becomes necessary for top management to develop a testing framework for judging proposals against strategic criteria, rather than financial criteria alone. In other words, a concept of capital budgeting which argues for acceptance of all projects above a particular cut-off point, or the selection of projects ranked solely by rate of return, is inadequate as a decision framework. If a strategic testing framework is to be understood in the organization, a necessity if subsequent decisions are to be perceived as being rationally guided, then it must be explicit and capable of being communicated.

This line of argument leads us back to the section on strategic formulation and expands the role of an explicit strategy (see page 27). In this earlier section, it was suggested that top management needed to develop in explicit terms a purpose, objective, and goals. In the reality of large organizations where many proposals are likely to emanate from subsidiary units, the value of such a structure of thinking lies in its further use as a testing framework to apply strategic criteria.

The second difficulty for top management centres on their relative bargaining position as determined by the information available to them. When a subsidiary unit puts forward a significant proposal, it will normally have carried out a fairly sophisticated appraisal and evaluation and will stand possessed of substantially greater relevant information than will exist at the centre. Under these circumstances, even with an explicit strategic framework for testing, top management will find itself at a disadvantage unless it can maintain its own sources of information relevant to strategic choice. In one sense, this is one of the roles which specialist staff must perform. However, the information flows to specialist staffs and their perception of the interests of the whole will be limited and influenced by their specialist roles. Thus, top management may find itself faced with the carefully evaluated proposals of a subsidiary unit and only specialist sources of information and advice against which to test them. What they may well lack as they face their decision is the relevant strategic information

It is partly the need for solutions of these two problems which has led to the development of 'planning, programming, budgeting' systems which were introduced into the Ministry of Defence in 1964 following their effective use in the United States Department of Defense. Since that time they have spread rapidly. They are described in the article by David Novick[11] on page 195 of this book. Essentially, they consist of three elements: a structure of objectives with associated programmes of activities expressed in cost benefit terms; an information matrix or cross-walk through which financial information compiled for accounting purposes appropriate for operational planning and control is transformed into a pattern appropriate for strategic review; and a system of conventions concerning the allocation of costs within the programme structure.

A simple structure demonstrating the difference in presentation of information is the United Kingdom's defence budget for 1969 presented in the two forms.* Figure 1.10 shows the defence budget expressed in conventional accounting terms, built round the need for controlling expenditure through costs of personnel, buildings, or purchases. Historically, each of the services and the other government ministries compiled and presented their budgets in this form. The motivational attachment of each service or ministry to its own proposals was great, and the balance of power, in terms of information, lay strongly with the subsidiary units. How, for example, could a minister deduce from figures prepared in this way the cost of any identifiable entity such as a group of dockyards or the forces in Germany? He would be forced to conduct a series of special studies, each of which would be complex and which, without standard conventions for cost determination, would not necessarily be comparable. But special studies of this nature offer no continuing framework for strategic review—merely a continuing series of special analyses.

Now consider the alternative structure of presentation arising from the conversion of the information in Fig. 1.10 to a programme budget format as in Fig. 1.11. One can swiftly identify the relation between costs and

* Figures 1.10 and 1.11 are taken from: *Statement of The Defence Estimates 1969* (HMSO).

Financial Year 1969-70 (£ million)

(1) Item	(2) MINISTRY OF DEFENCE												(3) MINISTRY OF TECHNOLOGY			(4) MINISTRY OF PUBLIC BUILDING AND WORKS			(5) TOTALS		
	(a) Central			(b) Navy			(c) Army			(d) Air											
	Gross	A.inA.	Net	Gross	A.inA.	Net	Gross	A.inA.	Net	Gross	A.inA.	Net	Gross	A.inA.	Net	Gross	A.inA.	Net	Gross	A.inA.	Net
1. Pay etc. of service personnel	11.94	—	11.94	112.71	3.75	108.96	200.24	12.74	187.50	154.23	8.43	145.80	2.13	—	2.13	—	—	—	481.25	24.92	456.33
2. Pay, etc. of reserve, territorial and auxiliary forces, and grants for administration, etc.	—	—	—	0.85	—	0.85	10.79	0.12	10.67	0.67	0.01	0.66	—	—	—	—	—	—	12.31	0.13	12.18
3. Pay, etc., of civilians (i)	12.43	—	12.43	136.59	1.27	135.32	179.04	2.34	176.70	61.00	4.41	56.59	37.82	—	37.82	20.90	—	20.90	447.78	8.02	439.76
4. Movements	0.57	—	0.57	13.49	0.09	13.40	24.16	1.03	23.13	15.50	2.70	12.80	2.72	—	2.72	—	—	—	56.44	3.82	52.62
5. Supplies:																					
(a) Petrol, oil, and lubricants	—	—	—	17.60	1.58	16.02	6.96	0.68	6.28	31.00	2.34	28.66	1.10	—	1.10	—	—	—	56.66	4.60	52.06
(b) Food and ration allowance	—	—	—	62.88	6.32	56.56	16.50	3.50	13.00	9.88	3.22	6.66	—	—	—	—	—	—	89.26	13.04	76.22
(c) Fuel and light	—	—	—	6.71	0.17	6.54	13.55	0.24	13.31	6.24	1.23	5.01	—	—	—	—	—	—	26.50	1.64	24.86
(d) Miscellaneous	0.08	—	0.08	5.29	—	5.29	—	—	—	—	—	—	1.47	—	1.47	—	—	—	6.84	—	6.84
6. Production and research																					
(a) Production (ii)	40.21	49.39	Cr. 9.18	259.92	20.34	239.58	(iii)194.05	(iii)104.20	89.85	313.24	14.07	299.17	(iii)373.15	(iii)340.60	32.55	—	—	—	(iv)805.66	(iv)153.69	651.97
(b) Research and development (v)	—	3.31	Cr. 3.31	27.97	0.40	27.57	11.31	0.80	10.51	—	—	—	150.10	15.29	134.81	—	—	—	189.38	19.80	169.58
7. (a) Works, buildings, and land	10.52	1.00	9.52	—	2.52	Cr. 2.52	22.23	23.58	Cr. 1.35	—	7.73	Cr. 7.73	4.60	4.79	Cr. 0.19	169.21	13.93	155.28	206.56	53.55	153.01
(b) Associated expenditure	—	—	—	—	—	—	—	—	—	—	—	—	—	—	—	3.62	—	3.62	3.62	—	3.62
8. Miscellaneous effective services	11.87	0.25	11.62	11.23	3.64	7.59	15.91	3.90	12.01	14.31	1.93	12.38	1.80	—	1.80	—	—	—	55.12	9.72	45.40
9. Non-effective charges	—	—	—	30.56	0.10	30.46	59.11	0.17	58.94	32.17	0.17	32.00	—	—	—	—	—	—	121.84	0.44	121.40
TOTALS	87.62	53.95	33.67	685.80	40.18	645.62	(iii)753.85	(iii)153.30	600.55	638.24	46.24	592.00	(iii)574.89	(iii)360.68	(iii)214.21	193.73	13.93	179.80	(iv)2,559.22	(iv)293.37	2,265.85

NOTES:
(i) Includes pay of directly employed in civilians totalling £81.71 million in naval dockyards, ROFs and other production establishments and £42.99 million in research and development establishments.
(ii) Includes the costs of Royal Ordnance Factories, the Ministry of Technology Special Materials Vote and Defence Sales transactions.
(iii) Includes defence expenditure on behalf of, and receipts from Defence Departments and non-Exchequer Customers carried on the respective Purchasing (Repayment) Services Vote (Civil Estimates Class IV 21 for Ministry of Technology).
(iv) To avoid double counting of payments by the Defence Departments to the Ministries of Technology and Defence (Army) Purchasing (Repayment) Services Votes the cross totals of columns 2-4 have been reduced by £374.91 million.
(v) Includes the cost of development work undertaken by industry under contract and the purchase of certain stores and plant for research and development establishments.

Source: Defence Estimates 1969 (HMSO)

Figure 1.10 Division of the defence budget under the principal headings

31

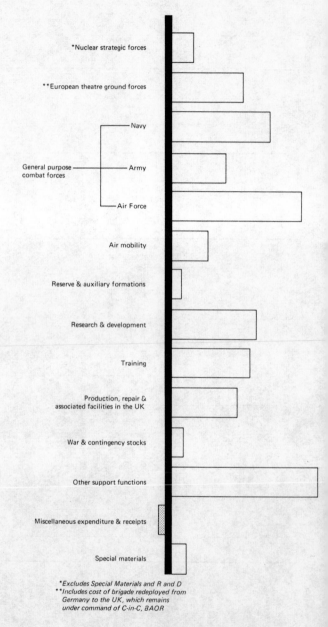

*Nuclear strategic forces

**European theatre ground forces

General purpose combat forces
— Navy
— Army
— Air Force

Air mobility

Reserve & auxiliary formations

Research & development

Training

Production, repair & associated facilities in the UK

War & contingency stocks

Other support functions

Miscellaneous expenditure & receipts

Special materials

*Excludes Special Materials and R and D
**Includes cost of brigade redeployed from
Germany to the UK, which remains
under command of C-in-C, BAOR

Figure 1.11   Functional analysis of defence expenditure 1969

32

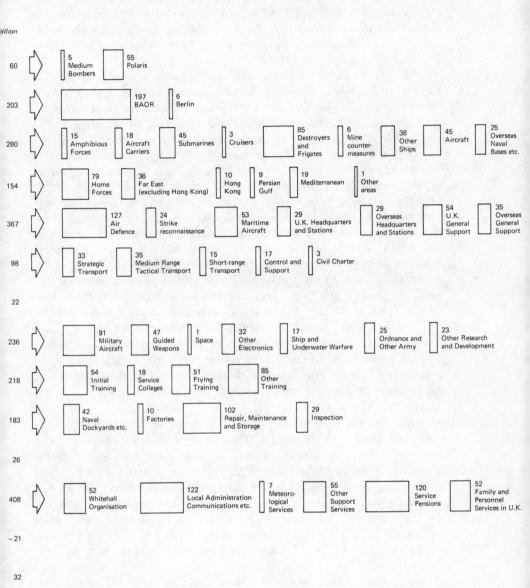

Figure 1.11—cont.   Source: *Defence Estimates 1969* (HMSO)

programmes, and because the conventions are standard, have some confidence in their comparability. For example, the cost of the nuclear deterrent can easily be isolated and seen in relation to the whole. For any given change in resource availability, the strategic effects of reducing expenditure in any area can much more readily be gauged.

While the problems of government and business in this field are not entirely similar, largely because of different objectives and the lesser freedom of government for political and social reasons to organize its activities in coherent elements related to programme objectives, nevertheless, many aspects of the problems of top management in both fields remain the same. Although the special need for planning, programming, budgeting systems arises partly as a response to the diverse organizational structures associated with government programmes, the need for an explicit framework of objectives and goals against which to test proposals, and the presentation of proposals in a form which has relevance to those goals, is similar. Thus, while it is probably unnecessary for business firms to emulate in detail the system increasingly being brought into governmental service, there is sufficient value in the method for consideration to be given to its vital elements.

Reverting, now, to the problems of the corporate political arena and the need for coordination, it was suggested that top management needs a clear strategy plus a method of examining proposals against a framework of information relevant to top management's strategic concerns. While a clear strategy and a relevant information and presentation system do not solve the political problems which require value-oriented decisions determined by a process of bargaining, it is suggested that where they exist, the ability of top management to take rational decisions and to explain them will be substantially increased.

If this line of argument is accepted, then the role of the corporate planner changes somewhat in concept. A structure for considering the work of a corporate planning department is given in chapter 14. But over and above consideration of what responsibility he should carry for different types of work is a more basic role. In simple terms, this is the creation of a forum for bargaining where the interests of the parts are explicitly considered in relation to the interests of the whole. Such a forum requires relevant information systems and explicit criteria if the political process is to be kept within acceptable limits and if political defeat is to be accepted as being rational rather than arbitrary.

It is a personal belief that one of the critical functions of those who find themselves faced with the task of corporate planning is the creation and maintenance of a political arena where the bargaining process can be carried out within stated and explicit criteria. This implies the probability that the corporate planner will develop into something akin to the military chief-of-staff, advising the board and the chief executive on the basis of relevant

34

information and analysis about the maintenance of the strategic interest of the company as a whole.

This short review of different types of planning, with emphasis on the strategic task and the top management as a political system, is introduced as a focus to which the various articles in this book can be related. Few books can hope to be totally comprehensive in coverage of a subject of this nature, and, as explained earlier, an attempt has been made to highlight certain aspects of corporate long-range planning from the point of view of the practitioner. Systematic corporate long-range planning, by virtue of greater analysis and fuller understanding of consequences frequently increases the difficulty of the decision-making task of top management, and its introduction may have a profound and initially unsettling effect on the political system of an organization. On the other hand, in a large and complex organization, it is difficult to see any other managerial system which will allow top management effectively to carry out its own particular and special responsibilities for the development and progress of the company as a whole.

References

1. AGUILAR, JOSEPH, *Scanning the Business Environment*. Macmillan, 1967.
2. DANIEL, D. RONALD, 'Reorganizing for Results.' *Harvard Bsns Rev.*, December 1966.
3. KITCHING, JOHN, 'Why Do Mergers Miscarry?' *Harvard Bsns Rev.*, November/ December 1967.
4. LIEN, A. P., ANTON, P., and DUNCAN, J. W. 'Technological Forecasting: Tools, Techniques and Applications.' *AMA Mgmt Bull.*, No. 115, 1968.
5. WAGLE, B. 'The Use of Models for Environmental and Corporate Planning.' *OR Quarterly*, September 1969.
6. GRANGER, CHARLES H. 'The Hierarchy of Objectives.' *Harvard Bsns Rev.*, May/June 1964.
7. STEINER, G. A. *Top Management Planning*. Chapters 6 and 7. London: Macmillan, 1969.
8. DENNING, B. W. 'The Integration of Business Studies at the Conceptual Level.' *J. Mgmt. Studies*, Vol. 5, No. 1, February 1968.
9. VICKERS, SIR GEOFFREY, *The Art of Management*. London: Chapman & Hall, 1965.
10. BAILEY, PROF. F. G. *Stratagems and Spoils*. Oxford: Blackwell 1959.
11. NOVICK, DAVID, ed. *Program Budgeting*. 2nd Edn. New York: Holt, Rinehart, Winston, 1969.

PART ONE: The concept of corporate planning

Few deliberate managerial activities are likely to be effective or maintained over any period of time unless the concepts on which they are founded have some validity. Planning is no exception. In my experience, clarification of concept can frequently be a first and critical step in making any change, and confusion of concept has a multiplier effect in producing confusion of behaviour. Part 1 concentrates attention on some concepts critical to effective planning.

In the first chapter, Robert Murdick inspects some of the differences between 'planning' and 'plans'. He stresses the fact that planning is a process. One end result of planning may be a piece of paper called a plan, but the most important value of planning may centre in the process itself. This vital distinction is one which needs constantly to be borne in mind in evaluating the effectiveness of any planning system.

The second chapter moves forward to examine the role of a comprehensive planning process in the context of the top management task. The distinction between plan and process is maintained, and it will be noted that the important identifiable outputs of the process are not in fact plans in the conventionally understood sense. The critical argument is that, in today's world, top management requires a comprehensive planning system if it is to carry out its own special task with the greatest probability of success.

The third chapter may puzzle readers who approach this book with an expectation of a quick 'How to do it' kitbag. In the introduction, stress is laid on the fact that corporate planning takes place within a political system and raises crucial value considerations. Virtually no writers have examined corporate planning in this context, and I have found it necessary to step outside the corporate framework to an area in which it is permissible to state that planning takes place within a political system. Within this legitimized context, a variety of patterns and roles for planning are identified, all at the level of the nation state.

The corporate reader will need to translate a number of terms; for example, for 'central government' read 'head office', for 'political institution' read 'top management', for 'politician' read 'policy-maker', for 'institution' read 'product division' or 'subsidiary'. Accepting this translation, important and relevant distinctions are drawn between developmental and adaptive planning, between allocative and innovative planning, and between different methods of inducement; attention is focused on the fact that planning involves a form of negotiation and the development of a system of bargains, and the different roles expected of planners in different types of planning are sketched out. All these distinctions and areas of concern are, I suggest, entirely valid in the context of a large complex corporation; and the fact that the model is developed primarily for examination of the behaviour of a national planning system should only deter those who are unable to see a business as a social and political system as well as a technical and financial system.

The importance of a model of this nature is that it raises in explicit form some of the more important considerations about alternative purposes of planning and some of the key choices in the design of a process relevant to perceived needs.   (Editor)

2. Nature of planning and plans
Robert G. Murdick

Universality of planning

Plans are the means by which objectives are ultimately achieved. Planning, as the term is usually understood, is carried out daily by almost every human being. In our personal life, we think of certain things we must do for the coming day, for this week, or for this month. We do not randomly make decisions for our next action after we have just completed our current activity. In general, human beings seek goals and objectives within some conceived time limits, not by cut-and-try processes or random motions, but usually by thinking in advance of acting.

We plan our personal activities and affairs most often in an informal way without usually documenting the plan. In business, the professions, or governmental administration, planning is more thorough, more complex, and more formal. Risks and gains are relatively large. The consequences of plans of an executive or leadership group may affect the lives of many people. It is in these areas that good planning is highly important. Therefore, the theory and techniques of executive planning deserve careful study.

What is 'planning'?

Concepts of planning

Planning is a process. Planning is concerned with the future, but planning is not the same as forecasting. 'Planning is intellectual in nature; it is mental work. Reflective thinking is required; imagination and foresight are extremely helpful.'[1]

• Reproduced with permission from the *Advanced Management Journal*, Vol. 30, No. 4, October 1965, pp. 36-46.

Planning, it is generally agreed, depends upon the selecting and relating of 'facts'. Facts are objective, verifiable objectively, and measurable. But facts as used by people depend upon people's perception of facts. It is in the process of this perception that facts become different things to different people. Psychologists today have proposed that there is no fixed correlation between data in the environment of the perceiver and data as they are perceived. Thus attitudes, beliefs, sentiments, and values are treated as facts upon which the planning process is structured.

The planning process also is structured upon a sequence of decisions extending into the future. How closely planning is related to decision-making depends mainly upon the definition of decision-making. If an individual concludes that he likes milk better than coffee, is this a decision? If we are to attempt to construct a logical theory of planning, we would not call the process by which we arrived at this conclusion a decision-making process. It is rather a crystallization of a belief, a recognition of a sensory discrimination, or, at most, an evaluation.

Decision-making must represent a choice of future actions. One author defines 'decision' as follows: 'We shall think of a decision as a course of action chosen by the decider as the most effective means at his disposal for achieving the goals or goal he is currently emphasizing—for solving the problem that is bothering him.'[2] If planning consists of creating alternative courses of action for the future, then we conclude that decision-making is an evaluation and selection process which terminates a phase of planning and eventually the complete planning process. Since 'decide' is derived from the Latin meaning to 'cut off', the concept of decision-making as the process of rational evaluation terminating in selection of one of two or more alternatives appears to be reasonable.

How, then, for the purpose of scientific inquiry, do we distinguish planning from decision-making, since both relate to future action? First, we note from what we have said above that decision-making is basically the termination of an evaluation and selection procedure. Decision-making results in a course of action, but a specified time is not necessarily involved. Planning is a much more comprehensive process. It consists of establishing objectives, determining various (and possibly numerous) lines of action to achieve the objectives, determining decision points through the pattern of alternative actions, and finally, selecting a single primary pattern for action based upon sequential decisions and a decision among total possible patterns of action. Further, timing of action is a necessary requisite of planning. Planning may also include establishing a list of plans and their priority. The highest ranked plan is considered to be the plan which stipulates the action. Before the first ranked plan is put into action, however, conditions may have changed so that an alternate plan will be substituted instead. We can see that planning involves complex relationships among decisions.

From the above discussion, we may now define planning as follows:

Planning is a conscious intellectual process characterized by (a) identification of a need or reflection of a stimulus, (b) accumulation of information, (c) relating of bits of information and beliefs, (d) establishing objectives, (e) establishing premises, (f) forecasting future conditions, (g) structuring alternative chains of actions based upon sequential decisions, (h) ranking or selecting total plans which will achieve the best balance of ultimate objective and subsidiary objectives, (i) establishing policies, and (j) establishing standards and means for the measurement of adherence to the plan of action.

Types of Planning

Since planning may apply to practically any activity, it will be useful for analysis to determine the basic types of planning. We find that there are six main classifications of planning. (See also Terry.[1])

One type of planning is physical planning. Physical planning deals with spatial arrangements of objects. Office layout planning, city layout planning, building location, and equipment location are examples. While other considerations may enter into physical planning, this type of planning is distinguished by its primary objective of spatial arrangement.

Organizational planning is concerned with the grouping of activities, development of a pattern or structure of working relationships among people in the enterprise, establishment of channels of communication and lines of authority, staffing of positions in the organization, and development of the people.

Process planning has as its major objective the development of a method or process which may be required. The process might be a manufacturing method, a procedure for operating a chemical plant, or a procedure for firing a satellite into space. Process planning might be thought of as operations planning. It is concerned primarily with sequences of motions, rather than arrangements of things or relationships among people. Physical distribution of goods might be considered mainly process planning although considerations of spatial planning, organizational planning, and financial planning are interwoven.

Financial planning, like the previous classifications, may occur in nearly a pure form or in combination with other types of planning. Financial planning is concerned only with obtaining the right amount of money at the right time, the management of money available so that it does not lie idle, the investment of money in terms of risk-return ratios, and the preservation of money from waste and other forms of loss. In short, financial planning is directed towards providing a service in terms of dollars to other people, parts

41

of an organization, or the organization as a whole. Financial plans, in other than purely financial institutions or estate management, are usually closely tied in with other functional plans of an organization.

Functional planning is directed towards a major type of work which the organization carries out, usually on a continuing basis. For example, in an industrial firm, major functions are marketing, manufacturing, and engineering. Functional planning represents a slice of physical, organizational, and financial planning applied to functional objectives.

General planning is total planning. It is the master planning for the firm, institution, or organisation as a whole. It is the summation and integration of functional plans in one sense and the establishment of the framework for functional plans in another sense. General planning is a combination of all four preceding types of planning. General planning is the process by means of which the organization adapts to its environment in time to insure its existence. General planning solves and prevents present and future problems, internal and external in nature.

What is a 'plan'?

Definition of a plan

A plan is a predetermined course of action over a specified period of time which represents a projected response to an anticipated environment in order to accomplish a specific set of adaptive objectives. Since a plan describes a course of action, it must provide answers to the questions of what, when, how, where, and who. The details of the course of action may or may not be spelled out in a plan. The plan may consist of a bare outline of the course of action to be taken. This outline may be filled in by others than the original planners and at a later time. 'A plan is nothing more than an ordered sequence of events (or activities) necessary to achieve a stated objective. To be complete, this ordered sequence of events must show *all* significant interrelationships that exist among those events beyond simple sequence.'[3]

Whereas planning is a process, the immediate result is an entity, namely, the plan. The plan is intended to be an intermediate event between the planning process and the implementation process. If the plan is not implemented, the plan becomes the end result (a somewhat sterile result, perhaps) rather than an intermediate event. 'All plans have a common purpose: the forecasting, programming, and coordination of a logical sequence of events, which, if successful, will accomplish the commander's mission.'[4]

What if several overall 'plans' are developed, but only one is considered feasible? Are the rejected 'plans', which do not represent the action, to be taken really as plans? For the purpose of definition, they should be included within the meaning of plan on the basis that they outline a course of action.

42

This idea of plans which are never put into effect is common to military operations. A vigilant country during peace time will have available plans defining action to be taken in the case of assumed threatening events. As conditions change, such plans will become obsolete and new plans must be developed. Yet we would certainly consider the discarded outlines for action 'plans' even though they are not put into effect.

The view is sometimes taken that 'no plan' is also a plan. By definition, however, a plan is a predetermined course of action over a period of time. If action is not predetermined for some specified time in the future, then *ad hoc* decisions cannot be said to constitute a plan.

Plans and forecasts

While forecasts are necessary for the process of planning, a forecast does not constitute a plan. A forecast is a prediction of anticipated future external events. Normally, forecasts of future conditions are first made without considering the effect or consequences of the action to be taken by the planner. It may be that the action prescribed by the plan will have only an infinitesimal effect on the environment forecasted. On the other hand, revised forecasts may have to be made when the effects of alternative plans are considered. In the latter case, plans may have to be revised in the light of revised forecasts and an alternative process employed until a stable point is reached.

Plans are concerned with lines of action to be taken by the executor of the plans, while forecasts are passive in that they are purely predictive. Plans are predictive in that the course of action laid out represents a prediction of future action by the executor of the plans. Thus, plans consist of specified courses of action for the future and, in a sense, represent a forecast of the executor's actions. Forecasting predicts environmental conditions at future times based upon the actions, nature, external factors in the environment, and the effector of the plans.

Forecasts are derived from facts, assumptions, creativity, and deduction. In turn, forecasts become assumptions upon which the plans are based. Forecasts and plans, while distinct, will often interact with each other. Plans may be such that they will, when implemented, affect the environment in which they act so that the forecast needs to be revised in this light. Under a revised forecast the plan may need revision. This dynamic relationship is typical of planning where conflicting participants are acting.

Formal, written and undocumented plans

A proposed sequence of actions may be set down in a highly formalized and systematic manner. The more complex the plan, the more important that the plan be expressed in such a formal manner. Otherwise, for complex plans, part of the plan may be forgotten or may be changed unknowingly, or may lack many other characteristics necessary for a plan to be effective. If a complex plan loses form and changes because it cannot be recalled by those implementing it, it is doubtful if it can truly be identified as a plan.

Plans may be written out in general terms and in an incomplete and informal fashion. Such plans may be in the form of notes or memoranda. For simple plans, this may be adequate to define the course of action.

For even simpler, short-range plans, particularly those of individuals in their everyday activities outside of business, plans may not be written down at all. Because of single objectives involved in each plan and because of few alternative courses of actions available at decision points, these plans can be easily stored in the memory. Yet the courses of action are presumed to be formulated mentally in a clear manner based upon forecast conditions, and these undocumented courses may represent true plans.

Objectives, goals, events, milestones, and missions

Part of the planning process is the establishment of objectives and goals. Hence, part of the plan is the statement or recognition of specific objectives and goals. For purposes of definition, we will take 'objective' to mean the ultimate end result which is to be accomplished by the overall plan over a specified period of time. The objective represents a state or condition which we desire to exist when the plan has been completely implemented. The objective may be a rather complex statement describing the desired situation. For example, a business objective may be to achieve a certain sales volume at a specified future time, to make its name known to a percentage of the population, to be a leader in its field, and to expand its product line. The objective may be considered, in discrete terms, to represent a set of goals to be achieved.

Objectives may be either tangible or intangible. A tangible objective may be the development and construction of a nuclear reactor, a space vehicle, or a chemical plant. On the other hand, an intangible objective might be the achievement of a certain market position, an established brand image, a new social security system, or a favorable balance of world power. Whatever the objective is, it must be completely defined and identified with a point in time in order that a meaningful plan may be developed.

A goal is defined as an intermediate result to be achieved by a certain time as part of the grand plan. A plan can therefore have many goals. For large engineering projects employing modern management planning techniques, goals are usually called 'events' or 'milestones'. The latter term, in particular, provides the flavour of meaning to the term 'goals' as we will use it to distinguish it from 'objective'. 'Event' emphasizes the occurrence of a situation in the real world.

44

The word 'mission' is sometimes used to denote 'objective'. The military writers have adopted this term to designate various assignments of people or special projects. In fact, according to some reports, it has been stated that inanimate objects have 'missions'. A mission is, according to the dictionary, a sending forth; a group of persons or envoy sent to perform some task; or an errand or commission. A mission may be considered to be a statement of a task and its objective assigned to an individual or group of people.

Policies, regulations, procedures, and methods

Is a policy a plan or only part of a plan? The view we take here is that a policy is *not* a plan. A plan is directed toward achievement of specific objectives over a specified period of time. A policy is a guide which delimits action, but does not specify time. It is open-ended, in that it is not a plan of action leading to specific objectives over a given period of time; rather, policies are timeless. This view has been stated simply: 'A policy is not a plan but a guiding cannon of interest.'[5]

A policy is a definition of common purposes of an organization which establishes guidelines and limits for discretionary action by individuals responsible for implementing overall plans. Policies may be written or implied. Policies may be identified by the following criteria:

1 Does it permit discretionary action and exercise of good judgement?

2 Are the provisions positive but permissive within clearly defined limits so that exceptions need not be made in implementing overall plans?

3 Is it timeless? That is, does it apply without any specification of how long it is to be in force?

Sometimes, for the sake of achieving uniformity of action in some area, an organization may issue a directive policy. A directive policy states a specific obligatory course of action which does not require interpretation by those who may be called upon to implement it. Despite the greater specificity, the directive policy is not a plan since it is designed to limit a process, not to reach a specific goal within a specific time.

Some organizations are guided by 'regulations'. When a question arises as to what should be done or how to do something, we would look in a book of regulations. Regulations may be policies which must guide actions. Some regulations constitute plans since they define sequences of actions or methods for achieving objectives within a limited time period.

Procedures, as the term is commonly understood, are plans. A procedure is a series of detailed steps telling how to accomplish a task or reach a goal, contingent upon the decision being made to accomplish the particular task or goal. Thus, procedures are really subplans to larger plans. Procedures, because

45

of their detailed nature, are ordinarily written down and made available to those who may use them. Actually, for a procedure to be a plan, according to our definition, the procedure must be one that is accomplished within a specified time period once it has been started.

A 'method' describes the process of performing one step of a procedure in terms of facilities, manpower, and time available. Since a method describes an action thought out in advance, a method may be considered to be a plan of action. Actually, it is a subplan of a procedure.

In summary, a plan may consist of many subplans with different degrees of detail. Policies, which are necessary for the accomplishment of a series of plans are important to the accomplishment of plans. They are a part of the plans, but they are not plans or subplans themselves. Procedures and methods, on the other hand, constitute detailed plans which are usually part of general plans. The general plan provides the time element for the procedure or method. A distinguishing feature of a plan is that a definite time limit is involved.

Tactics and strategies

There are other terms in common use which relate to a plan and which need to be examined. Tactics represent a short-range plan for operations where an element of conflict is involved. Tactics represent a plan which has emphasis on counter-actions of other players or actors in the environment. Tactics are adroit devices for achieving a goal. Thus, tactics represent a special type of short-range plan.

The term 'strategy' is founded upon military science which still has the greatest claim to the concept. Strategy in the military sense means 'the art of the general' and is derived from the Greek *strategos* formed from *stratos* (army) and *agein* (to lead). In the military sense, strategy is the overriding long-range plan. Strategy in the military sense is said to have direction, compass point, or intent. This direction is known as the 'strategic concept'.

Schelling gives the most elegant discussion of the meaning of strategy:

Among diverse theories of conflict—corresponding to the diverse meanings of the word 'conflict'—a main dividing line is between those that treat conflict as a pathological state and seek its causes and treatment, and those that take conflict for granted and study the behaviour associated with it. Among the latter there is a further division between those that examine the participants in a conflict in all their complexity—with regard to both 'rational' and 'irrational' behavior, conscious and unconscious, and to motivations as well as to calculations—and those that focus on the more rational, conscious artful kind of behaviour. Crudely speaking, the latter

46

treat conflict as a kind of contest, in which the participants are trying to 'win'. A study of conscious, intelligent, sophisticated conflict behaviour— of successful behavior—is like a search for rules of 'correct' behaviour in a contest winning sense.

We can call this field of study the 'strategy of conflict'.[6]

A recent definition of strategy has been developed in the theory of games, and while different authors give slightly different flavors to the term, their meanings are essentially the same. For example, John D. McDonald writes: 'The strategical situation in game theory lies in the interaction between two or more persons, each of whose actions is based on an expectation concerning the actions of others over whom he has no control. The outcome is dependent upon the personal moves of the participants. The policy followed in making these moves is the strategy.'[7] W. J. Baumol places considerable emphasis on the rules involved: 'The strategy really becomes an extensive book of rules indicating what the player intends to do, in every contingency, from the beginning of the game to the end. Thus the strategy commits the player to an entire sequence of moves which is contingent in a fully specified manner upon what is done by the other player.'[8]

For the purpose of our definition here, strategy includes the element of sophisticated conflict behavior. It includes a set of interrelated decisions. It includes a temporal dimension which is not included in game theory. Strategy, while long range, is flexible in that it is continually reviewed in terms of new information so it represents sequential decision-making. Thus, strategy may be considered a long-range plan or pattern of action by means of which the planner seeks to optimize achievement of his goals within a field of mutually conflicting and cooperating participants and varying unknown states of nature. It is a particular type of plan.

Programs

The word 'program' is often used in connection with the concept of plan. In engineering development work, the term PERT or Program Evaluation Review Technique, appears. According to a description of programming by a spokesman in the Polaris project.

The POLARIS Management Sequence consists of three principal phases; definition of program objectives, program planning and implementation, and program evaluation.[9] [*The Polaris Management* publication goes on to say] They (program management plans) present specific tasks, responsibilities, and key milestones within a logical structure deriving from the total program objectives; establish a uniform basis for performance reporting in the Special Projects Management Center; provide a common frame of reference for presenting effects (of performance facts on planned effort) in major areas of effort; and provide a basis for decision making. They are an official expression of top level and branch level planning.[10]

PERT was developed to minimize and control the time for large projects. One of its basic attributes is the statistical estimates of time for completion of each event and for the entire project.

It appears from a study of the literature of planning for research, development, and engineering projects that a program in this context may be a plan which is quite detailed, is characterized by defining the interrelationships of goals in terms of sequence and timing, and involves concurrent networks of actions which define times at which major decisions must be made. Yet, this is not always the case. For example, R. K. Stolz writes, '*Programming* develops specific research objectives and guidelines that make possible sound decisions on project selection. It defines the fields that should be studied and the emphasis that should be placed on the different kinds of research within each field.[11] If the output of programming is assumed to be a program, then a program consists of objectives and outlines for achieving these objectives.

Another form of 'program' is the output of a linear programming model. Linear programming is used to help solve problems where limited resources are specified in order to obtain a particular objective such as least cost, least time, or highest profit. While linear programming is problem-solving rather than planning, the question might be raised as to whether the outcome, a proposed course of action, is a plan. In general, the answer is that it is *not* a plan. While a course of action is specified, the timing of action is not. Even when a minimum-time problem is solved, the result is not a plan, since no starting and ending date or interval of time for accomplishment of the action appears in the representation of the result.

In administrative fields, 'program' may designate a large-scale course of action or set of integrated projects for achieving a major objective. For example, in the Report of the President's Commission on National Goals (1960), the Commission refers in its letter of transmittal to the Report as an outline of coordinated national policies and *programs*. However, in the Report itself, no time schedules are given and no deadlines for completion of action are mentioned. The subtitle of the popular publication of the Report does generalize the time aspect—'Programs for Action in the Sixties'. This is so vague that we could not deduce that a program as used in this context must include a schedule.

A less technical but common use of the word program occurs in the arts, entertainment, and sports worlds. The program is a description of events which will take place at a given time. Often, additional information is included in the program, such as the characters involved, location, and starting time. Usually, the termination time is not specified.

In attempting to develop the theory of management, it is important that terms be clearly defined. We find that the word 'program' is used with quite variable meanings by people engaged in executive planning. The problem is to determine whether 'program' should be identified as synonymous with 'plan' or whether it should have a different meaning. In the final analysis, this can only be an arbitrary choice. We believe that a commonly used term is desirable to describe courses of action which are interrelated but which have not been scheduled. We will therefore, assign this meaning to 'program'. A plan may then be considered to be a (time) scheduled program.

Types of plans

Plans may be categorized as single use, repeat, standing, standby, or rejected. The single-use plan is one that serves a particular purpose and is never used again. In a rapidly changing environment, there will be many single-use plans designed to achieve objectives arising from new problems. A repeat plan is used under more stable conditions or under parallel conditions. For example, a company may develop a recruiting plan. Whenever it is necessary to recruit a number of professional people as the firm expands, it puts its recruiting plan into effect. Suppose that a company's sales force is geographically decentralized. A new sales plan may be developed which is to be put into effect in each territory. Thus the plan is repeated in a parallel rather than series time sequence.

The standing plan is a repeat plan, but one that automatically goes into effect. Standing plans are best exemplified by the procedures spelled out in a business firm's operating manual. Thus, the operating manual may specify a plan for processing grievances. Each step of the process and the maximum time allowed for each step would be given. Whenever a grievance is initiated by an employee, the plan becomes effective automatically. In the case of the repeat plan, a decision must be made each time as to whether to put the plan into effect. The repeat plan must be triggered off by someone in authority; it is not put into operation each time automatically.

As for the standby plan, we could argue that all standby plans are part of the total plan. Yet, since the standby plan is a parallel plan to accomplish the same objective as the chosen plan, and since it may be a general plan itself, it appears advisable to distinguish it for analytical reasons. The standby plan may become the operative plan if (a) conditions change so that the standby plan is more appropriate or (b) if the operative plan appears inadequate during testing or beginning of operations.

Actually the standby plan may be identical to the operative plan up to a certain point. Therefore, we may substitute the standby plan for the operative plan with no difficulty at any time before the two diverge.

49

Characteristics of a plan

A plan may be described in terms of a number of characteristics. These characteristics describe both the plan itself and considerations involved in its formulation. The characteristics of a plan are listed below.[1,2]

1 Scope.
2 Complexity.
3 Depth.
4 Organizational level or preparation.
5 Organizational level at which plan is to apply.
6 Environment in which plan is made.
7 Environment in which plan will be operative.
8 Resources (men, money, materials, time) involved in the plan.
9 Forward time or projection into the future.
10 Timing of the plan (when it will start).
11 Decision points.
12 Certainty, risk, and uncertainty involved in the premises.
13 Balance.
14 Integration.
15 Value of the plan.
16 Cost of the planning process.
17 Authorship.
18 Acceptance.
19 Ease of implementation.
20 Ease of control.
21 Measurement—features.

The development of a set of characteristics of a plan is essential to the development of a science of planning. First of all, such characteristics allow us to define a plan to a far greater extent than is possible on the basis of popular usage in business publications. Second, such characteristics are valuable not only for theoretical reasons, but for practical reasons in the process of planning. For example, in the planning process, the characteristics provide a checklist to insure that the plan is as complete as is desired. We may check the completed plan to make sure that each quantitative characteristic is present in the desired amount or to the desired degree. Clear definition of the elements which make up a plan cannot help but lead to better planning by the serious manager.

Conclusion

A basic characteristic of scientific method is the initial definition of terms to be used and classification of knowledge concerning these terms. In the area of planning, there is a voluminous body of literature, but little attempt has been made to establish a foundation of understanding for the purpose of inquiry and communication. The above discussion is intended to stimulate thinking about basic concepts of planning and plans rather than offer the ultimate answer.

References

1. TERRY, GEORGE R. *Principles of Management.* 3rd edn. Homewood, Illinois: Irwin, 1960, p. 123.
2. JONES, MANLEY HOWE, *Executive Decision-Making.* Homewood, Illinois: Irwin, 1957.
3. *Summary Report Phase 1,* Special Projects Office, Bureau of Naval Weapons, Dept. of the Navy, July 1958, p. 3.
4. NICHOLAS, COLONEL JACK D. *et al. The Joint and Combined Staff Officer's Manual.* Harrisburg, Pa.: Stackpole, 1959, p. 105.
5. GLOVER, JOHN G. *Fundamentals of Professional Management.* New York: Republic Book Co., 1954, p. 71.
6. SCHELLING, THOMAS C. *The Strategy of Conflict.* Cambridge, Mass.: Harvard UP, 1960.
7. MacDONALD, JOHN D. *Strategy in Poker, Business and War.* New York: Norton, 1955, p. 16.
8. BAUMOL, WILLIAM J. *Economic Theory and Operations.* Englewood Cliffs, N.J.: Prentice-Hall, 1961, p. 359.
9. Special Projects Office, Dept. of the Navy, *POLARIS Management.* Washington DC: US Government Printing Office, Rev. February 1961, p. 4.
10. Ibid., p. 10.
11. STOLZ, ROBERT K. 'Planning—Key to Research Success.' *Harvard Bsns Rev.,* May/June 1957.
12. See also DAVIS, RALPH C. *The Fundamentals of Top Management.* New York: Harper, 1951, pp. 46-51; and LeBRETON, PRESTON P. and HENNING, DALE A. *Planning Theory.* Englewood Cliff, N.J.: Prentice-Hall, 1951, p. 23.

3. Top management and long-range planning

Basil W. Denning

Since 1964, there has been much discussion about long-range planning and the greater need for it in national, educational, industrial, and commercial activities. This upsurge of interest has produced two major misconceptions. One of these is that long-range planning is a totally new activity. Yet, in practice, it is clear that various types of long-range planning have always been carried out by most sizeable organizations. Oil refineries have been built to last for 15 or 20 years, forests that will produce mature wood 50 years hence have been planted, sophisticated research and development work has been undertaken in areas such as colour television and the development of nuclear energy to produce usable products or services 7, 10 or 15 years later, and individual companies have carefully exploited certain competitive advantages without immediate return over periods of years before achieving their pay-off. In the armed services, long-range planning of officer structures has been practised and the level of officer entry determined on this basis for decades.

The second misconception seems to assume that long-range planning involves the application of a series of new management techniques, but that these techniques have marginal relevance to the real problems of running a business organization. It is suggested that both these sets of ideas badly misrepresent the aims of and the needs for corporate long-range planning.

An alternative view, which has more direct relevance to the board function, stems from the increasingly difficult challenge facing the top manager in carrying out the key elements in his managerial task. Most companies today are required to deal with an accelerating rate of techno-

• Reproduced from *The Director's Handbook*. Maidenhead: McGraw-Hill, 1969.

logical change, a rapid rate of social and market change, increasing capital intensity, and increasing international competition. Managerial responses to these factors have varied, but among them have been:

1 An increasing tendency to concentrate into a small number of dominating large units in each industry.

2 The resulting development of more complicated organizational structures.

3 An increasing need to employ more sophisticated analytical approaches to the long-term problems of the company.

These responses have, in turn, created their complications for top management and, in conjunction with the factors that brought them about, have greatly increased the risks attached to poor management decisions. Thus, many companies have in the past years introduced 'long-range planning' as a separate specific activity. Thus, the aspect of 'long-range planning' that appears to be new is the development of formal long-range planning systems for the company as a whole, designed:

1 To ensure that top management's task is aided as much as possible by careful analysis and consideration of alternative courses of action and, perhaps more important, to ensure that corporate objectives and strategy are regularly and systematically reappraised.

2 To ensure that the most careful evaluation is made of projects (broadly defined to include building a new plant, acquiring another company, developing a new product, or entering a new market) most of which now require the commitment of large capital sums for long periods of time.

3 To develop an organizational process that coordinates the future activities of different units in large diverse organizations and increases top management's ability to control these activities.

It may be of interest here to indicate the rate of growth of long-range planning systems. In research carried out by questionnaire, in 1967, to the 'Top 300' companies in *The Times* list, 65 companies were carrying out systematic long-range planning over three years or more. Of these 65 companies, 22 had introduced long-range planning of this type between 1964 and 1967. Furthermore, out of 136 companies who replied, but did not complete the questionnaire, 27 stated that they were in the process of introducing systematic long-range planning.

What sort of formal long-range planning systems have been introduced and how have they been organized? As with all organizational processes it is not possible to set out general rules that should always be followed. Nevertheless, it is possible to develop an approach to the creation of a long-range planning system for application in particular situations, and the remainder of this section will concentrate on describing this approach.

The elements of a long-range planning process

A long-range planning process should be designed to organize three separate types of planning into one coherent pattern. These types of planning are:

1 Strategic planning. The function of strategic planning is to determine the future posture of the business in relation to its changing environment.

2 Project planning. The function of project planning is to assess new projects, to integrate new projects into the firm and to execute the projects efficiently.

3 Operational planning. The function of operational planning is to translate strategic plans into action, to coordinate diverse activities, and to allow top management consideration of future operations in specific terms.

A properly organized long-range planning process will ensure that all these planning activities are integrated in such a way that top management can:

1 Make strategic and project decisions after proper analysis of the best information available.

2 Approve projects which conform to the strategic plan and are economically attractive.

3 View the business as a whole in terms of size, market share, profitability, managerial strength, etc., at a point of time three, five, or seven years hence.

4 Approve the proposed activities of operational units in specific terms.

5 Compare the actual results of operational activities and new projects against planned results, thus exercising more effective control.

The activities involved in the long-range planning process

A diagram of a long-range planning process is given in Fig. 3.1. The diagram has deliberately been kept simple, and would need substantial amplification if it was intended to be used by any one organization, but it does draw attention to the key aspects of the planning process, and it can be viewed as a simple system defined by inputs, processes, and outputs.

1. Inputs

There are three basic inputs into the planning process: environmental information, new project information, and operational plans and forecasts.

Environmental information is needed on a systematic basis about the long-term economic position; developments in the technology appropriate to the business and any other technology likely to produce products that may replace the present product line; changes in the educational and social system with forecasts of the resulting changes in skills, abilities, and expectations of future personnel; political changes and influences, and the probabilities of new government regulations and taxation; actual and possible developments by competition, including changes in the structure of an industry. Increasingly, with the rapid development of large international companies this information needs to be collected systematically on a global basis.

New project information is required about all types of major new projects, a project being broadly defined. During the course of a year, many projects may be under consideration, such as research and development for new

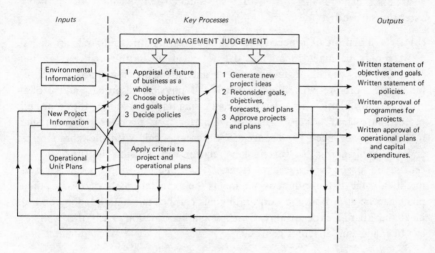

Figure 3.1 Simple flow diagram of a long-range planning process

products, plans to enter new markets, the licensing of new products, the development of new manufacturing facilities, or examination of companies for acquisition. In practice, project ideas will tend to be generated in many parts of the organization and, normally, some criteria are required to decide which projects must be evaluated and decided centrally. These criteria normally include a minimum size in terms of finance and company rules about projects that can be regarded as having strategic importance.

The last major series of inputs arise from the forward projection of the operating units of the business. Within a company that is planning forward on a regular basis, it will be normal for every unit, division, or subsidiary annually to prepare plans for three, five, or seven years ahead. The bringing together of these plans at the organization's centre enables a detailed examination to be made of the key measures of the business, turnover, product line, profitability, number of employees, strength of management structure, at a future point of time.

55

2. Corporate planning processes involving top management

The various informational inputs noted above enable top management to carry out its principal planning tasks. These can briefly be described as follows:

(a) Appraisal of the future of the company as a whole—By drawing together the operational projections, plus those new projects appraised centrally, a picture of the whole company at a future point in time can be established and the question raised as to whether this is a satisfactory picture. Strengths and weaknesses can be analysed with respect to current business and possible extensions of activity.

(b) Determination of objectives and goals—During this appraisal, an assessment should be made in quantitative terms of the future market standing (e.g., market shares, total turnover, and growth), the product range, innovation, productivity, the financial and physical resources, and profitability. Judgements can also be made qualitatively about the required performance and development of managers or the need for outside recruitment, the need for changes in the relationship with the labour force and the implications for certain key relationships outside the firm, such as central or local government relations. If examination of proposed achievements in each of these dimensions meets the expectations of the Board, then plans can be approved and corporate goals can be enunciated. If they do not meet the Board's expectations, then, reexamination along each of these lines can be made, and different goals set.

(c) Determination of policies—With objectives and goals defined, top management is in a position to develop its policies. In the limited sense of long-range planning, these can be regarded as being of two types: the setting of criteria for selection and choice of projects, and the development of standards for overall performance by subsidiary units. Policies are most realistically viewed as long-term decisions to guide action by others, and, in this sense, the establishment of selection criteria and standards of performance are important policy decisions.

(d) Application of criteria—Final judgement may now be reached by top management on the proposals submitted by operational and functional units, project teams, or other special staff units. In practice, few of the final decisions can ever be made by the mechanistic application of strict criteria, but decision-making is eased by agreed understanding of the criteria that will be used by the board.

At this stage, the planning process is likely to involve a further cycle, with project and operational proposals being sent back for reappraisal and reexamination before going through the same cycle a second or third time.

3. Outputs

The identifiable outputs of a corporate planning process are fourfold:

- (a) A written statement of objectives and goals.
- (b) A written statement of planning criteria.
- (c) Written approval of programmes for new projects.
- (d) Written approval of operational plans and delegated capital expenditures.

The last two of these are important, not only because they give final top management approval for action but also because they provide the basic standards against which subsequent action and performance can be measured. Some of the final plans will be in budgetary form, and in this sense, the planning cycle can be regarded as a lengthening out of a normal budgeting cycle. Long-range plans should not, however, be confined merely to financial figures, and should include the other dimensions of required action against which progress can subsequently be measured.

The timespan of planning

Different companies plan out to different time horizons for many reasons. There is a general tendency to choose five years as a reasonable compromise between the need for an adequate time perspective and the costs of planning in detail to time periods when, because of so many unknowns, the exercise would be unrealistic.

Whereas there are few prescriptive rules about the length of time over which planning should be carried out, there are some guides on how to reach a decision on this point. They are:

1 The planning cycle should be long enough to include the full time for bringing new large capital projects into existence, including the time required for negotiating the necessary outside finance.

2 The planning cycle should be long enough to allow reasoned consideration of major technological changes.

3 The planning cycle should be longer than any cyclical patterns that may exist in the economy if the product sold is affected by cyclical swings.

4 Special planning cycles and processes may be necessary to deal with projects of especial length, such as forest plantations, development of shipping fleets, life insurance, or oil-field exploration and research.

5 Long-range planning should be a continuous process. This means that while three, five, or seven years may be selected as the time period over which planning takes place, the forward planning for this time period should be carried out every year. In other words, the concept of a rolling plan should be adopted.

There are few sizeable companies that can afford not to indulge in systematic planning over less than three years.

The organization of long-range planning

The organization of long-range planning is carried out in a wide variety of different ways in different companies. There are few general statements of value about what is, of necessity, an intensely individual corporate process, but there are one or two factors that should always be borne in mind.

1 No effective long-range planning process is likely to be maintained in the face of operational pressures unless one man at a senior level is appointed to ensure that planning is effectively carried out.

2 There is no record of long-range planning being carried out effectively unless the activity has had the active support of the chief executive.

3 The introduction of systematic long-range planning will have an impact on the real power-structure of the company and may cause concern to managers of decentralized units. For this reason, it is a mistake to use long-range planning as a method of reorganization, and wiser to introduce it after any needed organizational changes have been made.

4 The responsibility for the detailed work involved in long-range planning may be carried out centrally or be decentralized to operating units. The question as to who should take responsibility for the different aspects of long-range planning involves organizational decisions similar to those required for any systematic process, such as management development or cost control. It will usually be necessary, however, to create a small central staff to assist the executive in charge of planning. Companies with experience of long-range planning have usually provided a small central staff with expertise in economic assessment, the relevant technology, operations research, market research, and finance.

5 Whereas the initial thrust for long-range planning tends to arise from the finance department, American experience suggests that corporate planning is best if it is not headed by the chief accountant or controller. The reason for this lies in the attitudes needed in the two jobs. One is a guardian of the company's assets. The other is the explorer of new areas of activity, and this calls for imagination, flexibility, and risk-taking. Increasingly, the tendency is to appoint a man of general managerial capability who commands the respect of other senior executives in the company, and to provide the necessary technical expertise through specialist subordinates.

6 In a decentralized organizational structure, it will be necessary to appoint to groups or divisions the equivalent of a long-range planning manager to assist group or divisional chief executives with their planning. It may not be necessary for this to be a full-time job, but the responsibility should be clearly defined.

58

7 Systematic long-range planning can be built only on a basis of efficient budgeting and control systems and a thorough understanding of the financial and economic aspects of operations. Where this underpinning is missing or is unrealistic, the quality of long-range plans will be poor.

8 The introduction of systematic long-range planning rarely produces immediate results since it is a difficult managerial exercise, frequently requires changes in the time horizons over which operating managers think, involving an attitudinal change, and is rarely carried out effectively in the first cycle.

9 The aim should be to have longer-range planning regarded as a normal part of the overall process of managing the company rather than a special separate exercise. This is likely to be achieved only after several cycles have been completed.

Techniques for long-range planning

Comparatively few techniques can specifically be regarded as being applicable to long-term planning only. Within each functional area there are specific techniques of forecasting for short, medium, and long-range purposes. Increasingly, mathematical models are being used for many types of forecast, but these models require substantial and crucial top management judgements if they are to give helpful results.

Certain forms of analysis and helpful structured approaches to these problems can be found in the literature quoted at the end of this section, but long-range planning should draw widely on any relevant managerial technique. The major problems in this area are conceptual, organizational, and judgemental.

Summary

Directors carry specific managerial responsibilities in addition to their legal responsibilities. In the increasingly complex industrial and commercial world, the fulfilling of these responsibilities requires special assistance. An important form of help large companies are increasingly adopting is the development of systematic long-range planning processes that incorporate strategic, project, and operational planning. Properly used and organized, these processes can assist top management in their key tasks of setting objectives and goals, formulating policy, deciding on major projects, and coordinating and controlling large organizations.

4. A conceptual model for the analysis of planning behavior

John Friedmann

Until a few years ago, discussions of planning were restricted to consideration of an abstract model of perfect rationality in social decision-making.[1] In use, however, this model turned out to be unsatisfactory. As a theoretical model, it failed to lead to fruitful hypotheses and, because of its logical rigidity, it was incapable of substantial modification. As a normative model it failed because rationality in real life is always 'bounded', so that the recipes for planning that could be drawn from the model were frequently inapplicable.[2]

With the recent upsurge of interest in national planning, however, social scientists have begun to study the actual workings of the planning process. Some students are focusing on the substantive contents of national plans and on the propriety of the strategies adopted; others are doing research on the administrative machinery evolved; still others are curious about how planning got started in particular societies and how the first plans came to be made.[3] But where the earlier theorists erred in ignoring planning practice, the new empiricists are leaning too much in the other direction: they simply look at activities called planning and describe what they see. Although this is leading to the collection of much information, it is also giving rise to unwitting distortions when basic preconceptions have not been made explicit. Simple descriptions of something as ephemeral as national planning is scarcely even of historical value, and certainly does not add significantly to *verifiable* knowledge, which alone is capable of serving as a sound foundation for a theory of planning.* The importance of these studies lies primarily in their

---

* Planning theory was formerly little more than an exercise in the logic of rational decision making; its reformulation on an empirical basis will involve extensive work in the description and explanation of planning phenomena and in generalizations derived from these data.

● Reproduced with permission from *Administrative Science Quarterly*, Vol. 12, September 1967, pp. 225-52.

fresh approach, which has brought the study of planning within the scope of empirical social research.

The present paper is an attempt to create that minimum of conceptual order which is necessary for a scientifically more disciplined study of planning.[4] There are various ways of defining planning.[5] Here planning will be considered as the *guidance of change within a social system.*[6] Specifically, this means a process of self-guidance that may involve *promoting differential growth* of subsystem components (sectors), *activating the transformation of system structures* (political, economic, social), and *maintaining system boundaries* during the course of change.* Accordingly, the idea of planning involves a confrontation of expected with intended performance, the application of controls to accomplish the intention when expectations are not met, the observation of possible variances from the prescribed path of change, and the repetition of this cycle each time significant variations are perceived.[7]

To this view of planning as a self-guidance system, a still more general conception may be added that will lead directly into the structure of the model. Planning may be simply regarded as reason acting on a network of ongoing activities through the intervention of certain decision structures and processes. The emphasis here is on intervention and, hence, on *planning for change.* This intervention is made on the basis of an intellectual effort or, more simply, of thought. 'Introducing' planning, then, means specifically the introduction of ways and means for using technical intelligence to bring about changes that otherwise would not occur.

This is fundamental in my view. Society is a going concern. The ongoing stream of life does not wait for planners to give it direction. Planners must act upon social and economic processes with the fragile instrument of their minds (amplified by whatever practical means they may command) to guide society towards desired objectives. A comprehensive model of planning must, therefore, include forms of thought as an important category for analysis.

The model

The model proposed here for the analysis of planning behavior has three general characteristics (see Fig. 4.1): First, it is valid only for what is here called planning for change. Other forms of planning may be identified, such as operations research, but these are not included. Second, it is an attempt to distinguish among different forms of planning for change and to show the relationships among them. Third, the model is intended as an aid to empirical research. On the basis of the actual findings, it will almost certainly need to

* The distinction between self-guidance systems and those in which guidance is imposed by agents external to the system is of theoretical and practical importance, but will not be pursued further in this paper.

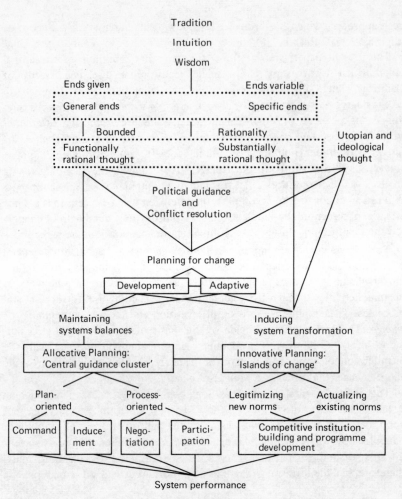

Tradition

Intuition

Wisdom

Ends given .... Ends variable

General ends   Specific ends

Bounded .... Rationality   Utopian and
                                                                   ideological
Functionally   Substantially   thought
rational thought   rational thought

Political guidance
and
Conflict resolution

Planning for change

Development ⎯ Adaptive

Maintaining   Inducing
systems balances   system transformation

Allocative Planning: Innovative Planning:
'Central guidance cluster'   'Islands of change'

Plan-   Process-   Legitimizing   Actualizing
oriented   oriented   new norms   existing norms

Command | Induce-   Nego- | Partici-   Competitive institution-
          ment   tiation pation   building and programme
                                          development

System performance

Figure 4.1   A conceptual model for the analysis of planning behavior

be refined, modified, and expanded. Specifically absent from the model are the institutional forms of planning and explicit recognition of the time dimension in which planning processes occur.

Forms of planning

A convenient way for entering the model is to consider the two major forms of planning for change. The criterion for distinguishing between them is the relative autonomy of planning units in the making of decisions. Under *developmental planning*, there is a high degree of autonomy with respect to the setting of ends and the choice of means; under *adaptive planning*, most

62

decisions are heavily contingent on the actions of others external to the planning system. In practice, of course, most planning decisions are made along the continuum between complete autonomy and complete dependency, and the behavior of planning systems will differ according to the distribution of decision functions between the two extremes. For instance, planning for urban development at the level of the city will usually be more adaptive than developmental: to a great extent, it will need to respond or adapt to external forces, such as shifts in the locational preferences of national industries, which the municipality cannot significantly influence through its own actions. In planning for national development, on the other hand, the public authorities are able to control a larger number of the variables relevant to its own objectives, so that the nation is much more independent than any of its municipalities. Even among nations, however, there may be differences in the degree of dependency on external forces; and a small, weak nation, such as Haiti, has to plan more adaptively with respect to international conditions—if it is planning at all—than the city of Sao Paulo with respect to Brazil.

What are the main differences in the expected behavior between developmental and adaptive planning?

Adaptive planning

In adaptive planning, there will be a tendency to push decisions upward to centers of developmental planning where the parameters for choice at lower levels may be changed. In attempting this, lower-level planning systems will generally rely on political manipulation to achieve their ends. So that negotiations with the central authorities may be conducted with equal technical competence, however, counterplanning may be added to political action. Since, on the government's side, any bargaining in a complex advanced economic system is usually done by qualified technical experts, the contending parties must enter negotiations at least as well prepared.*

At the same time, the gradual recognition of interdependence within the system may lead the separate, partisan interests—each engaged in a measure of adaptive planning—to discover a common or public interest. Such an interest, as the work of the Bureau of Economic Research, the Brookings Institution, the Committee for Economic Development, and the National Planning

* A typical example of counterplanning is the large number of national planning agencies that were set up in Latin America when it became known that the Alliance for Progress would make financial aid contingent on the preparation of national plans. In order to deal with the international agencies in Washington, a country had to send economists who could negotiate for aid on the basis of a logical program for development. This program was then compared to the Alliance's own planning for Latin America, whether by the Committee of Nine, the Agency for International Development, or the Interamerican Development Bank. In many Latin American countries today, national planning is primarily a means of obtaining international assistance rather than a means of guiding the use of resources within the country.

Association in the United States clearly demonstrates, will lead partisan interests gradually in the direction of quasi-governmental policy planning, although the interests they nominally represent are private. Thus, on the technical side at least, adaptive planning may become fused with developmental planning, that is, sub-system with system planning.

Finally, adaptive planning is typically opportunistic. For instance, one reason for the frequently noted instability of long-term capital improvement programs for municipalities in the United States is that cities cannot afford to lose the federal or state financial aid that frequently plays a decisive part in municipal public works. Since funds from external sources often become available only upon short notice, are tied to specific performance criteria, and normally require matching contributions, significant modifications in the program are frequently made to accommodate the emergence of sudden opportunities for external financing.[8] Similarly so-called national planning is often related to the availability of funds and the requirements of international sources, as, for example, the sudden creation of national planning agencies in Latin America in response to a call for national plans as a basis for Alliance for Progress assistance. These plans closely reflect what each country believes will, at a given time, be the most persuasive program for obtaining funds from the Alliance; they are not necessarily related to the priorities of domestic needs.

Different degrees of autonomy and dependency in decision-making tend to be mirrored in a hierarchy of planning authorities which stand in more or less systematic technical and political relation to one another, each level having its appropriate function and decision power. Since each higher level is capable of changing some of the relevant conditions for decisions at all lower levels, and since every change of this sort represents some change of policy, policy planning tends to be emphasized at higher decision levels and programming— the detailed specification of investments in volume, time, and place—at lower levels. Or, put in another way, developmental planning tends to shade off into policy-making, adaptive planning into programming. In fact, however, the two become mixed in varying proportion, according to the point on the autonomy-dependency continuum where planning occurs.

Developmental planning

In developmental planning, the role of political institutions for guidance and conflict resolution obviously becomes crucial; for it is here that the basic policy decisions are made and that the clashing interests of adaptive planners must be resolved. Developmental planning is not only a technical, but also, and to a large degree, a political function. The relationship between planning and politics is therefore a crucial one.[9]

First, an effective decision process almost always involves both experts and politicians (or policy-makers) simultaneously in close interdependency. No politician who values the services of an expert can afford consistently to disregard his judgement, nor will any expert desiring influence, systematically oppose the wishes of his employer. Therefore, every decision will be influenced by political interests in varying degrees, and, at the same time, it must satisfy some technical criteria. Once a decision is made, it becomes exceedingly difficult to separate the contributions made by each group, for it represents a synthesis of political and expert judgement. Failure to achieve this synthesis will mean that the plans are not carried out or, that policies adopted, being exclusively political, will be inadequate or inappropriate.[10]

Second, successful planning in its more technical aspects must meet certain needs internal to the political process itself. Although these uses of planning are not usually made explicit, they are nevertheless real. They may include: (a) symbolic representation of progress, modernity, and so on; (b) mobilization of external resources; (c) redistribution of the relative influence or weight of participants in a diffused power structure (for example, strengthening the role of the Presidency, of technicians, of the industrial sector, and so forth); (d) helping to build a national consensus on fundamental values; (e) stimulating an acceptance of development; and (f) encouraging counterplanning.[11]

For example, in his recent study on planning in Tanzania, Anthony Rweyemamu writes:

In a new nation like Tanzania, a national plan is a major, albeit incomplete, substitute for the goods which were promised explicitly or implicitly during the struggle for independence. In so far as it is indicative of a future of abundance, a national plan serves as a unifying agent of an otherwise loose and fragile society.... Therefore, even if the economic and social goals are not completely realized, a plan is successful to the extent to which it serves to mobilize the people's energies, bring about national integration and a measure of political consensus.[12]

These varied uses of planning are frequently not only more important than the explicit purposes for which planning is undertaken (more rapid growth, greater efficiency, better coordination), but also inconsistent with these purposes. It is evident that they will also define the respective roles of experts and politicians and help to shape the institutional framework of planning.

In any system, there are large areas of indifference where political behavior is possible without planned intervention. The relative influence of a technical planning function in guiding social and economic change will depend chiefly on five variables: (a) the clarity of system objectives, (b) the extent of consensus about them, (c) the relative importance that politicians attach to them, (d) the degree of variance relative to objectives expected in the performance of the system, and (e) the extent to which a technical (as contrasted with a purely political) approach is believed capable of making system performance conform to these objectives. Technical planning, therefore, moves temporarily into the foreground whenever goals are clear, widely held, and deemed to be important; whenever in such a situation system performance is believed to depart significantly from the norm; and whenever, given all of these conditions, expert judgement coupled with a variety of control mechanisms is held to be more effective than political manipulation. Where these conditions do not occur, planning is likely to be reduced to a vestigial function only.

Relation of kinds of thinking to planning

All political and planning activities are in varying degree influenced by different kinds of thinking that may be classified as rational or extra-rational. Rational thought can be further considered as bounded or non-bounded. And bounded rationality may be considered as functionally or substantially rational. Far from being superfluous categories for the analysis of planning, these kinds of thinking are decisive in influencing both the prevailing styles of planning and the actual behavior of planners.

Bounded rationality. This refers to the fact that thought and consequent action intended to be rational are contingent on environmental conditions—the social context of planning—which represent the medium in and through which planning decisions are made.[13] This environment for decision is often discussed in terms of so-called obstacles to planning, but it seems preferable to speak of it simply as the specific set of structural conditions under which planning must occur.[14] In discussing planning in Italy, Joseph LaPalombara underlines the critical importance of the decision environment. He writes: No one with even the most cursory knowledge of the Italian bureaucracy could seriously hold that, within its present structure, it is able to support state intervention in the economic sphere, much less to direct and to coordinate economic planning on a national scale.[15]

But, in fact, the limitations of bureaucracy are only one aspect of the decision environment, which is more adequately described in categories such as the following:

1 The number and diversity of organized interest groups and their power to influence decisions.

2 The degree to which political opposition is tolerated or accepted, and the role assigned to it.

3 The dependence of the economic system on private enterprise, and the characteristics of enterprise (size, monopoly, and others) and of entrepreneurial behavior.

4 The efficiency of the relevant information systems: their capacity, load, reliability, promptness, secrecy, etc.

5 The structure of bureaucratic institutions and their performance.

6 The educational level of the population and size of the university-educated elite.

7 The availability of relevant information and its reliability.

8 The predictability of change within the system and of external changes that will affect its performance.

In short, to be 'bounded' means that a decision can be no more rational than the conditions under which it is made; the most that planners can hope for is the most rational decision *under the circumstances.* 'Until administrative improvements are clearly foreseeable,' writes Albert Waterston, 'planners must prepare plans which take account of administrative capacity. This means, among other things, that complex forms of planning must be avoided when a country's administration is not ready for them.'[16] The author might have broadened this statement to include all conditions that provide the social context for decisions and action.

The concept of bounded rationality suggests the possibility of identifying a number of discrete planning styles which result from the adaptation of the institutional forms and procedures of planning to relatively stable characteristics of their institutional environment. These environments and the forms of planning adapted to them can both be reduced to a few general types. The study of planning styles would therefore be helpful in formulating hypotheses for the comparative study of planning behavior.

It is useful to distinguish two basic forms of bounded rationality.

Functionally rational thought is rational with respect to the means only; the ends are assumed by the planner to be given and may be more or less rational or even, according to certain criteria, irrational.[17] The ends must remain fairly stable, however, because the decision must appear rational not only before but also *after* implementation. As a rule, the more general the objective, the more stable it will tend to be. It may therefore be concluded that functional rationality in planning is found chiefly in connection with stable, general ends that are applicable to the system as a whole or at least to major portions of it. For example, the general ends of national economic development usually include such values as growth, more equitable income distribution, and full employment. These ends undergo relatively little change through time; but at the same time, they point only in a general direction. Functionally rational thought will try to guide the evolution of the system in this direction.

Substantially rational thought is rational with respect to both the ends and means of action. But this clearly implies the possibility of altering the ends during the action as a result of changing circumstances or new information.

One would therefore expect to meet with frequent modifications of the ends. Since only specific ends are capable of being modified in this way, it is permissible to posit a strong correlation between substantial rationality and variable ends.

In any planning system, both forms of rationality will usually occur: functional rationality with respect to system ends and substantial rationality with respect to more specific, subsystem ends; that is, one would expect to find stability in the general direction of the planning effort and adaptability in detailed planning. For example, lengthy conferences operate on what might be called 'daily blueprints', that is, frequent revisions of the detailed schedule to accommodate unforeseen events, yet the main purposes of the conference will usually remain the same, although the course towards them may be tortuous and seemingly anarchic.

Non-bounded rationality—The non-bounded form of reason, free from temporal constraints, may be called *utopian and ideological thought.* In such thinking, there is a picture of an ideal social order, often in considerable detail, and almost always as a final state existing in a perfect equilibrium outside of historical time. The images of perfect communism and perfect capitalism are such utopias, as are the corporate state, national socialism and participant democracy.

Utopian and ideological thought may be considered rational in two senses. Its constructions are not only logical and coherent; they are also concrete representations of abstract social values, such as equality, freedom, and social justice, and it is primarily these qualities that make this kind of thinking so often persuasive.[18] Forms of planning are often historical precipitates of utopian and ideological thought. Agricultural planning in the United States, for instance, can be illuminated by analyzing it against a background of Jeffersonian democratic thought; national planning in Spanish-speaking Latin America needs to be viewed in the light of the philosophy of the corporate state; and Indian planning still reflects the influence of Gandhi's social philosophy. What is still more significant is that many of the internal conflicts that rage about specific planning proposals turn precisely on philosophical issues such as these rather than on more pragmatic problems. The outcomes of these conflicts are usually decisive in setting the direction of development for an entire sector or even the whole nation.[19]

Extra-rational thought—The category of extra-rational thought includes what may be loosely called *tradition, intuition,* and *wisdom.* These forms of thought are not derived from coherent, logical structures, nor based on specific technical expertise. They are, however, the source of most political decisions and, therefore, play an exceptionally large part in planning processes. It must be admitted, however, that recently there has been a steady diminution of the role of extra-rational thought in public decision-making. Measurement and calculation are driving intuition and wisdom into more and more exclusive spheres, whereas the rapidity of change renders tradition meaningless as a source of decisions oriented towards the future. The result appears to be a weakening of the political elements in planning accompanied by a strengthening of the role of the technician. How this trend should be assessed is not yet clear.

Allocative planning

Allocative planning is the assigning of resource increments among competing uses. Typically, this is the task of national planning institutions and, for many people, it is the only task with which planning should be properly concerned. Four characteristics of allocative planning help to define it.

1 Comprehensiveness. Allocative planning must be comprehensive with respect to at least the following: (a) the interdependence among all of the explicitly stated objectives of the system (or subsystem), (b) the interdependence in the use of all available resources of the system (or subsystem), and (c) the influence of all external variables on the setting of intermediate targets.[20]

Comprehensiveness has become a preoccupation with allocative planners. They believe that their special contribution to social decision-making derives mainly from their ability to manipulate a comprehensive set of variables and objectives and to acquire, as a result, a point of view that necessarily coincides with the interests of the system (or subsystem) as a whole, that is, with the public interest. Their close association with executive power reinforces this conception of themselves. Thus, far from being mere experts, neutral with respect to values, allocative planners will often defend a set of value propositions as essential to the survival and well-being of the system (or subsystem). Since the concept of a public interest is difficult to maintain, however, especially in pluralistic or in non-integrated societies, the powers of allocative planning are often resented by groups whose partial concerns are threatened by an insistence on public values arrived at independently of any political process.

2 Systemwide balances. The optimality criterion, the basic norm for allocative planning, requires a balance among the variable components of the planning system. The model with which allocative planners customarily work is necessarily in equilibrium. Thus, planned investment must not exceed the capacity to invest; total imports must not exceed projected exports; employment gains must not be less than the increase of the labor force; electric energy production must meet projected power consumption. It is a question of determining the right magnitudes as the targets of the economic system. Accompanying a set of carefully worked out quantitative targets is

usually a text suggesting changes in existing policies that are thought necessary for their achievement.

3 Synthesis. Neither comprehensiveness nor systematic balance can be obtained without the aid of one or more synthetic models of the economy. These models allow study of the functioning of the system under quasi-experimental conditions as different conditions are considered and their implications are observed. The most common models include national economic accounts, input-output matrices, simulation models, and econometric policy models.[21] These models are abstracted from the institutional and legal framework of the economic system and from the persons through whom the system works.

4 Functional rationality. Allocative planning is an attempt to be functionally rational in that the objectives of the system are supposed to be determined externally through a political process that does not significantly involve the planners themselves. Planning, therefore, appears as only a working out of the implications for public policy of norms established independently. As a well-known economist has recently explained it:

> The tendency now is to abandon the effort to determine through economic analysis, what is the best form of economic organization or the 'best' set of economic policies, and to accept goals established through the political process and stated by governments—full employment, price stability,more rapid economic growth, elimination of pockets of poverty or distressed areas, and the like. For the most part, such goals seem reasonable to economists, but by starting their analysis at the point where government policy is already determined, they avoid value judgements of their own. They may point out inconsistencies among goals, or worry about such new dilemmas as the rising cost of living and increasing unemployment side by side, but choice between goals is left to the government, as is the establishment of priorities. Usually some set of measures of achieving goals—once priorities are established—can be suggested, even if there remains doubt as to whether they constitute the best possible set of measures.[22]

The impossibility of remaining uninfluenced by values has already been pointed out. Nevertheless, by shifting the major burden of choice among values to the political process, allocative planning can appear as an activity intended in large measure to be functionally rational and thus, presumably, objective.

Implementation

The institutions charged with implementation of the plans must remain constantly aware of the need to carry out the policies and advance towards the targets of the models. Implementation, however, is not an independent step taken subsequent to plan-making; *the kind of implementing mechanism adopted will itself influence the character of the plan and the way it is formulated.* The formulation and implementation of plans are closely interdependent processes, so that the choice of one will in large measure also determine the second. For this reason, allocative planning will be either *plan-oriented or process-oriented.* [23]

In Italy, where central planning has not yet advanced very far, the question of the appropriate mechanisms for plan implementation, and consequently for the whole structure of the planning system, is basic to the present controversy. According to LaPalombara,

> The question of control is a critical one. Is planning to be by 'inducement' or 'indication', as some Italians claim, or is it to have 'compulsive' dimensions? If the latter, will compulsion apply only to the public sector or will it be extended to the private sector as well? If planning is to be compulsory or obligatory for the public sector, what instruments will the government utilize to enforce private-sector adherence to the plan? Will the plan encompass the whole economy or will it be limited to only particularly important sectors? These are merely a few of the questions. Although the 1965 plan provides some tentative answers, many of them remain unclear. [24]

The production of a blueprint and adherence to its basic structure of goals may be viewed as so essential by the political leadership of a country that the maximum use will be made of the available powers of command and inducement in the endeavor to carry out the plan. In *command planning*, sanctions are applied to compel adherence to clearly formulated objectives and targets. The plan itself may have legal force or may be promulgated in a series of executive decrees in order to obtain specific results. [25] For Jean Maynaud, for instance,

> A plan is not a plan unless it is central and global, involving specific objectives, and directly inserted in the existing socio-economic context even if it anticipates some social change .... Public authorities must make a strong effort to assure that the results of planning will be close to what is predicted. This suggests that some compulsion is essential, even in places like Italy, where it appears that the forces of the free market have created rapid economic expansion. [26]

Inducement is a weaker form of activation in that its effects are not, as a rule, experienced as coercion. It arranges the decision environment of others in such a way that one kind of decision will tend to be preferred over possible alternative decisions. Typical instruments of inducement are special lines of credit, interest manipulation, subsidies, exchange-rate policies, tax exemptions, and preferential import tariffs.

71

Both command and inducement are clearly plan-oriented in that the plan will tend to be regarded as a serious long-term commitment in which changes can be made, but not made easily. However, where the performance of subsystems is important for the attainment of system-wide goals (where the carrying out of the plan depends, for instance, on the actions of the private sector), and the imposition of sanctions or indirect controls is impracticable, allocative planners will tend to stress *process* over plan. In this case, the participation of all the principal interests will be enlisted in the formulation of the plan itself. This has come to be known, following the recent French experience, as 'indicative planning'.[27] And, according to LaPalombara, 'The very fact that planning procedures will include pluralistic participation undercuts the idea of compulsion.'[28]

Both strong and weak forms of process-oriented planning are encountered. The strong form makes extensive use of bargaining; planning appears, therefore, as a process of continuous *negotiation,* with central government agencies among the list of main protagonists. According to Neil W. Chamberlain,

> There are few policies which are so 'technical', so independent of people's reactions, that they can be instituted without question. Most matters of any consequence involve discussion and compromise. The views of those on whom the functioning of the system depends cannot be wholly ignored unless the system is prepared to part with their services—in which case it must come to terms with their replacements.
>
> A system of bargains among people must be contrived, and it presumably can be contrived more or less efficiently from the viewpoint of achieving the objectives of the system—that is, with varying degrees of sacrifice of system objectives to subsystem (individual) goals.[29]

The weaker form of process-oriented planning depends for its implementation on nothing more persuasive than the participation of key actors in the planning process, those who will be charged with implementation. There is but a minimum of negotiation, and the plan document itself will come to be regarded as less important than the possible benefits resulting from a joint consideration of targets, policies, and instruments. These benefits include establishing a dialogue among contending sectors, creating a wider awareness of national problems, providing the main economic actors with a common information base, encouraging socially more responsible decision-making, reducing uncertainty in the calculation of sectoral investment programs, and so on.

In the pure case, process-oriented planning would probably not need to have a plan at all except as an informal discussion document which would register the temporary consensus of all the parties involved. But the pure case of process-oriented planning is rare; usually it will be found strongly mixed with a command and inducement, so that a formally adopted plan may have some substance, after all.

Hagen and White in their appreciation of French experience, write:

> On approval of the plan, comprehensive and vigorous intervention by the government began to see that the targets were attained. Or rather, the intervention under the preceding plans continued. French planning, M. Pierre Masse, the present director of the *Commissariat au Pian*, has said, is 'more than indicative and less than imperative.' The phrases are correct, but how much more than indicative, even though also much less than imperative, is the actual process! In M. Masse's delicate Gallic phraseology in another place, 'the heart of the matter is that French planning is active; it ... regulates the stimuli and aids at the disposal of the public departments in such a manner that the objectives assigned to the private sector are achieved.'[30]

Choice of kind of planning

Which kind of planning predominates will depend on the nature of the decision environment and the urgency of the problems to be solved. Allocative planning can occur under either developmental or adaptive planning. In adaptive planning, planners will be chiefly concerned with predicting the behavior of external variables and with adjusting the available policy instruments in order to maintain the system in some sort of equilibrium under the impact of changes which may impinge upon the subsystem (for example, national economic plans are not yet drawn up so as to optimize development potentials concurrently at national and local levels; the local impact of national plans is therefore determined largely by chance). The actual scope for allocative planning under these conditions is quite limited, since adaptations are made to external conditions, special opportunities are seized, and decisions are made about what are probably matters of only secondary importance to the community and, hence, are politically more vulnerable.[31]

Under developmental planning, allocative planners perform a quite different role, although they continue to build models or set targets. Their functions in this case can be best understood with reference to innovative planning.

Innovative planning

This appears as a form of social action intended to produce major changes in an existing social system. According to Neil W. Chamberlain, it creates 'wholly new categories of activity, usually large in scale, so that they cannot be reached by increments of present activity, but only by initiating a new line of activity which eventually leads to the conceived result.'[32] Unlike allocative planning, it is not *preliminary* to action but a fusion or synthesis of plan-making and plan-implementing activities within an organizational frame. Four characteristics help to distinguish innovative from allocative planning.[33]

1 Innovative planning seeks to introduce and *legitimize new social objectives*. Its central attention is, therefore, on the main points of leverage that will accomplish this task. By concentrating on only a few variables, innovative planners inevitably ignore large parts of the total value spectrum of the society into which the innovation is to be introduced. At the same time, only the most general consequences are considered, with attention to those which relate to expected structural changes in the system. The emphasis, therefore, is on the guidance of change through a selective repatterning of the influences on social action rather than on the multiple consequences of alternative allocations.

2 Innovative planning is also concerned with *translating general value propositions into new institutional arrangements and concrete action programs*. This difficult task usually falls upon a creative minority, which is basically dissatisfied with the existing situation. The organization of these groups, their self-articulation, and their functioning—until they themselves become subject to inevitable routinization—may all be thought of as part of the process of innovative planning.

For example, Bertram Gross referring to what he calls an 'institutionalized capacity to build other institutions', writes in his introduction to Robert Shafer's treatment of Mexican planning:

A new institutional infrastructure was needed. To build it in small pieces, however disconnected, seemed infinitely superior to the piling up of a vast hierarchical bureaucracy in a small number of ministries. It provided more upward career channels for people with ability and ambition. By placing scarce eggs in many baskets, there was more room for trial and error, more protection against failure. Promotion of new institutions took precedence over their coordination.

This kind of institution building has a pulse rate of its own. The more successful it is in getting things done, the more problems the new institutions create. This leads to increasing pressure to pull things together a little more tightly . . . . But then the effort to get important things done leads once again to new spurts of decentralized institution building. Central promotion of decentralized institutions once again races ahead of central coordination.[34]

3 From this, it follows that innovative planners are public entrepreneurs, who are likely to have more interest in *mobilizing resources* than in their optimal allocation among competing uses. They will seek to redirect financial and human resources to those areas which promise to lead to significant

74

changes in the system. In contrast to allocative planners who strive for equal marginal returns, innovative planners seek to obtain the largest amount of resources for their projects, even if this should mean weakening the purposes of competing organizations. Innovative planners are only peripherally concerned with these other purposes; by weakening other parts of the system, they may even gain a temporary advantage for themselves and facilitate the process of transformation.

4 Innovative planners propose to guide the process of change and the consequent adjustments within the system through the feedback of information regarding the actual consequences of innovation, in contrast to allocative planners, whose main endeavor is accurately to predict the chain of consequences resulting from incremental policies and then to adapt these policies to the prospective changes. To state the difference more succinctly: innovative planners are not, as a rule, interested in gradually modifying existing policies to conform to expected results. Innovative planners are more limited in focusing mainly on the immediate and narrowly defined results of the proposed innovation, and more ambitious in advancing a major project and laboring diligently to introduce it into society. Modifications of this project will tend to occur only as a result of political compromise in the course of getting it accepted and the actual consequences of the policy in operation that suggest the desirability of change in its original form. In place of experiments *in vitro* (through the manipulation of econometric models), innovative planners prefer the device of pilot schemes, the utility of an idea can be observed in action.

Innovative planning is especially prevalent in rapidly changing social systems. It is, in fact, a method for coping with problems that arise under conditions of rapid change, and it will tend to disrupt existing balances. There is much still to be learned about the different ways that major changes are introduced into an established society or how new social systems emerge. But it is certain that equal progress cannot be made on all fronts simultaneously. Rather, the image that comes to mind is that of successive waves and wavelets of innovation spreading outwards from a number of unrelated focal points, or innovating institutions, from Clarence Thurber's 'islands of development'.[35] Since it is difficult to sustain innovation at any of these points over prolonged periods, there may be frequent shifts of emphasis in innovation, one wave succeeding another, but in a different direction. It is even more difficult to succeed in establishing effective organizational linkages among institutions engaged in innovative planning, although clearly, where a massive effort for change is intended, this is a necessary condition for the successful transformation of the system.

The strategic problem is to identify the critical points for system transformation and to activate innovative planning at these points. But if a system is already undergoing rapid change, the importance of this strategic problem decreases sharply; for the system generates changes automatically. It is engaged in what Akzin and Dror call 'high pressure' planning. Speaking of Israeli experience, they write:

> The high rate of unpredicted change and the central social roles of government activities impose a fast pace of operation upon the civil service. Although nearly all ministries are overloaded with pressing day-to-day problems, energetic senior civil servants continue to launch relatively large numbers of new projects and activities. The constant pressure of issues necessarily lessens systematic long-range thinking and encourages a problem-by-problem manner of decision-making.[36]

But this pragmatic approach, they say, 'is frequently the optimal master strategy. For many problems in the economic, social, political, and technological fields, no applicable knowledge is available. Rather than be misled by theories and recommendations based on quite different circumstances, it is wiser to proceed pragmatically.'[37]

Under high-pressure planning, detailed target achievement is not possible. The general ends will remain fairly stable and give rise to efforts of allocative planners to keep the system in balance and generally moving in the desired direction. But specific ends may be frequently revised in the light of changing conditions and a constant reevaluation of the action. Innovative planning thus appears as a concrete form of substantial rationality.

Innovative planning is typically uncoordinated and competitive, and this is yet another reason why target achievement is, in any functional sense, unattainable. The top leaders of the Israeli government, writes Bertram Gross,

> have deliberately nourished the institution-building, empire-constructing, resource-grabbing expansionism of organizations in all sectors of society, including science and education as well as the trade union movement, political parties, and private business. This has meant the promotion of sectoral (or facet) planning. The result has been more and more high-pressure planning and implementation by competitive institutions. Under such circumstances clear-cut coordination by command of central authorities has been neither feasible, essential, nor desirable.[38]

Role of allocative planners in innovative planning

But not all systems find themselves already engulfed in a process of rapid internal transformation. Allocative planning is sometimes advanced as a means of generating more rapid changes, especially in the economic field. Dissident young engineers and economists, eager to transform traditional stagnation into dynamic industrial systems, regard the creation of central planning agencies as in itself a major act of innovative planning. For them a central planning agency represents a 'permanent institutionalized symbol of the Government's sustained commitment' to the goal of rapid economic growth.[39]

But in their enthusiasm, they may forget that their comprehensive econometric models accommodate discontinuous change only with difficulty. The more allocative planning relies on such models, the more conservative is it likely to be. Detailed awareness of interrelations tends to make experts cautious and hesitant to prescribe radical solutions. Allocative planners, then, confront essentially two choices: either to remain satisfied with the *symbol* they have created and to move gradually towards the bureaucratization of the planning function—but, at the same time, to forfeit ambitious goals, or to risk the seeming anarchy of rapid change, consciously using allocative planning for compelling and inducing maximum efforts in key areas and for endeavoring to maintain only a reduced number of strategic balances throughout the system. In the second case, allocative planners will not only resort increasingly to command as a form of implementation, but will encourage large-scale innovative planning to carry out major elements of the plan or to respond to new problems that are generated by rapid change.

In this vitally important interrelationship between allocative and innovative planning, the role of allocative planners is to develop new kinds of leadership, to channel resources to priority areas or points of change, to facilitate communication among the highly competitive innovative organizations, to search for areas of agreement, to help resolve interinstitutional conflicts, especially with regard to the use of limited resources, and to encourage organizational links among the many 'islands of development'. Over time, and as the pace of change slows down, allocative planning tends to replace innovation in the management not only of organizations, but also in the social system as a whole.

In general, then, we may conclude, first, the innovative planning is needed to accomplish a major—as compared to only a marginal—reallocation of resources. New institutions and new programs are needed if money is to be spent in radically different ways. The second conclusion concerns the process of translating abstract values into specific projects and programmed activities (goal reduction). Contrary to the belief of some theorists, this is not inherently a logical process, but one that requires institutional innovation.

Conclusion

The model suggested furnishes a skeleton for the analysis of planning. But why carry out such an analysis in the first place? What may be gained from an analysis of planning behavior?

First, *empirical findings may be incorporated into a positive theory of guided system change.* Many of the elements of such a theory already exist; what has been lacking up to now is a preliminary theoretical framework for

77

ordering the available data and for supplementing them with studies that will ask theoretically relevant questions and begin to test promising hypotheses. In this paper, some of the hypotheses suggested are:

1 Under adaptive planning, there will be a tendency to push decisions upward towards centers of developmental decision-making where the conditions for choice at lower levels may be changed.
2 The formulation and implementation of plans are closely interdependent processes, so that the choice of one will, in large measure, also determine the second.
3 General, system-wide objectives are modified less frequently than more specific subsystem objectives.
4 Innovative planning is typically uncoordinated and competitive.

Second, *empirical findings will permit a systematic analysis of planning pathologies.* What leads to the breakdown of guided system change? Under what conditions and for what reasons does planning cease to be effective? The reasons may include such variables as the failure of planning to adapt itself optimally to its decision environment, the resilience of this environment to change, conflicting relations between experts and policy-makers, failure to achieve an optimal distribution of planning functions according to their position on the dependency-autonomy continuum, neglect of either innovative or allocative planning functions, rigidity in planners' attitudes and procedures, and inappropriate mix between plan-oriented and process-oriented forms of implementation.

Third, *empirical findings may serve as a basis for formulating a prescriptive planning theory.* In the light of positive theory and a systematic knowledge of planning pathologies, a normative theory of planning may be formulated that should be superior to existing formulations. Such a theory will have to be expressed as a function of the decision environment of planning.

On the basis of these several purposes, the model raises important questions that can serve as a useful starting point for any research into planning behavior:

1 What is the role of political institutions in goal formulation policy-making, and conflict resolution under different planning systems? (The analysis will have to specify not only the social context of planning, but also whether planning is developmental or adaptive, and the relations between allocative and innovative planning.)
2 What is the relation of planning institutions and processes to their social context? Can typical planning styles be identified, especially in relation to the the mix of implementation procedures? What is the relative importance of allocative and innovative planning under different environmental conditions?

3 What are the political uses served by planning under different systems and how do these uses influence planning behavior?

4 What is the influence of utopian and ideological thought on the formulation, implementation, and substance of planning decisions?

5 What are the dynamic relations between developmental and adaptive planning under different environmental conditions? Under what circumstances does counterplanning appear, and how are the resulting conflicts resolved? Does something like a public or common interest arise from a system in which counterplanning is prevalent? How are planning functions distributed along a centralization-decentralization continuum, and what are their relations horizontally at each level as well as vertically among a hierarchy of ordered centers?

6 What is the relation of policy-makers (or politicians) to experts (or technicians) under different planning systems? How does this relationship influence the effectiveness of planning? Does planning lead inevitably to a 'depolitization' of major developmental issues?

7 What is the relation of allocative to innovative planning? What are the roles of either type of planning in guiding system change?

8 What are the relations of competitive innovative planning units to each other? What conditions are conducive to greater coordination among them, and which may be claimed to represent 'obstacles to change'?

9 What are the self-images of planners in contrast to the images of planners held by others, and how do these images affect behavior?

Perhaps a philosophical postcript will be permitted. If planning is accepted as the attempted intervention of reason in history, then it is clear that such intervention cannot be immediate and direct, but must be filtered through a series of complex structures and processes to be effective. A definitely anti-heroic picture of reason emerges. It is not the great mind that intervenes, but a multitude of individual actors, each playing his role in a collective process that he does not fully comprehend because he is involved in it himself and lacks perspective. Reason, therefore, to the extent that it operates on society, is a 'collective representation' in Durkheim's sense, whose functioning is contingent on structures and forces which are independent of itself.

References

1. A concise description of this model will be found in BANFIELD, EDWARD 'Note on Conceptual Scheme' in MAYERSON, MARTIN and BANFIELD, EDWARD C. eds. *Politics, Planning and the Public Interest: The Case of Public Housing in Chicago.* Glencoe, Illinois: The Free Press, 1955, pp. 303-30. In a more sophisticated version, this model also underlies much of TINBERGEN, JAN. The influential work of *Economic Policy: Principles and Design.* Amsterdam: North Holland, 1964. For a critique of classical decision theory, see LINDBLOM, CHARLES, *The Intelligence of Democracy.* New York: The Free Press, 1965.

2. On the concept of 'bounded rationality', see MARCH, JAMES G. and SIMON, HERBERT A. *Organizations.* New York: Wiley, 1958, pp. 203-10.
3. Recent examples include HAGEN, EVERETT E. *Planning Economic Development,* Homewood, Illinois: Irwin, 1963; HACKETT, JOHN and ANNE-MARIE, *Economic Planning in France,* Cambridge, Mass.: Harvard UP, 1963; chapters on the Netherlands, France, and Japan in HICKMAN, BERT G. ed., *Quantitative Planning of Economic Policy,* Washington: Brookings Institution, 1965; WATERSTON, ALBERT, *Development Planning: Lessons of Experience,* Baltimore: Johns Hopkins University, 1965; and the several volumes in the National Planning Series published by Syracuse University Press under the general editorship of Bertram M. Gross.
4. A study complementary to the present one, and fundamental for any serious research into planning, is GROSS, BERTRAM M. 'The Managers of National Economic Change.' In MARTIN, ROSCOE C. ed., *Public Administration and Democracy: Essays in Honor of Paul H. Appleby.* Syracuse: Syracuse University, 1965.
5. For some frequently used definitions of planning, see DROR, YEHEZKEL, 'The Planning Process: a Facet Design.' *International Review of Administrative Sciences,* Vol. 24, 1963, pp. 1-13.
6. This definition is in line with, if somewhat more general than, Bertram M. Gross' definition of planning as the 'processes whereby national governments try to carry out responsibilities for the guidance of significant economic change'. See his 'National Planning: Findings and Fallacies, *Public Administration Review,* Vol. 25, 1965, p. 264.
7. This description of the logic of planning coincides with Neil W. Chamberlain's model as developed in his *Private and Public Planning.* New York: McGraw-Hill, 1965, especially ch. 7.
8. BROWN, W. H. and GILBERT, C. E., *Planning Municipal Investment: A Case Study of Philadelphia.* Philadelphia: University of Pennsylvania, 1961, ch. 8.
9. For excellent discussions of the relation of planning to politics, see ALTSCHULER, ALAN, *The City Planning Process: A Political Analysis.* Ithaca: Cornell University, 1966. At the national level, one of the best accounts will be found in the forthcoming study by DALAND, ROBERT T., *Brazilian Planning: A Study of Development Politics and Administration.* Chapel Hill: University of North Carolina, February 1966, mimeographed.
10. PAJESTKA, JOSEF, 'Dialogue Between Planning Experts and Policy Makers in the Process of Plan Formulation.' Paper presented to the International Group for Studies in National Planning, 15-22 November, 1966, Caracas, Venezuela.
11. These and other functions are discussed in FRIEDMANN, J., *Venezuela: From Doctrine to Dialogue.* Syracuse: Syracuse University, 1965. For corroborative evidence, see DALAND, ROBERT T., *Op. cit.,* ch. 6.
12. Quoted in Bertram M. Gross's preface to BURKE, FRED G., *Tanganyika: Pre-planning.* Syracuse: Syracuse University, 1965, pp. 19, 20.
13. Reference to 'adaptive' rationality is made in FRIEDMANN, J., 'The Institutional Context.' In GROSS, BERTRAM M. ed., *Action Under Planning.* New York: McGraw-Hill, 1966, ch. 2. The equivalent concept of *bounded* rationality was introduced into the literature by Herbert Simon (see footnote 2). The importance of 'context' for planning has also been stressed by RIGGS, FRED W., *The Ecology of Development.* Comparative Administration Group, American Society for Public Administration, Occasional Papers. Bloomington, Indiana: 1964.
14. WATERSTON, ALBERT, *Development Planning: Lessons in Experience,* Baltimore: John Hopkins University, 1965, ch. 8.
15. LAPALOMBARA, JOSEPH, *Italy: The Politics of Planning.* Syracuse: Syracuse University, 1966, p. 106.
16. WATERSTON, ALBERT, *op. cit.,* p. 292.
17. This is Karl Mannheim's terminology for describing the two forms of rationality, in *Man and Society in an Age of Reconstruction.* New York: Harcourt, Brace, 1949, pp. 51-60.

18. MEYERSON, MARTIN, 'Utopian Traditions and the Planning of Cities.' *Daedalus,* Winter 1961, 180-93. The influence of utopian thought on economic planning has barely been recognized, and merits a full study.
19. KAUTSKY, JOHN H., ed. *Political Change in Underdeveloped Countries: Nationalism and Communism,* New York: Wiley, 1962. See also FRIEDMANN, J., 'Intellectuals in Developing Societies.' *Kyklos,* Vol. 13, 1960, 513-44.
20. TINBERGEN, JAN, *op. cit., passim.*
21. See HICKMANN, BERT G., *op. cit.,* for a discussion of the current planning models.
22. HIGGINS, BENJAMIN, 'An Economist's View.' In PHILLIPS, H. M. ed., *Social Aspects of Economic Development in Latin America.* UNESCO, 1963, p. 247.
23. The best current discussion of problems of planning implementation is that of GROSS, BERTRAM M., 'Activating National Plans.' In his *Action Under Planning, op. cit.* The terminology adopted in the present paper, however, differs from that of Gross.
24. LAPALOMBARA, JOSEPH, *op. cit.,* p. 103.
25. The concept of command planning has been suggested by WILES, PETER in his brilliant analysis of *The Political Economy of Communism* (Cambridge, Mass.: Harvard UP, 1962. See also his 'Economic Activation, Economic Planning, and the Social Order.' In the aforementioned volume edited by Bertram M. Gross, as well as BAUMAN, ZYGMUNT, 'The Limitations of "Perfect Planning".' in the same volume.
26. LAPALOMBARA, JOSEPH, *op. cit.,* p. 104.
27. HACKETT, JOHN and ANNE-MARIE, *op. cit.,* for a comprehensive account of French planning.
28. LAPALOMBARA, JOSEPH, *op. cit.,* p. 104.
29. CHAMBERLAIN, NEIL W., *op. cit.,* pp. 7 and 8.
30. HAGEN, EVERETT E. and WHITE, STEPHANIE, F. T. *Great Britain: Quiet Revolution in Planning.* Syracuse: Syracuse University, 1966, p. 105.
31. BROWN, W. H. and GILBERT, C. E., *op. cit.*
32. CHAMBERLAIN, NEIL W., *op. cit.,* p. 175.
33. This form of planning is discussed more fully in FRIEDMANN, J., 'Planning for Innovation: the Chilean Case.' *Journal of the American Institute of Planners,* Vol. 32, June 1966, pp. 194-203.
34. GROSS, BERTRAM M., 'The Dynamics of Competitive Planning.' Preface to SHAFER, ROBERT J. *Mexico: Mutual Adjustment Planning,* National Planning Series No. 4, Syracuse: Syracuse University, 1966, p. xix.
35. THURBER, CLARENCE E., 'Islands of Development: A Political and Social Approach to Development Administration in Latin America,' paper presented to the National Conference of the Comparative Administration Group, 17 April, 1966.
36. AKZIN, BENJAMIN and DROR, YEHEZKEL, *Israel: High Pressure Planning.* Syracuse: Syracuse University, 1966, p. 17.
37. *Ibid.,* pp. 16-17.
38. In the preface to AKZIN and DROR, *op. cit.,* pp. 26-27.
39. GROSS, BERTRAM M. In SHAFER, ROBERT J., *op. cit.,* p. 13.

PART TWO: Strategic planning

As argued in the introduction, one of the essentially new features in the development of corporate planning is a more systematic and analytical approach to the question of strategy. This part of the book examines three views of strategy-making from different vantage points.

In chapter 5, 'The science of strategy-making', Henry Mintzberg examines several approaches to strategic formulation. By artificially separating the manager from the planner, he is able to examine clinically some of the more systematic approaches and appraise their value and their limitations. In his final section, where he examines the state of integrated strategic planning, he properly concludes that the planner has serious limitations in his present approaches and that he must firmly maintain an adaptive as well as a deterministic philosophy if he is to help the manager with the problems and opportunities which he faces.

In chapter 6, W. H. Newman offers an essentially verbal description of strategy-making. The key questions are raised, examples of answers by different companies in different circumstances are quoted, and the difficult question of timing is examined. Readers who respond primarily to verbal statements rather than diagrammatic flowcharts will find some useful pointers to shaping their own thinking.

In chapter 7, Seymour Tilles offers a questioning approach to the difficulty of evaluating strategy. After a short definition of terms, six questions against which to test a strategy are listed, followed by a discussion of how they apply in specific situations. While testing any one situation against these questions calls for art, judgement and science, and specific criteria are not easily found, the article provides a sound starting point for evaluation of a present or future strategic posture.

(Editor)

5. The science of strategy-making

Henry Mintzberg

Introduction to strategy-making

Man's beginnings were described in the Bible in terms of conscious planning and grand strategy. The opposing theory, developed by Darwin, suggested that no such grand design existed but that environmental forces gradually shaped man's evolution.

The disagreement between the biblical and Darwinian theorists is parallel on a more mundane level in the study of strategy-making. There are those who envision grand calculated designs for the corporate entity, and there are those who cite current practice to argue that organizational strategy evolves, shaped less by man than by his environment.

This paper is written in an attempt to review and draw together the various views of strategy-making in organizations. Strategy-making is defined simply as the process of making important organizational decisions (e.g., to reorganize, develop a new product line, embark on an expansion program). Strategy is the sum total of these decisions, and may evolve as *independent* decisions are made over time, or may result from the process of making *integrated* decisions plans.

We shall begin by describing the manager as strategy-maker, from both entrepreneurial and 'fire-fighting' points of view. We shall then focus on the planner in order to investigate the role of formal analysis in the strategy-making process. Specifically, we shall discuss planner 'programs', systematic sets of procedures to produce answers to specific strategy questions. These programs will be classified as 'adaptive' or 'integrative', depending on whether they are designed to help the manager make independent decisions, or to develop integrated decision plans. Four of the most common adaptive

● Reproduced with permission from *Industrial Management Review,* Vol. 8, No. 2, Spring 1967, pp. 71-91.

rograms—forecasting, market research, systems analysis, and mathematical modeling, and two integrative programs—capital budgeting and integrated strategic planning—will be discussed.

This paper is written for two groups: the manager interested in understanding the programs and problems of the planner, and the planner interested in investigating the differences between his approach and that of the manager. A framework is developed with which to view these approaches to strategy-making.

A framework for strategy-making

Intelligence-design-choice activity

A proper understanding of the strategy-making process will require a decision framework. We shall use the intelligence-design-choice framework. [1]

Intelligence activity sets the stage for a strategic decision by discovering a problem in need of solution or an opportunity available for development. In general, intelligence activity involves scanning the environment and collecting and analyzing information on various trends.

Design activity begins once the area of action has been determined by intelligence activity. The two stages of design activity are search: inventing, finding, and developing alternative means of solving the problem or of exploiting the opportunity; and evaluation: determining the consequences of using these alternatives.

Choice activity is concerned with choosing one from the alternatives that have been developed and evaluated. The 'integration' of the various strategic decisions into a unified strategy is included in this category.

Although the intelligence, design, and choice activity are clearly delineated above, such is not always the case in practice. For example, a manager may first decide what he wishes to do and then develop alternatives and analyses to rationalize his choice. Nevertheless, the framework is a basically useful one for classifying strategy-making activity.

A working framework requires two further distinctions—that of the manager versus the planner and that of adaptive versus integrative programs.

Manager versus planner

For purposes of illustration, an overly sharp distinction is made in this paper between managers and planners. Managers will be viewed as those who must maintain the organizations that they head. They must react quickly to the variety of pressures, information, problems, and opportunities that continually bombard them, and they must, therefore, work informally. Planners are assumed to be autonomous and analytical, prepared to invoke a formal program when the need arises. Thus, we shall assume in this paper that managers do not plan, and that planners do not manage.

One may compare the informal approach of the manager with the programmed approach of the planner by using the intelligence-design-choice framework. Managers are continually performing *intelligence* activity as they interpret the natural flow of information (magazines, opinions of subordinates, newspaper reports, etc.), while planners use mathematical and behavioral theories to study environmental changes (e.g., forecasting, market research). *Design* activity takes place as managers debate new alternatives in the boardroom, or as an operations research team delves into a problem. *Choices* may be made informally in the mind of one man, or formally, by a capital budgeting program which chooses the highest return-on-investment alternatives.

Adaptive versus integrative programs

Each formal planner program will be categorized as either 'adaptive' or 'integrative'. Using an adaptive program, the planner responds to one specific stimulus and works in 'real-time' with the manager. For example, a market research program may be invoked to study a new product opportunity currently facing a company, or a planner's model may be used during labor negotiations to determine the cost of various strategies.

Integrative programs are not related to specific stimuli. They are invoked by the clock (usually annually), and they draw together a large number of problems and opportunities to work out one integrated plan. The capital budgeting procedure is an integrative program, since all proposed projects are approved, not when they are first conceived, but during the annual budget review.

Before discussing the various planner programs, we shall investigate the methods that managers use in developing strategy.

The manager as strategy-maker

'Intuition' and 'judgement', terms we use to suggest that the mind houses some processes that are still mysterious to use, are probably the most valid words for describing the contemporary strategy-making process. In other words, the strategy evolves in the mind of the chief executive without ever being explicitly stated, and without the aid of formalized procedures. Anthony discusses possible reasons:

> Strategic planning is essentially *irregular*. Problems, opportunities, and 'bright ideas' do not arise according to some set timetable; they have to be dealt with whenever they happen to be perceived. The appropriate

analytical techniques depend on the nature of the problem being analyzed, and currently there is no general approach (such as a mathematical model) that is of much help in the analysis of all types of strategic problems. Indeed, any attempt to introduce a systematic approach is quite likely to dampen the essential element of creativity.

Few companies have a systematic approach to strategic planning. Most companies react to changes in their environment *after* they experience the changes; they do not have an organized means of attempting to foresee changes and to take action in anticipation of them.[2]

This describes the context in which the manager operates, but it tells us little about his methods. Two pictures, one painted by Charles E. Lindblom and the other by Peter F. Drucker, provide some insight into managerial methods.

Lindblom's 'muddling through' manager[3]

Lindblom describes the manager who 'muddles through', a passive individual with no clear goals. He acts only when forced to, and then he can only consider a few convenient alternatives, each of which will cause only small, non-disruptive changes in his organization. He is careless in evaluating the consequences of each alternative, considering only those which are important, interesting, and easily understandable. Furthermore, he examines only the marginal consequences, making no attempt to 'comprehend strictly and literally present states of affairs or the consequences of present policies. . . . He attempts no more than to understand the respects in which various possible states differ from each other and from the status quo.' In Lindblom's opinion the analytical approach to strategy-making—careful analysis of many alternatives in terms of explicit goals—fails because it does not recognize man's inability to cope with complex problems, the lack of information, the cost of analysis, the problems of timing, and the difficulties of stating realistic goals.

Drucker's entrepreneurial manager[4]

At the other extreme the manager is depicted as an entrepreneur, controlling his environment, actively searching for significant opportunities, and relating them to his vision of strategy. Perhaps more than any other management writer, Drucker speaks for the entrepreneurial manager:

Entrepreneurship is essentially the acceptance of change as an opportunity and the acceptance of 'the leadership in change' as the unique task of the entrepreneur. Entrepreneurship in effect means finding and utilizing opportunity. It is opportunity-focused and not problem-focused. Management deals with problems. Entrepreneurship deals with opportunity.

The entrepreneur is the systematic risk-maker and risk-taker. And he discharges this function by looking for and finding opportunity.

Although the descriptions of the entrepreneurial manager tend to be vague, they leave little doubt about the writer's belief in his freedom to act.

The composite manager

The above two views leave much to the imagination. In one case, we see the manager sitting at his desk, somewhat harassed, hoping for a moment of relief. In the other case, the manager, free of problems, roams the world searching for grand opportunities, returning occasionally to implement painlessly the best of his discoveries.

However overemphasized, these views do help us to piece together a theory of managerial strategy-making:

1 Strategy evolves. An organization's strategy changes over time as managers make new significant decisions.

2 Strategy results from two kinds of *intelligence* activity. Certain strategic decisions are motivated by problems forced on the manager; others result from entrepreneurship—management's active searching for new opportunities.

3 Strategy decisions are not scheduled; they are made when problems and opportunities happen to occur.

4 Because it is not possible to predict with accuracy what problems and opportunities will arise, it is extremely difficult to integrate different decisions into an explicit, comprehensive strategy.

5 Managers are busy people with many demands on their time. In effect, they are continually bombarded with information, ideas, and problems. Furthermore, the strategy-making environment is very complex. Therefore managers are unable to delve deeply into analysis of strategy questions. It may be concluded that *design* activity—development of alternatives to solve problems and evaluation of the consequences of these alternatives—is generally conducted without precision.

6 Managers have no rigid programs for handling given issues. Each strategic *choice* is made in a different context with new and uncertain information. The manager may have a loose vision of the direction in which he would like to take his organization, and, in an imprecise way, opportunities are evaluated in terms of this vision. But problems are not handled in terms of the vision. When a problem arises, the manager is primarily concerned with reducing the pressures that are acting. Any convenient means of solving the problem will satisfy him.

7 The manager alternates between opportunity-finding and problem-solving. To the extent that problems occur infrequently, and to the extent

that the manager is effective in finding relevant opportunities, his vision of organizational strategy is turned into reality.

Once stated, these are simple, almost platitudinous notions of strategy-making. Nevertheless, we shall make practical use of them in the concluding sections.

Adaptive programs

Recognizing the manager's time constraints and the complexity of strategic decisions, planners have developed a number of programs to aid the manager in his quest for opportunities and his efforts to solve problems. In this section, we discuss the adaptive programs: forecasting, market research, systems analysis, and mathematical modeling.

Forecasting

Because of the complexities of environmental changes, many large corporations have turned to forecasting as an analytical method. Using various mathematical techniques ranging from arithmetic to Markov process models, the forecaster attempts to predict economic growth, market growth, product demand, resource availability, and so on. This data is fed to the manager, who uses it to determine the problems that will face the organization, and the opportunities that are available. As such, forecasting is straightforward *intelligence* activity. The first phase of forecasting, trend determination, is a well-developed science. The second phase, analyzing the trends to determine problems and opportunities, does not appear to be highly programmed and is, therefore, often left to the manager.

Market research

Market research, broadly defined, is concerned with the study of various aspects of a company's marketing functions. This involves *intelligence* activity—studying the product line and the company's markets to determine specific marketing problems and opportunities; and *design* activity—searching for and evaluating product, promotion, and price alternatives.

For example, a market research group in an airline company may conduct a study of the travel market and discover that the customers are discouraged by city to airport transportation. This defines a problem area for the management. A series of interviews may establish that passengers believe that helicopters and subways are desirable alternative means of transportation. Finally, the market research may partially evaluate the alternatives by determining the demand curves as a function of city to airport travel time.

Market research is a useful and well-developed set of programs. From a management point of view, however, market research information must first be related to a wealth of other information (e.g., finance and manufacturing information) before decisions can be made. In general, market research studies tend to be *ad hoc,* and management is left to relate them to each other and to the overall strategy picture.

Systems analysis

A number of organizations have developed special groups, under the title 'Systems Analysis' or 'Operations Research', to conduct *ad hoc* studies of individual strategy problems. These groups tend to conduct relatively intricate analyses and, thereby draw fairly tight bounds around their studies.

In the early 'fifties, the Rand Corporation developed the idea of applying the operations research approach of problem-solving to strategic problems. The emphasis was on military problems, and the approach came to be called 'Systems Analysis'. Hitch and McKean have outlined the role and methods of systems analysis in their book, *The Economics of Defense in the Nuclear Age.*[5] When Robert McNamara became US Secretary of Defense, he hired Hitch to implement the book's recommendations.

Systems analysis is the natural outgrowth of the economic or 'rational' approach to decision-making. The analyst takes a problem defined by management and begins by studying the objectives of the organization in terms of the problem. If the problem for a Department of Defense systems analyst is 'developing a defensive strategy to protect against nuclear attack', the objectives may be defined as 'minimizing death and property losses'. The next step is to develop criteria to measure the consequences of alternatives. In this case, the criteria might be 'number of lives lost, and dollar value of property destroyed'. The analyst then develops alternatives—in this case, perhaps, (a) an anti-missile system, and (b) a series of fallout shelters. Each alternative is evaluated in terms of each criterion. Thus, management would be told the extent of human and property losses given that either system was available during nuclear attack.

Systems analysis is most well-developed in the area of evaluation, where extensive use is made of statistical and economic concepts. The key concept employed is 'cost-benefit', which assesses the greatest benefit for a given cost (e.g., number of lives saved for a ten billion dollar expenditure), or the minimum cost for a given benefit (e.g., cost of keeping property losses to 100 billion dollars).

Secretary McNamara has received much publicity for allowing 'whiz kids' to become involved in high-level defense strategy-making, and, no doubt, this publicity will eventually influence many business organizations. However, the number of firms using systems analysis to study *strategy* problems is probably

91

quite small at the present time. One such firm is General Electric, which has set up a group numbering 300, called 'Tempo', to conduct analyses on a consulting basis for various parts of the organization.[6]

With respect to the role that systems analysts actually play in strategy-making, four criticisms may be put forth:

1 The problems to be studied are initially defined by management. No programmed procedure for problem-finding (i.e., *intelligence* activity) exists.

2 The studies are actually formal means of suboptimizing. Generally each study is independent; no means are used to interrelate various studies.

3 While it is well known that systems analysts generate alternatives, nowhere in the literature is there any mention of how search is conducted. It must be concluded, therefore, that the analyst's search procedures are no more programmed than the manager's search procedures.

4 Systems analysts are quick to state that they do not make choices, rather that they clarify the issues and analyze the alternatives such that management's job of making choices is easier. *Choice* activity implicitly involves trading off objectives in deciding between alternatives (e.g., the anti-missile system saves more property, but the shelter system saves more lives) and the analyst has no means of guiding the manager in these decisions.

Given these four deficiencies, it must be concluded that systems analysis is essentially *design* activity, and is concerned mainly with evaluating alternatives in the context of specific strategy problems.

Mathematical modeling

Mathematics is a rigorous language, and the ability to use it in describing a situation indicates high-level understanding of the subject concerned. It is, therefore, not surprising that little use is made of mathematical models in the process of strategy-making.[7] Nevertheless, much research work is being done in this area, and there is little doubt that the importance of modeling will increase.

Mathematical modeling serves one basic purpose in the development of strategy. It provides to the manager a simulated environment in which he may determine the consequences of different strategies before actually implementing them, or ascertain the consequences of various environmental changes before they occur.

PERT and industrial dynamics represent two extremes in model-building. The PERT system represents the times taken to complete, and the interrelationships among, the various activities of a project. It is used primarily as a device to plan and control the scheduling of a project. With a PERT model, NASA management is able to determine, for example, the effect of a strike on a scheduled satellite launching, or the effects of different testing procedures on the completion of the Apollo program. Industrial dynamics employs feedback theory in the building of dynamic models of a firm's environment and operations. For example, if sales, inventory, and production parameters are built into the model, management can assess the effects of a change in inventory rules on company performance.

Basically, mathematical modeling is used in the *design* phase of strategy-making to evaluate alternatives. To be accepted by management, models must be recognized as accurate. Unfortunately, at present we have so little understanding of the strategy environment that it is not possible to be optimistic about the widespread development of accurate and useful models in the near future.

In this section, we have shown how certain programs are used to increase the power of the manager while he makes strategy. Forecasting collects data on environmental trends and presents it to the manager in systematic form, leaving the manager to decide what the problems and opportunities are. Market research is used to define problems and opportunities in the marketing area, and may be used as well to generate marketing alternatives and to evaluate them. Systems analysis is programmed problem-solving, with its real usefulness lying in its evaluation procedures. The mathematical models that are available are used to determine the consequences of particular strategies or the impacts of possible environmental changes.

Integrative programs

In addition to the adaptive programs described in the previous section, programs have been designed to develop strategic plans, that is, to make a number of different strategic decisions at one point in time. In theory, these programs replace managerial intuition with fully formalized decision-making procedures. In this section, this premise is investigated by analyzing two plan-producing programs: capital budgeting and integrated strategic planning.

Capital budgeting

Capital budgeting was probably the first programmed procedure used in the determination of strategy, and it is probably the most widely used today. Ideally, the program works as follows: the various division managers of an organization determine that certain projects, such as building a new plant or marketing a new product, are worth considering. The added operating costs and revenues (or savings) which would result from the project are predicted. Net revenue for each year of the project life is determined, and this flow of funds is discounted. By comparing the resultant revenue with the investment necessary to start the project, a return on investment (ROI) figure is calculated. The headquarters' executives then review all the divisional proposals and accept, within the total budgetary constraint, the most profitable ones.

Two criticisms of capital budgeting may be presented:[8]

1 Choices are really made, not by headquarters' executives using the ROI figures, but by division executives. Knowing that the cost and revenue data are very inaccurate, they can choose to propose any project and make it look profitable.

2 The one choice criterion, return on investment, is inadequate. It presupposes that all information relevant to the choice can be reduced to monetary terms. Social objectives and risk and timing factors are therefore usually ignored.

One recent improvement has been 'planning by mission'. In the early 'sixties, Theodore Leavitt[9] argued that companies should think about the service they perform rather than the products they produce (e.g., providing energy, not refining oil). Robert McNamara made popular this notion when he changed the Department of Defense budgeting system from one based on a departmental allocation (army, navy, etc.) to one based on a mission allocation (strategic retaliatory forces, civil defense, etc.). This allowed for a more objective analysis of projects, since funds were no longer allocated along divisional lines.

Another variation in the McNamara system, called planning-programming-budgeting, replaces the return on investment criterion with a cost-benefit criterion. This aids governmental organizations, which are frequently unable to state project benefits in dollar terms. Here, systems analysis is used to compare similar projects in cost-benefit terms, and strategic choices are made on such a basis. The problem of multiple criteria is not solved, however, for no means are available to compare projects across missions. For example, although President Johnson wishes to extend planning-programming-budgeting to the entire government, he has no analytical means by which to decide how much to allocate to a poverty project as compared to a military project. A common benefit measure (i.e., some measure of the 'social good') would have to be developed first to afford a means of comparison.

Capital budgeting is an integrative program because it is designed to make a series of strategic decisions at one point in time. All major projects for the year are accepted or rejected when the funds are allocated. Unfortunately, the capital budgeting program is of marginal use in making strategic decisions. The *intelligence* activity and the search phase of *design* activity are not part of the program. The program formalizes (a) the evaluation phase, by evaluating each proposed alternative on a cost-benefit or ROI basis, and (b) in theory, the choice phase, by using the firm rule of choosing only the highest pay-off projects. The program loosely integrates the alternatives by ensuring

94

that, taken all together, they do not violate a budgetary constraint. Other than this, however, no attempt is made to relate one project to another.

Integrated Strategic Planning

The planning process reaches its highest degree of sophistication when the planner has available a well-defined program for designing corporate strategy. He would follow his formal procedure, much as an engineer does in designing a bridge. The result would be a unified strategic plan. A number of theorists have been working on such programs, and their work should, at the very least, provide more insight into the strategy-making process.

Gilmore and Brandenburg[10] propose a four-part program comprising (a) reappraisal, (b) economic mission, (c) competitive strategy, and (d) program of action phases. H. Igor Ansoff[11] presents a highly detailed procedure for making expansion-diversification plans.

The integrated strategic planning programs usually make use of the intelligence-design-choice framework and frequently consist of some variant of the following:

1 Quantitative objectives are stated by management. For example, the organization may choose eight per cent profit and three per cent growth as objectives.

2 The strengths and weaknesses of the organization are studied.

3 Environmental trends (e.g., economic, social, competitive trends) relevant to the operation of the organization are investigated.

4 The information collected in steps 2 and 3 is used to define problem and opportunity areas. For example, a shift in consumer tastes may indicate a problem or an opportunity for a company, and an exploitable strength for a company, and an exploitable strength may give rise to an opportunity. Thus, IBM, with its strengths in designing and selling tabulating equipment and its recognition of the trend toward high-speed computing equipment, was able to enter the computer industry at an opportune time.

5 Given the listing of problem and opportunity areas, the next step is to generate alternatives to solve the problems and exploit the opportunities. Thus, if the company organizational structure is recognized as a weakness, a number of alternative structures are proposed. If oceanography is recognized as an opportunity area, a technological company may generate a number of alternative types of seawater recording instruments that it is capable of producing.

6 By combining the various alternatives in each of the problem and opportunity areas, a number of alternative unified strategies are developed. Thus, the technological company may decide that one organizational structure suits the production of one type of oceanographic equipment,

while a different structure will be necessary to produce and market another type of equipment.

7 The next step is to evaluate each unified strategy in terms of the organizational objectives developed in step 1. It may be determined, for example, that one strategy will satisfy the growth objective, but fall short on the profit objective.

8 The strategy that best satisfies the objectives is chosen.

While this description of the planning program may seem vague and inadequate, it does, by and large, represent the state of the art. Effective means are available to tabulate strengths, weaknesses, and environmental trends, but there exist no subprograms for detailing the search (step 5) and integration (step 6) phases. The planner who applies the integrated strategic planning program finds himself using his intuition in much of his work. Indeed, asking the planner to develop strategic plans today is tantamount to letting him 'muddle through', instead of the manager.

Another issue open to debate is step 1, the statement of objectives. Those who favor this step argue that explicit quantitative objectives serve to guide subsequent planning steps. The counter-argument questions the stating of objectives at the outset. Management may say that it wants 20 per cent profit and 10 per cent growth, but analysis may indicate that these objectives are unrealistic. It may be found, for example, that one alternative strategy offers 2 per cent profit and 13 per cent growth, while the other offers 6 per cent profit and 8 per cent growth. Management determines the true corporate objectives—the relative preference for growth over profit—when it chooses one of these strategies over the other. But management cannot state this preference in the absence of actual alternatives. Thus, it may be concluded that objectives cannot be inputs to the analysis, rather they result from the analysis.

In this section, two integrative programs have been discussed. Capital budgeting ostensibly uses a return on investment (or cost-benefit) criterion to accept or reject various proposals, while integrated strategic planning presents a vaguely defined set of steps to produce unified strategic plans.

Summary

Figure 5.1 summarizes the various views of strategy-making presented in this paper. A survey of the chart will show that a wide variety of organizational strategy-making behaviors are possible. The two extremes, the 'muddling through' manager and integrated strategic planning, represent the difference between the totally passive, judgemental approach and the active, quasi-programmed approach. In reality, any large organization would use different

	Program	Intelligence Activity (initiating action)	Design Activity (searching and evaluating)	Choice (choosing and integrating)
Manager	'Muddling through' manager	Problems forced on manager	Brief search, marginal analysis	First satisfactory alternative chosen; no integration
	Entre-preneurial manager	Consequential opportunities actively sought by manager	Opportunities compared to vision of strategy	Opportunities chosen which satisfy aims
Planner adaptive	Forecasting	Environmental changes predicted		
	Market research	Products and markets studied to define marketing opportunities and problems	Consumers studied to find alternatives and determine consumer preferences	
	Systems analysis		Alternative solutions to individual problems cost/benefit basis	
	Mathematical modeling		Alternatives tested in simulated environment	
Planner integrative	Capital budgeting		ROI figures calculated for proposed projects	Highest ROI projects chosen, subject to overall budget constraint
	Integrated strategic planning	Problems and opportunities identified by studying organizational strengths and weaknesses and environmental trends	Alternatives generated to exploit opportunities and solve problems; alternatives evaluated against stated objectives	Alternatives combined in logical sets for evaluation; set chosen which best satisfies stated objectives

Figure 5.1

mixtures of the programmed and managerial approaches, depending on the particular situation at hand. Consider the following examples:

A problem faces the manager ('muddling through' manager). He asks a team of analysts to find and evaluate different means of solving the problem (systems analysis). Their recommendations are presented in ROI terms, and are dealt with during the annual budget review (capital budgeting).

Sales predictions indicate a possible slump (forecasting). A marketing group begins to search for new products (market research), and management accepts the first reasonable alternative that the group finds ('muddling through' manager).

Management discovers a new process for saving time in constructing facilities (entrepreneurial manager). Using the PERT model, these time-savings are assessed on a project basis (mathematical modeling). Valuing time, management adopts the new process (entrepreneurial manager).

Figure 5.1 indicates that there has been little evidence of programming in *intelligence* activity, except, perhaps, in the marketing area. This activity consists primarily of managers finding opportunities and reacting to problems. Search is, by and large, an unprogrammed activity, but there has been much analytical activity in the evaluation phase of *design* activity. Unless the organization uses capital budgeting, choices are made informally by managers who satisfice, or who attempt to achieve certain strategy aims.

The present: Conclusions

Planners play a relatively minor role in strategy-making for two reasons:

1 Their programs are loose and ill-defined. In most cases, the important work is left to the manager. For example, the manager must define the projects for capital budgeting; he must interrelate the various *ad hoc* market research and systems analysis studies. In other cases, planner methods are no more formal than traditional managerial methods. For example, search is a critical part of any systems study, yet there are no formal search programs. The planner 'muddles through'.

2 The information necessary for strategy-making flows to the manager. Much of this information—problems, opportunities, pressures, values, opinions, etc.—is unavailable to the planner.

Given the current weaknesses of planning, it must be concluded that a Darwinist evolutionary theory is more realistic than a biblical 'grand plan' theory. Strategy evolves as managers react to stimuli. It is worthwhile to do research on methods of developing integrative plans on a periodic basis, but practitioners must recognize the manager's need to react to problems and pressures as they arise and to be exposed to feedback as problems are gradually solved.

The future: Recommendations

1 Until we have a fully developed understanding of the manager's strategy-making environment, and until we can develop much stronger integrative programs, planners will find the adaptive programs to be most useful. Let us return to the intelligence-design-choice framework:

(a) If the planner can effectively tap the flow of information to the manager, he can be very helpful in the area of *intelligence* activity. Managers lack the time to analyze carefully all the information that bombards them.

(b) Search activity, if it is to be effective, is very time-consuming. Planners can play a vital role here, not because of their analytical abilities, but simply because they have the time.

(c) Evaluation and choice are highly complex activities. The growth of systems analysis has shown that planners can do an effective job of evaluation, given that time is available to conduct intricate analyses. However, the planner lacks the formal authority to trade off organizational objectives, and so cannot openly participate in *choice* activity.

2 Planning theorists must now concentrate on studies of current managerial methods. There is a great need to know how managers define problems, how they search for opportunities, and how (and if) they integrate *ad hoc* decisions. Currently, the literature offers the reader much more on strategy-making as it should be than as it actually is.

3 The long-run future of the science of strategy-making can best be understood by turning to the past. In 1911, Frederick W. Taylor, referring to the use of analysis in physical work, used a set of arguments which could well have been used in this paper:

It is true that whenever intelligent and educated men find that the responsibility for making progress in any of the mechanic arts rests with them, instead of upon the workmen who are actually laboring at the trade, that they almost invariably start on the road which leads to the development of a science where, in the past, has existed mere traditional or rule-of-thumb knowledge. When men, whose education has given them the habit of generalizing and everywhere looking for laws, find themselves confronted with a multitude of problems, such as exist in every other trade and which have a general similarity one to another, it is inevitable that they should try to gather these problems into certain logical groups, and then search for some general laws or rules to guide them in the solution. ... The workman's whole time is each day taken in actually doing the work with his hands, so that even if he had the necessary

99

education and habits of generalizing in his thought, he lacks the time and the opportunity for developing these laws. . .

Planning foremen of necessity spend most of their time in the planning department, because they must be close to their records and data which they continually use in their work, and because this work requires the use of a desk and freedom from interruption.[12]

The development of the field of industrial engineering, as a direct result of Taylor's urgings, stands as a vivid example of those who support the 'grand plan' approach today.

References

1. SIMON, HERBERT A. *The New Science of Management Decision.* New York: Harper & Row, 1960.
2. ANTHONY, ROBERT N. *Planning and Control Systems: A Framework for Analysis.* Boston: Division of Research, Graduate School of Business Administration, Harvard University, 1965.
3. BRAYBROOKE, DAVID and LINDBLOM, CHARLES E. *A strategy of Decision.* Glencoe, N.Y.: The Free Press, 1963.
4. DRUCKER, PETER F. 'Entrepreneurship in the Business Enterprise.' Lecture delivered at the University of Toronto on 3 March, 1965. Reprinted in *Commercial Letter.* Toronto: Canadian Imperial Bank of Commerce, March 1965.
5. HITCH, CHARLES J. and McKEAN, ROLAND N. *The Economics of Defense in the Nuclear Age.*
6. 'Where GE Peers Far into the Future,' *Business Week,* 11 September, 1965, p. 46.
7. STARR, MARTIN K. 'Planning Models.' *Management Science,* Vol. XIII, No. 4. December 1966, pp. 115-141.
8. BERG, NORMAN, 'Strategic Planning in Conglomerate Companies.' *Harvard Bsns. Rev.,* May/June 1965, pp. 79-92.
   TILLES, SEYMOUR. 'Strategies for Allocating Funds.' *Harvard Bsns. Rev.,* January/February 1966, pp. 72-80.
9. LEAVITT, THEODORE. 'Marketing Myopia.' *Harvard Bsns. Rev.,* July/August 1960, pp. 45-56.
10. GILMORE, FRANK F. and BRANDENBURG, RICHARD G. 'Anatomy of Corporate Planning.' *Harvard Bsns. Rev.,* November/December 1962, pp. 61-69.
11. ANSOFF, H. IGOR. *Corporate Strategy.* New York: McGraw-Hill, 1965.
12. TAYLOR, FREDRICK W. *Scientific Management.* New York: Harper & Row, 1947.

6. Shaping the master strategy of your firm

William H. Newman

Every enterprise needs a central purpose expressed in terms of the services it will render to society. And it needs a basic concept of how it will create these services. Since it will be competing with other enterprises for resources, it must have some distinctive advantages—in its services or in its methods of creating them. Moreover, since it will inevitably cooperate with other firms, it must have the means for maintaining viable coalitions with them. In addition, there are the elements of change, growth, and adaptation. Master strategy is a company's basic plan for dealing with these factors.

One familiar way of delving into company strategy is to ask, 'What business are we in or do we want to be in? Why should society tolerate our existence?' Answers are often difficult. A company producing only grass seed had very modest growth until it shifted its focus to 'lawn care' and provided the suburban homeowner with a full line of fertilizers, pesticides, and related products. Less fortunate was a cooperage firm that defined its business in terms of wooden boxes and barrels and went bankrupt when paperboard containers took over in the field.

Product line is only part of the picture, however. An ability to supply services economically is also crucial. For example, most local bakeries have shut down, not for lack of demand for bread, but because they became technologically inefficient. Many a paper mill has exhausted its sources of pulpwood. The independent motel operator is having difficulty meeting competition from franchised chains. Yet in all these industries some firms have prospered—the ones that have had the foresight and adaptability (and probably some luck, too) to take advantage of their changing environment.

• © 1967 by The Regents of the University of California. Reprinted from *California Management Review,* Vol. IX, No. 3, pp. 77-88, by permission of The Regents.

These firms pursued a master strategy which enabled them to increase the services rendered and attract greater resources.

Most central managers recognize that master strategy is of cardinal importance. But they are less certain about how to formulate a strategy for their particular firm. This article seeks to help in the shaping of master strategies. It outlines key elements and an approach to defining these. Most of our illustrations will be business enterprises; nevertheless, the central concept is just as crucial for hospitals, universities, and other non-profit ventures.

A practical way to develop a master strategy is to:

1 Pick particular roles or niches that are appropriate in view of competition and the company's resources.

2 Combine various facets of the company's efforts to obtain synergistic effects.

3 Set up sequences and timing of changes that reflect company capabilities and external conditions.

4 Provide for frequent reappraisal and adaptation to evolving opportunities.

New markets or services

Picking propitious niches

Most companies fill more than one niche. Often, they sell several lines of products; even when a single line is produced an enterprise may sell it to several distinct types of customers. Especially as a firm grows, it seeks expansion by tapping new markets or selling different services to its existing customers. In designing a company strategy, we can avoid pitfalls by first examining each of these markets separately.

Basically, we are searching for customer needs—preferably growing ones—where adroit use of our unique resources will make our services distinctive and, in that sense, give us a competitive advantage. In these particular spots, we hope to give the customer an irresistible value and to do so at relatively low expense. A bank, for example, may devise a way of financing the purchase of an automobile that is particularly well-suited to farmers; it must then consider whether it is in a good position to serve such a market.

Identifying such propitious niches is not easy. Here is one approach that works well in various situations: focus first on the industry—growth prospects, competition, key factors required for success—then on the strengths and weaknesses of the specific company as matched against these key success factors. As we describe this approach more fully, keep in mind that we are interested in segments of markets as well as entire markets.

The sales volume and profits of an industry or one of its segments depend on the demand for its services, the supply of these services, and the competitive conditions. (We use 'service' here to include both physical products and intangible values provided by an enterprise.) Predicting future demand, supply, and competition is an exciting endeavor. In the following paragraphs, we suggest a few of the important considerations that may vitally affect the strategy of a company.

Elements of demand

Demand for industry services

The strength of the desire for a service affects its demand. For instance, we keenly want a small amount of salt, but care little for additional quantities. Our desire for more and better automobiles does not have this same sort of cut-off level, and our desires for pay-television (no commercials, select programs) or supersonic air travel are highly uncertain, falling in quite a different category from that of salt.

Possible substitutes to satisfy a given desire must be weighed—beef for lamb, motorboats for baseball, gas for coal, aureomycin for sulfa, weldments for castings, and so forth. The frequency of such substitution is affected, of course, by the relative prices.

Desire has to be backed up by ability to pay, and here business cycles enter in. Also, in some industries large amounts of capital are necessarily tied up in equipment. The relative efficiency, quality of work, and nature of machinery already in place influence the money that will be available for new equipment. Another consideration: If we hope to sell in foreign markets, foreign-exchange issues arise.

The structure of markets also requires analysis. Where, on what terms, and in response to what appeals do people buy jet planes, sulphuric acid, or dental floss? Does a manufacturer deal directly with consumers or are intermediaries, such as retailers or brokers, a more effective means of distribution?

Although an entire industry is often affected by such factors—desire, substitutes, ability to pay, structure of markets—a local variation in demand sometimes provides a unique opportunity for a particular firm. Thus, most drugstores carry cosmetics, candy, and a wide variety of items besides drugs, but a store located in a medical center might develop a highly profitable business by dealing exclusively with prescriptions and other medical supplies.

All these elements of demand are subject to change—some quite rapidly. Since the kind of strategic plans we are considering here usually extends over several years, we need both an identification of the key factors that will affect industry demand and an estimate of how they will change over a span of time.

103

Supply situation

Supply related to demand

The attractiveness of any industry depends on more than potential growth arising from strong demand. In designing a company strategy, we also must consider the probable supply of services and the conditions under which they will be offered.

The capacity of an industry to fill demand for its services clearly affects profit margins. The importance of over- or undercapacity, however, depends on the ease of entry and withdrawal from the industry. When capital costs are high, as in the hotel or cement business, adjustments to demand tend to lag. Thus, overcapacity may depress profits for a long period; even bankruptcies do not remove the capacity if plants are bought up—at bargain prices—and operated by new owners. On the other hand, low capital requirements—as in electronic assembly work—permit new firms to enter quickly, and shortages of supply tend to be short-lived. Of course, more than the physical plant is involved; an effective organization of competent people is also necessary. Here again, the case of expansion or contraction should be appraised.

Costs also need to be predicted—labor costs, material costs, and, for some industries, transportation costs or excise taxes. If increases in operating costs affect all members of an industry alike and can be passed on to the consumer in the form of higher prices, this factor becomes less significant in company strategy. However, rarely do both conditions prevail. Sharp rises in labor costs in Hawaii, for example, place its sugar industry at a disadvantage on the world market.

A highly dynamic aspect of supply is technology. New methods for producing established products—for example, basic oxygen conversion of steel displacing open-hearth furnaces and mechanical cotton pickers displacing century-old hand-picking techniques—are part of the picture. Technology may change the availability and price of raw materials; witness the growth of synthetic rubber and industrial diamonds. Similarly, air cargo planes and other new forms of transportation are expanding the sources of supply that may serve a given market.

For an individual producer, anticipating these shifts in the industry supply situation may be a matter of prosperity or death.

Climate of industry

Competitive conditions in the industry

The way the interplay between demand and supply works out depends partly on the nature of competition in the industry. Size, strength, and attitude of companies in one industry—the dress industry where entrance is easy and style is critical—may lead to very sharp competition. On the other hand, oligopolistic competition among the giants of the aluminum industry produces a more stable situation, at least in the short run. The resources and managerial talent needed to enter one industry differ greatly from what it takes to get ahead in the other.

A strong trade association often helps to create a favorable climate in its industry. The Independent Oil Producers' Association, to cite one case, has been unusually effective in restricting imports of crude oil into the United States. Other associations compile valuable industry statistics, help reduce unnecessary variations in size of products, run training conferences, hold trade shows, and aid members in a variety of other ways.

Government regulation also modifies competition. A few industries like banking and insurance are supervised by national or state bodies that place limits on prices, sales promotion, and the variety of services rendered. Airlines are both regulated as a utility and subsidized as an infant industry. Farm subsidies affect large segments of agriculture, and tariffs have long protected selected manufacturers. Our patent laws also bear directly on the nature of competition, as is evident in the heated discussion of how pharmaceutical patents may be used. Clearly, future government action is a significant factor in the outlook of many industries.

Crucial factors

Key factors for success in the industry

This brief review suggests the dynamic nature of business and uncertainties in the outlook for virtually all industries. A crucial task of every top management is to assess the forces at play in its industry, and to identify those factors that will be crucial for future success. These we call 'key success factors'. Leadership in research and development may be very important in one industry, low costs in another, and adaptability to local need in a third; large financial resources may be a *sine qua non* for mining, whereas creative imagination is the touchstone in advertising.

We stressed earlier the desirability of making such analyses for narrow segments as well as broad industry categories. The success factors for each segment are likely to differ in at least one or two respects from those for other segments. For example, General Foods Corporation discovered to its sorrow that the key success factors in gourmet foods differ significantly from those for coffee and Jello.

Moreover, the analysis of industry outlook should provide a forecast of the growth potentials and the profit prospects for the various industry segments. These conclusions, along with key success factors, are vital guideposts in setting up a company's master strategy.

The range of opportunities for distinctive service is wide. Naturally, in picking its particular niche out of this array, a company favors those opportunities which will utilize its strength and bypass its limitations. This calls for a candid appraisal of the company itself.

Position in market

Market strengths of company

A direct measure of market position is the percentage that company sales are of industry sales and of major competitors' sales. Such figures quickly indicate whether our company is so big that its activities are likely to bring prompt responses from other leading companies. Or our company may be small enough to enjoy independent manoeuvrability. Of course, to be most meaningful, these percentages should be computed separately for geographical areas, product lines, and types of customer—if suitable industry data are available.

More intangible, but no less significant, are the relative standing of company products and their reputation in major markets. Kodak products, for instance, are widely and favorably known; they enjoy a reputation for both high quality and dependability. Clearly, this reputation will be a factor in Eastman Kodak Company strategy. And any new, unknown firm must overcome this prestige if it seeks even a small share in one segment of the film market. Market reputation is tenacious. Especially when we try to 'trade up', our previous low quality, service, and sharp dealing will be an obstacle. Any strategy we adopt must have enough persistence and consistency, so that our firm is assigned a 'role' in the minds of the customers we wish to reach.

The relationship between a company and the distribution system is another vital aspect of market position. The big United States automobile companies, for example, are strong partly because each has a set of dealers throughout the country. In contrast, foreign car manufacturers have difficulty selling here until they can arrange with dealers to provide dependable service. A similar problem confronted Whirlpool Corporation when it wanted to sell its trademarked appliances publicly. (For years its only customer had been Sears, Roebuck, and Company.) Whirlpool made an unusual arrangement with Radio Corporation of America which led to the establishment of RCA-Whirlpool distributors and dealers. Considering the strong competition, Whirlpool could not have entered this new market without using marketing channels such as RCA's.

All these aspects of market position—a relative share of the market, comparative quality of product, reputation with consumers, and ties with a distributive system—help define the strengths and limitations of a company.

Service abilities

Supply strengths of a company

To pick propitious niches, we also should appraise our company's relative strength in creating goods and services. Such ability to supply services fitted to consumer needs will be built largely on the firm's resources of labor and material, effective productive facilities, and, perhaps, pioneering research and development.

Labor in the United States is fairly mobile. Men tend to gravitate to good jobs. But the process takes time—a southern shoe plant needed ten years to build up an adequate number of skilled workers—and it may be expensive. Consequently, immediate availability of competent men at normal industry wages is a source of strength. In addition, the relationships between the company and its workforce are important. All too often both custom and formal agreements freeze inefficient practices. The classic example is New England textiles; here, union-supported work habits give even mills high labor costs. Only recently have a few companies been able to match their more flourishing competitors in the South.

Access to low-cost materials is often a significant factor in a company's supply position. The development of the southern paper industry, for example, is keyed to the use of fast-growing forests which can be cut on a rotational basis to provide a continuing supply of pulpwood. Of course, if raw materials can be easily transported, such as iron ore and crude oil by enormous ships, plants need not be located at the original source.

Availability of materials involves more than physical handling. Ownership, or long-term contracts with those who do own, may assure a continuing source at low cost. Much of the strategy of companies producing basic metals—iron, copper, aluminium, or nickel—includes huge investments in ore properties. But all sorts of companies are concerned with the availability of materials. So whenever supplies are scarce a potential opportunity exists. Even in retailing, Sears, Roebuck, and Company discovered, in its Latin American expansion, that a continuing flow of merchandise of standard quality was difficult to assure, but once established, such sources became a great advantage.

Physical facilities—office buildings, plants, mines—often tie up a large portion of a company's assets. In the short run, at least, these facilities may be an advantage or a disadvantage. The character of many colleges, for instance, has been shaped by their location, whether in a plush suburb or in a degenerating urban area, and the cost of moving facilities is so great that adaptation to the existing neighborhood becomes necessary. A steel company, to cite another case, delayed modernizing its plant so long that it had to abandon its share of the basic steel market and seek volume in specialty products.

107

Established organizations of highly talented people to perform particular tasks also give a company a distinctive capability. Thus, a good research and development department may enable a company to expand in pharmaceuticals, whereas a processing firm without such a technical staff is barred from this profitable field.

Perhaps the company we are analyzing will enjoy other distinctive abilities to produce services. Our central concern at this point is to identify strengths and see how these compare with strengths of other firms.

Finances and management

Other company resources

The propitious niche for a company also depends on its financial strength and the character of its management.

Some strategies will require large quantities of capital. Any oil company that seeks foreign sources of crude oil, for instance, must be prepared to invest millions of dollars. Five firms maintain cash reserves of this size, so financial capacity to enter this kind of business depends on: an ability to attract new capital—through borrowing or sale of stock—or a flow of profits (and depreciation allowances) from existing operations that can be allocated to the new venture. On the other hand, perhaps a strategy can be devised that calls for relatively small cash advances, and in these fields a company that has low financial strength will still be able to compete with the affluent firms.

A more subtle factor in company capacity is its management. The age and vitality of key executives, their willingness to risk profit and capital, their urge to gain personal prestige through company growth, their desire to insure stable employment for present workers—all affect the suitability of any proposed strategy. For example, the expansion of Hilton Hotels Corporation into a worldwide chain certainly reflects the personality of Conrad Hilton; with a different management at the helm, a modification in strategy is most appropriate because Conrad Hilton's successors do not have his particular set of drives and values.

Related to the capabilities of key executives is the organization structure of the company. A decentralized structure, for instance, facilitates movement into new fields of business, whereas a functional structure with fine specialization is better suited to expansion in closely related lines.

Picking a niche

Matching company strengths with key success factors

Armed with a careful analysis of the strengths and limitations of our company, we are prepared to pick desirable niches for company concentration. Naturally, we will look for fields where company strengths correspond with the key factors for success that have been developed in our industry analyses described in the preceding section. And in the process we will set aside possibilities in which company limitations create serious handicaps.

Potential growth and profits in each niche must, of course, be added to the synthesis. Clearly, a low potential will make a niche unattractive, even though the company strengths and success factors fit neatly. And we may become keenly interested in a niche where the fit is only fair if the potential is great.

Typically, several intriguing possibilities emerge. These are all the niches—in terms of market lines, market segments, or combinations of production functions—that the company might pursue. Also typically, a series of positive actions is necessary in order for the company to move into each area. So we need to list not only each niche and its potential, but the limitations that will have to be overcome and other steps necessary for the company to succeed in each area. These are our propitious niches—nestled in anticipated business conditions and tailored to the strengths and limitations of our particular company.

An enterprise always pursues a variety of efforts to serve even a single niche, and, typically, it tries to fill several related niches. Considerable choice is possible, at least in the degree to which these many efforts are pushed. In other words, management decides how many markets to cover, to what degree to automate production, what stress to place on consumer engineering, and a host of other actions. One vital aspect of master strategy is fitting these numerous efforts together. In fact, our choice of niches will depend, in part, on how well we can combine the total effort they require.

Synergy is a powerful ally for this purpose. Basically, synergy means that the combined effect of two or more cooperative acts is greater than the sum which would result if the actions were taken independently. A simple example in marketing is that widespread dealer stocks combined with advertising will produce much greater sales volume than widespread dealer stocks in, say, Virginia and advertising in, say, Minnesota. Often, the possibility of obtaining synergistic effects will shape the master strategy of the company—as the following examples will suggest.

Combination of services

Total service to customers—A customer rarely buys merely a physical product. Other attributes of the transaction often include delivery, credit terms, return privileges, repair service, operating instructions, conspicuous consumption, psychological experience of purchasing, and the like. Many services involve no physical product at all. The crucial question is what combination of attributes will have high synergistic value for the customers we serve.

International Business Machines, for instance, has found a winning combination. Its products are well designed and of high quality. But so are the products of several of its competitors. In addition, IBM provides salesmen who understand the customer's problems and how IBM equipment can help solve them, and fast, dependable repair service. The synergistic effect of these three services is of high value to many customers.

Each niche calls for its own combination of services. For example, Chock Full o' Nuts expanded its restaurant chain on the basis of three attributes: good quality food, cleanliness, and fast service. This combination appealed to a particular group of customers; a very limited selection, crowded space, and lack of frills did not matter. However, if any one of the three characteristics slips at an outlet, the synergistic effort is lost.

Adding to capabilities

Fuller use of existing resources—Synergistic effects are possible in any phase of company operations. One possibility is that present activities include a 'capability' that can be applied to additional uses. Thus, American watch companies have undertaken the manufacture of tiny gyroscopes and electronic components for spacecraft because they already possessed technical skill in the production of miniature precision products. They adopted this strategy on the premise that they could make both watches and components for spacecraft with less effort than could separate firms devoted to only one line of products.

The original concept of General Foods Corporation sought a similar synergistic effect in marketing. Here, the basic capability was marketing prepared foods. By having the same sales organization handle several product lines, a larger and more effective sales effort could be provided and/or the selling cost per product line should be reduced. Clearly, the combined sales activity was more powerful than separate sales efforts for each product line would have been.

Vertical integration

Expansion to obtain a resource—Vertical integration may have synergistic effects. This occurred when the Apollo Printing Machine Company bought a foundry. Apollo was unsatisfied with the quality and tardy delivery of its castings and was looking for a new supplier. In its search, it learned that a nearby foundry could be purchased. The foundry was just breaking even, primarily because the volume of its work fluctuated widely. Following the purchase, Apollo gave the foundry a more steady backlog of work, and, through close technical cooperation, the quality of castings received by them was improved. The consolidated set-up was better for both enterprises than the previous independent operations.

110

The results of vertical integration are not always so good, however; problems of balance, flexibility, and managerial capacity must be carefully weighed. Nevertheless, control of a critical resource is often a significant part of company strategy.

Unique services

Expansion to enhance market position—Efforts to improve market position provide many examples of 'the whole being better than the sum of its parts'. The leading can companies, for example, moved from exclusive concentration on metal containers into glass, plastic, and paper containers. They expected their new divisions to be profitable by themselves, but an additional reason for the expansion lay in anticipated synergistic effects of being able to supply a customer's total container requirements. With the entire packaging field changing so rapidly, a company that can quickly shift from one type of container to another offers a distinctive service to its customers.

International Harvester, to cite another case, added a very large tractor to its line a few years ago. The prospects for profit on this line alone were far from certain. However, the new tractor was important to give dealers 'a full line'; its availability removed the temptation for dealers to carry some products of competing manufacturers. So, when viewed in combination with other International Harvester products, the new tractor looked much more significant than it did as an isolated project.

Negative synergy

Compatibility of efforts

In considering additional niches for a company, we may be confronted with negative synergy—that is, the combined effort is worse than the sum of independent efforts. This occurred when a producer of high quality television and hi-fi sets introduced a small color television receiver. When first offered, the small unit was as good as most competing sets and probably had an attractive potential market. However, it was definitely inferior in performance to other products of the company and, consequently, undermined public confidence in the quality of the entire line. Moreover, customers had high expectations for the small set because of the general reputation of the company, and they became very critical when the new product did not live up to their expectations. Both the former products and the new product suffered.

Compatibility of operations within the company should also be considered. A large department store, for instance, ran into serious trouble when it tried to add a high-quality dress shop to its mass merchandising activities. The ordering and physical handling of merchandise, the approach to sales promotion, the sales compensation plan, and many other procedures which

111

worked well for the established type of business were unsuited to the new shop. And friction arose each time the shop received special treatment. Clearly, the new shop created an excessive number of problems because it was incompatible with existing customs and attitudes.

Broad company goals

Summarizing briefly: we have seen that some combinations of efforts are strongly reinforcing. The combination accelerates the total effect or reduces the cost for the same effect or solidifies our supply or market position. On the other hand, we must watch for incompatible efforts which may have a disruptive effect in the same cumulative manner. So, when we select niches—as a part of our master strategy—one vital aspect is the possibility of such synergistic effects.

Master strategy sets broad company goals. One firm may decide to seek preeminence in a narrow specialty while another undertakes to be a leader in several niches or perhaps in all phases of its industry. We have recommended that this definition of 'scope' be clear in terms of:

1 Services offered to customers.
2 Operations performed by the company.
3 Relationships with suppliers of necessary resources.
4 The desirability of defining this mission so as to obtain synergistic effects.

But master strategy involves more than defining our desired role in society. Many activities will be necessary to achieve this desired spot, and senior executives must decide what to do first, how many activities can be done concurrently, how fast to move, what risks to run, and what to postpone. These questions of sequence and timing must be resolved to make the strategy operational.

Strategy of sequence

Choice of sequence—Especially in technical areas, sequence of actions may be dictated by technology. Thus, process research must precede equipment designs, product specifications must precede cost estimation, and so forth. Other actions, such as the steps necessary to form a new corporation, likewise give management little choice in sequence. When this occurs, normal programming or possibly PERT analysis may be employed. Little room—or need—exists for strategy.

Preordained sequences, however, are exceptional in the master strategy area. A perennial issue when entering a new niche, for instance, is whether to develop markets before working on production economies, or vice versa. The production executive will probably say, 'Let's be sure we can produce the

112

product at a low cost before committing ourselves to customers,' whereas the typical marketing man will advise, 'Better be sure it will sell before tooling up for a big output.'

A striking example of strategy involving sequence confronted the Boeing company when it first conceived of a large four-engine jet plane suitable for handling cargo or large passenger loads. Hindsight makes the issue appear simple, but at the time, Air Force officers saw little need for such a plane. The belief was that propeller-driven planes provided the most desirable means for carrying cargo. In other words, the company got no support for its prediction of future market requirements. Most companies would have stopped at this point. However, Boeing executives decided to invest several million dollars to develop the new plane. A significant portion of the company's liquid assets went into the project. Over two years later, Boeing was able to present evidence that caused the Air Force officials to change their minds—and the KC 135 was born. Only Boeing was prepared to produce the new type of craft which proved to be both faster and more economical than propeller-driven planes. Moreover, the company was able to convert the design into the Boeing 707 passenger plane which, within a few years, dominated the airline passenger business. Competing firms were left far behind, and Convair almost went bankrupt in its attempt to catch up. In this instance, a decision to let engineering and production run far ahead of marketing paid off handsomely.

No simple guide exists for selecting a strategic sequence. Nevertheless, the following comments do sharpen the issue:

1 Resist the temptation to do first what is easiest simply because it requires the least initiative. Each of us typically has a bias for what he does well. A good sequence of activities, however, is more likely to emerge from an objective analysis.

2 If a head start is especially valuable on one front, start early there. Sometimes, being the first in the market is particularly desirable (there may be room for only one company). In other cases, the strategic place to begin is the acquiring of key resources; at a later date, limited raw materials may already be bought up or the best sites occupied by competitors. The importance of a head start is usually hard to estimate, but probably more money is lost in trying to be first than in catching up with someone else.

3 Move into uncertain areas promptly, preferably before making any major commitments. For instance, companies have been so entranced with a desired expansion that they committed substantial funds to new plants before uncertainties regarding the production processes were removed.

4 If a particular uncertainty can be investigated quickly and inexpensively, get it out of the way promptly.

5 Start early with processes involving long lead-times. For example, if a

113

new synthetic food product must have government approval, the tedious process of testing and reviewing evidence may take a year or two longer than preparation for manufacturing and marketing.

6 Delay revealing plans publicly if other companies can easily copy a novel idea. If substantial social readjustment is necessary, however, an early public announcement is often helpful.

In a particular case, these guides may actually conflict with each other, or other considerations may be dominant. And, as the Boeing 707 example suggests, the possible gains may be large enough to justify following a very risky sequence. Probably the greatest value of the above list is to stimulate careful thought about the sequence that is incorporated into a company's master strategy.

Resource limitations

Straining scarce resources

A hard-driving executive does not like to admit that an objective cannot be achieved. He prefers to believe, 'Where there's a will there's a way.' Yet, an essential aspect of master strategy is deciding what can be done and how fast.

Every enterprise has limits—perhaps severe limits—on its resources. The amount of capital, the number and quality of key personnel, the physical production capacity, or the adaptability of its social structure—none of these is boundless. The tricky issue is how to use these limited resources to the best advantage. We must devise a strategy which is feasible within the inherent restraints.

A household-appliance manufacturer went bankrupt because he failed to adapt his rate of growth to his financial resources. This man had a first-rate product and a wise plan for moving with an 'economy model' into an expanding market (following rural electrification). But, to achieve low production costs, he built an oversized plant and launched sales efforts in 10 states. His contention was that the kind of company he conceived could not start out on a small scale. Possibly all of these judgements were correct, but they resulted in cash requirements that drained all of his resources before any momentum was achieved. Cost of the partially used plant and of widely scattered sales efforts was so high that no one was willing to bail out the financially strapped venture. His master strategy simply did not fit his resources.

The scarce resource affecting master strategy may be managerial personnel. A management consulting firm, for instance, reluctantly postponed entry into the international arena because only two of its partners had the combination of interest, capacity, and vitality to spend a large amount of time abroad, and these men were also needed to assure continuity of the United States practice. The firm felt that a later start would be better than weak action immediately—even though this probably meant the loss of several desirable clients.

The weight we should attach to scarce resources in the timing of master strategy often requires delicate judgement. Some strain may be endured. But, how much, how long? For example, in its switch from purchased to company-produced tyres, a European rubber company fell behind on deliveries for six months, but, through heroic efforts and pleading with customers, the company weathered the squeeze. Now, company executives believe the timing was wise! If the delay had lasted a full year—and this was a real possibility—the consequence would have approached a catastrophe.

Forming coalitions

A cooperative agreement with firms in related fields occasionally provides a way to overcome scarce resources. We have already referred to the RCA-Whirlpool arrangement for distributing Whirlpool products. Clearly, in this instance, the timing of Whirlpool's entrance into the market with its own brand depended on forming a coalition with RCA.

Examples of coalitions—The early development of frozen foods provides us with two other examples of fruitful coalitions. A key element in Birdseye master strategy was to obtain the help of cold-storage warehouses; grocery wholesalers were not equipped to handle frozen foods, and before the demand was clearly established they were slow to move into the new activity. And the Birdseye division of General Foods lacked both managerial and financial resources to venture into national wholesaling.

Similarly, Birdseye had to get freezer cabinets into retail stores, but it lacked the capability to produce them. So, it entered into a coalition with a refrigerator manufacturer to make and sell (or lease) the cabinets to retail stores. This mutual agreement enabled Birdseye to move ahead with its marketing program much faster. With the tremendous growth of frozen foods, neither the cold storage warehouse nor the cabinet manufacturer continued to be necessary, but without them in the early days widespread use of frozen foods would have been delayed three to five years.

Coalitions may be formed for reasons other than 'buying time'. Nevertheless, when we are trying to round out a workable master strategy, coalitions—or even mergers—may provide the quickest way to overcome a serious deficiency in vital resources.

The right time to act

Receptive environment

Conditions in a firm's environment affect the 'right time' to make a change. Mr Ralph Cordiner, for example, testifies that he launched his basic reorganization of General Electric Company only when he felt confident of three years of high business activity because, in his opinion, the company could not have absorbed all the internal readjustments during a period of declining volume and profits.

Judging the right time to act is difficult. Thus, one of the contributing factors to the multimillion-dollar Edsel car fiasco was poor timing. The same automobile launched a year or two earlier might have been favorably received. But buyer tastes changed between the time elaborate market research studies were made and the time when the new car finally appeared in dealer showrooms. By then, preference was swinging away from a big car that 'had everything' toward compacts. This mistake in timing and associated errors in strategy cost the Ford Motor Company over a hundred million dollars.

A major move can be too early, as well as too late. We know, for instance, that a forerunner of the modern, self-service supermarket—the Piggly Wiggly—was born too soon. In its day, only a few housewives drove automobiles to shopping centers; and those that could afford cars usually shunned the do-it-yourself made so prevalent today. In other words, the environment at that time simply was not receptive to what now performs so effectively. Other 'pioneers' have also received cool receptions—prefabricated housing and local medical clinics are two.

No simple rules

The preceding discussions of sequence and timing provide no simple rules for these critical aspects of basic strategy. The factors we have mentioned for deciding which front(s) to push first (where is a head start valuable, early attention to major uncertainties, lead-times, significance of secrecy) and for deciding how fast to move (strain on scarce resources, possible coalition to provide resources, and receptivity of the environment) bear directly on many strategy decisions. They also highlight the fundamental nature of sequence and timing in the master strategy for a firm.

Master strategy involves deliberately relating a company's efforts to its particular future environment. We recognize, of course, that both the company's capabilities and its environment continually evolve; consequently, strategy should always be based, not on existing conditions, but on forecasts. Such forecasts, however, are never 100 per cent correct; instead, strategy often seeks to take advantage of uncertainty about future conditions.

This dynamic aspect of strategy should be underscored. The industry outlook will shift for any of numerous reasons. These forces may accelerate growth in some sectors and spell decline in others, may squeeze material supply, may make old sources obsolete, may open new possibilities and snuff out others. Meanwhile, the company itself is also changing—due to the success

116

or failure of its own efforts and to actions of competitors and cooperating firms. And with all of these internal and external changes the combination of thrusts that will provide optimum synergistic effects undoubtedly will be altered. Timing of actions is the most volatile element of all. It should be adjusted to both the new external situation and the degrees of internal progress on various fronts.

Consequently, frequent reappraisal of master strategy is essential. We must build into the planning mechanisms sources of fresh data that will tell us how well we are doing and what new opportunities and obstacles are appearing on the horizon. The feedback features of control will provide some of these data. In addition, senior managers and others who have contact with various parts of the environment must be ever-sensitive to new developments that established screening devices might not detect.

Hopefully, such reappraisal will not call for sharp reversals in strategy. Typically, a master strategy requires several years to execute and some features may endure much longer. The kind of plan I am discussing here sets the direction for a whole host of company actions, and external reputations and relations often persist for many years. Quick reversals break momentum, require repeated relearning, and dissipate favorable cumulative effects. To be sure, occasionally a sharp break may be necessary. But, if my forecasts are reasonably sound, the adaptations to new opportunities will be more evolution than revolution. Once embarked on a course, we make our reappraisal from our new position—and this introduces an advantage in continuing in at least the same general direction. So, normally, the adaptation is more an unfolding than a completely new start.

Even though drastic modification of our master strategy may be unnecessary, frequent incremental changes will certainly be required to keep abreast of the times. Especially desirable are shifts that anticipate change before the pressures build up. And such farsighted adjustments are possible only if we periodically reappraise and adapt present strategy to new opportunities.

Master strategy is the pivotal planning instrument for large and small enterprises alike. The giant corporations provide us with examples on a grand scale, but the same kind of thinking is just as vital for small firms.

An example

A terse sketch of the central strategy of one small firm will illustrate this point. The partners of an accounting firm in a city with a quarter-million population predicted faster growth in data-processing than in their normal auditing and tax work, yet they knew that most of their clients were too small to use an electronic computer individually. So they foresaw the need for a single, cooperative computer center serving several companies. And they believed that their intimate knowledge of the procedures and the needs of several of these companies, plus the specialized ability of one partner in data processing, put them in a unique position to operate such a center. Competition was anticipated from two directions: New models of computers much smaller in size would eventually come on the market—but even if the clients could rent such equipment they would still need programmers and other specialized skills. Also, telephonic hook-ups with International Business Machines service centers appeared likely—but the accounting firm felt its local and more intimate knowledge of each company would give it an advantage over such competition. So, the cooperative computer center looked like a propitious niche.

The chief obstacle was developing a relatively stable volume of work that would carry the monthly rental on the proposed computer. A local insurance company was by far the best prospect for this purpose; it might use half the computer capacity, and then the work for other, smaller companies could be fitted into the remaining time. Consequently, the first major move was to make a deal—a coalition—with the insurance company. One partner was to devote almost his entire time working on details for such an arrangement; meanwhile, the other two partners supported him through their established accounting practice.

We have seen in this brief example:

1 The picking of a propitious niche for expansion.

2 The anticipated synergistic effect of combining auditing services with computing service.

3 The sequence and timing of efforts to overcome the major limiting factor.

The project had not advanced far enough for much reappraisal, but the fact that two partners were supporting the third provided a built-in check on the question of 'How are we doing?'

References

This article is adapted from a new chapter in *The Process of Management* (Englewood Cliffs, N.J.: Prentice-Hall, 1967).

Executives who wish to explore the meaning and method of shaping master strategies still further can consult the following materials:

REILLEY, E. W. 'Planning the Strategy of Business.' *Advanced Management,* Vol. 20, December 1955, pp. 8-12.

LEVITT, THEODORE, 'Marketing Myopia.' *Harvard Bsns Rev.,* Vol. 38, No. 4, July/August 1960, pp. 45-66.

GILMORE, F. F. and BRANDENBURG, R. G. 'Anatomy of Corporate Planning.' *Harvard Bsns Rev.,* Vol. 41, No. 6, November/December 1962, pp. 61-9.

MEWMAN, H. W. and BERG, T. L. 'Managing External Relations.' *California Management Review,* Vol. 5, No. 3, Spring 1963, pp. 81-6.

7. How to evaluate corporate strategy

Seymour Tilles

No good military officer would undertake even a small-scale attack on a limited objective without a clear concept of his strategy. No seasoned politician would undertake a campaign for a major office without an equally clear concept of his strategy. In the field of business management, however, we frequently find men deploying resources on a large scale without any clear notion of what their strategy is. And yet a company's strategy is a vital ingredient in determining its future. A valid strategy will yield growth, profit, or whatever other objectives the managers have established. An inappropriate strategy not only will fail to yield benefits, but also may result in disaster.

In this paper, I will try to demonstrate the truth of these contentions by examining the experience of a number of companies. I shall discuss what strategy is, how it can be evaluated, and how, by evaluating its strategy, a management can do much to assure the future of the enterprise.

Decisive impact

The influence of strategy can be seen in every age and in every area of industry. Here are some examples:

1 From the time it was started in 1911 as the Computing-Tabulating-Recording Co., International Business Machines Corporation has demonstrated the significance of a soundly conceived strategy. Seeing itself in the data-system business at a time when most manufacturers were still preoccupied with individual pieces of equipment, IBM developed a set of policies which resulted in its dominating the office equipment industry.

2 By contrast, Packard in the 'thirties was to the automobile industry everything that IBM is today to the office machine industry. In 1937, it sold over 109 000 cars, compared with about 11 000 for Cadillac. In 1954, it had disappeared as an independent producer.

Strategy is, of course, not the only factor determining a company's success or failure. The competence of its managerial leadership is significant as well. Luck can be a factor, too, although often what people call good luck is really the product of good strategy. But a valid strategy can gain extraordinary results for the company whose general level of competence is only average. And, conversely, the most inspiring leaders who are locked into an inappropriate strategy will have to exert their full competence and energy merely in order to keep from losing ground.

When Hannibal inflicted the humiliating defeat on the Roman army at Cannae in 216 BC, he led a ragged band against soldiers who were in possession of superior arms, better training, and competent 'noncoms'. His strategy, however, was so superior that all of those advantages proved to be relatively insignificant. Similarly, when Jacob Borowsky made Lestoil the hottest selling detergent in New England some years ago, he was performing a similar feat—relying on strategy to battle competition with superior resources.

Strategy is important not only for aspiring Davids who need an offensive device to combat corporate Goliaths, it is significant also for the large organization faced with a wide range of choice in domestic and international operations. For instance, the following corporations are all in the midst of strategic changes, the implications of which are worldwide in scope:

1 Massey-Ferguson, Ltd, with 26 factories located around the world, and vying for leadership in the farm-equipment industry.

2 General Electric Company and Westinghouse Electric Corporation, the giant producers of electrical equipment who are recasting their competitive policies.

3 Singer Sewing Machine Company, trying to make its vast assets yield a greater return.

Dynamic concept

A strategy is a set of goals and major policies. The definition is as simple as that. But while the notion of a strategy is extremely easy to grasp, working out an agreed-upon statement for a given company can be a fundamental contribution to the organization's future success.

In order to develop such a statement, managers must be able to identify precisely what is meant by a goal and what is meant by a major policy. Otherwise, the process of strategy determination may degenerate into what it

120

so often becomes—the solemn recording of platitudes, useless for either the clarification of direction or the achievement of consensus.

Identifying goals

Corporate goals are an indication of what the company as a whole is trying to *achieve* and to *become*. Both parts—the achieving and the becoming—are important for a full understanding of what a company hopes to attain. For example:

1 Under the leadership of Alfred Sloan, General Motors achieved a considerable degree of external success; this was accomplished because Sloan worked out a pattern for the kind of company he wanted it to be internally.

2 Similarly, the remarkable record of Du Pont in the twentieth century and the growth of Sears, Roebuck under Julius Rosenwald were as much a tribute to their modified structure as to their external strategy.[1]

Achieving. In order to state what a company expects to achieve, it is important to state what it hopes to do with respect to its environment. For instance: Ernest Breech, chairman of the board of Ford Motor Company, said that the strategy formulated by his company in 1946 was based on a desire to hold our own in what we foresaw would be a rich but hotly competitive market'.[2] The view of the environment implicit in this statement is unmistakable: an expanding overall demand, increasing competition, and emphasis on market share as a measure of performance against competitors.

Clearly, a statement of what a company hopes to achieve may be much more varied and complex than can be contained in a single sentence. This will be especially true for those managers who are sophisticated enough to perceive that a company operates in more external 'systems' than the market. The firm is part not only of a market but also of an industry, the community, the economy, and other systems. In each case, there are unique relationships to observe (e.g., with competitors, municipal leaders, Congress, and so on). A more complete discussion of this point is contained in a previous HBR article.[3]

Becoming—If you ask young men what they want to accomplish by the time they are 40, the answers you get fall into two distinct categories. There are those—the great majority—who will respond in terms of what they want to *have*. This is especially true of graduate students of business administration. There are some men, however, who will answer in terms of the kind of men they hope to *be*. These are the only ones who have a clear idea of where they are going.

The same is true of companies. For far too many companies, what little thinking goes on about the future is done primarily in money terms. There is nothing wrong with financial planning; most companies should do more of it.

But there is a basic fallacy in confusing a financial plan with thinking about the kind of company you want yours to become. It is like saying, 'When I'm 40, I'm going to be *rich.*' It leaves too many basic questions unanswered. Rich in what way? Rich doing what?

The other major fallacy in stating what you want to become is to say it only in terms of a product. The number of companies who have got themselves into trouble by falling in love with a particular product is distressingly great. Perhaps the saddest examples are those giants of American industry who defined their future in terms of continuing to be the major suppliers of steam locomotives to the nation's railroads. In fact, these companies were so wedded to this concept of their future that they formed a cartel in order to keep General Motors out of the steam locomotive business. When the diesel locomotive proved its superiority to steam, these companies all but disappeared.

The lesson of these experiences is that a key element of setting goals is the ability to see them in terms of more than a single dimension. Both money and product policy are part of a statement of objectives; but it is essential that these be viewed as the concrete expressions of a more abstract set of goals—the satisfaction of the needs of significant groups which cooperate to ensure the company's continued existence.

Who are these groups? There are many—customers, managers, employees, stockholders, to mention just the major ones. The key to corporate success is the company's ability to identify the important needs of each of these groups, to establish some balance among them, and to work out a set of operating policies which permits their satisfaction. This set of policies, as a pattern, identifies what the company is trying to be.

The growth fad

Many managers have a view of their company's future which is strikingly analogous to the child's view of himself. When asked what they want their companies to become over the next few years, they reply, 'Bigger'.

There are a great many rationalizations for this preoccupation with growth. Probably the one most frequently voiced is that which says, 'You have to grow or die.' What must be appreciated, however, is that 'bigger' for a company has enormous implications for management. It involves a different way of life, and one which many managers may not be suited for—either in terms of temperament or skills.

Moreover, whether for a large company or a small one, 'bigger', by itself, may not make economic sense. Companies which are highly profitable at their present size may grow into bankruptcy very easily; witness the case of Grayson-Robinson Stores, Inc., a chain of retail stores. Starting out as a small but profitable chain, it grew rapidly into receivership. Conversely, a company

122

which is not now profitable may more successfully seek its survival in cost reduction than in sales growth. Chrysler is a striking example of this approach.

There is, in the United States, a business philosophy which reflects the frontier heritage of the country. It is one which places a high value on growth, in physical terms. The manager whose corporate sales are not increasing, the number of whose subordinates is not growing, whose plants are not expanding, feels that he is not successful. But there is a dangerous trap in this kind of thinking. More of the same is not necessarily progress. In addition, few managers are capable of running units several times larger than the ones they now head.

The great danger of wholehearted consumer acceptance or an astute programme of corporate acquisition is that it frequently propels managers into situations that are beyond their present competence. Such cases—and they are legion—emphasize that in stating corporate objectives, bigger is not always better. A dramatic example is that of the Ampex Corporation. From 1950 to 1960, Ampex's annual sales went from less than $1 000 000 to more than $73 000 000. Its earnings went from $115 000 to nearly $4 000 000. The following year, the company reported a decline in sales to $70 000 000, and a net loss of $3 900 000. The *Wall Street Journal* reported: 'As one source close to the company put it, Ampex's former management "was intelligent and well-educated, but simply lacked the experience necessary to control" the company's rapid development.'[5]

Role of policy

A policy says something about *how* goals will be attained. It is what statisticians would call a 'decision rule', and what systems engineers would call a 'standing plan'. It tells people what they should and should not do in order to contribute to achievement of corporate goals.

A policy should be more than just a platitude. It should be a helpful guide to making strategy explicit, and providing direction to subordinates. Consequently, the more definite it is, the more helpful it can be. 'We will provide our stockholders with a fair return,' is a policy no one could possibly disagree with—or be helped by. What *is* a fair return? This is the type of question that must be answered before the company's intentions become clear.

The job of management is not merely the preparation of valid policies for a standard set of activities; it is the much more challenging one of first deciding what activities are so strategically significant that explicit decision-rules in that area are mandatory. No standard set of policies can be considered major for all companies. Each company is a unique situation. It must decide for itself which aspects of corporate life are most relevant to its own aspirations and work out policy statements for them. For example, advertising may be insignificant to a company which provides research services to the Defense Department, but critical to a firm trying to mass-merchandise luxury goods.

It is difficult to generalize about which policies are major, even within a particular industry, because a number of extraordinarily successful companies appear to violate all the rules. To illustrate:

1 In the candy industry, it would seem safe to generalize that advertising should be a major policy area. However, the Hershey Company, which is so successful that its name is practically the generic term for the product, has persistently followed a policy of no advertising.

2 Similarly, in the field of high-fidelity components, one would expect that dealer relations would be a critical policy area. But Acoustics Research, Inc., has built an enviable record of sales growth and of profitability by relying entirely on consumer pull.

Need to be explicit

The first thing to be said about corporate strategy is that having one is a step forward. Any strategy, once made explicit, can quickly be evaluated and improved. But if no attempt is ever made to commit it to paper, there is always the danger that the strategy is either incomplete or misunderstood.

Many successful companies are not aware of the strategy that underlies their success. It is quite possible for a company to achieve initial success without real awareness of its causes. However, it is much more difficult to successfully *branch out into new ventures* without a precise appreciation of their strategic significance. This is why many established companies fail miserably when they attempt a program of corporate acquisition, product diversification, or market expansion. One illustration of this is cited by Myles L. Mace and George G. Montgomery in their recent study of corporate acquisitions:

A basic resin company . . . bought a plastic boat manufacturer because this seemed to present a controlled market for a portion of the resin it produced. It soon found that the boat business was considerably different from the manufacture and sale of basic chemicals. After a short but unpleasant experience in manufacturing and trying to market what was essentially a consumer's item, the management concluded that its experience and abilities lay essentially in industrial rather than consumer-type products.[6]

Another reason for making strategy explicit is the assistance it provides for delegation and for coordination. To an ever-increasing extent, management is a team activity, whereby groups of executives contribute to corporate success. Making strategy explicit makes it far easier for each executive to appreciate what the overall goals are, and what his own contribution to them must be.

Making an evaluation

Is your strategy right for you? There are six criteria on which to base an answer. These are:

1 Internal consistency.
2 Consistency with the environment.
3 Appropriateness in the light of available resources.
4 Satisfactory degree of risk.
5 Appropriate time horizon.
6 Workability.

If all of these criteria are met, you have a strategy that is right for you. This is as much as can be asked. There is no such thing as a good strategy in any absolute, objective sense. In the remainder of this article I shall discuss the criteria in some detail.

Is the strategy internally consistent?

Internal consistency refers to the cumulative impact of individual policies on corporate goals. In a well-worked-out strategy, each policy fits into an integrated pattern. It should be judged not only in terms of itself, but also in terms of how it relates to other policies which the company has established and to the goals it is pursuing.

In a dynamic company consistency can never be taken for granted. For example: many family owned organizations pursue a pair of policies which soon become inconsistent: rapid expansion and retention of exclusive family control of the firm. If they are successful in expanding, the need for additional financing soon raises major problems concerning the extent to which exclusive family control can be maintained.

While this pair of policies is especially prevalent among smaller firms, it is by no means limited to them. The Ford Motor Company after the Second World War and the *New York Times* today are examples of quite large, family-controlled organizations that have had to reconcile the two conflicting aims.

The criterion of internal consistency is an especially important one for evaluating strategies because it identifies those areas where strategic choices will eventually have to be made. An inconsistent strategy does *not* necessarily mean that the company is currently in difficulty. But it does mean that unless management keeps its eye on a particular area of operation, it may well find itself forced to make a choice without enough time either to search for or to prepare attractive alternatives.

Is the strategy consistent with the environment?

A firm which has a certain product policy, price policy, or advertising policy is saying that it has chosen to relate itself to its customers—actual and potential—in a certain way. Similarly, its policies with respect to government contracts, collective bargaining, foreign investment, and so forth, are expressions of relationship with other groups and forces. Hence, an important test of strategy is whether the chosen policies are consistent with the environment—whether they really make sense with respect to what is going on outside.

Consistency with the environment has both a static and a dynamic aspect. In a static sense, it implies judging the efficacy of policies with respect to the environment as it exists *now*. In a dynamic sense, it means judging the efficacy of policies with respect to the environment *as it appears to be changing*. One purpose of a viable strategy is to ensure the long-run success of an organization. Since the environment of a company is constantly changing, ensuring success over the long run means that management must constantly be assessing the degree to which policies previously established are consistent with the environment as it exists now; and whether current policies take into account the environment as it will be in the future. In one sense, therefore, establishing a strategy is like aiming at a moving target: you have to be concerned not only with present position but also with the speed and direction of movement.

Failure to have a strategy consistent with the environment can be costly to the organization. Ford's sad experience with the Edsel is by now a textbook example of such failure. Certainly, had Ford pushed the Falcon at the time when it was pushing the Edsel, and with the same resources, it would have a far stronger position in the world automobile market today.

Illustrations of strategies that have not been consistent with the environment are easy to find by using hindsight. *But the reason that such examples are plentiful is not that foresight is difficult to apply.* It is because even today few companies are seriously engaged in analyzing environmental trends and using this intelligence as a basis for managing their own futures.

Is the strategy appropriate in view of the available resources?

Resources are those things that a company *is* or *has* and that help it to achieve its corporate objectives. Included are money, competence, and facilities; but these by no means complete the list. In companies selling consumer goods, for example, the major resource may be the name of the product. In any case, there are two basic issues which management must decide in relating strategy and resources. These are:

(a) What are our critical resources?
(b) Is the proposed strategy appropriate for available resources?

Let us look now at what is meant by a 'critical resource', and at how the criterion of resource utilization can be used as a basis for evaluating strategy.

Critical resources—The essential strategic attribute of resources is that they represent action potential. Taken together, a company's resources represent its capacity to respond to threats and opportunities that may be perceived in the environment. In other words, resources are the bundle of chips that the company has to play with in the serious game of business.

From an action-potential point of view, a resource may be critical in two senses: first, as the factor limiting the achievement of corporate goals; and, second, as that which the company will exploit as the basis for its strategy. Thus, critical resources are both what the company has most of and what it has least of.

The three resources most frequently identified as critical are money, competence, and physical facilities. Let us look at the strategic significance of each.

Money. Money is a particularly valuable resource because it provides the greatest flexibility of response to events as they arise. It may be considered the 'safest' resource, in that safety may be equated with the freedom to choose from among the widest variety of future alternatives. Companies that wish to reduce their short-run risk will therefore attempt to accumulate the greatest reservoir of funds they can.

However, it is important to remember that while the accumulation of funds may offer shortrun security, it may place the company at a serious competitive disadvantage with respect to other companies which are following a higher-risk course.

The classical illustration of this kind of outcome is the strategy pursued by Montgomery Ward under the late Sewell Avery. As reported in *Fortune*:

> While Sears confidently bet on a new and expanding America, Avery developed an *idée fixe* that postwar inflation would end in a crash no less serious than that of 1929. Following this idea, he opened no new stores but rather piled up cash to the ceiling in preparation for an economic debacle that never came. In these years, Ward's balance sheet gave a somewhat misleading picture of its prospects. Net earnings remained respectably high, and were generally higher than those of Sears as a percentage of sales. In 1946, earnings after taxes were $52 million. They rose to $74 million in 1950, and then declined to $35 million in 1954. Meanwhile, however, sales remained static, and in Avery's administration profits and liquidity were maintained at the expense of growth. In 1954, Ward had $327 million in cash and securities, $147 million in receivables, and $216 million in inventory, giving it a total current-asset position of $690 million and net worth of $639 million. It was liquid, all right, but it was also the shell of a once great company.[7]

127

Competence. Organizations survive because they are good at doing those things which are necessary to keep them alive. However, the degree of competence of a given organization is by no means uniform across the broad range of skills necessary to stay in business. Some companies are particularly good at marketing, others especially good at engineering, still others depend primarily on their financial sophistication. Philip Selznick refers to that which a company is particularly good at as its 'distinctive competence'.[8]

In determining a strategy, management must carefully appraise its own skill profile in order to determine where its strengths and weaknesses lie. It must then adopt a strategy which makes the greatest use of its strengths. To illustrate:

1 The competence of *The New York Times* lies primarily in giving extensive and insightful coverage of events—the ability to report 'all the news that's fit to print'. It is neither highly profitable (earning only 1.5 per cent of revenues in 1960—far less than, say, the *Wall Street Journal*), nor aggressively sold. Its decision to publish a West Coast and an international edition is a gamble that the strength of its 'distinctive competence' will make it accepted even outside of New York.

2 Because of a declining demand for soft coal, many producers of soft coal are diversifying into other fields. All of them, however, are remaining true to some central skill that they have developed over the years. For instance, Consolidation Coal is moving from simply the mining of soft coal to the mining *and transportation* of soft coal. It is planning with Texas Eastern Transmission Corporation to build a $100 million pipeline that would carry a mixture of powdered coal and water from West Virginia to the East Coast. The North American Coal Company, on the other hand, is moving towards becoming a chemical company. It recently joined with Strategic Materials Corporation to perfect a process for extracting aluminum sulfate from the mine shale that North American produces in its coal-running operations.

James L. Hamilton, president of the Island Creek Coal Co., has summed up the concept of distinctive competence in a colorful way: 'We are a career company dedicated to coal, and we have some very definite ideas about growth and expansion within the industry. We're not thinking of buying a cotton mill and starting to make shirts.'[9]

Physical Facilities. Physical facilities are the resource whose strategic influence is perhaps most frequently misunderstood. Managers seem to be divided among those, usually technical men, who are enamored of physical facilities as the tangible symbol of the corporate entity; and those, usually financial men, who view physical facilities as an undesirable but necessary freezing of part of the company's funds. The latter group is dominant. In many companies, return on investment has emerged as virtually the sole criterion for deciding whether or not a particular facility should be acquired.

Actually, this is putting the cart before the horse. Physical facilities have significance primarily in relationship to overall corporate strategy. It is, therefore, only in relationship to *other* aspects of corporate strategy that the acquisition or disposition of physical facilities can be determined. The total investment required and the projected return on it have a place in this determination—but only as an indication of the financial implications of a particular strategic decision and not as an exclusive criterion for its own sake.

Any appraisal of a company's physical facilities as a strategic resource must consider the relationship of the company to its environment. Facilities have no intrinsic value for their own sake. Their value to the company is either in their location relative to markets, to sources of labor, or to materials; or in their efficiency relative to existing or impending competitive installations. Thus, the essential considerations in any decision regarding physical facilities are a projection of changes likely to occur in the environment and a prediction about what the company's responses to these are likely to be.

Here are two examples of the necessity for relating an evaluation of facilities to environmental changes:

1 Following the end of the Second World War, all domestic producers of typewriters in the United States invested heavily in plant facilities in this country. They hypothesized a rapid increase of sales throughout the world. This indeed took place, but it was short-lived. The rise of vigorous overseas competitors, especially Olivetti and Olympia, went hand in hand with a booming overseas market. At home, IBM's electric typewriter took more and more of the domestic market. Squeezed between these two pressures, the rest of the US typewriter industry found itself with a great deal of excess capacity following the Korean conflict. Excess capacity is today still a major problem in this field.

2 The steady decline in the number of farms in the United States and the emergence of vigorous overseas competition have forced most domestic full-line manufacturers of farm equipment to sharply curtail total plant area. For example, in less than four years, International Harvester eliminated more than a third of its capacity (as measured in square feet of plant space) for the production of farm machinery.

The close relationship between physical facilities and environmental trends emphasizes one of the most significant attributes of fixed assets—their temporal utility. Accounting practice recognizes this in its treatment of depreciation allowances. But even when the tax laws permit generous write-offs, they should not be used as the sole basis for setting the time period over which the investment must be justified. Environmental considerations may reveal that a different time horizon is more relevant for strategy determination. For example, as Armstrong Cork Company moved away from

129

natural cork to synthetic materials during the early 'fifties, management considered buying facilities for the production of its raw materials—particularly polyvinyl chloride. However, before doing so, it surveyed the chemical industry and concluded that producers were overbuilding. It therefore decided not to invest in facilities for the manufacture of this material. The projections were valid; since 1956 polyvinyl chloride has dropped 50 per cent in price.

A strategic approach to facilities may not only change the time horizon; it may also change the whole basis of asset valuation: recently, a substantial portion of Loew's theaters was acquired by the Tisch brothers, owners and operators of a number of successful hotels, including the Americana in Florida.[10] As long as the assets of Loew's theaters were viewed only as places for the projection of films, its theaters, however conservatively valued, seemed to be not much of a bargain. But to a keen appraiser of hotel properties, the theater sites, on rather expensive real estate in downtown city areas, had considerable appeal. Whether this appraisal will be borne out is as yet unknown. At any rate, the stock, which was originally purchased at $14 (with a book value of $22), was selling at $23 in October 1962.

Achieving the right balance—One of the most difficult issues in strategy determination is that of achieving a balance between strategic goals and available resources. This requires a set of necessarily empirical, but critical, estimates of the total resources required to achieve particular ojectives, the rate at which they will have to be committed, and the likelihood that they will be available. The most common errors are either to fail to make these estimates at all or to be excessively optimistic about them.

One example of the unfortunate results of being wrong on these estimates is the case of Royal McBee and the computer market. In January 1956, Royal McBee and the General Precision Equipment Corporation formed a jointly owned company—the Royal Precision Corporation—to enter the market for electronic data-processing equipment. This joint operation was a logical pooling of complementary talents. General Precision had a great deal of experience in developing and producing computers. Its Librascope Division had been selling them to the government for years. However, it lacked a commercial distribution system. Royal McBee, on the other hand, had a great deal of experience in marketing data-processing equipment, but lacked the technical competence to develop and produce a computer.

The joint venture was eminently successful, and within a short time the Royal Precision LPG-30 was the leader in the small-computer field. However, the very success of the computer venture caused Royal McBee some serious problems. The success of the Royal Precision subsidiary demanded that the partners put more and more money into it. This was no problem for General Precision, but it became an ever more serious problem for Royal McBee, which found itself in an increasingly critical cash bind. In March 1962, it sold its interest in Royal Precision to General Precision for $5 million—a price which represented a reported $6.9 million loss on the investment. Concluding that it simply did not have sufficient resources to stay with the new venture, it decided to return to its traditional strengths: typewriters and simple data-processing systems.

Another place where optimistic estimates of resources frequently cause problems is in small businesses. Surveys of the causes of small-business failure reveal that a most frequent cause of bankruptcy is inadequate resources to weather either the early period of establishment or unforeseen downturns in business conditions.

It is apparent from the preceding discussion that a critical strategic decision involves deciding: (a) how much of the company's resources to commit to opportunities currently perceived, and (b) how much to keep uncommitted as a reserve against the appearance of unanticipated demands. This decision is closely related to two other criteria for the evaluation of strategy: risk and timing. I shall now discuss these.

Does the strategy involve an acceptable degree of risk?

Strategy and resources, taken together, determine the degree of risk which the company is undertaking. This is a critical managerial choice. For example, when the old Underwood Corporation decided to enter the computer field, it was making what might have been an extremely astute strategic choice. However, the fact that it ran out of money before it could accomplish anything in that field turned its pursuit of opportunity into the prelude to disaster. This is not to say that the strategy was 'bad'. However, the course of action pursued *was* a high-risk strategy. Had it been successful, the payoff would have been lush. The fact that it was a stupendous failure instead does not mean that it was senseless to take the gamble.

Each company must decide for itself how much risk it wants to live with. In attempting to assess the degree of risk associated with a particular strategy, management may use a variety of techniques. For example, mathematicians have developed an elegant set of techniques for choosing among a variety of strategies where you are willing to estimate the payoffs and the probabilities associated with them. However, our concern here is not with these quantitative aspects, but with the identification of some qualitative factors which may serve as a rough basis for evaluating the degree of risk inherent in a strategy. These factors are:

1 The amount of resources (on which the strategy is based) whose continued existence or value is not assured.

2 The length of the time periods to which resources are committed.

3 The proportion of resources committed to a single venture.

The greater these quantities, the greater the degree of risk that is involved.

Uncertain term of existence—Since a strategy is based on resources, any resource which may disappear before the payoff has been obtained may constitute a danger to the organization. Resources may disappear for various reasons. For example, they may lose their value. This frequently happens to such resources as physical facilities and product features. Again, they may be accidentally destroyed. The most vulnerable resource here is competence. The possible crash of the company plane or the blip on the president's electrocardiogram are what make many organizations essentially speculative ventures. In fact, one of the critical attributes of highly centralized organizations is that the more centralized they are, the more speculative they are. The disappearance of the top executive, or the disruption of communication with him, may wreak havoc at subordinate levels.

However, for many companies, the possibility that critical resources may lose their value stems not so much from internal developments as from shifts in the environment. Take specialized production know-how, for example. It has value only because of demand for the product by customers—and customers may change their minds. This is cause for acute concern among the increasing number of companies whose futures depend so heavily on their ability to participate in defense contracts. A familiar case is the plight of the airframe industry following the Second World War. Some of the companies succeeded in making the shift from aircraft to missiles, but this has only resulted in their being faced with the same problem on a larger scale.

Duration of commitment—Financial analysts often look at the ratio of fixed assets to current assets in order to assess the extent to which resources are committed to long-term programs. This may or may not give a satisfactory answer. How important are the assets? When will they be paid for?

The reasons for the risk increasing as the time for payoff increases is, of course, the inherent uncertainty in any venture. Resources committed over long timespans make the company vulnerable to changes in the environment. Since the difficulty of predicting such changes increases as the timespan increases, long-term projects are basically more risky than are short ones. This is especially true of companies whose environments are unstable. And today, either because of technological, political, or economic shifts, most companies are decidedly in the category of those that face major upheaval in their corporate environments. The company building its future around technological equipment, the company selling primarily to the government, the company investing in underdeveloped nations, the company selling to the Common Market, the company with a plant in the South—all these have this prospect in common.

The harsh dilemma of modern management is that the timespan of decision is increasing at the same time as the corporate environment is becoming increasingly unstable. It is this dilemma which places such a

132

premium on the manager's sensitivity to external trends today. Much has been written about his role as a commander and administrator. But it is no less important that he be a *strategist*.

Size of the stakes—The more of its resources a company commits to a particular strategy, the more pronounced the consequences. If the strategy is successful, the payoff will be great—both to managers and investors. If the strategy fails, the consequences will be dire—both to managers and investors. Thus, a critical decision for the executive group is: What proportion of available resources should be committed to a particular course of action?

This decision may be handled in a variety of ways. For example, faced with a project that requires more of its resources than it is willing to commit, a company either may choose to refrain from undertaking the project or, alternatively, may seek to reduce the total resources required by undertaking a joint venture or by going the route of merger or acquisition in order to broaden the resource base.

The amount of resources management stands ready to commit is of particular significance where there is some likelihood that larger competitors, having greater resources, may choose to enter the company's field. Thus, those companies which entered the small-computer field in the past few years are now faced with the penetration into this area of the data-processing giants. (Both IBM and Remington Rand have recently introduced new small computers.)

I do not mean to imply that the 'best' strategy is the one with the least risk. High pay-offs are frequently associated with high-risk strategies. Moreover, it is a frequent but dangerous assumption to think that inaction, or lack of change, is a low-risk strategy. Failure to exploit its resources to the fullest may well be the riskiest strategy of all that an organization may pursue, as Montgomery Ward and other companies have amply demonstrated.

Does the strategy have an appropriate time horizon?

A significant part of every strategy is the time horizon on which it is based. A viable strategy not only reveals what goals are to be accomplished; it says something about *when* the aims are to be achieved.

Goals, like resources, have time-based utility. A new product developed, a plant put on stream, a degree of market objectives penetration, become significant strategic objectives only if accomplished by a certain time. Delay may deprive them of all strategic significance. A perfect example of this in the military sphere is the Sinai campaign of 1956. The strategic objective of the Israelis was not only to conquer the entire Sinai Peninsula; it also was to do it in seven days. By contrast, the lethargic movement of the British troops made the operation a futile one for both England and France.

133

In choosing an appropriate time horizon, we must pay careful attention to the goals being pursued, and to the particular organization involved. Goals must be established far enough in advance to allow the organization to adjust to them. Organizations, like ships, cannot be 'spun on a dime'. Consequently, the larger the organization, the further its strategic time horizon must extend, since its adjustment time is longer. It is no mere managerial whim that the major contributions to long-range planning have emerged from the larger organizations—especially those large organizations such as Lockheed, North American Aviation, and RCA that traditionally have had to deal with highly unstable environments.

The observation that large corporations plan far ahead while small ones can get away without doing so has frequently been made. However, the significance of planning for the small but growing company has frequently been overlooked. As a company gets bigger, it must not only change the way it operates; it must also steadily push ahead its time horizon—and this is a difficult thing to do. The manager who has built a successful enterprise by his skill at 'putting out fires', or the wheeler—dealer whose firm has grown by a quick succession of financial *coups,* is seldom able to make the transition to the long look ahead.

In many cases, even if the executive were inclined to take a longer range view of events, the formal reward system seriously militates against doing so. In most companies the system of management rewards is closely related to currently reported profits. Where this is the case, executives may understandably be so preoccupied with reporting a profit year by year that they fail to spend as much time as they should in managing the company's long-term future. But if we seriously accept the thesis that the essence of managerial responsibility is the extended time lapse between decision and result, currently reported profits are hardly a reasonable basis on which to compensate top executives. Such a basis simply serves to shorten the time horizon with which the executive is concerned.

The importance of an extended time horizon derives not only from the fact that an organization changes slowly and needs time to work through basic modifications in its strategy; it derives also from the fact that there is a considerable advantage in a certain consistency of strategy maintained over long periods of time. The great danger to companies which do not carefully formulate strategies well in advance is that they are prone to fling themselves toward chaos by drastic changes in policy—and in personnel—at frequent intervals. A parade of presidents is a clear indication of a board that has not really decided what its strategy should be. It is a common harbinger of serious corporate difficulty as well.

The time horizon is also important because of its impact on the selection of policies. The greater the time horizon, the greater the range in choice of tactics. If, for instance, the goals desired must be achieved in a relatively short

134

time, steps like acquisition and merger may become virtually mandatory. An interesting illustration is the decision of National Cash Register to enter the market for electronic data-processing equipment. As reported in *Forbes*: 'Once committed to EDP, NCR wasted no time. To buy talent and experience in 1953 it acquired Computer Research Corp. of Hawthorne, California. . . . For speed's sake, the manufacture of the 304's central units was turned over to GE. . . . NCR's research and development outlays also began curving steeply upwards.'[11]

Is the strategy workable?

At first glance, it would seem that the simplest way to evaluate a corporate strategy is the completely pragmatic one of asking: Does it work? However, further reflection should reveal that if we try to answer that question, we are immediately faced with a quest for criteria. What is the evidence of a strategy 'working'?

Quantitative indices of performance are a good start, but they really measure the influence of two critical factors combined: the strategy selected and the skill with which it is being executed. Faced with the failure to achieve anticipated results, both of these influences must be critically examined. One interesting illustration of this is a recent survey of the Chrysler Corporation after it suffered a period of serious loss: 'In 1959, during one of the frequent reorganizations at Chrysler Corp., aimed at halting the company's slide, a management consultant concluded: "The only thing wrong with Chrysler is people. The corporation needs some good top executives." '[12]

By contrast, when Olivetti acquired the Underwood Corporation, it was able to reduce the cost of producing typewriters by one-third. And it did it without changing any of the top people in the production group. However, it did introduce a drastically revised set of policies.

If a strategy cannot be evaluated by results alone, there are some other indications that may be used to assess its contribution to corporate progress:

1 The degree of consensus which exists among executives concerning corporate goals and policies

2 The extent to which major areas of managerial choice are identified in advance, while there is still time to explore a variety of alternatives.

3 The extent to which resource requirements are discovered well before the last minute, necessitating neither crash programs of cost reduction nor the elimination of planned programs. The widespread popularity of the meat-axe approach to cost reduction is a clear indication of the frequent failure of corporate strategic planning.

Conclusion

The modern organization must deploy expensive and complex resources in the pursuit of transitory opportunities. The time required to develop resources is so extended, and the timescale of opportunities is so brief and fleeting, that a company which has not carefully delineated and appraised its strategy is adrift in white water.

In short, while a set of goals and major policies that meets the criteria listed above does not guarantee success, it can be of considerable value in giving management both the time and the room to manoeuvre.

References

1. For an interesting discussion of this relationship, see CHANDLER, A. D. JR, *Strategy and Structure.* Cambridge, Mass.: Institute of Technology Press, 1962, pp. 1-17.
2. See BURSK, EDWARD C. and FENN, DAN H. *Planning the Future Strategy of Your Business.* New York: McGraw-Hill, 1956, p. 8.
3. TILLES, SEYMOUR, 'The Manager's Job—A Systems Approach.' *Harvard Bsns Rev.,* January/February 1963, p. 73.
4. See LEVITT, THEODORE, 'Marketing Myopia.' *Harvard Bsns Rev.,* July/August 1960, p. 45.
5. 'R for Ampex: Drastic Changes Help Solve Big Headache of Fast Corporate Growth.' *Wall Street Journal,* September 1962, p. 1.
6. *Management Problems of Corporate Acquisitions.* Boston: Division of Research, Harvard Business School, 1962, p. 60.
7. 'Montgomery Ward: Prosperity Is Still Around the Corner.' *Fortune,* November 1960, p. 140.
8. *Leadership in Administration.* Evanston, Illinois: Row, Peterson, 1957, p. 42.
9. *Wall Street Journal,* 11 September 1962, p. 30.
10. See 'The Tisches Eye Their Next Million.' *Fortune,* January 1960, p. 140.
11. 'NCR and the Computer Sweepstakes.' *Forbes,* 15 October 1962, p. 21.
12. 'How Chrysler Hopes to Rebound.' *Business Week,* 6 October 1962, p. 45.

PART THREE: Selected planning tasks and techniques

With the definition of corporate planning advanced in the introduction, it is clear that the subject must embrace an immense variety of special planning tasks and techniques. Indeed, within the definition, it is difficult to argue that there are any specific techniques of corporate planning. Such a view raises obvious difficulties for a writer or editor attempting to offer some view of the field.

In this part, a limited number of areas have been selected for examination because of their importance in the process, their neglect in the literature, their newness, or the need for an appreciation of their contribution. Chapter 8, by M. J. Cetron and D. N. Dick, offers a workable approach to a currently fashionable area without making irresponsible claims about the results to be obtained from technological forecasting. Emphasis is properly laid on the purpose of the forecast and the problem of structuring for forecasting, while individual techniques are swiftly reviewed before raising important organizational and communication problems.

To discuss corporate planning without explicit consideration of the capital appropriation procedure would be to ignore a critical area of resource allocation. In chapter 9, A. W. Lucas and W. G. Livingston move swiftly through the broader work of environmental and strategic appraisal to the formulation of objectives; they subsequently examine the next steps in the development of programmes requiring capital investment or operational programmes, such as cost reduction or technical effort. Financial evaluation of present trends and existing programmes leads into an examination of profitability and a projection of desired results. From this approach develops the need for a specific pattern of major investment directed at achievement of specific goals. The reader can usefully compare this approach to capital investment, where explicit strategic considerations dictate the size and pattern of investment, with much of the writing about capital allocation in which attention is concentrated on the selection of projects purely on financial grounds and with comparison of return on investment with the cost of capital implicitly being assumed as the only useful criterion.

If finance is one of the key resources, manpower is obviously a further essential. Yet the practice of systematic manpower planning is in its infancy and only a minority of leading companies have even begun to tackle the problems involved. C. P. Johnston and H. A. Meredith place some of the efforts in this field in focus, demonstrate the increasing need for this activity in a world of change, emphasize the importance of defining the 'key people' as a first priority for planning, and present a framework within which this activity can be seen in relation to the other planning activities of the firm.

The last chapter in this part (chapter 11) is of a different nature. In it, David Novick examines the developing area of planning, programming, budgeting. PPB systems tend to be associated primarily with governmental planning, and have been somewhat ignored by business executives. This is a mistake. The importance of PPB as a system does not lie in any superiority in dealing with trade-offs between intangibles, such as education or defence, but in the approach which it allows to the structuring and grouping of activities in different organizations directed at the same end, and the development of cost and other information in such a way that reasoned choices can be made between major activities. An alternative view is to argue that organizations are primarily structured to conduct specific tasks efficiently. The efficient conduct of operations requires the development of relevant, task-directed planning and control systems such as budgeting. But the information system so created may have little relevance to the needs of those charged with achieving overall effectiveness, frequently a responsibility held at some central unit such as a major ministry or a top management group. At this level of decision-making, a different concept of relevant information, and its presentation geared to the needs of the centre, becomes critical. PPB offers an approach to such needs.

It should be noted that several areas properly associated with corporate planning have been omitted in this part. These would include questions such as risk and sensitivity analysis, market planning, mergers and acquisitions, new product planning, and organizational planning. The omission is deliberate in the sense of being a choice within the constraints of a reasonable length of book. There are many good articles on these subjects, but the areas chosen for the present columns have been selected as being of especial importance in developing an effective system of planning for the whole.

(Editor)

8. Technological forecasting: Practical problems and pitfalls

Marvin J. Cetron and Donald N. Dick

When a corporation decides to utilize a technological forecast as an input to planning decisions, the administrators are faced with some very fundamental questions. *What do we ask for? How is it accomplished? Who should be assigned the task? How can we insure a useful product?* Or as one questioning manager put it, 'How much time will it take from productive work?'

A primary consideration that affects all of these questions is the forecast content. The prescription for the contents can determine its overall utility. During 1968, the US Navy prepared and published its first technological forecast. Other military services and several corporations had prepared forecasts prior to this, and the Navy had profited from these efforts. The Navy's product covered three different types of forecasts, comprising over 600 individual forecasts prepared by 23 separate R and D activities. The format used by the Navy required a complete assessment of each field of technology as well as a forecast of the state-of-the-art. In retrospect, this work did present some experiences that can contribute to the learning process of management and the technical communities, and can be used as a vehicle for discussion of the practical problems and pitfalls that can develop in the preparation of technological forecasts.

The forecast—something for everyone?

To insure that a technology forecast is useful to technical, operational, and management personnel, the Navy required that each forecast be *'the prediction, with a stated level of confidence, of the anticipated occurrence of*

• Reproduced with permission from *European Business*, Vol. 21, April 1969, pp. 13-24.

a technological achievement, within a given time frame with a specified level of support'. Supporting information was required for all forecasts. Each forecast comprised *five* categories. The categories covered all aspects of the technology under examination from the history of its application to the implications of the forecast to the areas of application. The following paragraphs discuss the five major categories and their desired contents from corporate and military viewpoints.

Background

This section should identify the *organizational goals* and other objectives to which the fields of technology being forecast can contribute. It should discuss the present fields of application of the technology in areas of interest to the organization. A description of the significant factors influencing past developments, and those factors which would tend to emphasize or deemphasize further developments should be included.

Present status

Here, the field of technology's *current state-of-the-art* should be quantitatively described. The inherent advantages or disadvantages (safety, stability, etc.) must be listed, and a description of existing or potentially troublesome technological barriers or gaps should be included. Also, this section should describe the effort made by competitors to utilize the technology and how these efforts have affected their share of market. One example of technology utilization with a marketable difference is the varied approaches to the construction of television sets. The hand-wired and printed circuit technologies are each advertised as having greater advantages than the other.

The military planner must consider the technological advantages, disadvantages, and susceptibility to counteractions by potential aggressors. This involves quantitative statements of current status of a nation compared with its potential adversaries, and identification of gaps where technological advances over present barriers would present clear advantages.

Forecasts

The forecast consists of a *projection of the state-of-the-art* as a function of time and cost with an indicated level of confidence. Only relevant and accurately identified pacing technological parameters should be projected. These parameters could be strength, weight, specific impulse, shaft horsepower, per unit volume, or any other parameter that typifies the advance of the technology areas. The discussion of the pacing parameter should be quantitative and directed to the effects of changes in complexity, cost, performance, and any other factors that may alleviate or cause limitations. Charts and graphs should be used to clarify projections and enhance communication. Adequate supporting data is an essential requirement for preparation of a valid forecast.

Product implications

This section should describe *the effect on the corporation* of the technological advances projected in the forecast. The corporate or product goals discussed in the 'Background' section should be quantitatively related to the forecast. Factors affecting manpower requirements, training, effectiveness, or operating efficiency should be described. Graphic techniques should be used where applicable. The implications of new products, market share, profits, economics of scale should be discussed quantitatively.

In military forecasts, this section would discuss the implications to operating forces.

References and associated activities

The publications from which authoritative direction has been elicited should be cited. List the technical documents in the field which add credibility (hence utility) to the forecast. The corporate divisions and competitors who have contributed or have interest in this technological area are to be included. Also, government activities, universities, consultants and their point of contact should be listed. The Navy forecast requires its contributors to identify all laboratory reports. The reference section also includes other applicable references with the names of the contributory activities.

The factual content of the forecasts is quite extensive. For each technological field, a history of its application, projections of the state-of-the-art, relative corporate goals, marketing information, possible new applications, and present shortcomings are essential parts of the package. *It is this breadth of the technological assessment that allows the forecasts to be beneficial to a diverse audience.* The manager, technical expert, systems analyst, and marketing expert each use the forecast as an aid in planning. In contrast, if the content of the forecast were just a state-of-the-art projection of a technological area without background, present status, and operational implications, its usefulness would probably be limited to the technical community.

In recognizing a technological forecast designed for wide utilization, we gain an appreciation of the nature and extent of the effort involved. The actual mechanics of conducting such a task must be directed by the talents and training of the specific individuals involved. No attempt to prescribe an all encompassing step by step procedure to avoid pitfalls will (or can) be made, but a discussion of what appear to be the inherent problems to such an undertaking and an indication of some solutions that were found to be applicable in preparing the Navy forecast are presented here.

Structuring—the key to understanding

Perhaps the most important factor to consider in directing or preparing a forecast is the problem of structuring. In technological forecasting, the aspects of structuring permeate all levels of effort. It begins when management states the areas in which forecasts are to be prepared. (Here we assume that the implementation of a technological forecasting program would attempt to assess a broad corporate technological base.) The manner in which the various fields of technology are defined will affect the type of forecasts prepared, their content, and the overall effect of policy and goals of the corporation.

Structuring, as used here, is the art of putting one's mind and communications in order. It is the attempt to describe the mutually exclusive and collectively exhaustive sets that define the breadth and depth of the forecasting effort. Stated another way, *a good technological forecast structure will be a good definition of the technological areas to be forecast. As an example of the nature of structuring,* consider the hierarchy of the various factors that can be used to describe food for human consumption. A conventional arrangement may begin with the categories of fruit, vegetable, meat, etc. These major categories are then broken into their parts, and these parts are further broken into their parts. Fruit could be divided into apples, oranges, bananas, etc. Apples, in turn, can be structured into different varieties. The structure, to have high utility, must be as complete as possible. In general, the first few items fall into place quite easily, then as completeness is approached the task is much more demanding as the inevitable rearrangements occur and the search for all encompassing terminology is conducted.

When attempting to define a structure to accommodate an area to be forecast, it is convenient *to view the corporate product* (or groups of products) *as a system or systems.* This system view simply means the product is viewed as being composed of separate items that are fully integrated in their contribution to the product. The task is to take each product, separate it (mentally, of course) into its components, look for commonality across product components, and request a forecast for each component. As an example, an automobile can be viewed as being composed of a transmission, engine, body, and so on. Any structuring problem in the example appears to be one of fineness of division, which might be considered trivial in such a well-defined product. This would be true if the problem in hand were so well constrained.

Here, the main object is to separate a forecast. This implies that concern is directed towards the future. The dependence upon presentday configurations of products becomes uncertain and complexity is added to the forecasting task as we move our forecasting further into the future.

The Navy forecast covered operating capabilities 20 years ahead. During such a lengthy period, supporting technologies can change drastically.

The problem of future uncertainty is not insurmountable, but it does complicate forecasting. It will require the corporate product to be viewed as a system in a broader sense than just its physical components. It should be visualized in terms of the functions necessary to accomplish the product objectives while the product is in operation in its environment. The fundamental premise of the functional approach is: 'components may come and go, but basic functions remain and need to be satisfied.' This look at *system functions* in an operational environment is sometimes referred to as the *systems approach*. In prior times, it was probably regarded as part of competence. As an example of the difference between the views one can take, let us return to the automobile. The individual who views the auto as an integration of components, such as the engine, steering, brakes, and so on, is indeed thinking 'systems'. There are many variations available within this framework to accomplish the desired product performance. However, the individual who views the auto as one part of a transportation system, composed of propulsion, guidance, and control, and so on, is thinking functionally. *Long-range forecasting requires functional thinking.*

The distinction between components and functions is a relative matter. Words, such as function, component, and system, are multi-level. One man's system is another man's subsystem or one man's function is another's system. Functions, as used here for technological forecasting, are the product requirements, independent of technological approach. (For example, a function could be defined as a market share increase, and attainment need not be tied to any particular product or products. As a military illustration one could define a neutralization function to be achieved without specifying the particular weapons required.) Thinking functionally for the major portion of the forecast areas will not solve all problems. It will, by taking that first big step, help avoid many dead ends and much wheel-spinning.

One should be aware of some effects of this process. Structuring of the type discussed here can set the framework for creative contributions to end products. *It will not guarantee creativity; however, it will provide a field for its development.* A good functional structure will point out gaps or holes and will tend to insure completeness of product coverage. Further, everyone will be looking at the corporate product from a common but individually different view. This in itself may be worth the forecasting effort. Another effect will be a definite need to state explicity and quantitatively the corporate operational objectives. *A valid structure cannot be obtained without a clear understanding of the objectives.* Product functional structuring may also force consideration of the company's future direction. As an example, if a group is required to think functionally about house refrigerators and house air-conditioners, it will not be too long before the consideration of house refrigeration as a corporate product could arise. It is not a small effort to determine whether the company should be going in this direction in the future. Creativity and explicit product (or corporate) goals seem to be the type of activity that any corporation would encourage. The fact is, many establishments do not have a formalized procedure to handle such demands. The result can be overall frustration for both the manager and the technical innovators.

What areas are to be forecast?

A fairly logical argument can be made for structuring a product as if it consisted of a series of functions operating as a total system within a described environment. The extension of this concept to the actual forecast may not be as straightforward. As a matter of fact, strict adherence to a set of functions may artificially constrain the broad view inherent in a forecast. In general, much of this concern can be alleviated when one addresses the question of 'what is technology?'

A general consensus of the scientific, technical, and management communities will agree that solid state electronics, lasers, and hydrodynamics are fields of technology. Also, communications, automatic data-processing, and ship hull design are regarded as fields of technology. We are faced with the chicken/egg problem when considering that solid state electronics can contribute to automatic data-processing, but there is no functional relationship—just one of several techniques. This suggests that the functional area forecasts should be complemented with other forecasts. These are forecasts of technologies that in one way or another contribute across several functions. They are multipurpose technologies and can be described as 'support technologies'. As an example, an automobile functional forecast would be complemented by forecasts in areas such as organic materials and materials fabrication. The support technologies should, as a minimum, cover: (a) areas that can constitute the physical end product, (b) the activities necessary to produce the product, and (c) the *total* environment in which the product operates (human, natural, competitive...).

To summarize the thoughts on the identification and definition of technological areas to be forecast, there are two complementary approaches. One is the *functional structure based upon the corporate product(s)*. These are forecasts of scientific applications to specific corporate problem areas. The other approach is the preparation of *forecasts in technology areas that support product development and use.* These tend to be forecasts of scientific engineering areas such as materials, hydrodynamics, acoustics, and so on. For

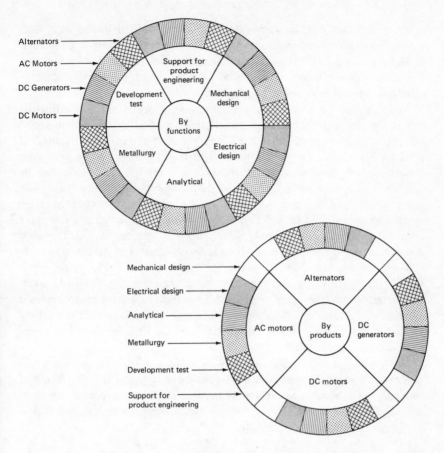

Figure 8.1 Two different R and D structures

a complete assessment of technology impact upon the corporation both are required. When defining the technology areas of interest to a corporation, it is important to consider the ramifications of the various ways it can be done. Two illustrations of structuring are shown in Fig. 8.1. Note that one major category is concerned with support for product engineering. This is composed of the multipurpose technologies that support products developed under either structure. Note also that the structures in the illustrations are the type that might be developed by a production-oriented manager. A research engineer would probably view the corporation as being in the energy conversion business and proceed from there. Both views are necessary to develop a common structure. For conflicting views, as in this example, corporate goals would be the modifier between the views.

With an understanding of what areas are to be forecast, the question of the type of forecast can be addressed. The depth of penetration into each technological area will be variable. Also, no one person or group of people has or should have a peer's license in identifying technology areas of interest to the corporation. These considerations can be accommodated by allowing different types of forecasts to be prepared.

The corporate goals indicate a certain area for operations, and a forecast should be prepared for each functional area identified by the structuring of the product. This insures that the corporate strategy (as it is visualized at present) is covered. The functional area forecasts will tend to be normative (need-oriented) forecasts. They should provide a reasonable indication of the corporate technological capabilities in the product field. Further, to insure completeness and because functional forecasts are product-oriented, additional forecasts should be solicited for technological areas that could support several functions or that could have an effect on the overall corporate operations. These forecasts would tend to be exploratory in nature.

Both the functional area and support forecasts should be at broad level. For simplicity, this type of forecast can be identified as a *broad area forecast*. The definition of the areas to be forecast should be a joint effort between management and technical departments. Any one breakout will not satisfy everyone, but each should be able to interpret the final framework in terms of their area of responsibility.

A second type of forecast should be included to allow excursions in depth into each functional or support area as need dictates, and also as a forum to express new product ideas. These *In-Depth Forecasts* can be considered as avenues for spontaneous efforts of technological opportunities, as well as part of the overall program of forecasting.

Forecasting methods

The forecast presentation will, to a large extent, be governed by the methodology used to project the field of technology. The methods used to forecast the future state-of-the-art are generally categorized as intuitive, growth analogy, trend extrapolation, and trend correlation. Within each of these categories, there are several techniques.

Intuitive forecasting projects the state-of-the-art by expert advice using one or a group of individuals who are experts on a technology area. Figure 8.2 represents the time projection of ship shaft horsepower per unit weight. The curve is based upon a consensus of technical experts in the ship propulsion area. The curve also indicates the step-wise nature of some technological innovation developments.

Growth Analogies represent forecasts where the projection is based upon the familiar S-shaped saturation curve. Figure 8.3 indicates a projection of fuel cell power plants that follow this type trend. Generally, the saturation

146

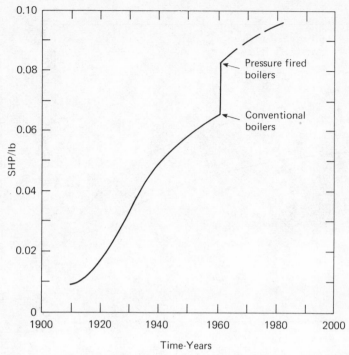

Source: Long-Range Research and Development Planning

Figure 8.2 Typical intuitive forecast curve: Marine steam propulsion systems

level is a theoretical or practical limit which the curve approaches asymptotically. A great number of developments can be represented in this way.

Trend Correlation uses the comparison between two or more trends to confirm one or determine a third. Figure 8.4 is an example of trend correlation where it is assumed that marine technology for gas turbines in the future will follow the known development of aircraft gas turbines. Trend correlation has the advantage that the extent of correlation between trends can be established statistically.

The *Trend Extrapolation* forecasts are projections using curve fitting techniques or simply extensions of present trends. Trend extrapolation assumes that present and past data define the future.

The 'a picture is worth a thousand words' guidance is especially valid in presenting a technology forecast. By intent, the forecast will be reviewed (and interpreted) by people with diverse needs and backgrounds. The forecaster should present the projection of the state-of-the-art and product implications in a graphic display, if at all possible. Further, the forecaster should use the display to convey as much qualification as is deemed necessary and to bring

147

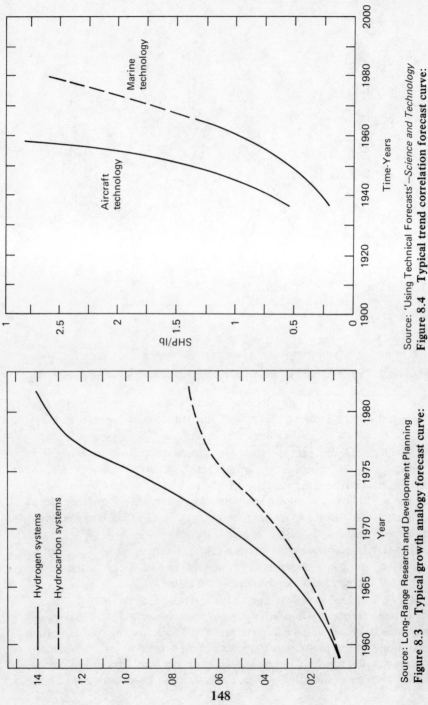

Source: 'Using Technical Forecasts'—*Science and Technology*
**Figure 8.4   Typical trend correlation forecast curve:
Simple cycle gas turbine**

Source: Long-Range Research and Development Planning
**Figure 8.3   Typical growth analogy forecast curve:
Fuel cell power plants**

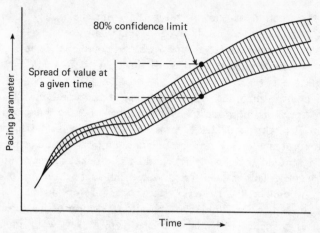

Figure 8.5   Level of confidence shown where time is a critical parameter

attention to significant points. For example, consider the Navy forecast requirement to express the forecast as a *level of confidence*. The requirement can be used by a forecaster to insure his forecast is interpreted as a projection to an area—not a point. Figure 8.5 indicates how confidence limits about a 'best-estimate' (spread of value at a given time) can be displayed to portray the approximate nature of the projection where time is critical. Figure 8.6 is a way to indicate confidence of time (spread of time for a given value) where the value is critical. Display techniques can be used to guard against misinterpretation or to crystallize concepts. For instance, a planner wants to know how fast a train could travel in the year 1975. The forecaster would

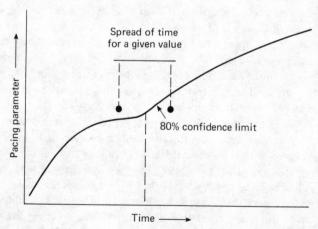

Figure 8.6   Level of confidence shown where value of the pacing parameter is the critical factor

149

present the projection as shown in Fig. 8.5 with the pacing parameter, operating speed, given as a spread (say, 175 to 200 miles per hour). If, on the other hand, the planner wanted to know what he could operate at 200 MPH, the forecast would be given as a spread of time (say, 1974 to 1976) for the operating speed as in Fig. 8.6.

At some point in time, the top management of a corporation will want to *review the technological forecast.* It would be wiser to present to top management the portion of the forecast which will be useful in making decisions at corporate level. For this, a separate summary should be prepared. The summary should cover new ideas and an assessment of what corporate goals can be met. This is a different view from that which the technical community would desire. However, the needs of top management are reasonably covered in the 'Product Implications' section of the forecast. If the section is prepared with the top management review in mind, the executive summary can be composed entirely of that section.

Who should do it?

Having covered what a forecast should contain, the areas to be forecast, and the various types of forecasts available to serve the corporate needs, our attention can turn to who should do it. It is doubtful whether a general request will generate a stampede of volunteers. The reaction of the technical community is likely to be unenthusiastic. The initial response of many technical people in laboratories to a request for technological forecasts could be described as pessimism. However, after preparing the forecasts, many found it to be a useful experience. It appears that a considerable portion of the 'conversion' was due mainly to the recognition that technological forecasting is really a formalization of what is done (or should be done) in the natural process of technical planning.

At present, there appear to be two approaches on the question of *who* should prepare the forecast. One is that the forecast should be prepared by a technical expert in the field. The other is that the forecast should be prepared by a product-oriented technical staff (generalists) or operations research staff. Both approaches were used in preparing the Navy forecast, with most activities using the 'technical expert' approach. Several activities used technical experts to prepare the forecast with assistance from an operations research group to determine operational implications (product implications).

Referring to the five categories of the forecast content discussed previously, it should be observed that the information desired covers a broad range. Corporate goals are discussed in the section on background with the entire 'Product Implications' section devoted to a discussion of the effect of advances in technology on the corporate operations. At the other end of the spectrum, the 'Present Status' and 'Forecast' sections require rather detailed discussions of the technology area. If any one type of person prepares the forecast, it is likely to make severe demands on his depth and breadth of knowledge.

This demand was reflected in the results of the Navy's forecast. Figure 8.7 shows the relationship between the five sections of the forecast and desired quality. Quality was measured as actual content versus requested content. As indicated in the figure, the relative quantitative quality of the 'Background', 'Present Status', and 'References' was more than adequate. The 'Forecast' section drops off from the desired quantitative (not quantity) level of the

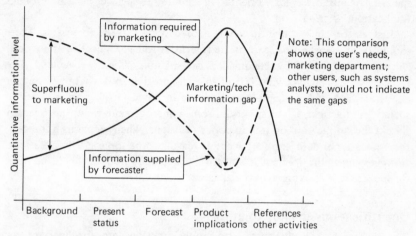

Figure 8.7 Forecast sections: Comparing outputs and inputs

specific user with the 'Product Implications' section low enough to require additional effort beyond the first submission of most forecasts. It is apparent that the individual technical experts encounter difficulty in translating their technical expertise into 'Product Implications' terms.

On the basis of the Navy experience, and on consideration of the extent of information required to prepare a technology assessment type of forecast, it appears that *the preparation may require the joint effort of two distinct types of people.* One, a *technological area expert* to be primarily concerned with the 'Present Status' and 'Forecast' sections. The other, a *systems analyst* (OR, generalist,...) to assist in the 'Background' and 'Product Implications' section. A joint effort of the two can have some beneficial side-effects. A communication problem always seems to exist between people in general or managers and the technical community, as is illustrated in Fig. 8.8. The joint effort can help open a dialogue between the two groups. It is not coincidental that the forecasting format is in itself a forcing function between the two groups to help to insure overall utility.

The task of anyone preparing a forecast can be lightened by a good, clear statement of specific and quantitative corporate or product goals. The Navy's recently published *Exploratory Development Goals* provided the product goals for the Navy Technological Forecast. The goals allow the forecast to be related directly to the needs, resulting in a normative (need-oriented) forecast. Although a normative forecast has many advantages, it does have one distinct disadvantage. If the goals change (or are misstated or misinterpreted), the forecast may have minimal utility or be entirely misleading. A reasonable compromise is to have the actual forecast of the state-of-the-art (the 'Forecast' section) exploratory to the greatest extent possible. All specific quantitative goal orientation should be placed in the 'Product Implications' section.

Just as the goals can influence the forecast, so can the forecaster. There should be an effort on the part of the forecaster to be as objective as possible. 'Axe-grinding', either by commission or omission, should be avoided. The forecast should predict what is probable and possible, not what one wants or does not want. This concern is exemplified in the scientist's responsibility to society in the area of weaponry. From a management view, the scientist should 'be on tap—not on top' in policy decisions. When preparing a forecast, the.forecaster should consider what is feasible, not the social implications. However, once the forecast is objectively prepared, avenues should be open for the scientist to express his social views.

Quantification—the key to unity

The 'Forecast' and 'Product Implications' sections are the heart of the technology assessment type of technological forecast. The first indicates, within the stated probability limits, the growth of the technology. The latter is a projection of the effect of this growth on the corporation. It should not take a great deal of persuasion to convince most people that a forecast increases in utility according to the degree with which it is quantified. A statement such as 'Commercial aircraft will fly higher, faster, and carry more passengers than at present' does not contain information of great value, whereas the statement, 'Commercial aircraft will be capable of speeds of Mach 3 at altitudes of 70 000 feet while carrying up to 400 passengers' contains information that can be used by a diverse audience.

It may appear simple and straightforward to state the need for, and obtain, quantification of forecasts. Experience has indicated otherwise. One reason quantification of the forecast is difficult is because the pacing parameter(s) to quantify is usually not apparent. The forecaster should spend a considerable portion of the time allowed for the task identifying the pacing (key) parameters of the technology. Pacing parameter identification may require a trade-off study between all major technology parameters. In general, it is not a simple task. When the pacing parameters are not identified, a technique

the typical dialogue! . .

Figure 8.8

153

used by some forecasters is to project many parameters. Going the extreme in this direction and overpowering the reader with data will severely limit the forecast's usefulness. Another factor influencing quantitative discussions is the natural reluctance of the technical community to state a precise number in a forecast when there is doubt about overall accuracy of the projection. Any quantitative discussion, or any forecast, is expressed as a prediction with a *level of confidence.* This qualification must be kept in mind by both the user and the forecaster.

Is technological forecasting needed and useful?

Many technological forecasts have been prepared by government and industry. An area of concern is their utilization. One issue is whether the preparation of the forecast will be self-fulfilling. Will the forecast, consciously or unconsciously, be used to guide development? We do not know of any correlation studies that indicate they are or are not. Certainly, there have been forecasts stating certain things could not be done which did not stop others from doing them. On the other hand, if the forecast was prepared by a laureate in the field, the chances for self-fulfillment increase, and if the forecast is prepared by an individual who has equal competence, but little recognition in the technology area, the chances decrease.

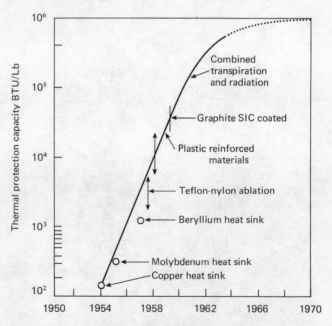

Figure 8.9   'Wrong forecast': Thermal-protective **materials**

Another issue concerns the development of forecasting methodology to insure a reasonable degree of *credibility*. There have been some forecasts which were completely out of phase with actual developments. We can assume forecasts of this type will continue. However, if the forecasting is approached in an objective scientific manner, one can place a reasonable degree of confidence in the forecast. Figures 8.9 and 8.10 are curves taken from forecasts prepared eight years ago. With each curve is the comment of a technical reviewer's 1968 hindsight. The figures indicate a cross-section of forecast usefulness. They represent projections of what was feasible in 1961. Note that feasibility does not mean advancement will happen. A need must be present to insure development.

The preparation of a technological forecast is not a single-shot affair. It should be considered a continuing effort. *Each forecast should be reviewed periodically and updated as required.* A specific time period cannot be stated for all forecasts. It will depend upon the dynamic nature of the area. Any updating procedure should include a reassessment of the areas to be forecast to insure compatibility with current needs.

Finally, there seems to be an issue over whether one should attempt to forecast technology at all. It is a relatively new field where military and industry have expanded in a hasty and haphazard fashion. Consequently,

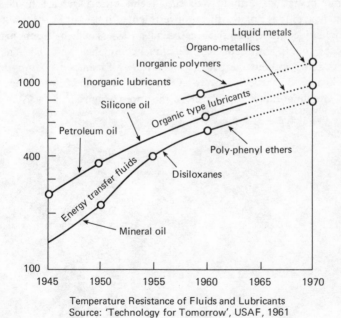

Temperature Resistance of Fluids and Lubricants
Source: 'Technology for Tomorrow', USAF, 1961

Figure 8.10 'Good forecast'

155

technological forecasting bears close scrutiny, if for no other reason than it may not warrant the load on the time of the people required to prepare them. Critical to the entire issue *is the need and utility of forecasting.* As to the need, decisions are made that require an assessment of technology whether a forecast exists or not. As was indicated previously, a forecast is nothing more than a formalized scientific procedure of activities that are normally utilized either in a fragmented manner or informally in making decisions concerning the future state-of-the-art of technology. As to the utility, this is a function of the overall effort. If a valid, objective, quantitative forecast is available it will be used. Quantification and objectivity can be attempted. Validity cannot be guaranteed, but face validity can be approached by iterative updating. Actual validity can never be proven because of self-fulfillment. Technological forecasting is not a panacea, but neither is it useless. It is, like other systematic analyses, an attempt to quantify to the extent possible the state of technology. As such, it can aid in decisions that might be made as well if the forecast did not exist.

The various types of problems discussed here should crystallize several important points about technological forecasting. *First,* there is no cheap and quick way of producing a technological forecast. There are many factors to consider. The forecast effort should be planned and conducted with entire corporate operations in mind. *Second,* a technological forecast should serve a wide audience. It is not worth the investment if it cannot be, or is not, used. The forecast content should be as broad an assessment of technology as is practicable within corporate goals. *Finally,* a comprehensive forecasting effort is not possible without the backing of *all levels* of management. An objective technological forecast can provide a valuable input to the future direction—an area of vital importance to all levels of the corporation.

9. Long-range planning and the capital appropriations program

Arthur W. Lucas and William G. Livingston

Before you can have a capital appropriations program, you must have a sound plan for the future progress of the corporation as a whole. Just how far ahead such a plan should look is something that every company must decide for itself, in light of its own peculiar needs and circumstances. In some kinds of business, you can turn the faucet off today and back on again tomorrow without any trouble at all; in a business of this sort, decisions can be made on a day to day basis, and there is probably no need for long-range planning at all. Most businesses today, however, are so dynamic and complex that decisions must be made well in advance of accomplishment, and in such businesses long-range planning is an absolute necessity. In this paper, we shall be dealing exclusively with businesses of this second type.

An approach to long-range planning

A plan presumes a purpose. In long-range planning, our purpose is not to predict the future precisely but rather to determine the effect that the results forecast will have upon the scope and direction of our company; not to lay down a rigid and inflexible course of navigation but rather to identify clearly those things that we must look at soon and those that we can postpone for a while.

General objectives must be established for the corporation as a whole. Such objectives might include, for example, a statement of the desired size and scope of the business and its desired industry position at the end of the period covered by the plan; a general profitability target; and some indication of the means by which the company wishes to accomplish the growth desired.

• Reprinted by permission of the publisher from *Management Report No. 44, Financial Planning for Greater Profits,* © 1960 by the American Management Association, Inc.

The nature of these objectives will vary, of course, from industry to industry and from company to company.

Once the general objectives have been established, the company's markets and the markets of its industry as a whole must be studied. A thorough analysis of all markets in which the company presently sells, or proposes to sell its products or services, is an absolute *must* for effective long-range planning. Such analysis (including market research to determine the potential size and nature of end-use markets) helps to identify those factors that significantly affect the sales potential of the company and the industry as a whole.

Specific goals and objectives must then be established for each functional part of the corporation. For the marketing function, for example, a certain share of the market may be specified; for the manufacturing function, a certain level of cost reduction and/or efficiency improvement; for the engineering function, a certain amount of facilities expansion within a fixed limit of capital expenditure; and for the research and development function, a certain number of profitable new products and processes and/or modifications of existing products and processes.

Alternative means of achieving these functional objectives and the objectives of the corporation as a whole must then be considered, and their probable effects compared. Once an overall plan has been selected from among these various alternatives, individual plans must be prepared accordingly for each major function or organizational segment of the company. This process of considering alternatives, comparing their probable effects, and developing definitive plans may necessitate the revision of previously established targets and goals. The final result will be the establishment of '*the* plan' for the direction and guidance of all future activities of the corporation.

The plan is then divided into functional, departmental, and/or divisional segments, depending upon the nature of the company's organization structure. Each of these segments consists of specific goals and plans for the function or organizational unit involved.

From time to time, an orderly review and follow-up of results, should be made. This will require coordination of all corporation activities, review of plans, resetting of goals, and measurement of performance.

Developing a long-range plan: A hypothetical case study

In the pages that follow we shall attempt to describe, in what we think is their proper sequence, the various phases of the development of a long-range plan for Smithco, an imaginary company in a mythical industry. Any similarity between Smithco's products, plans, or operations and those of any real company or industry is purely coincidental. Our object in this hypothetical case study is to demonstrate the general method of planning, not to suggest the planning procedure of any given company or industry.

To begin with, let us briefly describe the company and the industry of which it is a part. As the reader may have surmised, 'Smithco' is an abbreviated form of 'The Smith Company' which is used as a trademark in product advertising. The company manufactures a non-durable consumer product called 'glunk'. There are four different types of glunk produced by the US glunk industry: natural, wabe, tove, and synthetic. Collectively, these four types account for the total glunk consumption in the United States. Smithco produces synthetic glunk, of which there are several varieties, the most important being snerls, gyres, and brillig. It is a medium-size company, with sales in the low seven figures, earnings in the low six figures, and assets in the low seven figures.

Imagine, if you will, that you are a member of Smithco's board of directors, and that the authors are Smithco's president and vice-president in charge of planning. We are going to present to you in summary form our most current estimate of what we think the future holds for Smithco and its industry, and what we hope to do about it. This summary is offered to bring you up to date on our plans and to establish a basis for your understanding of the decisions and capital projects that will be forthcoming.

It is 16 October 1959. We have just reviewed our plans for the next four years, added 1964 to the previous plan, measured our performance for 1959, and made fairly definitive plans for the year 1960. What we are presenting to you now is the Smithco five year plan for the period 1960-64.

Charting general economic and industry trends

We need, first of all, to know what the general trend of business and economic activity in the United States is expected to be in the next five years. Figure 9.1 shows, in terms of dollar volume, what the gross national product, consumers' disposable income, and consumers' non-durable expenditures have been for the past seven years. It also shows the outlook for the end of 1959, which by now 16 October 1959, that is) is reasonably firm. Our economic consultants, upon whom we depend for information regarding trends in general business activity for the country as a whole, have told us what the future holds in the way of economic activity for the next five years. We shall present all projected data in constant (1958) dollars so that the trend lines will demonstrate real growth.

We are interested in consumers' disposable income because this is the measure of our ultimate customers' spending power; we are also interested in trends in consumers' total expenditures for non-durables, since this is the part of the consumer's dollar for which we compete. Business did, of course, drop off in 1958, as demonstrated by the gross national product line, but active

159

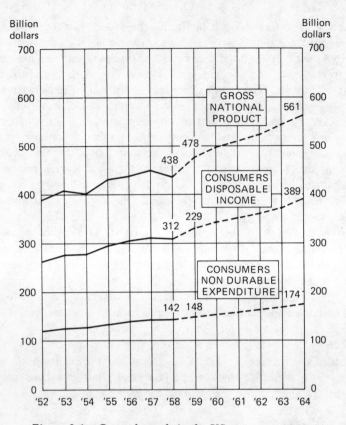

Figure 9.1   General trends in the US economy 1952-64

recovery began in 1959. Consumers disposable income merely stayed level in 1958, and expenditures for non-durables were relatively unaffected by the reduction in business activity. Consumers' income and non-durable expenditures are expected to increase at a rate approximately parallel to the rate of growth of the economy—that is, by a factor of about 18 per cent over the next five years.

This rate of growth is contingent in part upon an increase in population, as well as some increase in overall income levels. As shown in Fig. 9.2, the population is expected to rise to 190 million by 1964—some 8 per cent above the present level of 176 million. As the exhibit also shows, per capita consumption of glunk (in terms of physical units) has been declining over the past five years. This decline is expected to continue because the consumer will be spending an increasingly large part of his dollar on leisure activities, on services, and on durables. Although, as the exhibit indicates, our part of the glunk industry has been experiencing an increasing rate of per capita consumption and is expected to continue in this trend during the next five

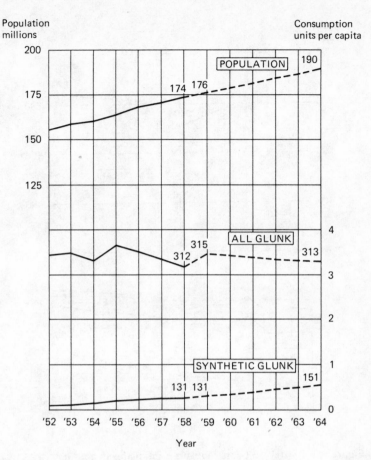

Figure 9.2   US population and per capita Glunk consumption 1952-64

years, the synthetic glunk industry is a very small factor in total glunk consumption. Even if per capita consumption of synthetic glunk increases by more than 60 per cent in the next five years, as we expect it to, it will still account for only some 15 per cent of total glunk consumption, as compared with 9 per cent at present.

This upward trend in synthetic glunk consumption is at the expense of all other types, as indicated in Fig. 9.3, which shows trends in total glunk consumption and its major components. The top line represents total glunk consumption; the area between the top line and the next line represents natural glunk consumption; and so forth, until we reach the bottom-most layer, which represents synthetic glunk consumption. Even though per capita consumption has been declining and is expected to continue to decline, total glunk consumption in physical units is increasing. Natural glunk is expected

161

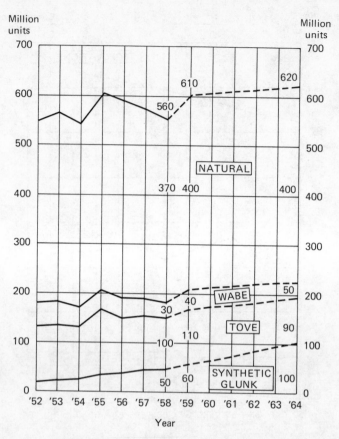

Figure 9.3   Total US Glunk consumption major components 1952-64

to hold its own, wabe and tove to decline, and all the increase to be absorbed by the synthetic glunk industry, of which Smithco is a part. The synthetic glunk industry, in other words, is the only growth factor in this commodity. Impressive as the rate of growth in synthetic glunk consumption may look, however, it still represents only a very small portion of total glunk consumption.

Let us look a little more closely at our synthetic glunk industry. Figure 9.4 illustrates past trends in the sale of various types of synthetic glunk: snerls, gyres, brillig, and 'other'. We have projected these trends on the basis of market research work done by our own people. They tell us where the industry is expected to go, and what consumption will be over the next five years. As you can see, snerls constitute the bulk of synthetic glunk sold in the United States. Sales of snerls are expected to continue to grow but will begin to taper off around 1963. The new growth areas in synthetic glunk sales will

162

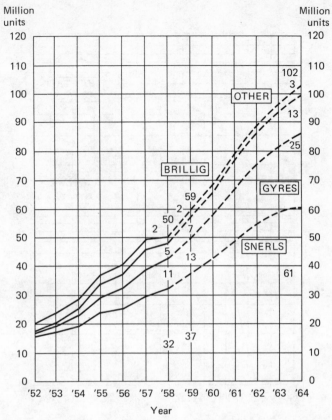

Figure 9.4   Synthetic Glunk sales major components 1952-64

be gyres and, increasingly, brillig. New products yet to be developed will swell the total in the 'other' category by late 1963 and 1964.

Plotting Smithco's course

Now that we have some idea of where the synthetic glunk industry can be expected to go in the next five years, we must plot Smithco's course. As Fig. 9.5 indicates, and as we have seen in previous charts, the glunk industry has been doubling in size every five years. The slopes of the two lines indicate that our company has been growing more rapidly than the industry. We now account for a little more than 20 per cent of synthetic glunk sales in the United States. Achievement of our objectives for the next five years will take us up to almost 30 per cent of industry sales by 1964. We thus plan not only to keep pace with the industry but to go a little faster. The bulk of the exhibits which follow will define the plans and activities necessary to accomplish this objective.

163

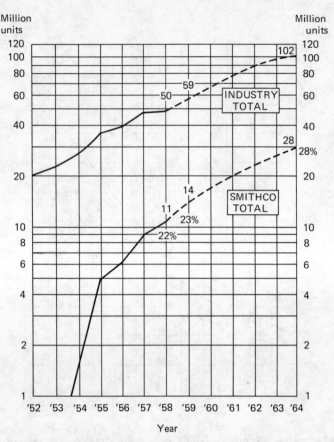

Figure 9.5 Growth in synthetic Glunk sales Smithco versus industry 1952-64

With our goals for share of market established within the framework of forecasted industry growth, we can now determine what Smithco glunk sales will be for the next five years. In developing Fig. 9.6, we quickly realized that a logical extension of everything that we are doing, or expect to do, in the existing snerls and gyres areas will not meet our objectives for increasing our market share by 1963-64. It is apparent, therefore, that we need a new product to keep that line from tapering off and that, to do so, we must have it on the market on a commercial scale by 1962. This will require extensive research and development effort, as well as market development and promotion.

Measuring the market for snerls

Having outlined our goals for Smithco sales within the framework of forecasted industry growth and general business and economic conditions, we

164

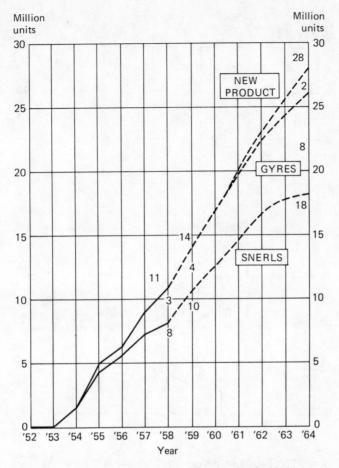

Figure 9.6   Total Smithco Glunk sales 1952-64

shall now present our five year program for the snerls product area and describe the plans that we expect to accomplish during that period for this one product.

In preparing Fig. 9.7, we began with market research forecasts which indicate where sales of snerls are expected to go in the next five years. As the chart shows, we expect sales to increase by about 40 per cent during that time. Against this industry growth pattern, we have plotted our own increase, and, as the lower line on the chart suggests, we expect to increase our market share from 31 per cent at present to about 33 per cent in 1964—an increase of something more than 40 per cent within this five year period.

If we are to achieve this increase, we must take a closer look at end-product markets for snerls. Shown in the two lefthand columns of Fig. 9.8 are the end-product markets and the actual industry sales for the years

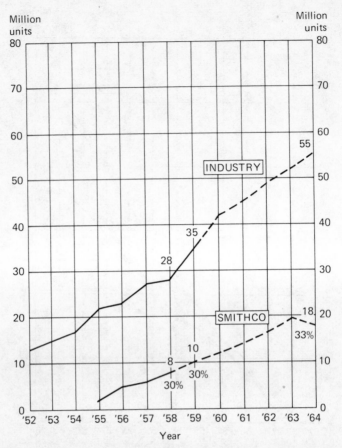

Figure 9.7   Total Snerls sales Smithco versus Industry 1952-64

1958 and 1959, as well as the estimated sales for 1964. The figures in the two righthand columns indicate Smithco's actual sales experience and its expected results for 1964, with the shares they represent of the total industry market. What is immediately apparent is that market A and B represent the largest part of industry sales. Although Smithco is established in these markets, its share is not nearly as great as its present share of markets D, E, and F. Markets A and B are not expected to grow much during the next five years. Market C is expected to increase significantly, but real industry growth will come in markets D and E. Market F will remain static. Therefore, it is in markets C, D, and E that Smithco will attempt to obtain a substantially higher market share to bring its overall market share from 31 per cent up to 33 per cent in five years.

We expect to increase our share of market A, and to lose a little in market B, because of competitive conditions; we hope to hold our own in market F,

End product	Industry			Smithco sales			Smithco share		
market	*'58*	*'59*	*'64*	*'58*	*'59*	*'64*	*'58*	*'59*	*'64*
A	5	5	6	1	1	1½	20%	20%	25%
B	7	7	8	1	1	1	15	15	12
C	2	3	5	½	1	2½	25	33	50
D	1	2	6	½	1	2	50	50	33
E	3	3	4	2	2	2	67	67	50
F	2	2	2	1	1	1	50	50	50
Total	20	22	31	6	7	10	30%	31%	33%

Figure 9.8   Snerls sales by end product market Smithco versus industry

of which we have a better than average share; and in market E we already occupy a preeminent position and can expect to hold on to this much of the market in the coming five year period. The real growth in Smithco sales will come in markets C and D: we anticipate less of a reduction in our share of market D, but a more rapidly growing market C. In short, we plan to hold onto the better than average market share that we now enjoy, and to increase our share of the markets in which it is now somewhat below average. Our greatest effort, however, will be directed toward the end-product markets that we expected to grow rapidly. It is here that we will concentrate the bulk of our promotion and technological efforts for Smithco snerls.

Holding the line on the profit margin

Such a marketing program will have to be supported, of course, by sufficient technical work and research and development to furnish the improvements in existing processes, the cost reductions, and the additions to our product line that will be necessary by the end of 1964. The timetable that we have set for

	Target date		
Project	*Research*	*Develop.*	*Comm'l*
Improved process A	1/61	1/62	6/62
Modified product B	1/62	1/63	1/64
New product C	1/60	1/61	1/62
Lower-cost process D	—	1/63	6/63
New packaging E	—	—	6/60

Figure 9.9   Snerls research and development program

ourselves for the research, development, and commercialization of these new major projects is shown in Fig. 9.9. Heavy emphasis will be placed on new product C, followed by an improved process for product A and modification

167

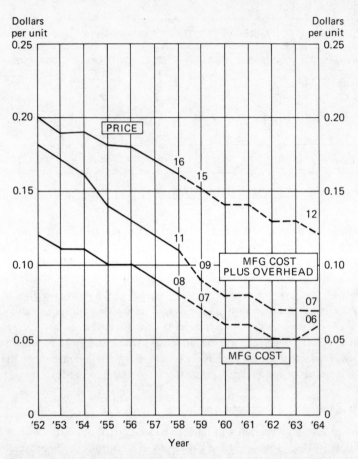

Figure 9.10 Snerls price and cost trends per unit sold 1952-64

of product B. Cost reduction through an improved process for product D, now in the development stage, will be commercial by mid-1963. New packaging E will be available for marketing by the middle of 1960. These are only the *major* technolgoical goals that must be achieved to support our marketing plans.

We do not, however, expect the price of our product to remain at its present level. As shown in the top line of Fig. 9.10, the trend of snerl prices has been down for the last seven years. We expect this trend to continue for the next five years, but at a somewhat diminishing rate, and with the change occurring in several big steps rather than gradually, as it has in the past. We anticipate that an aggressive cost-reduction program will result in lower manufacturing costs which, in combination with improved control of overhead expenses, will result in a lower cost per unit sold in 1964 than now.

168

These efforts, however, will not quite compensate for the reduction in price, so our profit per unit will be slightly less in 1964 than in 1959.

The snerls cost-reduction program is absolutely essential if we are to hold the line on our profit margin. Figure 9.11 shows, in broad terms, in what areas and by what means we expect to accomplish this objective. As you can see, most of our cost-reduction activity is aimed at labor costs, the largest single element of total manufacturing cost; at the same time, however, we expect to improve our materials yields and plant and equipment utilization. By putting the cost-reduction program into effect, fitting it to the estimate of sales (at lower prices anticipated) and investment necessary to support it, we expect to realize the return on investment indicated in Fig. 10.12. We anticipate a decline in return on investment for the next several years because

	Actual 1958	Projected		1959-1964 Reduction
		1959	1964	
By cost type				
Raw materials	1.5d	1.2d	1.0d	0.2d
Labor	4.5	3.5	3.0	0.5
Supplies	0.5	0.5	0.5	—
Utilities	0.5	0.5	0.5	—
Investment costs	1.0	0.8	0.5	0.3
Total	8.0d	6.5d	5.5d	1.0d
How				
Raw materials—	Lower purchase prices			
	Reduce waste			
Labor—	Increased efficiency			
	Minimize additions			
Investment costs—	Minimum cost expansion			
	Increased productivity			

Figure 9.11   Snerls cost-reduction program (d unit)

prices will be reduced faster than they can be compensated for by lower manufacturing cost and lower per-unit overhead. By mid-1962, however, we do expect to have improved the utilization of plant and equipment enough to show a marked increase in capacity, and to have begun to realize the benefits of lower costs. As a result, return on investment at the end of the five years (by 1964) will be better than we realized in 1959. This is fairly stern measure of progress, since 1959 is expected to be our best year since 1953 in terms of return on investment.

Plotting financial results

Supported by research and development and cost-reduction efforts, the snerls marketing program is expected to yield the financial results shown in Fig.

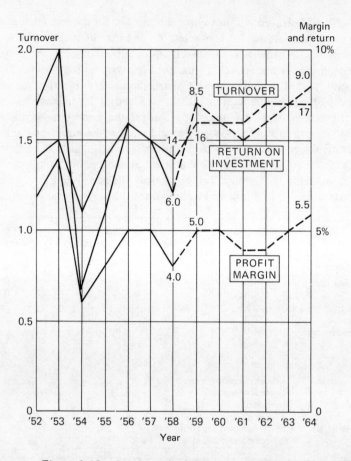

Figure 9.12   Snerls profitability trends 1952-64

9.13. This table is condensed to show the key items of major interest to our directors. We have plotted actual results for 1958, together with our latest forecast for 1959. The 1959 forecast is based upon nine months of actual experience, plus a reasonably good guess for the rest of the year. To provide a basis for comparison, we have included expected results for the first year of the five year plan (1960) and for its last year (1964).

Sales quantities are up in 1959, and we expect them to be up in 1960, and to have increased some 6 million units more by 1964. Sales in 1964 are expected to be some 80 per cent higher than the level achieved this year, but sales revenue will not increase by the same factor because of the anticipated reduction in the price schedule. Sales revenue will be up some 40 per cent and net income up 50 per cent in 1959 from the poor results of 1958. Net income will continue to increase in 1960 and achieve a 60 per cent increase by the end of 1964; this, of course, assumes substantial improvement in manu-

170

	1958	1959	5 yr. plan	
	Actual	Forecast	1960	1964
Sales quantities (units)	8000	10 000	12 000	18 000
Income ($)				
Sales revenue	$1280	$1500	$1740	$2150
Net income	50	75	80	120
Ratios				
Overhead (% sales)	15%	12%	12%	10%
Profit margin	4%	5%	5%	5½%
Capital turnover	1.4	1.6	1.6	1.7
Return on investment	6%	8½%	8%	9%
Unit values (d/unit)				
Average price	16d	15d	14d	12d
Mfg. cost	8d	6½¢	6d	5½¢

Figure 9.13   Snerls 5 year program: Financial results (amounts in thousands)

	1959 Actual	Projected				
		1960	1961	1962	1963	1964
Sales	10	12	14	16	17	18
Production capacity						
Plant X						
Crude	12	12	13	15	15	15
Finishing	10	10	10	11	11	12
Plant Y						
Crude	3	3	3	3	4	5
Finishing	2	5	5	5	5	5
New plant Z						
Crude	–	–	–	–	–	–
Finishing	–	–	–	–	2	3
Total						
Crude	15	15	16	18	19	20
Finishing	12	15	15	16	18	20

Figure 9.14   Snerls expansion program (million units)

facturing costs and overhead expenses. Significant ratios show that overhead expense, as a percentage of sales revenue, will decline for the five year period, and that our profit margin will increase somewhat. The real gain, however, will be made in capital turnover through better utilization of plant capacity, and this will result in improved return on investment. Average prices and manufacturing costs plotted on the previous chart are shown in this exhibit as well.

Planning for expansion

To realize the level of sales predicted for snerls over the next five years, we must provide for increased production capacity. Figure 9.14 shows in summary form where we intend to install more equipment, and the resulting balance between crude production and finishing capacity. By the end of 1959, completion of present projects will have given us about 20 per cent more crude capacity than finishing capacity, so we will be reasonably provided for in the area of crude capacity for the next year or so. Process

	Project Cost	Decision Point
Plant X		
1961—Increase crude plant capacity (2MM Units)	$200M	Jan. 1961
1963—Increase finishing plant capacity (1MM Units)	$200M	Sept. 1963
Plant Y		
1962—Increase crude plant capacity (2MM Units)	$300M	Jun. 1962
New plant Z		
Start finishing plant (3MM Units)	$500M	Mar. 1962

Figure 9.15   Snerls new-facilities timetable

improvements at plant X will add to this capacity, but expansion to 15 million units will require a capital project. We expect also to realize 1 million units of finishing capacity from increased productivity at plant X by 1962, but the expansion to 12 million units planned for 1964 will require another capital project. All new crude capacity beyond the requirements at plant X will be added at plant Y with no additional finishing capacity. New finishing capacity now under construction will be available next year. It is anticipated that this plant will be in balance at a five million unit level by 1964.

172

We must, however, provide for additional finishing capacity, and we propose to do this by installing facilities at plant Z, with the site yet to be determined. The first phase will be completed in 1963; by 1964, completion of the second phase will provide us with an overall balanced capacity of 20 million units. The timetable for these major projects and our preliminary estimates of expected project capital cost and levels are shown chronologically by plant in Fig. 9.15. The earliest decision point before us will be the crude-capacity project at plant X; it will require a board decision by 1961. Extensive work in engineering and evaluation in 1960 will be necessary to define this project more precisely. The next decision point occurs in 1962, when we will have to review the need and basis for increased crude capacity at plant Y, as well as start the finishing-capacity project for plant X. By late 1963, the extension of finishing capacity at plant X will, as we now see it, be submitted for approval. These are the major decision points required for new facilities in our timetable for the next five years.

(At this point, similar summaries of our five year program for gyres and for the new glunk product would have been presented. These have been omitted here, since the comments would be quite similar to those we have already made regarding the snerls program.)

Summarizing the overall plan

In Fig. 9.16, we have summarized the capital requirements of the combined projects in terms of their influence on present resources. In setting up the program for each product, we have compiled an overall timetable for all new facilities during the next five years, indicating by production area the specific projects that will be coming before us for decision and their approximate cost. The totals shown in this summary suggest the areas of concentration. We estimate that $500 000 in capital expenditures will come before us for decision in 1960; $1 250 000 in 1961; $800 000 in 1962; $450 000 in 1963; and $500 000 in 1964.

The overall financial results of Smithco's five year plan in terms of income, cash position, and significant ratios are shown in thumbnail form in Fig. 9.17. Actual results for 1958 and present experience for 1959 are shown under the column marked 'Current'. Projected results for the first, middle, and last year of the five year plan, together with significant five year totals, are shown in the righthand column. Significant factors again are increased growth in sales revenue, an even larger increase in net income, and the need for $4.5 million for the total capital program, with $4.35 million in new financing to support this. Return on assets will increase from 7 per cent to 10 per cent—a good measure of overall improvement. The return on owner equity will increase from 14 per cent to 20 per cent, with debt/equity ratios remaining the same.

	Project cost	Decision point
1960		
Gyres		
Increase capacity—		
plant A	$500M	Jun. 1960
1961		
Snerls		
Increase crude capacity—		
plant X	$200M	Jan. 1961
Gyres		
Modify equipment—plant B	$300M	Jun. 1961
New product		
Initial installation—		
new plant	$750M	Sept. 1961
1962		
Snerls		
Start new finishing plant	$500M	Mar. 1962
Increase crude capacity—		
plant Y	$300M	Jun. 1962
1963		
Snerls		
Increase finishing capacity—		
plant X	$200M	Sept. 1963
New product		
Increase plant capacity	$250M	Mar. 1963
1964		
Gyres		
Install new process—plant C	$500M	Jun. 1964

Figure 9.16   Smithco new-facilities timetable

Developing a capital appropriations program

By now it should be apparent that all of these steps are essential prerequisites to a capital appropriations program. They provide a solid foundation and demonstrate the need for, as well as the desirable timing and scope of, such a program.

Our long-range plan suggests the need for new facilities and provides a basis for developing a capital appropriations program. We cannot, however, simply write up a series of projects and let it go at that. We must first go back

	Current		Projected			
Income	1958	1959	1960	1962	1964	5 Yr. Total
Sales revenue	$3500	$4000	$4500	$6000	$7000	—
Net income	175	220	245	350	420	—
Cash position						
Requirements	$200	$150	$500	$900	$600	$4500
Capital program						
Debt repayment	200	250	300	400	500	2000
Working capital	—	130	200	250	300	1250
Dividends	75	90	100	150	180	750
Total	$475	$620	$1100	$1700	$1580	$8500
Sources						
Income	$175	220	245	350	420	1750
Depreciation	300	400	400	500	600	2500
New financing	—	—	500	850	560	4350
Total	$475	620	1145	1700	—	8600
Cash Balance	$500	$500	$545	$545	$600	—
Ratios						
Return on assets	5%	7%	7½%	8½%	10%	
Return on owner equity	10%	14%	15%	17%	20%	
Debt to equity ratio	1.0	1.0	1.0	1.0	1.0	

Figure 9.17   Smithco financial results (amounts in thousands)

and reexamine our position—the nature of the need—and define more precisely the environment of each project. This will involve a series of steps similar to the following:

1 Timing is continually reassessed.

2 Markets, market potentials, and research and development activity are appraised further.

3 Capacity alternatives within the framework of the newly appraised need are suggested.

4 A comparative evaluation is made of each of these alternatives.

5 Selection of the optimum course of action is followed by detailed engineering and evaluation of specific projects.

6 With these details smoothed out, the project has now been defined and is ready to be submitted for approval.

7 After approval, the project becomes something tangible as construction begins.

8 With completion of the project and start-up of the project facilities, a final closing report is submitted to give a complete, detailed analysis of the results.

Back to Smithco

To illustrate the development of a capital appropriations program, let us refer back to the Smithco five year plan, and specifically to the five year program for snerls. In Fig. 9.7, page 167, you will recall, we plotted the rate of growth anticipated for sales in the snerls industry. We charted the course for Smithco and predicted an increase in our share of the market from 31 per cent to 33 per cent and an increase in our sales from 10 million units in 1959 to 18 million units in 1964.

In Fig. 9.14, we showed how we intended to provide additional capacity to support the anticipated increase in sales volume. Total production capacity was substantially above sales for the early part of the five year plan, but narrowed down to about 10 per cent excess in 1964. This amount of excess should be carefully evaluated to determine what influence it might have on our profits. The deployment of expansion at three different plants involves some coordinated planning of current and future capacity, as well as consideration of the desirability of expansion at one plant versus another and the location of a new plant. All of these matters must be subjected to careful and definitive engineering and evaluation. Our market outlook in the preliminary evaluation suggested that our plans were economical and logical, but the basic need must be defined more thoroughly before we can commit ourselves to spend the money.

Post-appraisal

We have all heard the expression, ' . . . and they all lived happily ever after.' In business, post-appraisal is required to prove out the fairytale ending. The process of post-appraisal should follow completion of the individual projects as well as major segments of the program. Its purpose is to keep the estimators honest and provide better control. Depending upon the size of the project, it may take a year or two of operation to determine how effective the results have been. Sometimes it may be difficult to isolate a specific project, since in many cases it becomes part of a major facility. The project audit should cover all areas contributing to the development and approval of the project: marketing estimates, capital expenditures estimates, selling prices, manufacturing costs, financial results, and timing.

Certain specific areas should be audited for each project, with the content of the audit depending upon the size and type of the project. These would include at least some of the following:

1 *Capital expenditures.* These should, of course, be checked throughout the project.

2 *Timing.* Was the deadline for completion met?

3 *Equipment performance.* Did equipment perform as designed?

176

4 *Operating costs.* Did they exceed expectations?
5 *Sales results.* Did sales materialize as forecasted?
6 *Financial results.* Were predicted results achieved?

This is not to suggest that, if we merely audit each project, the program will take care of itself. An essential element in the planning function is continuing reappraisal of the capital appropriations program and the overall picture into which a specific project fits. Such reappraisal will suggest revisions in plans, and perhaps even in individual projects.

No financial or capital appropriations program is any better than the plan upon which it is based. If long-range planning is taken seriously, and if top management thinking is forward-oriented, plans will be sufficiently hedged for successful results. The footings of a good foundation include:

1 A thorough appraisal of markets.
2 Well-defined goals set high enough that they must be striven for.
3 Sufficient resources and capabilities to accomplish objectives.
4 Thorough evaluation of project results and of the way various plans measure up to objectives.

The functions of long-range planning, forecasting, and evaluating must be performed in most companies. If the organization does not include the coordination influence of a department devoted exclusively to these functions, they are usually performed by the finance department and its top financial staff. The reason is obvious: all financial executives need to anticipate the demands that will be made on them to raise money or to reinvest funds. It is the prime objective of long-range planning to encourage the climate, attitude, and thinking in the top management ranks that will make the financial executive's task of securing money easier.

At the same time, the financial executive provides a major contribution by evaluating profitability and estimating its effect on the company's operating profits. He will, as a result, have a better basis for evaluating his company's financial needs and comparing them with his own estimate of the money supply situation. He may even recommend changes in the timing of specific projects to take advantage of the money market or to obviate financing under disadvantageous terms.

In closing, we would offer two quotations. The first is: 'Plan or panic.' The second is from President Eisenhower: '*Plans* are worthless, but *planning* is everything.'

10. Manpower planning— strategy and implications

C. P. Johnston and H. A. Meridith

Manpower planning has been carried out intuitively for years by many progressive companies as an ongoing but unnamed process. With rare exceptions, a systematic approach has been developed only in the past decade. Because of the rapidity with which change is occurring, the only effective control left to management is the planning process. Companies and products come and go, seemingly at the whim of chance and circumstance. Over half of the largest US companies of 30 years ago are no longer in existence. Two-thirds of the sales volume of Dupont is in products developed within the past 10 years! Sputnik introduced whole new industries in space research and communications which now directly or indirectly employ hundreds of thousands of persons.

While companies may spend substantial amounts of time and money in production, research and development, marketing and facilities planning, very little is yet being done in the crucial area of manpower. Management has apparently assumed that skilled manpower will always be available, or that people will be sufficiently—and infinitely—flexible to adapt immediately to new situations and requirements. This attitude, perhaps at one time valid, is no longer so. Today the methods and tools for anticipating and planning for change are available to companies who do not wish to rely solely on tenuous reflex action to survive and prosper.

This paper is intended primarily as an exposition of the state of the art of manpower planning in its broadest sense.

Manpower planning has two major elements. First, there is the identification of the strengths and weaknesses in the human resources of the

• Reproduced with permission from *The Business Quarterly*, Vol. 33, No. 4, Winter 1968.

organization, both quantitatively and qualitatively, in relation to forecast manpower requirements and changing internal and external conditions. Second, from this analysis the necessary plans and action programs must be formulated to ensure that projected requirements are met.

Two examples might help to illustrate the major aspects of manpower planning.

Study 1

A recent study carried out for a major Canadian service organization, employing a workforce of 4000 and anticipating a growth rate of less than four per cent per annum, indicated that some 5200 new employees would have to be recruited over a five year period. This activity, in turn, would require well over 10 000 internal personnel moves. These two figures were arrived at by projecting attrition* (turnover and retirements), growth in new jobs, and the consequent number of transfers, promotions, and new appointments to be made to meet staff requirements.

Following these projections, an examination of the labor market revealed that due to increased competition from business, government, and universities, the probability of filling the entrance level openings from traditional sources was extremely low. (The company's policy had always been one of recruiting at the lowest level with high school graduates and promotion from within.) The ramifications were obvious: in order to meet projected manpower requirements, the total package of manpower planning policies of the firm had to be completely reevaluated.

The resultant manpower plan involved the introduction of more accurate and comprehensive means for developing and maintaining personnel information, a completely redesigned performance appraisal system to better identify potential and career objectives, a revitalized training and development program, some significant changes in the organization setup, and a radical departure from the previous hiring, promotion, and transfer policies. New emphasis was placed on reducing turnover, particularly among managerial and technical staff, and in increasing productivity and morale through the introduction of more modern management practices.

Following these studies, the role of the corporate planning department was reevaluated. While performing commendably, the human resources aspects of planning had been largely ignored. The manpower input into the corporate plan necessitated major changes in strategy and direction.

A further example illustrates how the lack of preparation to meet new situations with flexibility and realism can be disastrous.

* The term 'attrition' is sometimes used to signify those who will leave the company through the normal course of events, either voluntarily or involuntarily, and are not replaced from outside or whose positions then become redundant. Attrition as it is used here refers to all people who leave the company for reasons other than lay-off.

Study 2

In the process of becoming a major conglomerate, a large consumer (manufacturing) organization began buying up smaller companies in unrelated industries. As part of its policy, it dropped the executives of these acquired organizations, and provided staff from the parent organization. The skills, knowledge, and abilities of the new management were insufficient for the demands placed upon them. Profits in several of the new companies began to drop. At the same time, the staffing policy had precipitated turnover in the lower levels with the consequent need to transfer more people and to increase recruiting from outside. In the process, the radical change in the company's staff and method of operations created concern in the marketplace and an undesirable image for the parent concern and its subsidiaries. The outside market for skilled and experienced personnel became seriously restricted.

The costs of replacement and training which accrued to this company were only part of the total costs paid for the lack of manpower planning. They were small in comparison to the losses of markets, internal disruptions and chaos, and the poor morale and consequent inefficiency of those remaining.

Some practical questions

Who should be included in the manpower plan?

The 'key people'. The definition of this group depends on the objectives and orientation of the organization. In a technologically advanced company, engineers and foremen may be more important than more senior support staff; in a consumer products company, sales and market personnel may comprise the key group.

Manpower planning tends to start with management—down to first level supervision. More elaborate and advanced plans may involve the entire workforce, particularly in organizations such as railroads with strong unions, substantial skill and experience requirements at all levels, and labor redundancy problems.

Some companies use an A B C system of selective inventory control.· Senior management, scientific and key people are placed in the A category, lower management, technicians and staff in the B category and all others in the C category. The kind and extent of information for each of these categories differs, as does the way in which the information is used and evaluated.

What period should the plan cover?

Plans are dependent on objectives and forecasts. These must be continually updated; consequently, the manpower plan must be continually examined in

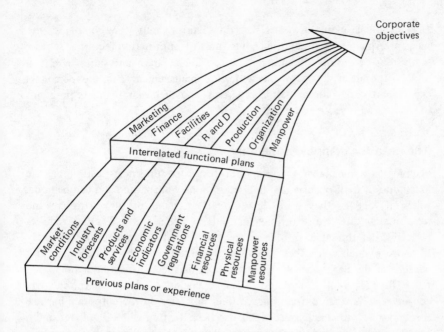

Figure 10.1 Manpower planning and its relation to the total planning process

the light of changing needs and circumstances. Some aspects may not change; for example, the numbers of people who will be forced to leave through retirement. Turnover, for other reasons, however, can fluctuate widely. Technological innovations or economic conditions can radically alter needs.

The purpose of the plan, nevertheless, is to anticipate these needs and meet them before they produce undesirable repercussions. The value of the plan will be determined not only by how accurately it projects, but by how flexible it is in meeting changing manpower requirements. In initiating formal manpower planning, it is probably wisest to aim at three to five years, with the greatest emphasis being put on the initial one year period. The real time determinant will be the level of overall planning existing within the organization.

Who should devise and implement the plan?

Manpower planning (as it is here understood) should be coordinated and implemented by a corporate staff responding directly to top management. There is as yet no established pattern as to what organizational unit the manpower planner should belong. In some instances, he may be part of personnel; in others, corporate planning, and, in still others, the function has been combined with organizational planning.

The actual planning must be done throughout the company; the manpower planner will determine the kinds of information required, act as a catalyst in obtaining this information, collate, analyze and summarize it in total corporation terms, work with line management and the personnel department in developing action programs, and then monitor these programs to ensure that objectives are met.

The need for manpower planning

Planning is a means of preparing for future contingencies, estimating the likelihood of their occurrence, and determining what should and can be done, when, if, and as they arise. It is, in effect, a means of controlling and manipulating the future through minimizing uncertainty. Planning requires foresight, determination and an awareness of what is happening and is likely to happen which will affect the life of the enterprise. This is a difficult task because of the nature of our changing circumstances—a reading is no sooner taken than another is required. These changing conditions have, and will continue to have, an extraordinary effect not only on the corporate balance sheet, but in our daily lives. Much has been written on this subject and a general understanding of the major dimensions of change is probably a prerequisite to carrying out manpower planning. These dimensions may be categorized as follows:

Communications and knowledge explosion

The ego boundaries of an individual 50 years ago could be defined as the distance a man could cover between sunrise and sunset. Anything beyond that distance was psychologically in another universe and affected very little the day to day life of the average individual. Today, we can watch a football game in France as it is actually being played or be eye witnesses of presidential assassinations.

Information is increasing at an enormous pace and conventional knowledge and 'facts' are every day being discarded. Scientific knowledge doubles every 10 years and the human brain is constantly bewildered. The threat of obsolescence is with each of us. Without proper planning and direction, we will either become bogged down in a jungle of trivia, or swamped in a sea of inconsistencies.

Changes in age and educational distributions

Concurrently, we are rapidly becoming a more youthful society. By 1970, the median age in the United States will be 25 and the value of experience as the prime teacher will be even more questioned and less respected than today.

182

Companies with a high rate of growth will suffer from acute managerial malnutrition, particularly in the 35-45 year age group. Bimodal age curves will be commonplace and competition for middle management personnel will increase.

Thirty-five years ago high school leaving was a respected level of educational achievement. Very few—probably less than five per cent of the population—had acquired a university education. Today, a Master's degree is a standard requirement for many jobs. In 1968 in the United States, 60 per cent of those eligible will enter college; at least 30 per cent will graduate. The arithmetical effect of so many being removed from the historic labor supply is easily calculated. The consequent demands placed upon industry and government to accommodate those graduating, and to avoid managerial obsolescence of those already employed, is overwhelming.

Socio-psychological changes

Youth today is better educated than at any time in the history of mankind, not only in terms of numbers, but in terms of critical thinking capacity. The old regimented stereotyped kind of bureaucratic thinking prevalent in so many companies is no longer tolerable to an aggressive, accomplishment-oriented graduate.

The days of the paternalistic manager are gone; yet many of the policies, rules and philosophies lingering on in many companies emanate from these bygone eras. Social, religious, and cultural mores are being rent apart, and the total fabric of society is being threatened. Security as a motivating force for the educated person has disappeared—basic needs are guaranteed, and the concepts of loyalty to a firm no longer have the same meanings.

Performance-oriented companies do not guarantee tenure of employment. Intercompany mobility has become a way of life (20 per cent of US citizens change their residences annually). The modern manager or professional owes his fundamental loyalty to himself, derives his security from his educational investment and his strength from his identity in that great new fraternity—management. He is upward striving and if he is good (and knows he is good) and cannot reach his objectives in one company, he will in another. Fear as either a motivator or as an inhibitor no longer really exists for the competent individual.

Technological organizational changes

The lead-time for war was, not too far back, months or even years: today, it is calculated in minutes and even seconds. The computer and instant data have revolutionized the workings of entire companies and have placed greater and greater stress on its decision-makers. The methods available for making

183

decisions and picking alternatives are equally elaborate. In order to operate, whole new departments and professions have come into being to supply, analyze and evaluate this idea. Organization structures have had to adapt to their presence and their purpose.

Mergers and acquisitions, occurring at an unprecedented rate, are placing managers in entirely new operating environments, making new demands on their talents and abilities, and placing new stresses and pressures on their professional shoulders. Shareholders are conscious of performance and products are often obsolete before they hit the market.

Change is virulent and its demands will substantially alter the 'mix' of the characteristics of personnel available to the organization, both internally and externally. The personnel man can no longer function as historian, pacifier, or wage clerk. Today, he must become an analyst and planner as well. Manpower will be his source, material planning his tool, and return on investment his reference point.

Financial considerations

Little is known of the costs involved in the manpower resourcing or the direct and indirect tangible benefits to be earned or saved through effective selection, utilization, and development of human resources. Yet all agree that such resources are a company's most valuable asset. In some service industries, as much as 70-75 per cent of total operating costs are directly related to the selection, training, and remuneration of personnel.

Each time a company issues a paycheck to an employee, it is implicitly saying: 'We have made a decision, we are going to retain your services as this is the best use of our resources in keeping with our management philosophy'. When considered in this light, the most effective (profitable) use of personnel is a resource allocation problem. Continuity of employment is merely the result of allocating resources in a certain manner.

An executive earning an average salary of $15 000 over a lifetime constitutes a total salary expense of $600 000. If roughly 25 per cent is added to this amount to cover fringe benefits, etc., the figure rises to over $750 000. But what is his asset value? How can his replacement cost be estimated?

While turnover is a problem which has been inadequately researched, some estimate of direct costs can be made within broad limits. But, the indirect costs of turnover are particularly difficult to assess. Excessive or unusual turnover has a profound effect on the morale and expectations of those remaining. It creates dissonance in the workforce and reappraisals of implicit decisions to remain. It can adversely affect productivity and efficiency, and is often harmful to the company's ability to attract suitable replacements from the market place. While such effects are largely intangible and difficult to evaluate in terms of dollars and cents, new methods and techniques are being developed that will soon become commonplace in the hands of the sophisticated manpower planner. Indications of these have appeared in some recent publications. [1,2,3,6,11]

The direct costs of turnover are perhaps easiest to calculate provided enough information is available. Such costs may be thought of in terms of 'replacement' or 'displacement' costs.

In Fig. 10.2, replacement costs include recruiting, induction, and training costs. Displacement costs are those related to promoting, transferring, and

Turnover rate	5%	10%	15%	20%	25%
Total turnover (5 yrs.)	500	1 000	1 500	2 000	2 500
Estimated replacement costs	750 000	1 500 000	2 250 000	3 000 000	3 750 000
Estimated displacement costs	250 000	500 000	750 000	1 000 000	2 250 000
Total turnover costs	1 000 000	2 000 000	3 000 000	4 000 000	5 000 000

Figure 10.2   Estimated cost of turnover

shifting employees to fill the gaps left by those who leave. Depending on the position and its level in the organization, as many as five or six employees may be directly affected by an incident of turnover. For purposes of presentation, arbitrary costs have been set at $1500 per person for replacement and $500 for displacement. These figures are probably highly conservative; some well-researched studies have estimated direct replacement costs at over $10 000 for mid-management personnel in certain industries. The costs are assumed to be in arithmetical progression—that is the costs per unit remain constant regardless of the level of turnover.

Relating these 'direct' costs to a company of 2000 people in a non-growth situation (i.e., the only new employees are replacements for those who leave) over a five year period, the costs in Fig. 10.2 may be calculated according to different turnover rates.

In any organization, there is probably an optimum level of turnover which should occur over any given period of time depending on whether the company is in a period of growth or expansion, stability or stagnation, constriction or disintegration. High turnover in certain situations may, in effect, be less costly than no turnover at all. Practically, the problem is again one of evaluating alternatives and of controlling excess or undesirable turnover and its related costs—financial and otherwise.

Most of the activities of the personnel manager are therapeutic and remedial in nature. Personnel budgets are usually set by precedent and not in the light of well-planned objectives. Without such objectives and an estimate of the cost involved these questions cannot be answered. How much could legitimately be spent in turnover research in the attempt to reduce turnover? What would be the payoff in actual dollars and cents? How much should be spent in training and development to ensure manpower needs are met at some given time? Investment in job training and executive development is skyrocketing yearly. In the United States, annual investment for the male workforce alone is over one half of total expenditures for all primary, secondary, and university education. Yet by far the vast majority of firms have no means of evaluating the results of their expenditure, and few make any systematic attempts to do so. What monies should be allocated towards measuring attitude and morale and what efforts should be made to alleviate problems before they arise?

Such questions must be answered in order to bring manpower resourcing into its own. 'No organization which handles its employees as expense items can make as wise plans or as rational allocation decisions as the one which recognizes explicitly the asset characteristics of its human resources.'[1]

The framework for manpower planning

Corporate planning is usually the means for making decisions on long-term goals and priorities, and on the strategies to be adopted in reaching those goals. It lends direction to the company in terms of present and forecast realities; i.e., general socio-economic and political trends, foreign and domestic competition, technological developments, from all departments. Manpower must be an integral part of the total corporate planning process.

Manpower planning is concerned with:

1 Translating present and future corporate objectives into manpower requirements.

2 Identifying current and projected manpower strengths and weaknesses.

3 Ensuring both the development of manpower policies and plans necessary to meet projected requirements, and their integration with operating personnel programs.

The process of manpower planning

As represented in Fig. 10.3, there are a number of steps which must be logically undertaken in order to design specific action programs. These include:

1 Defining the personnel requirements of the organization for the period of the plan.

2 Cataloguing the present human resources of the organization—an inventory.

3 Calculating the expected attrition to the manpower inventory.

4 Developing a manpower forecast, from the three previous sources of information (assuming no changes in personnel policies).

5 Analyzing the ability of the labor market to meet the forecast.

6 Developing an integrated plan of action to meet the personnel requirements of the organization.

These are discussed separately in brief outline.

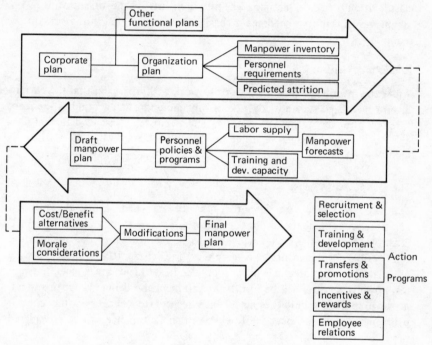

Figure 10.3 Major elements, processes, and outputs of manpower planning

The organization requirements

The personnel requirements of the organization must be developed by the manpower planner in detail for the period of the plan. The obvious first step is to define the present structure of jobs in the organization. This definition should include the skills, education, and experience required for each job, and special factors such as language. Then, based on the corporate plan for, say, a

187

five year period and on the organization plan for the same period, the manpower planner should develop detailed plans showing exactly what positions will be added and at what dates. Here again, manpower specifications must be outlined for each position.

The manpower inventory

The manpower planner must then tabulate and classify the current human resources of the organization. What is the age mix of the present personnel? What qualifications do they have? What experience do they have? What potential for advancement? To what jobs? In so far as possible, the classifications used for developing this information should parallel the classifications used in defining the requirements of the organization. This manpower inventory becomes a basic tool in planning to meet future requirements.

Predicting attrition

While the inventory is the basic tool to work with, it is clear that the current inventory will be substantially reduced by the end of the period of the plan, through turnover, retirements, death, and dismissals. Based on factual data and on historical trends, a projection can be made of what the attrition is likely to be.

The manpower forecast

Following this step, the inventory can be matched against the planned personnel requirements of the organization, after deducting the projected attrition. The numbers who will have to be recruited into the organization can easily be represented in graphic form (Fig. 10.4). In a growing organization, this forecast will inevitably indicate major areas where current manpower resources will be insufficient to meet the demands. At this point, no assumptions should be made with respect to changes in the current personnel policies to meet the forecast—other factors need to be considered first.

The labor market

The forecast will reveal shortages and suggest the need for upgrading the current inventory through training and development and through recruiting substantial numbers from outside the organization. A study of the labor market may reveal that efforts to recruit substantially greater numbers from traditional recruiting sources are impractical. For example, an organization which has depended heavily upon high school graduates may find, in projecting for a five year period, that it would be unrealistic to rely on this

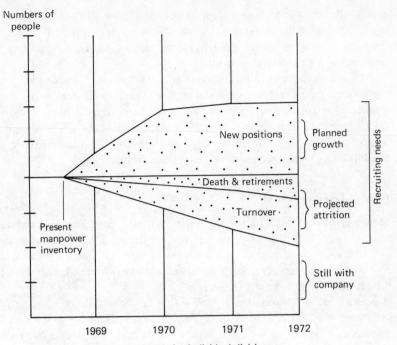

In calculating recruiting needs for individual divisions or departments transfers 'in and out' must be taken into consideration. 'Transfers out' are added to attrition and 'transfers in' are subtracted from total recruiting needs.

Hence:
Recruiting needs attrition · Transfers out · Growth −
Transfers in

Figure 10.4 Anticipated corporate recruitment needs

source of supply in view of the trends towards higher education. Or, a company relying heavily on recruiting outside its ranks in the 35-44 year age group, would have to consider seriously altering this policy over the next five years in view of the known decreasing numbers in this group.

Developing the plan

Once all the 'inputs' have been assembled, the organization will know its requirements, have a good understanding of what is likely to be available from within to meet those requirements, and some understanding of the labor market. Specific plans can now be drawn up to meet the demands. For example, in order to supply 30 computer specialists over five years, a decision may be taken to recruit 5 computer systems specialists per year and to train 3 internally (on the assumption that 10 will leave); a decision may be taken to recruit substantially increased numbers of MBA graduates for the period of the plan; it may be decided to identify outstanding potential within the organization and to undertake rapid development programs, including job rotation and accelerated promotion.

Provided the information gathering and analytical processes have been well carried out, the manpower plans can be worked out in remarkable detail and specific programs can be established. Subsidiary plans can be developed towards special programs to reduce turnover, to revise the salary administration program, to encourage outside recruiting or to revise training and development programs to meet overall company objectives.

Technical considerations

Various skills will be required to devise and implement a reliable and valid plan. It is unlikely that one man will possess them all. The systems analyst, the operations researcher, the behavioural scientist, among others, can provide valuable input into the plan, as well as those who are daily involved in the personnel function.

Knowledge in information-assembly is mandatory. The completion of a manpower or skills inventory, for example, for an organization of over 1000 persons makes indispensable the utilization of a computer or some readily accessible, simple to operate, manual system such as the Jonkers Termatrex, or the Royal McBee Kardex.

Because of the large number of variables and calculations involved in developing a comprehensive manpower plan, some of the techniques of the operations researcher may be particularly effective. Through the development of appropriate mathematical and heuristic models based on well-founded sets of assumptions and pertinent personnel data, decisions may be tested before actual commitments to action are made. Such applications are still in the development stage, not because of the lack of mathematical tools, but because of the lack of fundamental data and appropriate working assumptions. However, even with limited information, mathematical formulae can be constructed to assist in determining tenure on the job, recruitment quotas, and the like. One such technique would be the application of multivariable regression analysis to determine manpower requirements in relation to changes in sets of operating or end product variables, for example, dollar sales, customer miles, units produced.

The person knowledgeable in the theory and practice of what is euphemistically known as 'the behavioural sciences' may also prove to be a valuable resource. He can help to evaluate the internal climate of the organization, isolate and identify problems which may be contributing to turnover or employee dissatisfaction and recommend appropriate remedial action. He can also assist in identifying and developing potential, and provide

190

counsel on problems of development, motivation, and organizational change.[5,8,9,13]

The foregoing examples represent only some of the skills which can—and should—be brought to bear from other professional disciplines.

Summary

Manpower planning is a comparatively new addition to the planning process. It flows from, and is logically a part of, both corporate and organization planning and of the personnel function. In essence, it involves the forecasting of manpower requirements and the design and implementation of programs necessary to meet these requirements over a given span of time. It has many constituent elements and much remains to be learned of the techniques—essentially multidisciplinary—and the process involved.

The number of variables to be taken into consideration in developing a comprehensive manpower plan (many of which are unpredictable—such as changing socio-economic and technological conditions) make it doubtful that a manpower plan can be completely accurate beyond a year or two. Short-range planning can be demonstrated easily to more than pay its way, and longer-range planning, while inevitably making assumptions on as yet indiscernible trends, is nonetheless an indispensable tool in today's business environment.

The essential element in the planning process is that it be carried out continuously and that the assumptions made for the long-range plan are challenged as concrete evidence becomes available. Competent performance of the manpower planning function will enable top management to make optimum use of its human resources and to evaluate its manpower policies and decisions in hard economic terms.

References

1. BRUMMET, R. LEE, PYLE, WILLIAM C., and FLAMHOLTZ, ERIC G., 'Accounting for Human Resources.' *Michigan Bsns Rev.*, March 1968.
2. BRUMMET, R. LEE, PYLE, WILLIAM C., and FLAMHOLTZ, ERIC G., 'Human Resource Measurement—A Challenge for Accountants.' *The Accounting Review,* April 1968.
3. DOTY, JACK H., 'Human Capital Budgeting—Maximizing Returns on Training Investment.' *Journal of Industrial Engineering,* March/April, 1965.
4. GEISLER, EDWIN B., *Manpower Planning: An Emerging Staff Function,* American Management Association Bulletin No. 101, New York, 1967.
5. GELLERMAN, SAUL W., *Motivation and Productivity.* New York: American Management Association, 1963.
6. HAAS, FREDERICK C., *Executive Obsolescence.* New York: American Management Association, 1963.
7. JEKIMIAN, JAMES S. and JONES, CURTIS H., 'Put People on Your Balance Sheet,' *Harvard Bsns Rev.,* January/February 1967.

8. HOUSE, ROBERT H., *Management Development: Design, Evaluation and Implementation.* Ann Arbor: University of Michigan Press, 1967.
9. HUGHES, CHARLES L., *Goal Setting.* New York: American Management Association, 1965.
10. KYLE, J. D., 'Essentials of Management Development.' *The Business Quarterly,* Winter 1967.
11. KYLE, J. D., 'Manpower Planning for the Future.' *Canadian Personnel and Industrial Relations Journal,* January 1966.
12. LIKERT, RENSIS, *The Human Organization: Its Management and Value.* New York: McGraw-Hill, 1967.
13. ODIORNE, GEORGE S., *Management by Objectives.* New York: Pitman, 1965.

11. Long-range planning through program budgeting: A better way to allocate resources

David Novick

A plan for an organization, whether a government agency or a business firm, prescribes actions to be taken and activities to be carried on to advance the organization's perceived objectives. Plans vary widely in substance and form according to the nature of the organization, the scope of the plan, and the timespan to which it applies. However, one element is universal in the planning of any organization that produces goods or services: at some point, the plan must deal with the question, 'How shall the organization make use of its available resources?' This—the resource allocation question—is fundamental, because in every sphere of the organization's activity the amount of resources sets limits to what can be accomplished.

The strategic and most comprehensive form of planning is long-range planning of the organization's total program. In business, such planning may embrace the full set of product lines and productive functions of a diversified corporation. In government, it may encompass the programs of an entire department or ministry or, perhaps, the development of a 'five year plan' for an entire jurisdiction. This paper deals with a system for organizing the long-range planning function and for helping managers to reach the key resource allocation decisions that confront them in this context.

For more than 25 years, I have been developing a management tool—program budgeting—which is designed to strengthen an organization's

● Reproduced with permission from *Business Horizons,* Vol. 12, No. 1, February 1969, pp. 59-65.

capability to do long-range planning and to provide a systematic method for resolving major resource allocation issues.[1] Program budgeting—or the planning-programming-budgeting systems abbreviated to PPB—focuses on the basic function of management, which is to use the organization's available resources in the way that will be most effective in meeting its goals. Basically, the PPB system contributes to the planning process in two ways.

First, it establishes and makes explicit the relationships or linkages among the organization's objectives, its programs and activities, the resource implications of those activities, and their financial expression in a budget. In so doing, it provides much of the information needed for rational planning in an easily usable form. Second, PPB contributes directly to management decision-making by providing analyses of the consequences, in terms of estimated costs and expected benefits, of possible program decisions.

This may sound like a broad charter, but it should be borne in mind that PPB does not do a number of important things. As it is discussed here, PPB is an instrument for overall planning that utilizes existing systems for directing and controlling operations and therefore does not necessitate change in either the existing organization or methods of administration. In addition, PPB is specifically designed for long-range planning and budgeting; it is not primarily a tool for conducting the annual budgeting-accounting cycle, although next year's budget must be included in its purview, and accounting supplies part of the reports. Last, although PPB stresses the use of quantitative analytical methods and, in some cases, a rather extensive use of modern computer technology, it does not attempt to quantify every part of the problem or to computerize the decision-making process.[2]

PPB has been in operation for seven years in the US Department of Defense, and, since 1965, efforts have been under way to extend the system to other departments and agencies. Many state and local governments have applied PPB methods to their own planning problems, and similar methods are in use in major business firms. Nevertheless, in some organizations, the adoption of PPB has caused apprehension and insecurity, largely as the result of a misunderstanding of what PPB is and does. People assume program budgeting is revolutionary and complex. When in operation and understood, the real content comes through; it is revolutionary but simple, and based on common sense.

The program budget concept

The PPB system is constructed on a few basic concepts related to objectives, programs, resources, cost, effectiveness, and benefits.

Objectives are the organization's aims or purposes, which, collectively, define its *raison d'être*. They may be stated initially in broad and relatively abstract terms, as, for example, when we say that the objective of a defense program is to provide national security, or that the objectives of education are to provide good citizens and productive participants in the economy. However, objectives at this level are too remote from the organization's specific activities to be useful for formulating or evaluating programs to be operational; they must be translated into lower-level objectives that can be stated in concrete terms.

Programs are the sets of activities undertaken to accomplish objectives.[3] A program generally has an identifiable end product. (Some programs may be undertaken in support of others; if so, they have identifiable intermediate products.) Several programs may be associated with an objective, in which case they may be identified with distinct subobjectives or with complementary, but distinguishable, means for accomplishing the objective.

Resources are the goods and services consumed by program activities. They may be thought of as the inputs required to produce each program's end product. Program cost is the monetary value of resources identified with a program.

Effectiveness is a measure of the degree to which programs accomplish their objectives. It is related to benefit, which is a measure of the utility to be derived from each program.

Program budgeting for an organization begins with an effort to identify and define objectives, and group the organization's activities into programs that can be related to each objective. This is the revolutionary aspect, since it requires grouping by end product rather than by administrative organization or by function. This method allows us to look at *what* we produce—output—in addition to *how* we produce or what inputs we consume. The program budget itself presents resources and costs categorized according to the program or end product to which they apply. This contrasts with traditional budgets found in most organizations, that assemble costs by type of resource input (line item) and by organizational or functional categories. The point of this restructuring of budget information is that it aids planning by focusing attention on competition for resources among programs and on the effectiveness of resource use within programs. The entire process by which objectives are identified, programs are defined and quantitatively described, and the budget is recast into a program budget format is called the 'structural phase of planning-programming-budgeting'.

Often, both in government and in business, responsibility for the work required to accomplish a coherent set of objectives is divided among a number of organizations. In the government, for example, programs with objectives for health and education are each fragmented among a dozen bureaux and independent agencies. The activities of each one are sometimes complementary, sometimes contradictory, or in conflict with those of the others. As a result, there is no overall coordination of the resource allocation decisions relevant to program objectives. One of the strengths of program

195

budgeting is that it cuts across organizational boundaries, drawing together the information needed by decision-makers without regard to divisions in operating authority among jurisdictions. The advantage for planning is obvious: a program can be examined as a whole, contradictions are more likely to be recognized, and a context is supplied for consideration of changes that would alter or cut across existing agency lines.

One product of the structural phase is a conversion matrix or 'cross-walk' from the budget in program terms to the traditional or functional budget, which treats of organizations like departments and sections, in categories such as wages and salaries, equipment, and the like. Through the cross-walk, we are able to translate ongoing methods of record-keeping and reporting into data for program planning; we are also able to translate program decisions into existing methods for directing, authorizing, controlling, recording, and reporting operations. If existing management methods in any of these areas are inadequate or unsatisfactory, they should be upgraded and improved whether or not the organization has a PPB system. In any case, the program budget must derive information and relationships from existing management records and practices, and must rely on them for the implementation of the programs.

The long-range planner encounters problems of choice at several levels. At the highest level, the different programs and objectives compete for their shares of the organization's total resources or total budget. For example, in the government Transportation Ministry, programs for international transportation, domestic intercity transportation, and local transportation compete with each other. In a business firm, competition for investment funds may involve different product lines, different research and development projects, and so forth. At a lower level, the problem of choice focuses on decisions among alternative ways of carrying out a program. For instance, in connection with the Transportation Ministry's program of domestic intercity transportation, choices have to be made among alternative transport modes—railway, automobile, and air transport—or among alternative combinations of modes.

In program budgeting, the approach to this problem is to apply analysis wherever it is possible, so that decision-makers will be able to make the final judgements with as much objective information as can be assembled. Thus, a planning-programming-budgeting system subsumes a systems analysis capability with which the resource and cost implications of program alternatives, and their expected 'outputs' or accomplishments, may be estimated, examined, and compared. (When a systems analysis capability does not exist or is inadequate, it should be created or upgraded since analysis is perhaps the most important part of PPB.) A wide range of techniques is employed in these program analyses, including statistical analysis; modelling, gaming, and simulation; operations analysis; and econometric techniques. Systems analysis examines both the resource/cost side and the benefit/effectiveness side of program consequences.

An important aspect of systems analysis in connection with program planning is that it often goes far beyond the decision problem as initially given. Program analysis is not confined to examination of predetermined alternatives; development of new and better alternatives is part of the process. It is likely that analysis of possibilities A, B, and C will lead to the invention of alternatives D and E, which may be preferable (more cost/effective) to the original candidates. Therefore, the analytical aspect of PPB cannot be viewed merely as the application of a collection of well-defined analytical techniques to a problem. The process is much more flexible and subtle, and calls for creativity by the analyst and interaction between the analyst and the decision-maker during the decision process.

Other important features

Some other features of the PPB system will convey a fuller impression of the context in which these principles are applied. First, since program decisions that we make today often have implications that extend far into the future, and since program costs may be incurred and benefits enjoyed many years after a decision is made, meaningful planning requires a *long-time horizon*. Generally, the program budget itself, and the associated program analyses, cover at least a 5 year period and, where appropriate, should extend 10, 15, or more years into the future.

Planning, not forecasting, is the purpose of the PPB system. Our aim is to examine the cost and benefit implications for the future of relevant alternative courses of action. The program budget, which conveys a projection of existing programs and a display of decisions already made, provides a base line and serves as a frame of reference for specification and analysis of alternatives. It should not be thought of as a static extrapolation of a program.

Comparability rather than accuracy is the main consideration in our analysis of program cost and benefits. Because of intrinsic uncertainties in long-range planning, absolute accuracy is not attainable. The relevant criterion for analyses is consistency in treatment of different alternatives; this must be accompanied by explicit treatment of uncertainties, including tests of the sensitivity of analytical results to variations in circumstances. Excessive concentration on absolute accuracy is likely to be self-defeating, since it would tend to overwhelm the work with detail and make this kind of planning impracticable. In addition, aggregate, not detailed, data must generally be used in cost and benefit estimation. Examination of many alternatives is costly or impossible, so we must focus on variables that have important impacts on program consequences.

Several points may be made about the cost concepts that enter into program analysis. *Full costing* of programs and program alternatives is required if we are to achieve consistency in our estimates. Programs often have indirect cost implications that are difficult to trace; important interdependencies may exist between 'direct' and 'support' programs or among direct programs themselves (for example, joint cost situations). In order to sort out the full cost implications of alternatives, it is often necessary to have a cost model or its equivalent that is capable of translating the total program of the organization into resource and cost implications. The cost figures that will actually be compared with benefit estimates are incremental costs associated with specific program decisions, but these must be derived by comparing the full costs of either another program alternative or a base case.

Resources and costs are generally divided into three categories, corresponding to differences in the time pattern by which they are incurred and in the duration of their contribution to benefits. Research and development costs are the one-time outlays to create new capability, for example, studies of new products, services, or technologies, or of new methods for accomplishing programs. Investment costs are the non-recurring outlays required to install new capability, for example, construction of plants or facilities, purchase of equipment, or training of personnel for participation in new programs. Annual operating costs are the recurring costs required either to operate the new capability to be installed or the existing capability to be maintained. Each of these elements of cost enters into the full cost of a program. All three are projected on a year by year basis, and summed for each program and for the total program of the organization. Capital and operating cost implications of programs are looked at together, not separately, as is the traditional practice.

A planning-programming-budgeting system provides for communication between analysts and decision-makers and between analysts, operating organizations, and decision-makers at different organizational levels. Some specific documentary forms have been developed to facilitate this exchange of information. For example, *program memoranda* provide the communication between the analysts within a program area and the analytical staff that services the decision-making group. In these paper studies, the program group lays out the issues it identifies in the program area, the alternatives it recommends, and the pros and cons for its recommendations, as well as the data, analysis, and arguments for the possibilities it has rejected.

The topside analytical group reanalyzes the program memorandum and writes its memorandum in response. The reply may accept the recommendations for the same, different, or modified reasons; determine issues that have not been raised; suggest alternative program packages that have not been considered; or modify alternatives that were examined. After as much study, analysis, and reanalysis as time permits, the top staff, with concurrence or objection from the program manager, drafts the final program memorandum covering all issues and all alternatives for consideration by the decision-maker.

Special studies require more time and/or study resources than are available during the program memorandum period as scheduled. These areas are assigned for completion in the near future in order of importance, and will frequently (not always) cut across areas handled by two or more program managers. For reasons of time or specialized knowledge, parts or all of these studies may be contracted out.

Program change is another administrative step calling for analysis and study. Program budgeting aims at a continuing, fluid management process. This means setting up a 'base case' or set of decisions taken now, which are revised and updated as required. When change is or appears to be in order, the proposed change is considered in a total resource, overall time context, just as though it was a program memorandum in the original deliberations. Ideally, this would mean only one overall program budget exercise. Changes would be made as required, and the revised total plan would become the new base case, which would be used for the cross-walk from the program budget into the immediate changes in the budget as well as next year's organizational and functional operating budgets.

Introducing PPB

Two possible courses of action are open for the introduction of program budgeting. One is to set up a study group to examine the government's or company's objectives, develop a program structure tailored to those objectives, recommended alternative organization and administration schemes, examine the organization's analytical capabilities, and recommend education, training, and hiring policies to be followed in developing the analysis capacity required for program budgeting. (Reassignment, upgrading, and so on, would obviously be included.) This approach would aim at an operation to start eighteen months to two years in the future.

The other course of action starts with the assumption that program budgeting is the thing to do and to get on with it. This would mean taking some great leaps to put it in use in a current planning and budget cycle, and to learn in the process the answers the study group would otherwise have provided. This procedure is described in the following steps.

1 Set up a program structure that uses major activities or lines of business as final product programs, taking major government agencywide or company-wide activities like electronic data-processing (EDP), and calling them major support programs, and putting everything else, like research, planning, and executives, into a general support program category. This may or may not be the right program basis. Probably, it is not. However it will fit existing practice and is a satisfactory starting point for developing improvements.

2 Have several final product programs and major support programs made the subject of program memoranda to be completed in six to eight weeks. Use the existing analytic capability. The development of program memoranda and

the other communication materials of the program budget relies heavily on analysis. Therefore, if the analytic organization is either understaffed or inadequate, immediate steps should be taken to expand and upgrade.

3 Designate the individual or individuals to complete the program structure in order to accommodate all activities to the three major areas identified in step 1 above. These studies should be completed in eight to ten weeks.

4 Designate the individual or individuals to develop a first-cut study on alternatives available for organization and administration of program budgeting in the government unit or the business organization.

5 Agree on program identification, possible program manager, organization and administration, schedule of steps to be taken, and dates.

6 Get executive approval and move on.

One of the major advantages of this approach is that from the outset we get the required interaction between the operating, analytical, and decision-making parts of the organization; this interaction is essential to the development of an effective program-budgeting system. Time is saved and more intimate knowledge of the content of the administrative procedure is developed by both analytical and operating personnel.

Relationship described

The relationship between program and budget and planning, programming, and budgeting merits more complete description. It is rather commonplace in the literature on budgeting for business to say, 'The budget is the financial expression of a plan'. Many people apply the same definition for government. Nonetheless, we are all familiar with the budget that was developed without a plan (particularly a long-range plan). In fact, it is probably fair to say that in most budgets any planning is a projection of the *status quo* with increments added on the basis of the most current experience. A statement made by Roswell Gilpatric, when he was Deputy Secretary of Defense in 1961, typifies one of these situations: 'In the past, the Defense Department has often developed its force structure by starting with a budget and sending it off in search of a program.'[4] On the other hand, there are elaborate plans made by either government or business that never get beyond top-level approval—that is, are never budgeted.

Planning is the production of a range of meaningful potential courses of action through a systemic consideration of alternatives. In the short range, it deals with a limited number of alternatives because past actions have already locked in the available paths. However, for the long range (the major emphasis of program budgeting), the planning activity attempts to examine as many alternative courses of action as appear to be feasible and to project the future course of the organization against these in cost-benefit terms. Since the objective is not to make specific decisions, but rather to turn up likely possibilities, the work is done in a general and highly aggregative form.

Programming is the more detailed determination of the manpower, equipment, and facilities necessary for accomplishing a program-feasibility testing in terms of specific resources and time. The program and its elements used in the planning process in highly aggregative terms are moved down the scale to more detailed terms (as detailed as is appropriate) required for determining the feasibility of the possibilities. Even here, for most cost elements, we are at a level of aggregation above that required for the detailed determinations involved in next year's budget. That budget is the translation of program cost elements into the specific funding and time requirements identified in traditional terms, such as object class, function, and organization.

How do we distinguish the program budget from the traditional next year's budget? PPB is the development and preparation of a budget in a planning context, that is, with information about what is in store for the future. The planning context puts it in contrast to the short-range fiscal management and expenditure control objectives that categorize the traditional approach. This new method allows for major shifts among purposes for which resources are to be used, ranging from changes in funding levels to the introduction of completely new activities.

Under the program budget, annual allotments to administrative organizations allow them to take the next step along a path thoughtfully set by policy-makers at all levels. Probably more important, the direction of the path and the distance to be covered in the next year will have been established after considering a number of possible futures.

References

1. NOVICK, D. ed., *Program Budgeting: Program Analysis and the Federal Budget.* 2nd Edn. Cambridge, Mass.: Harvard UP, 1967, 'Introduction'.
2. NOVICK, D. *The Role of Quantitative Analysis and the Computer in Program Budgeting.* The RAND Corpn., P-3716, October 1967.
3. ANSHEN, M., NOVICK, D., and TRUPPNER, W. C. *Wartime Production Controls.* New York: Columbia UP, 1949, pp. 109-11.
4. GILPATRIC, ROSWELL C. 'Defense—How Much Will It Cost?' *California Management Review,* Vol. 5, Fall 1962, p. 53.

PART FOUR: Organizing for corporate planning

Part 4 concentrates attention on what is, in my experience, the most difficult practical aspect of corporate planning. Reverting to the definition in the introduction of 'a formal, systematic, managerial process organized by responsibility, time and information. . .', and given the size and scope of many firms, there are clearly substantial problems to be solved in determining who does what, over what timespan and with what information. Furthermore, there is the great singularity of different companies, and there is no reason to believe that the planning system developed in one company has any necessary relevance to the problems of another.

In chapter 12, C. E. Summer examines clinically some of the pressures causing more planning to take place, such as rapid change and organizational complexity, and deduces from these trends that those involved in corporate planning require certain qualities and aptitudes to be effective. He raises the issue of planning and authority, central power and semiautonomous divisions, and the impact of planning on bureaucracy.

W. B. Schaffir moves forward in chapter 13 to examine ways of relating any central planning function to the existing centres of power in such a way that the potential of corporate planning as an agent of deliberate change can have its greatest effect. The question of relationships with divisions in multidivisional companies and with other staff functions is examined, and the importance of the relationship between planning and budgeting, keeping them related but separate, is stressed. Finally, some comments about building a corporate planning department within a defined concept of role is offered.

Chapter 14 goes one stage further by suggesting that there are an indentifiable set of activities which must be carried out somewhere in the organization if any effective process is taking place, but that responsibility for different parts of the work may well be done in different places in companies with different needs. Within this structure of work and potential responsibilities, examples of organizational patterns in three companies are considered and the suggestion made that these observed organizational patterns are relevant responses to different needs of top management in the different situations. The importance of the paper centres on its attempt to offer a structure for reasoned decision as a way through delicate problems of power and personality.

Finally there is a very short chapter by G. A. Steiner concentrating on 25 fundamental and common reasons for faulty corporate planning. The reader may be interested to note that most of the 25 reasons are centred round failures of process rather than faulty technique. This lends support to the view that critical problems in obtaining effective corporate planning are associated with developing a 'systematic process organized by responsibility, time and information' relevant to the particular needs of the enterprise.

(Editor)

12. The future role of the corporate planner

Charles E. Summer, Jr

In the past five years, many companies have established full-time positions which perform a function variously referred to as 'top management planning' or 'long-range planning'. To date, this trend has progressed far enough that the Institute of Management Sciences now has a College on Long-Range Planning. The New York Chapter of this College can today muster, for its monthly meetings, some 30 to 40 men from different companies, whose principal duties revolve around the planning function.

The establishment of these positions, with titles, such as director of planning, or manager of corporate planning, represents the creation of a new role in the hierarchy of many US corporations. It is my purpose to look more closely at this role or position, and ask:

1 What is its function in the organization as a whole, and why has such a position evolved?

2 What work duties and behavior are required to carry out this function?

3 What qualities of mind are required if the planner is to function in the organization, behave successfully as an individual, and carry out the relationships required?

In considering these questions, I shall examine the present state of affairs, and hazard some predictions of things to come.

Charging someone in the organization with responsibility for planning is not a new idea, either in American business or in other types of organizations.

● ©1961 *California Management Review,* Winter 1961, pp. 17-31. Reprinted by permission of the Regents of the University of California.

Historically, whenever large complex organizations have committed them-selves to courses of action which could not easily be reversed without serious consequences, there have been people doing long-range planning. This was equally true of the campaigns of Alexander the Great, the construction of Rheims Cathedral, Harriman's building of the Union Pacific Railroad, and the US Government's participation in the Second World War.

In American business, so-called line executives have always been forced to do long-range planning, with the aid of staff specialists, each doing planning work in his own area—manufacturing, engineering, marketing, personnel-manpower, and so on. It is not even entirely new to find someone assigned the role of 'generalist type' planner, who is not a line executive, and yet who coordinates the information on plans from all line and all specialized staff departments.

For example, men with titles like 'assistant to the president', or 'executive vice-president—administration', have been concerned, at least on a part-time basis, with the general coordination of long-range planning throughout the whole company system, bringing together information from both line and staff departments. In some companies, through custom and because of qualifications and interests of incumbent officers, capital budget and product development departments have had the same approximate kind of duties as our 'managers of long-range planning' do today.

Line and staff

These positions have not been different from the long-standing practice of the military to install general staff men to coordinate plans of the various specialists, such as supply, personnel, operations, and intelligence. In fact, the general staff role in the military very closely approximates what is happening in American business today: that is, the relief of the line executive from much of the planning, by a person who integrates the whole organizational system, rather than plans only one of its specialized parts.

Because the military has had to move quickly as a coordinated whole, and because its organizations were so big and complex, it long ago was forced to establish such a role. These two things are, in my opinion, ones which are operating, along with others in American business today, as underlying causal factors in the establishment of positions such as 'manager of planning', 'director of long-range planning', and the like.

What is new, then, is the creation of positions in many corporations which are assigned planning as their full-time activity, which do not combine planning with other staff functions, which are 'generalist', in the sense that they integrate information from all other organizational units in the system, and which are not viewed as line executive positions.

206

Function of planning

At this point, I would like to describe in general terms the function of management planning in an organization. It is, first, that function which establishes goals, for all parts of the company, in terms of results to be accomplished and, at the same time, allocates physical, human, and financial resources throughout the company to attain those goals.

This is a very general statement—almost meaningless because it covers such a vast and complex system. It implies the 'coordination' of goals and resources for hundreds of thousands of individual physical items and human beings. It also implies both coordination at any one point of time, and coordination in a time series, so that the achievement of certain goals becomes the means to more distant goals. In later parts of this article, I will try to make more explicit what is involved in the establishment of the goals, and allocation of resources, in a complicated managerial system.

Second, top management planning has the function of initiating change of the total company system, moving forward as a coordinated whole, in an evolutionary sense, in response to changes in the environment (technological, social, economic, political) in which the company must survive, grow, or decline. It insures some speed of change in the company, overcoming the static forces that result from technological habit, red-tape types of bureaucracy, and what I shall later call technological and institutional commitment.

As I view US society, its government, and corporations, over the last 30 years, I see, in fact, an increase in the importance of the planning activity which must be done. This, in turn, has meant an increased number of manhours devoted to planning in business organizations. The establishment of planning positions in companies is simply one of the visible outgrowths of this increase in importance of the function and its concomitant requirement for manpower devoted to the activity.

These three things—increased importance of the planning function, increased manpower being devoted to planning, and an increase in the number of planning positions—are phenomena to be explained. I am not, in this article, saying that we should have more planning activity. Rather, I am saying, 'We, in fact, have experienced these things over the past 30 years.' It is not a question of moralizing as to whether more central planning is 'good' or 'bad'. It is simply that, whether we like it or not, planning is becoming more important, and this importance is reflecting itself in the organization structure of our corporations.

If we can isolate the underlying causal factors which have brought about the evolution of separate planning departments, these will allow us to predict the future of such roles and departments and to speculate about the qualifications of men who fill planning positions.

Growing importance

These causal factors, which I shall discuss separately, are as follows:

1 The increasing complexity and interdependence of the planning system.

2 The increase in planning work brought about through divisionalization.

3 The speed with which organizations must innovate new procedures as a coordinated system.

4 The static forces which are generated by technological and social commitment, and which oppose change and innovation.

5 The technical competence and knowledge required to do an effective planning job.

Technological complexity

The first factor which has important implications for long-range planning departments is the increasing complexity and interdependence in the system to be planned.

A system may be thought of as a number of variable parts, each of which is dependent on the other. That is, when one part changes, this affects other parts, and there is a chain reaction throughout the whole system. I view the internal part of the corporate system as a vast complex of three subsystems of variables.

Three variables

First, there are technological variables. This system includes everything from quality control, equipment type and layout, production line layout, to plant location. It also includes advertising, pricing, product characteristics, distributive facilities in marketing, and a host of subparts in personnel relations and manpower development. It would include all facilities for product and process research. Finally, it would include the sum total of the policies, procedures, and methods which the company has worked out to pass semifinished parts and paperwork from one person and department to another.

A second part of the internal corporate system is composed of social variables. This subsystem is composed of a large number of human beings, each with different characteristics, often bound together in informal groups. It is also composed of a number of globs of human effort which we call departments and divisions. Each person, and each department, has a specialized and unique set of activities, with special knowledge and skills required to perform the work.

A third subpart of the internal corporate system is composed of economic or financial variables. Money costs, and money prices, are attached to every single part of the technological system and the social system.

Interrelated key factors

Very few people have ever attempted to catalog how many major operating parts there are in a typical large corporation. E. G. Booz, in his management consulting work, developed what he called '70 key factors' in the operation of a company. Austin Grimshaw, Dean of the Business School at the University of Washington, arrived at about 50 key parts in the system. Now, assuming that each of these is related to every other, so that a change in one sets off a chain reaction in all others, I estimate that there are somewhere between 50 and 70 relationships which may have to be considered in making any one important long-range management plan.*

In addition to the integral operating variables in the corporate planning system, there is also an external system of variable factors to be considered. These factors do not appear in the legal organization system of the corporation, but they are in the planning system.

Here are a few examples among hundreds that could be cited: the entire range of government laws; regulations and tax levies; the many customs, and norms of society; the number, type, and quality of items purchased from other companies; the prices charged on purchases; the supply and cost of borrowing money; the quirks of men who head various money-lending institutions; the state of the economy in terms of both cyclical and growth indices; the power and personal characteristics of labor union leaders; the quantity and characteristics of the labor force; the efficiency and desirability of different wholesale and retail outlets, and so on.

Complexity fosters planning role

It was this type of complexity in the total planning system which contributed to the establishment of more and more traditional staff departments, each doing planning on one segment of the system and reporting to a line executive (perhaps the president). Personnel vice-presidents investigated manpower, labor organization, productivity, and so on. Treasurers investigated money supply, lending institutions, credit costs, etc. Headquarters engineering or manufacturing staffs looked at changing processes, quality standards, plant locations, and the like.

As technology, the US economy, the financial structure of the country, and other parts of the culture (e.g., labor unions) became more complex, the ability of the chief line executive to comprehend everything his specialist

---

* This estimate assumes that all variables are related to each other in one relationship. 'A' is a certain function of 'D', regardless of how many intervening variables there may be. Thus 50 and 70 represent the number of relationships. The estimate is conservative in that 'A' may well be related to 'D' in two different ways. Thus, the number of relationships between all parts of the firm could conceivably be, for the 50 part system, somewhere between a minimum of 50! and a maximum of (50! + 49! + 48! ... 2!).

planners told him was exceeded in many large corporations. Furthermore, even if he were technically competent, the sheer number of manhours necessary to integrate this diverse information could exceed all of the hours in a working day.

The next step, which generally occurred in the period 1940 to 1950, was to establish super-staff positions—generalist planners sometimes given the title 'assistant to the president' or 'executive vice-president—administration'. These men received summary information from the specialists, and fitted together long-range goals and resource allocations. The total planning activity was thus divided between abstract planners (sometimes referred to as integrative planners) and more specialized planners, such as manufacturing, personnel, marketing, financial, and research executives.

What's going to happen next?

I predict that the diversity of operations within most companies, due to technological progress, will continue to become more complex. I also believe that society and the economy, representing external variables in the planning system, will become more diverse and complex. What implications does this have for the planning role in the corporations in the United States?

1 For medium-sized companies, there will probably be more generalist planning positions established. These may combine all top management planning, both 'short-range' and 'long-range' and may have titles such as 'assistant to the president' or 'vice president-administration.'*

2 For the large corporations, there will probably be more staff positions created which are specifically devoted to long-range planning and given titles accordingly.

3 For governmental organizations, I see more central planning, whether we like it or not, since society is becoming more and more complex, and the parts of the total social system are becoming more interrelated.[1]

4 For the selection of men to fill the planning positions, complexity means that planners must have been exposed, in their experience, to a wide variety of company operations. Only men with relatively long service, and broad experience in the company will have the random pieces of knowledge of internal variables stored in memory, which are necessary to make sense out of the abstract summary information they must receive from all parts of the system.

5 The men who fill the planning positions will also need a wide variety of

---

* Actually, combining long-range planning with short-range planning, is the same job, has certain motivational disadvantages. Nevertheless, many companies simply may not be able to afford the luxury of separating the two by creating an additional executive position.

knowledge about the structure of US society. Not a detailed knowledge of business cycle theory—or population statistics or labor union tactics—but he should at least be acquainted with the structure of society and some of its many subparts and processes. This, to me, suggests a fairly good grounding in macroeconomics, sociology, history, and the philosophy of culture.

6 Generalist type planners must also communicate with many different other departments, in rapid-fire succession, and inspire trust on the part of other executives. Since communication with other humans is one of their principal research methods, this means, in common terms, a gregarious type of individual. It means a person who has a degree of social skill, a degree of 'other directedness', and a trusting, rather than a suspicious or fearful, view of the world. It also means selecting a person who has what the applied anthropologists call a high degree of interaction energy. Simply stated, this means that the man can sustain himself in a wide variety of social contacts, with high frequency and long duration, without losing his interest or propensity to communicate.

Divisionalization creates jobs

A second factor which has important implications for the planning activity is the current trend in organization structure commonly called decentralization, but, I believe, more accurately called divisionalization. This type of structure is characterized by 'divisions' of a company, each forming a relatively self-contained internal planning system, such as the Chevrolet Division of General Motors. It is also characterized by a new kind of planning at company headquarters which is more abstract or summarized, but which nevertheless sets goals and allocates resources among the various self-contained planning systems. It is interesting also, that the goals and resource allocations made at company headquarters, when viewed from the division manager's position, are parts of the division's external planning system.

It is my belief that what appears from one viewpoint to be decentralization of authority for planning detail, actually results in the creation of more planning work to be done, and a greater degree of central planning. This structure of organization also increases the manhours of planning to be done in the whole company organization, and may cause the creation of new positions or roles devoted to central planning.

Why does divisionalization result in greater amounts of planning activity in a company, and a greater degree of central planning? The answer lies in the fact that the resulting company organization permits a larger and more complex internal planning system to be created within the legal organization system which we call a corporation.

The company's goals are still set as usual, but there is a bigger job of

211

allocating diverse resources. Note that increased size may also affect the size of the planning job. But mere inclusion of more complexity in the resource allocation system can mean more manhours of planning required, and so can the creating of more layers of planning.

Mergers create planning jobs

Divisionalization can come about in two ways. First, it may evolve by taking a previously functionalized company organized in major divisions of manufacturing and sales, and regrouping the activities by product or territory (as in General Motors). (This is what is commonly called 'decentralization'.) Or, second, divisionalization may come about by merger or acquisition of smaller planning systems, bringing larger amounts and greater diversity of resources under the planning of one corporation; as in Textron, General Dynamics, Philadelphia and Reading, and Texas Instruments.*

In either case, the resulting organization structure is similar in that more diverse resources, and perhaps, greater amounts of resources, are brought into the internal planning system of the legal corporate organization. The principal difference in the two types of divisionalization is that, when it occurs through merger, this increase in size and complexity of the planning system occurs in the short run, while, in decentralization, it is less evident, and occurs in the long run.

Let me illustrate the merger or short-run case with a brief case history of Texas Instruments, Inc. In 1959, Texas Instruments acquired the Metals and Controls Corporation of Massachusetts. As a division of Texas Instruments, essentially the same kind of planning and amount of planning must be carried out in M & C as previously, but the goals toward which M & C's resources must be allocated are now the goals of the Texas Instruments Corporation. Consequently, someone at corporate level, who owes no allegiance to any one division, and who has a knowledge of what other divisions are doing, must help to integrate the allocation of resources in M & C with those of Texas Instruments.

One of the first things that TI management did was to reorganize the Metals and Controls Division into tertiary planning systems, each relatively self-contained. Thus, the General Plate Division, the Spencer Thermostat Division, and the Nuclear Division were created, each with a general manager.

Now stand back for a minute, and look what has happened in the space of

* The merger and acquisition movement, as a trend in US organization of production, is evidenced by such companies as Botany, US Hoffman, H. K. Porter, US Industries, George W. Helme Co., and many others. The last-named company, originally producing snuff products, has acquired divisions now producing 32 kinds of snuff products sold in 15 types of packages, the Bachman line of bakery products, 16 kinds of nuts in 45 types of packages, and a line of 16 different pretzel products.

212

a few months, and with little change in the sales volume or assets of the Metals and Controls system:

1 A larger planning system has been created in the Texas Instruments system—a greater complexity of manpower, different materials, and a diverse set of fixed capital must now be allocated in this system. New and different skills, personalities, raw materials, buildings, and machines must all be taken into account when setting a course of action for the whole corporation. It is my belief that the increased complexity and time required for planning work is more than proportionate to the increased sales of the total company. Thus the traditional measures of 'bigness'—assets and sales volume—are not good measures of the manhours of planning which must be added in a merger.

2 The ability of the President of Texas Instruments to plan, at any but the most abstract level, may be exceeded by the addition of more diverse resources which must be coordinated. Yet someone must fit M & C manpower, capital equipment, and money expenditures into the scheme of TI goals.

3 Part of the same effects are true at the next level. Mr Vetter, the general manager of M & C, does not have any greater quantity of resources, or greater diversity of resources, in his planning system, than did the former president of the independent corporation. But he has now pushed a certain amount of planning detail down to the Spencer Thermostat Division. There is consequently a new role of summary planning which must be performed at the divisional level. As the division grows, a point may be reached at which the division manager must also delegate this function in part to a planning department.

Planning hierarchy

What does this mean in terms of the duties performed, and the qualifications, of the planner? First, it means that the planners in the lower systems will be the ones who have a bent for empirical investigation and detail. You have seen some men who prefer to be thorough, working a problem through with precision, utilizing many facts and tables.

Second, the planners in the upper (and larger) systems will have to be a different breed of cat. They are the deductive thinkers, rather than the empirical investigators, whose mental predisposition is more like a philosopher than an empirical scientist. They will have less patience with facts, and a higher tolerance of ambiguity, otherwise their minds will be unwilling to take the risk of making decisions with broad, less precise (and what appears to the scientist as ambiguous) variables.

I also believe that the higher level planners should have IQ scores in a range which could be described as 'bright, creative, and intelligent', rather than in the higher ranges which could be described as 'brilliant'. Too much brilliance would result in the man's insisting on too much evidence and validity, both as to deductive reason and empirical fact, before the corporation could move forward with timely and speedy action.[2]

A second way in which divisionalization may come about is not through merger, but by regrouping the globs of human effort and physical resources, which we call divisions, into product or territorial planning systems. In the Texas Instruments example above, divisionalization of the Metals and Controls Division (the first echelon under the president of TI) came about through merger, but the divisionalization of Spencer Thermostat (the second echelon under the president of TI) came about through a regrouping of existing resources and goals. This is a well-known trend in US corporations, as exemplified by such companies as General Motors, DuPont, Johnson & Johnson, Massey-Ferguson, General Foods, IBM, RCA, Westinghouse, and many others.

In the merger case, both more diverse resources and a greater absolute quantity of resources were immediately, in the short run, brought under the planning sphere of the Texas Instruments goals, and were subsequently allocated toward this central set of goals.

Positions via decentralization

In the decentralization case, the same effects are indicated, except that they will come about only in the longer run, and will be caused by a growth of the company and of the economy. For example, after the 1957 reorganization of the IBM Corporation:

1 We might have expected that there would have been an absolute growth in the quantity of resources allocated toward the top goals of the IBM Corporation. The decentralized form arose in the first place because it was impossible for one human mind, or group of minds, at the top to comprehend and allocate such a large and diverse aggregate of resources, with the result that there was a limit put on the size of the firm. There was also a limit in the degree to which headquarters could change the behavior of such a large institution, which was interlocked so intricately in quality and timing of work of the specialized parts. Now, with the decentralized form, that limit is extended.

The degree to which more and more absolute amounts of resources can come under the allocation of one corporation's central goals cannot be disproved by statistics, which show that there is little increase in the relative proportion of wealth accounted for by large corporations. The percentage of national income or GNP accounted for by General Motors may not increase. But as society grows in total, the absolute dollars of capital investment, or the absolute number of people employed by GM, might well increase considerably in the decentralized form of organization, in the long run.

2 We might also expect that there would be an increase in the technological and social complexity of the resources which are allocated toward the corporation's goals. As science, product design, and the social structure of government and society become more complex, this will add to the amount of central planning which must be done. Therefore, quite independent of the 'long-run, size effect', we also have a 'long-run complexity effect'.

3 We might also expect a short-run increase in the planning which must be done. Decentralization actually creates a new planning level in the corporation. Whereas formerly details of planning were handled at headquarters by one set of staff people, we now have two planning jobs to be done. An abstract or summary set of resource allocations must be done at the top to coordinate the divisions, and a more detailed set of resource allocations must be done within the divisions. This gives rise to a third underlying cause of increase in planning work to be done in decentralized companies—the 'level effect'.

Speeds integrated changeovers

The next major factor which I see as having important implications for the planning role in business is the speed with which the entire corporation must move forward or change, as a coordinated whole, throughout all its complexity, in response to changes in its environment, or in pursuit of deterministic goals, which, in fact, change the environment.

Let us suppose that you go on a fishing trip to Florida with six friends. None of you has been to Florida before, and none has been on the kind of boat required, or caught the particular fish which is your goal, or used the type of equipment needed. Beforehand, there are many arrangements necessary—car-routing, spend-the-night points, arranging luggage in the car, motel reservations, and the like. Then, during the trip, there are many shorter-range plans necessary—where to stop for lunch and gas, sequence of unloading the baggage, selection of the charter boat, negotiations with the captain, purchase of provisions, and so on.

If there exist no one or two central planners or information centers, coordinating what the group is doing, each of these decisions will take a long time, and there will be much hashing back and forth. (Of course, if you are a group of retired executives, you may have leisurely committee meetings at lunch over a four month period, engaging in true 'group dynamics'. Then, you may make a leisurely drive to Florida, stopping during more long lunches to discuss what you will do next.)

If there is anything that study of small group dynamics has taught us, it is

215

that the emergence of courses of action, and the emergence of 'natural leader-planners', takes great amounts of time.[3]

On the other hand, if your fishing trip is to be accomplished in a limited time, some central planning, by someone, is a necessity—even if that person does not have authority and power, but merely acts as an information initiator and integrator between subparts of the action system.

While this is true of a small group, it is absolutely vital in a larger, complex, and impersonal organization, where one department has a difficult time knowing what others are doing, and where great amounts of time are required to start at the bottom of the pyramid; having workers thrash out their ideas and report to the foreman, foremen thrash out their ideas and report to the factory managers, factory managers meet and report to the manufacturing vice-president, all vice-presidents meet and work out plans with the president, and so on.

What I am saying is, the greater the speed with which organizations must act as an integrated whole, the more manhours must be devoted to some form of central planning. The time devoted to planning, and the number of personnel involved, vary with the speed of coordinated action.

Of course, there are times when greater speed is achieved without central planning. For example, when one division of GE is more acquainted with operating facts and local conditions than headquarters, decentralization of planning to the divisions increases speed of movement. Note, however, that this is speed of one subsystem moving as a unit, and it assumes that the divisions do not affect other divisions of the company in their actions. Whenever the General Electric Company, as a coordinated whole, must innovate and change, greater speed is achieved by central information clearance and central planning. This is precisely the most important reason for the controversy, since Sputnik, over the organization of the Defense Department and the nation's space program.

Takes planning to speed up

Let us look at what is happening to speed of change required of American corporations. The breakthrough in technology is the most important reason why this speed of change is increasing. New processes and new products by some companies, force their competitors to get busy and introduce major changes, affecting all segments of the company, in a limited time, or else. We see this particularly in the chemical, electronics, and allied industries.

But we see it also in some industries that are considered stable and conservative. Banks are an example, where development of new consumer loans, opening of branches, introduction of data-processing, and offering new services, are forcing some top to bottom innovation, in large banks as well as small. Insurance companies are another example, where the innovations and 'bombshells' of a few companies have caused some other companies to form long-range planning groups, to deal with long-term innovations.

Bosses or consultants?

What I see in the future, growing out of great dynamic changes in industry, is two different kinds of staff roles at company headquarters, depending on whether the company must move swiftly or relatively more slowly in changing its operations.

For the companies and industries where fast change is vital, I believe we will see greater centralization of the planning role, and in some cases the staff men will be given official authority, rather than held only to an advisory status.

It is significant, in the respect, that the new planning department heads in the divisions of IBM are given 'the right to demand' planning information from the division managers. Furthermore, in the industry with swiftly moving change, perhaps the staff planners must be selected with slightly different characteristics than in other industries. They may turn out to be more logicians, thinkers and rational beings, concerned more with the necessities of change, than they are concerned with social skills and committee meetings.

On the other hand, in those companies where change is less frequent and drastic, and where the company lives a more comfortable life, not bombarded so heavily or frequently from the environment, I foresee that planners will continue to be advisors. They will elicit help from the divisions more through social skills than through status as possessors of broad knowledge of current conditions, and status as skilled problem solvers and logicians.

Commitment time

The next major factor which I see affecting the role of professional planners is the commitment time involved in major decisions. We have all seen frequent references to the fact that labor unions, guaranteed annual wages, the increased size and expense of capital machinery, and the length of time required to research and develop new products—all mean that companies must take actions today which commit resources for longer periods of time. This, in turn, calls for more long-range planning to avoid the costly prospect of having to maintain a partially idle labor force, abandon the development of non-saleable products, or write off obsolescent plans and equipment. Since this subject is so well covered in management literature already, I will not deal with it further.

However, there is another kind of commitment which has not been given much attention, and which has an important bearing on how much top planning must be done, and what the role of planners will be. This can be called sociological, institutional or organizational commitment.

Institutional commitment

In simplest terms, institutional commitment is what is meant when we say that a company has grown big and inflexible, that it is tied down to routine, and that it is difficult and slow to change. Robert Merton, the sociologist, lists two of the dysfunctions of a bureaucracy as, first, inflexibility under changing conditions, and, second, the substitution of means (that is, the existing procedures and policies) for ultimate ends (goals of the company).[4] Another way of saying this is that large organizations tend to remain in habitual way of motion, until some force stimulates them to change direction, and to change the whole vast structure of policies, procedures, methods, and subobjectives.

To me, this has important implications for the role of the planner in business. There are two kinds of forces that can stimulate organizations to change: one is an outside force, generated by other organizations, by nature, or by technology. The second kind is the internal, deterministic ideas of men inside the organization.

The larger organizations get, the more they need men who have the time and capability, and interest to watch the external forces of technology, other organizations, and nature, and think through their implications for the company as an organization which must adapt to its environment.

Similarly, the larger and more complex organizations become, the more they need men who influence them through the power of new ideas. There is an old controversy in the study of history which poses the question, 'Do the times make the man or do men shape the times?'[5] There is no answer to this question—organizations do influence participants, sometimes to the point of stifling their vision of new ways of doing things. On the other hand, there is no question but that strong-minded creative men shape the structure and functioning of organizations.

While the smaller and less complex corporations of yesterday flourished on the creativity and imagination of Ford, Sarnoff, T. J. Watson, and Colonel Patterson, if you look closely today at the companies founded by these men, they each have staff men who devote time to long-range planning. This is no reflection on the former line executives' ability—instead, it reflects a necessity generated by the increasing complexity of external society and internal operations.

This turn of events also has one additional implication regarding the characteristic of the planners themselves. From early childhood on to maturity, the experiences in one's life tend to create characteristics in people of independence versus dependence. This is not an either-or proposition, where a person is either independent on the one hand or dependent on the other. However, there is a continuum of all shades of gray, with some people finding self-satisfaction with existing ways of doing things, and others who can live and develop only by being dissatisfied with the *status quo*. These are the independent thinkers, and they are somewhat self-centered. If they are too independent, of course, they may have trouble getting along in society, or even upset the company. And, by alienating their colleagues, they may fail to get their ideas across even though they are good. This was the case in the novel, *The Fountainhead,* where the architect failed to get his buildings constructed because he would not give in to social norms and the desires of others even in the slightest detail.

Independent thinkers needed

Too much independence also conflicts with the need for social skills, which I referred to previously. Perhaps what is needed for the planning role in companies of fast-moving change is a man who possesses a higher degree of independence on the continuum, and who possesses a mature, civil, but open-minded form of social behavior.

It is my contention that line executives in charge of product divisions, or even functional (sales, manufacturing) divisions, are generally more biased to the short-term *status quo* than are men especially assigned to top management planning of long-run programs.

This may occur because short-run objectives, such as this year's profits, often conflict with long-run objectives, such as profit 10 years hence. If a good profit showing is being made by existing products and operations, why not, in the minds of executives whose careers are tied to those operations, continue to make that profit? Why lower this year's profits by sinking valuable budget money into new product divisions when you do not know whether they are to be successful?

Must take the long view

I have seen this, for example, in an insurance company which faced the problem of new product development. For many years, the life insurance division of the company had been the biggest and most profitable money-maker. As group insurance was introduced in response to changes in the national society, many executives were reluctant to put large additional company resources and expenses into the group field.

What probably happened was that the competitive advantage of moving swiftly in the group business was somewhat retarded because the life executives naturally saw no reason to sacrifice their own budgetary position in favour of sinking more sales effort, advertising and research into this new and relatively untried product. This is not so much 'bad management'—as simply human nature.

In another case, in the wallboard business, the executives in charge of X

219

division, whose product was becoming obsolescent, successfully vetoed the entry of the company into new wallboard lines for three years. In an independent study by a Wall Street underwriting firm, the president was informed that X division was a 'dead duck', and that unless an orderly closing of the division were effected, the company would suffer severe losses within 10 years. Note, however, that the executives in X division could hardly be expected to recommend, on their own initiative, that their operations (and their jobs) be discontinued.

In each of these cases, a planner in company headquarters, whose responsibility was to look ahead, and who was rewarded for producing profits in 10 years rather than this year would have helped to prevent the institutional commitment of existing divisions from trying to stave off the inevitable. A planner with the time and interest to gather and disseminate valid facts on the demands of consumers, the actions of competitors, and the inevitability of change—showing, in effect, the 'writing on the wall' to all concerned might have increased the profitability of these companies through anticipating new goals, and convincing people throughout the company by weight of the evidence, that resources must be reallocated in an orderly long-range development program.

Summary

In summary, it seems to me that technological commitment definitely means more long-range planning if the company is to minimize the risk of sinking money into relatively fixed expenditures which may not later pay off. Plant, equipment, research and development, fixed labor forces, heavy advertising campaigns, all come in this category. It further seems that institutional commitment has these additional implications:

1 Large, bureaucratic social institutions are likely to become attached to existing ways of doing things, and to existing policy and procedures. They cannot swiftly adjust to changes in tastes of consumers, new products, and new actions by smaller and more agile competitors.

2 Part of the tendency is due to the natural bias of managers within divisions of the company to maintain their own 'empires' which are successful today, but may not be successful ten years hence.

3 Another part of the tendency is due to the conflict between this year's profits, for which line executives are responsible, and the profits of the company in the long run.

4 Provision for orderly change can be made by establishment of long-range planning positions, if

(a) the man in the position has the time and interest to watch future developments in the company and environment, and think through the effects of these on company operations;

(b) the man in the planning position has stronger than average characteristics of independence, a kind of natural dissatisfaction with the *status quo*, and a critical and inquiring mind;

(c) the man in the position is rewarded on the basis of creativity and intelligence in balancing long-run company goals, rather than concentrating exclusively on profits this year.

A new profession

The last factor which I see as affecting the future of the planning role in US corporations is the necessity for methodological knowledge to do adequate and thorough planning. Planning today is not an art into which you can throw a bright young man with common sense. Neither is it a science in which you can train men with depth and intensity of formulas, and then be assured that they will be effective.

Neither is planning a position where, as I have seen in some companies, you can promote a less capable executive when there does not appear to be any other place for him. When viewed correctly today, if the company expects a truly effective planning job, rather than a mediocre one, planning is a combination of three things:

1 A *Technology*, including a body of knowledge which helps the planner to do his work.

2 A group of *social and intellectual attitudes and skills*, a few of which are mentioned in this article.

3 *Wisdom*, which I define as an ability to know what knowledge and past experience are applicable to the problem at hand, and a willingness to abandon theoretical knowledge when it will not work (this could also be called a pragmatic attitude).

The technology to which I am referring here is not a body of substantive knowledge—the exposure to random facts in the internal and external planning systems. Earlier we saw that this kind of knowledge is also vital. Rather, I am referring now to various kinds of methodological knowledge, applicable in varying degrees to any planning system.

This is analagous to the chemical engineer who must know a wide variety of substantive principles and facts, such as the table of elements, properties of liquids and solids, families of compounds, such as halogens and hydrocarbons. But he must, in addition, know something about the scientific method and about the chemical processes of distillation, adsorption, filtration, in order to apply the substantive knowledge he has accumulated.

221

Accounting skill necessary

There is no doubt in my mind that, in spite of the many recent developments in applied mathematics, the most vital planning methodology for a total business or division of a business is at the present time, and will be for some years to come, the methodology of financial accounting.

I am referring to financial accounting in the sense of a means of allocating *physical* resources, as well as a means of figuring profits or expenses, in dollar terms. I am also speaking of it as a way of relating sales volume (physical and dollar) to the entire company structure of men, machinery and buildings, materials purchases, and money allocations.

Physical and dollar budgets, and their counterpart *pro formas* extended into the future, are the only comprehensive model of the firm we have.

I am no accountant, and I have no particular allegiance to the field. However, in all of the issues of *Management Science, Operations Research,* and *Econometrica* combined, I have never seen a model which can reduce every part of a company to numbers, in all its complexity, right down to the allocation of most detailed resources, and interrelate every part to every other part, as can a well-conceived system of expense budgets, capital budgets, and cash flows.

Any apology for financial accounting, which must be made in the face of newer developments, must be made either because the budget was misused as only a historical record, rather than as a *pro forma* prediction, or because the rules of public accounting have blinded the controllers and prevented them from being flexible in allocating money differently for internal planning purposes than they do for public balance sheet and profit statement purposes.

Wanted: methods plus intuition

If I were hiring a planning man to staff my headquarters planning department, I would want to make sure that he had at least a broad knowledge or acquaintance with financial accounting methods, if not a more detailed knowledge about how to enter transactions on the books. Perhaps accounting departments can also be criticized for not utilizing the methods of mathematics and statistics for improving the precision of forecasted figures that go into the balance sheet and income statement.

In line with this kind of knowledge, the techniques variously called 'managerial economics', and particularly knowledge of the discounted cashflow method of determining profitability of investment, seem to me to be mandatory for a good planner. I am not suggesting that this be applied blindly as a formula, but the staff man should at least know enough about the method to see whether or not it is wise to apply it to his specific company.

At the same time, I do not mean to belittle the methods of traditional statistics, such as correlation analysis, time series analysis, frequency distribution inference, and the like. Neither do I mean to imply that the higher level planner can get by today without some knowledge or acquaintance* with the mathematical techniques of linear programming, queuing theory, stochastic processes, and so on. Both statistics and mathematics can be used profitably to find which figures are most reliable for use in the *pro forma* balance sheet and income projections.

In addition to knowledge of this sort, I believe an intuitive kind of knowledge of the clinical or diagnostic method, starting with strengths and weaknesses of a company, is extremely helpful to the planner. This method, championed first by the Harvard Business School, is a fine way for the planner to avoid jumping to superficial conclusions, to stimulate his own depth-thinking, to promote creativity in solutions, to cut through a complex problem finding its essential important factors, and to develop a sense of timing in various decisions.

Decision matrix method

Finally, it seems to me that the decision matrix method, variously labeled part of 'operations research', 'game theory', or 'decision theory', represents a more important methodology for the high level planner than do the mathematical formulas in more empirical investigation.

This is definitely a logical method, not a factual or empirical method. As such, it is quite suited to the broad kind of thinking required in long-range, top-management, judgemental decisions.

It is important to recognize that all of these methodologies are becoming, in themselves, a competitive weapon. Those companies which can increase revenues or lower costs by their use will have a competitive advantage over those which ignore them. It is also important to recognize that they, in themselves, quite over and above the substantive complexity of the internal and external planning system, definitely add to the complexity of the planning task. This being true, it is even more unlikely that the line executives of organizations will have the degree of knowledge of them that I see as necessary.

Wisdom through security

One final point must be made about the mental qualities of the planner. We have already mentioned some social skills and attitudes, some personal

* This term, initiated by the psychologist Carl Rogers, implies a relatively broad kind of knowledge, rather than a 'scientific', 'knowledge about' these techniques. Someone, of course, must have this kind of knowledge also. But to say that all planners must have detailed specializations in operations research is equivalent to saying that all presidents should be accountants.

223

qualities of independence and dependence, and some substantive and methodological knowledge which the planner must have stored in his head.

At this point, we must inject some attitudes which he should hold regarding the use of his knowledge. In vast open-end, complex action problems, we all know that there are no formulas. At best, the planner can use these knowledge frameworks only as guides, and he must have the wisdom and judgement to know when they work and when they do not; when they are applicable and when common sense is preferable.

People who latch on to formulas and methods, and try to apply them with an almost fanatical zeal to action type problems, are people who have low degrees of personal security. One way this sort of person can make his world more orderly, more secure, and less confused as a place to live, is to catalog everything neatly into formulas. In such a situation, he has knowledge, but not wisdom; methodology, but not judgement.

Therefore, the last comment I would like to make about the qualifications of a person to fill the planning role is that he should have enough security, in other facets of his life, to maintain his judgement along with his science, logic, and brilliance. He should not have so much security, however, that he becomes dependent, self-satisfied, and content to conform to the usual ways of operating in the organization.

References

1. For a recent book which clarifies the reasons for the trend towards more planning, see HEILBRONNER, ROBERT L. *The Future as History.* New York: Harper, 1960.
2. For further substantiation of this reasoning, see SUMMER, C. E. 'The Managerial Mind.' *Harvard Bsns Rev.,* January 1959.
3 For a description of the managerial process, in terms of group dynamics, see LIPPITT, RONALD *et al. The Dynamics of Planned Change.* New York: Harcourt Brace, 1958.
4. An appreciation of the real complexity of large organizations, and the two tendencies mentioned, can be had from MERTON, ROBERT, *Social Theory and Social Structure.* Glencoe, Illinois: The Free Press, 1948.
5. For a penetrating study of this question, see HOOK, SIDNEY, *The Hero in History.* Beacon Press, 1953, especially pp. 113-18 and 153-4.

13. Planning for change: Organizing for companywide action

Walter B. Schaffir

The establishment of corporate planning as a more or less formalized function within a business enterprise is predicted, above all else, on the desire to bring about innovation and change. Bringing about change naturally requires many important steps other than organizational ones, but the structural arrangements within the company do much to help or hinder the introduction of change.

Over the past decade, a host of activities has sprung up in scores of companies, under such labels as 'long-range' or 'corporate' planning. These activities cover anything from long-range market projections to short-term budgeting, from acquisition search to internal management consultation, and from a parttime job of the assistant to the president to full-fledged planning staffs.

A systematic approach to corporate planning recognizes two key elements: first, the imposition of a planning discipline on the present operations (i.e., the establishment of a planning system for each division of the organization and the maintenance of this system); and, second, a reappraisal of the nature of the business and of the direction in which it should be heading.

Planning becomes long-range not because it attempts to span five or ten years rather than two or three, but rather because it comes to grips with the opportunities and problems that have a fundamental impact on the organization's long-range future. It must be solidly founded on, and be a

• Reprinted by permission of the publisher from *Management Review,* June 1965. © 1965 by the American Management Association, Inc.

logical extension of, planning for the immediate future. For this reason, the terms 'corporate planning' or 'corporate development' are probably more appropriate, since they denote concern for the entire range of business planning—both short- and long-range—and for the corporate enterprise as a whole.

A separate function?

Is it legitimate to single out and organize the planning function as a separate entity? Some managers believe that planning should not be carved away from other management activities, since planning is one of any manager's most important tasks. To organize for planning elsewhere not only encourages the particular manager to ignore this responsibility, but creates a cleavage between planning and execution that is detrimental to overall performance.

Others, however, believe that the manager who is charged with 'getting stuff out the door' by the end of the week, or producing a profit by the end of the quarter, is under the kind of constant pressure that makes planning difficult—and that places little reward on stopping and taking a fresh look at fundamental objectives, basically different modes of operation, and potential new opportunities.

Moreover, fundamental corporate planning usually requires the kind of background study that is possible only through full-time effort, painstaking research, and application of specialized skills and techniques for which the operating manager seldom has the time, training, or inclination.

A growing trend

In industry today, it is becoming increasingly popular to organize planning as a separate corporate activity. A recent survey by the Stanford Research Institute indicates that approximately 20 per cent of the 3600 US manufacturing firms, whose annual sales exceed ten million dollars, follow formal planning procedures and have some form of full-time planning staff. Among the largest publicly held US companies, 60 per cent are conducting their planning on a formal basis, and of those who do not, 60 per cent intend to institute a program in the near future.

The National Industrial Conference Board throws an interesting sidelight on these observations. They found corporate planning units in more than half of the decentralized, divisionalized companies they studied, and in less than a third of the centralized, functionally organized companies. The reason for this undoubtedly lies in the need to counteract the centrifugal forces of decentralization by providing a better basis for corporate unity and purpose.

226

The place of planning

It may seem trite to suggest that corporate planning should report 'to the top'; there is not a specialty in management that has not claimed this privilege as a requisite for its effectiveness. Nevertheless, it is clear that corporate planning, being concerned with the fundamental nature of the business and with the entire scope of the organization, cannot be effective unless it reports to top management. The real question is *where* at the top corporate planning can function most effectively. To locate corporate planning properly, two questions should be posed:

1 What is the real mission of corporate planning?

2 What particular individual (as distinct from the particular position) is best qualified and motivated, and enjoys the required prestige within the company, to make it successful?

Organizational location

If the principal mission of corporate planning is to undertake broad background studies for guidance of divisional efforts or to offer management consultation type assistance to divisions, reporting to the executive vice-president who is responsible for operating the divisions may be best. If the company's basic direction has already been determined, and the principal mission is to evaluate and negotiate acquisitions, placing corporate planning under the top financial executive may be appropriate. If planning is charged primarily with providing a basis for controlling divisions, the controller may be responsible for this. Where it is to determine the direction of central research as the primary means for expansion and growth, responsibility might be placed under the vice-president for research. Where the major mission of the planning group is to crystallize the direction of corporate development, it will work best directly under the chief executive.

Among *Fortune's* '500', according to the Stanford Research Institute, about 230 have a single individual in charge of corporate planning. Over three-quarters of these men report to the chief operating executive (president, executive vice-president, or chairman). The rest report to various vice-presidents.

Status in the company

In addition to organizational location, status of the responsible executive within the company's management must be considered. Location can be determined by looking at the company's organization chart; status can be found only from the reactions of key people. Organization and status are, of course, not unrelated. The status of an executive reporting to the president is ordinarily higher than that of a man further down the line. Nevertheless, an

227

assistant to the president, whose calibre or personal acceptance throughout the organization leaves something to be desired, cannot be expected to spearhead a major improvement program of this type sucessfully. Neither can the man whose glorious performance was in the past and who is now 'kicked upstairs' to do long-range planning while awaiting retirement. Sometimes, it is preferable to put corporate planning under an executive whose stature within the company is ideal for the purpose, even though his organizational location is not.

To be successful, corporate planning should be a dynamic influence on top management's decision-making process. It is relatively sterile, for example, to organize a corporate planning activity to develop and present recommendations that are then deliberated elsewhere. The corporate planning head should have the opportunity of participating in the top decision-making process. This is important not only because he must be 'in the know' and fully aware of top management's viewpoint in order to guide his planning intelligently, but also because he should be able to inject the longer-range viewpoint during the deliberation of key issues, whenever opportunities present themselves. In this manner, corporate planning becomes part of the organization's fabric, rather than merely a matter of formal reports. Corporate planning heads invariably consider the key to success as being not so much in their planning ability (good planners can be recruited), but rather in their rapport with top management and in their ability to sense and respond to what management wants to accomplish.

Relations with divisions

Establishing constructive relations between corporate planning and the product-type divisions within a decentralized business enterprise it important for several reasons:

1 Division heads are likely to be represented in the top council that will approve the recommendations of corporate planning, and many of the recommendations will undoubtedly concern the well-being and future growth of the divisions themselves.

2 The corporate group cannot hope to become expert in the fields of the company with which many divisional personnel have been associated for years. Corporate planning must rely on the divisions for much information, guidance, and advice.

3 A corporate staff group is always suspect—at least in the beginning. Not only does it constitute a threat of interference in local affairs, but its mere existence often tends to imply a criticism of divisional performance.

To keep this relationship clear and workable, it is necessary to have a well-thought-through concept of the role and responsibility of the corporate planner.

The planner's function

There appears to be rather general agreement on the futility of masterminding plans in one corner of the organization for obedient execution elsewhere. The successful corporate planner is most often the one who sees to it that there is a plan, that the planning gets done—rather than one who does the planning himself. Except for planning in the direction of new fields to enter (outside the scope of present divisional businesses) and for planning concerned with matters of overall corporate policy and concern, planning is best done by the organization that is to make those plans come true.

The corporate planner functions as a catalyst. He establishes the system and the discipline to make planning function successfully; he is instrumental in reviewing subplans and in pulling them together into a cohesive corporate plan. He provides format, structure, and basic premises. He controls the planning process, sees that deadlines are met, and requirements adhered to. Most importantly, he is the corporate conscience, representing the longer-range view and defending the company's longer-term interests and plans against encroachment by short-term decisions. But he recognizes the difference between a plan suggested, or even imposed from the top down, and one prepared and signed by the organization that must ensure its success. The former tend to remain a topic of conversation; the latter becomes a commitment to be executed.

The central staff

Ideally, then, the central corporate planning staff should be responsible for:

1 Developing overall corporate goals (i.e., growth, profit, other objectives).

2 Educating, stimulating, and counseling division management to undertake as much planning as possible within their own area of jurisdiction. Any headquarters staff must perform a missionary function and serve as management's nagging conscience within its scope of responsibility.

3 Reviewing divisional plans and proposals for completeness, consistency of argument, adequacy of goals, and so forth.

4 Integrating divisional plans into a total corporate plan. This requires the development of guides, formats, standards, and procedures as a basis for divisional plans, to insure that they will be capable of being integrated.

5 Providing broad background studies of a more fundamental and long-range nature than divisions can afford to undertake for themselves, or studies that are of benefit to two or more divisions. For example, a central staff may project the general business conditions and specify the basic assumptions on which divisional planning is to be based.

6 Coordinating problems and programs involving two or more divisions.

229

7 Providing specialized consultation, talent, and techniques to assist the divisions in their own planning.

8 Undertaking planning in areas outside the current scope of the divisions (i.e., plans to enter new fields).

9 Serving as consultants to help top corporate management evaluate the proposals of the divisions.

10 Auditing the planning activities of the divisions.

The divisional staffs

Divisional planning staffs should do all the planning that division management is willing and able to undertake, as long as it is not likely to interfere with the plans of other divisions or to jeopardize corporate goals. The principle of 'federalism' is applicable here, as it is to problems of decentralized management generally. Divisions of the corporate organization should be free to act, except in decision areas specifically reserved for top management.

The implementation of this division of planning responsibility requires divisional counterparts of the corporate planning group. These divisional focal points may be individuals or entire departments—or even part-time individuals. The basic requirement is for some one person to act as a point of divisional contact for the corporate group and, in turn, to promote the planning point of view within his own organization. The divisional planning activity's relation to division management and corporate planning is an organizational problem that is common to many staff functions. The general consensus appears to be that the divisional staff should have direct line responsibility to the division manager, but functional responsibility to the corporate staff. Most people in business today act as if they were certain what this means, and as if they accepted this semantic possibility as an organizational reality. In practice, it is probably an irreconcilable dilemma. The tone of this dual relationship will vary with the strength and status of the particular personalities involved and the pattern of other managerial relationships.

Lack of manpower

Another organizational problem in the area of headquarters-divisional relationships arises when there is simply not sufficient depth of managerial manpower and technical talent or time available within a division to establish a divisional counterpart to corporate planning. Should the corporate staff attempt to plug this gap by doing divisional planning itself—at the risk of possibly fostering local resistance? Or should the creation of a local planning activity be encouraged, even though the division may not want it or feel it can afford it at what may be a critical stage of the division's development?

The answer to this 'trade-off' will depend on the relative urgency, as well as the economics, of the situation. In the smaller company, particularly when the divisional situation requires a major study, but not necessarily a great deal of continuous attention over the years to come, it may be most economical to have members of the corporate staff undertake occasional projects for the division, much in the same way as an outside consultant would be asked to do.

Other staff groups

It is obvious that a corporate planning staff must cooperate closely and maintain constructive and mutually beneficial relationships with such other corporate staff groups as finance, industrial engineering, operations research, management development, methods improvement, data-processing, and market research. It certainly must make sure that all these groups understand its aims and purposes within the corporate structure. In turn, corporate planning must understand the functions of these other staff groups, in order to take advantage of information that may already be available and of the advice and consultation that members of such groups may be able to offer.

A serious organizational problem is likely to arise here only if there is real or perceived overlap in the missions and functions of any of these groups with those of corporate planning. This is more likely to occur in the larger organization in which various activities have come into being over the years, some of which may already have responsibility for various specialized aspects of planning.

The problem in such cases is essentially one of organization planning and allocation of functions. This can seldom be solved by corporate planning itself. It may involve strong personalities with clashing interests, ambitions, and prerogatives. The solution requires tact and patience. Sometimes it is possible to offer a rationale that enables more clear-cut division of responsibility.

Putting out fires

The opposite problem—a gap in management activities—is likely to occur in the smaller company that has lagged in the development of corporate services. Here, the planning staff will tend to be called on to perform a variety of functions that it may not consider germane to its principal mission. It is well to avoid a puritan attitude in this case. The opportunity to be of assistance is often a way to acceptance and cooperation, and it matters little in which area this assistance is rendered. Moreover, involvement in other divisional and corporate management problems is corporate planning's opportunity to acquire the background and insights that are prerequisites for intelligent

231

longer-range planning. The problem here is one of balance, and the danger arises from allowing the emphasis to swing from planning to putting out fires. It requires determination and well-developed priorities to stay on the course. However, some fire-fighting is good seasoning for the staff and helps them to keep their feet on the ground.

Planning and budgeting

The relationship between planning and budgeting is particularly important. There are cases where responsibility for both is lodged in the same department. However, different talents and backgrounds are required to make these functions work best. A budget is the essential and inescapable expression of a plan in financial terms. It brings into a common financial language—the only form in which final accountability can be rendered—the resources required and the pay-offs expected. Planning, on the other hand, makes sure that the budgets are appropriate to the goals desired.

The planning committee

An organizational device that is useful for introducing corporate planning and facilitating its acceptance, for opening channels of information, for fostering the divisional planning activities, and for guiding the planning effort, is the planning committee. Such a body usually consists of key executives who are influential within the organizational subunits they represent—men who can act as a sounding board for the corporate planning head and bridge the gap that may exist between the planning program and the established operations. By commenting on approaches and proposals, the members of the planning committee can help to fashion this program along lines that are productive in terms of existing concepts, traditions, and personalities; this may help to avoid ivory tower approaches which, though technically sound, may have little chance of acceptance within the culture of the organization involved. It is sometimes useful to include key individuals hostile to the program along with sympathetic members. Care must be taken, however, to prevent such a committee from being in a position to immobilize the corporate planning effort.

To strike an appropriate balance, the following points should be observed:

1 Have the corporate planning head serve as chairman of the planning committee, and limit the committee's role to one of advice only. The chairman will usually do well to heed such advice, but he is still free to make his own recommendations to the top.

2 To keep the agenda free of detail, the committee should consider specific proposals, not just meet for general discussion. Its attention should focus on broad issues, not matters of tactics and techniques.

3 Do not schedule committee meetings too frequently. Between meetings, the members of the committee should, of course, be accessible to the corporate planning head on an individual basis.

4 Meet on a carefully prepared agenda, and have proposed material distributed to members beforehand.

It is important that the initiative remain with the chairman, so that the committee does not become a vehicle for diluting the program, for passing the buck, for mutual backscratching, or, at worst, for bringing the program to a halt.

In spite of the many pitfalls of committee work, a steering committee of this type can serve a useful purpose. This role can also be filled by any top-management committee devoting some of its sessions to planning.

The planning department

A number of fundamental questions must be resolved in organizing a corporate planning department: size, composition, internal structure, and extent of responsibility.

How large an effort?

A concept that has met general acceptance today is that of 'minimum critical size' of effort. It has been found that in research, planning, and other improvement activities, it takes a certain minimum effort to obtain any significant results at all. In any research project—and corporate planning is just that—the relationship between input and output is not linear. One cannot hope to start with just a little bit of effort in the expectation that this will lead to a little bit of sound results. It is usually necessary to reach a certain plateau of effort before results become promising.

Minimal or sporadic research effort is likely to peter out and go to waste entirely. There is enough time to start some projects, but not enough to pursue them. There is neither enough opportunity to gather necessary background information nor enough time for following up and working out details of application. This inability to bring such an undersize effort to a significant conclusion, in turn, discourages further expenditure of time, and talents are diverted to 'more urgent' matters. The resulting vicious circle further dissipates effort until the project is abandoned entirely. Dribbles of planning here and there are usually a complete waste of time and effort.

This story of halfhearted improvement programs is commonplace in many organizations. It spans the entire scope from cost-reduction to long-range planning, and holds true in technical research as well. The problem is not that we cannot afford an adequate effort, but rather that we cannot afford to waste money on a halfhearted job.

What, then, is an adequate magnitude of effort? Obviously, this depends on the scope of problems to be solved and the types of results expected. A three-man acquisition group may be too large, but a ten-man internal consulting group, covering a wide range of services, may be inadequate. A smaller group with good project planning, a system of priorities, and the discipline to stick with them, is more productive than a larger group spread over a variety of frequently changing assignments. The size of the department depends also on the extent to which help is available from other staffs—both corporate and divisional.

Diversity is the key

Diversity rather than the size of the company is the crucial factor. For example, a company doing one-fifth the volume of another, in the same six fields, generally faces just as complex a corporate planning problem as its larger competitor. There are still six businesses to study and understand, six sets of division managements to deal with. It makes relatively little difference whether the size of any one of the divisions in question is 4000 or 400. On the other hand, the planning problem in the larger organization is certainly aggravated by sheer organizational and geographical distances, and by the number of subunits that must be serviced.

Another factor affecting the group's size is management's disposition to engage outside consultants. Despite the obvious advantages of having much of the planning activity performed by an internal staff for reasons of continuity, personal relationships, and proprietory aspects, outside consultants and similar services can be most useful and economical.

Under certain conditions, specific, well-delineated tasks within the long-range planning project may well be subcontracted. Among the advantages of doing this is that consultants are not as easily diverted to other tasks as are internal staff; and due to the periodic arrival of bills of frequently substantial magnitude, the time of the outside consultant is sometimes treated with greater care than that of the staff.

A minimum effort capable of producing significant results from a long-range planning program would probably consist of a head and one or two assistants. Since the man who heads the program is generally preoccupied with top-management liaison missionary work, and the development of a plan for planning, he tends to have little time for background research himself.

There is probably also a maximum effective size. This is determined by the rate at which the organization is able to absorb new concepts and ideas. There are probably few corporate planning groups whose professional planning staffs exceed a dozen or so.

Types of talent

Basically, planning staff members require personal qualities of imagination, initiative, organizational insight, independent judgement, and self-criticism. Also important is broad industrial experience and education, preferably with graduate work in one of the various management disciplines. Ideally, each individual member should be broadly flexible, yet contribute a particular speciality in depth.

As far as specific educational backgrounds are concerned, a corporate planning group should most likely include personnel trained in market research, industrial or management engineering, business administration, operations research, and economics. It should contain someone trained in the technologies in which the particular business operates, and probably someone with financial and accounting background, particularly if acquisition analysis or problems of management control are involved. Another possible requirement may be for someone with systems and procedures or data-processing experience. The diversity of backgrounds is, of course, a function of the size and mission of the group.

In recruiting the group, consideration should be given to a balance between individuals who know their way around the organization and enjoy a certain degree of acceptance and reputation, and fresh blood from the outside, who can bring new points of view and needed specialized skills.

Organizing the department

The alternatives in organizing a planning group are functional organization and task-force organization. In a functional set-up, the market research man does all market research, the industrial engineer all administrative analysis, etc. As the demand for market research or industrial engineering analysis increases, more specialists are added to the staff. As a result, the department soon grows into specialized subdivisions, each of which contributes its specialty to the problem at hand. These functional contributions are then coordinated and collated by the head of the group. This type of organization has many disadvantages:

1 It increases the burden on the chief, who cannot delegate any one project and who soon becomes a bottleneck.

2 It fosters a multilayer organizational hierarchy with its attending difficulties of communication, problems of status, and relative difficulty of access of members to each other.

3 Furthermore, it encourages parochialism and fails to foster the total management point of view so necessary in tackling corporate problems successfully.

Under the task-force pattern of organization, each team member has full responsibility for a particular project or for several projects. At the same time, each member serves as a consultant to other members of the group within his particular sphere of specialization. Thus, a man may be project leader of one task-force, possibly because this project has a predominant requirement for his particular specialty, and, at the same time, he may be a member of one or more other task-forces that also require his contribution. Each man is responsible for final results of his project, but also for bringing to bear effectively specialized advice available within the group.

The advantages of this form of organization are:

1 The corporate planning head can effectively delegate complete project responsiblity.

2 Each man is encouraged to adopt a total point of view and to integrate specialized advice (without becoming fully competent in all required specialities himself).

3 Everyone's job becomes enlarged and enriched, with the greater opportunity for career development and personal rewards and the satisfaction that this most likely entails.

4 The group's capability is broadened, as is the reservoir of potential successors to the post of the chief and to other positions of importance within the company.

Extent of responsibility

There is one more problem each management must face in setting up a corporate planning group: just what is to be its responsibility? Is it to be responsible for developing information for others to consider? For making recommendations and proposals? For seeing that such proposals are resolved and, once approved, are properly implemented? For monitoring performance after proposals are converted into action? What is the extent of the corporate planning group's responsibility in the event of failure?

The answer to these questions has organizational implications. A staff that must stay with its recommendations until they have proven themselves in the line of fire (a sound concept) requires different organization than one that leaves each project at the point of recommendation and goes on to the next.

Organizing for change

Corporate planning, then, is an organized, systematic approach to appraising the crucial problems and opportunities, the fundamental economic pattern, and the basic factors that underlie the business; to making explicit the policies and assumptions on which the business is to be based; and to clarifying the likely consequences of alternative, reasonable courses of action.

To implement this effectively requires many organizational considerations: the place of planning within the organization, corporate-divisional relations, interstaff relations, steering committees, and the organization of the planning department itself. All these require attention and deliberate decision. They are at the heart of the problem of organizing for change and innovation.

14. Organizing the corporate planning function

Basil W. Denning

A great many British companies have recently introduced or are in the process of introducing 'long-range planning'. The introduction of this activity on a systematic basis usually follows a fairly similar pattern whereby one senior executive feels the need for a more careful approach to problems of strategy and policy, informs himself about the nature of strategic and corporate planning and then persuades his senior colleagues to experiment with making a formal overall corporate plan for three, five, or seven years ahead.

Assuming that commitment is made to the experiment by top management, there immediately arises a host of organizational problems. Who is to do the planning? Do we need a special corporate planner and a new department? If, so, what will he and his department do that is not already done elsewhere? How will a planning department work with heads of divisions or functions who carry executive responsibility? Is corporate planning a staff or a line function?

American experience suggests that the answers to some of these problems are fairly clear. Corporate planning is a staff function which must have direct access to the chief executive. Indeed, it is more accurate to consider a corporate planner as an extension of the chief executive responsible for providing an objective analytical ability free from functional or executive responsibilities. Senior line executives must largely plan their own operations and projects while working within a framework of goals, objectives, policies, and standards set by top management, while special projects of a strategic nature may be planned at the centre. Any planning system must obtain

• Reproduced with permission from *Long-Range Planning*, Vol. 1, No. 4, June 1969.

executive involvement and motivation which is probably best achieved by dispersing planning responsibilities in this way.

Unfortunately, this general type of statement offers little detailed guidance to the corporate planner or to the chief executive with responsibility for organizing an effective planning process in his own company because of the organizational and personality structure, and the business characteristics of his particular firm. It is the purpose of this article to suggest a framework within which any company can systematically approach the definition of responsibility for those activities which need to be carried out in a full corporate planning process.

Corporate planning can most usefully be regarded as a process over time involving strategic planning, project planning and operational planning. As with any other process, planning can then be broken down into a number of discrete activities and with these activities isolated and defined, it becomes possible to attach formal responsibility to a particular person or group for that activity and to design the necessary information flows to enable that person or group to carry it out.

As part of some current research into the organization of corporate planning among the top 300 companies in Britain, information was sought along these lines with particular reference to the role of the corporate planning department, if one existed. (See Fig. 14.1) In the lefthand column, a list of activities which need to be carried out in any organization doing effective corporate planning was specified. It was assumed that the formal responsibilities of the corporate planning department in each of these areas could be one of four types:

1 Responsibility to initiate that activity with the detailed work being done elsewhere.

2 Responsibility to coordinate that activity with the detailed work being done elsewhere.

3 Responsibility to do the detailed work.

4 No responsibility.

In certain cases, the department could have responsibility for both initiation and the detailed work. No inquiry about the decision-making responsiblity of the planning department was made, on the assumption that decisions would be made by line executives with or without the help and advice of their planners. Companies were asked to mark the responsibility of the corporate planning department against each activity and some contrasting results in different companies are noted at the end of this article.

One of the points which emerged as a byproduct of the research was that, when companies were asked to delineate the responsibilities of their corporate planning departments by giving a highly specific statement of the responsibilities of the department, they were able to do so. A second relevant

Activity / Responsibility of corporate planning department	Responsibility for initiation	Responsibility for coordination	Responsibility for detailed work	No responsibility
Economic forecasting				
Technological forecasting				
Establishment of assumptions about the future				
Economic analysis of markets				
Sales forecasting				
Estimation of product life cycles				
Determination of corporate goals				
Appraisal of top management's attitudes				
Examination of company's strengths and weaknesses				
Evaluation of top management's proposals				
Determination of markets in which to operate				
Development of new products				
Market development				
Manpower projections				
Capital budgeting				
Preparation of investment proposals				
Planning new facilities				
Integration of divisional plans				

Figure 14.1   Framework for organizing long-range corporate planning

240

point was that companies were asked to indicate if any key activities of their corporate planning department were omitted. No suggestions were made that there were any additional activities. Clearly, this could arise from the broad interpretation which could be given to activities such as 'Evaluation of top management's proposals', and this item could usefully be broken down into more detailed areas such as: investigation of possible acquisitions, proposals to licence, or proposals to move outside the present field of business.

Nevertheless, it would seem that the use of this simple framework to specify more accurately the work of a corporate planning department stands up to the test of practice. If this is so, then it can provide a useful framework for considering the role that a corporate planning department should play in any one organization. For example, in a multidivisional organization it is possible to ask questions such as:

1 Are divisional managers to be responsible for the planning of new products or are these to be planned at the centre?

2 To what extent do we require a corporate planning department to prepare, assess, or coordinate, investment proposals?

3 Is it reasonable to expect operating divisions to have the expertise to make longer-term sales forecasts of key products?

The opportunity to ask precise questions of this type also enables top management to relate the design of the planning activity to another important dimension of top management's role, namely, the retention of planning power over key tasks. If, for example, in a highly technological company, decisions on product development are crucial, then it may be that the corporate planning staff needs to be given the function of detailed planning of new product development. Alternatively, if a company is constrained by shortage of capital and this is a key factor in a strategic development, it may be that the detailed work involved in capital budgeting needs to be carried out by the corporate planning staff. In other words, the adoption of a systematic approach to the analysis and synthesis of the planning process can be helpful to top management in applying the ideas of key task management to its organization for corporate planning.

The virtues of adopting a systematic approach along these lines lie in two fields. First, by detailed examination of the extent to which responsibility will be held by a division, a function or a planning department, the matter can perhaps be discussed rationally and an acceptable solution to the political problems be evolved. Second, if the role of the corporate planning department can be defined along these lines, it becomes possible to decide on the nature of staff and the information required to carry out the work allocated to them, two essentials of sound organizational practice.

It is not being suggested that the actual planning arrangements in any one company can be fully specified or that demarcation barriers should be erected and maintained. Nor, indeed, would this be desirable, since a large amount of the work done by an effective corporate planner is an influencing process carried out informally by virtue of the respect he commands at senior levels in the organization. Nevertheless, to rely entirely on informal processes in any organized activity can only too often be a recipe for ineffectiveness, and attempts to define boundaries of responsibility are usually an aid to efficiency in planning as in any other activity.

Some different organizational patterns

Underlying the research are some attempts to examine why companies introduce corporate planning and what they hope to achieve by it. Certainly, as a fact of life, one has to accept entirely different patterns of organization of the function as existing and being effective. To a great extent, these differences have historically been viewed as having no underlying rationale, or merely being preferences of particular chief executives.

An alternative approach to this puzzling problem of organizational differences would be to argue that the introduction of systematic long-range planning may be a response to quite different needs in different situations. Again, relating the long-range planning process to top management's role, there appear to be two vital parts of this role which planning systems can assist. The first is formal analytical consideration of strategy through the whole process of environmental and strategic appraisal and the formal setting of objectives and goals. The second arises in large complex organizations where a major task is faced in the coordination of diverse product groups, divisions, and subsidiary units into a coherent whole. Different companies, at different times, may find that one or other of these needs is dominant and under these circumstances it would be reasonable to expect that the organization of the planning function would differ markedly in response to the different needs.

Strategic planning is of the greatest importance where a company operates in an area of rapid market or technological change accompanied by high-capital intensity, since these conditions impose the greatest strategic risk. For companies in this technical-economic position, systematic strategic planning becomes a key managerial response if profitable survival is to be assured. It would not, therefore, be unreasonable to anticipate that under these circumstances a corporate planning department will be oriented primarily towards strategic planning, and the task which it will be required to perform will incorporate a great deal of detailed analytical work exploring strategic alternatives in key areas. This would give a particular role definition to the corporate planning function, and dictate the type and kind of staff considered necessary to execute this role.

This state of affairs would seem to be exemplified in the profile of the

242

corporate planning department shown in Fig. 14.2. Company A is a major operator in the area of computer and data-processing systems. The rate of technological change is very rapid, the investment in research and development for hardware is very high, and this is aggravated by substantial investment in the development of software, programmes and programming techniques. The risk element in the financial posture of such a company is not dissimilar to a company with more conventional characteristics of high capital intensity, normally thought of as possessing expensive single purpose assets with a high ratio of fixed capital per employee. Under these circumstances, the key role of systematic long-range planning would need to be strategic with a great deal of centralized effort and work in all key strategic areas.

A glance at Fig. 14.2 indicates that the corporate planning department in this company is responsible for detailed work in all the areas listed except for technological forecasting and appraisal of top management's attitudes. Technological forecasting involves a special knowledge and expertise which can probably best be performed by a small expert group with strong research links which would not necessarily fit inside the corporate planning department.

It seems reasonable to suggest that the way in which the corporate planning function has been organized in this company is primarily a response to the special needs of a company in a situation of major opportunity and high risk, where strategic considerations are of paramount importance and strategic rethinking is necessary at frequent intervals in an environment of rapid change.

Compare this situation with a company of quite different characteristics. Company B, whose planning department profile is shown in Fig. 14.3 was, at the time of inquiry, a large integrated steel and engineering concern with many subsidiaries both in the United Kingdom and abroad, covering a vast range of products and markets. In the United Kingdom, subsidiaries were organized into semiautonomous product groups, and each product group had several subsidiaries operating in related but separate fields. Through the group as a whole there was substantial intercompany trading, especially in the supply of steel to the engineering groups, and this imposed a requirement for vertical coordination. A further factor was that the demand for the products of many of the engineering companies was fundamentally derived from activities in other major industrial fields.

Under these circumstances, two of the most difficult and critical tasks of top management are the coordination of activities across an enormous product-market spectrum, and the need to assess the effects of investment in one area with activity in another. Under such circumstances, a critical function of formal long-range planning can well be the operation of a managerial system which allows more effective coordination of activity

Activity \ Responsibility of corporate planning department	Responsibility for initiation	Responsibility for coordination	Responsibility for detailed work	No responsibility
Economic forecasting	X		X	
Technological forecasting		X		
Establishment of assumptions about the future			X	
Economic analysis of markets			X	
Sales forecasting			X	
Estimation of product life cycles			X	
Determination of corporate goals			X	
Appraisal of top management's attitudes		X		
Examination of company's strengths and weaknesses			X	
Evaluation of top management's proposals			X	
Determination of markets in which to operate			X	
Development of new products			X	
Market development			X	
Manpower projections			X	
Capital budgeting			X	
Preparation of investment proposals			X	
Planning new facilities			X	
Integration of divisional plans			X	

Figure 14.2   Profile of company A: A large computer and data processing company

Activity / Responsibility of corporate planning department	Respon-sibility for initiation	Respon-sibility for coordination	Respon-sibility for detailed work	No respon-sibility
Economic forecasting				X
Technological forecasting				X
Establishment of assumptions about the future				X
Economic analysis of markets				X
Sales forecasting				X
Estimation of product life cycles				X
Determination of corporate goals		X		
Appraisal of top management's attitudes				X
Examination of company's strengths and weaknesses		X		
Evaluation of top management's proposals		X		
Determination of markets in which to operate				X
Development of new products				X
Market development				X
Manpower projections				X
Capital budgeting				X
Preparation of investment proposals		X		
Planning new facilities				X
Integration of divisional plans		X		

Figure 14.3   Profile of company B: A large integrated steel and engineering company

between product groups, between domestic and foreign companies, and between raw material producers and finished engineering goods companies.

The profile of the responsibilities of the corporate planning department in this company seems to reflect this essential coordinative need. The department has virtually no responsibility for detailed work, and its defined responsibilities lie entirely in the field of coordinating various activities. Operationally, these are concentrated in the area of coordinating investment proposals and divisional plans, and, at the strategic level, there is a responsibility to bring together heads of staff departments or chief executives of product groups for strategic review. This line of argument would be supported by other evidence arising from the present research where there is a marked tendency for systematic corporate planning to have been introduced where more complex organizational structures have been created due to size or the geographical dispersion of operations.

Even within the limits imposed by an attempt to define responsibilities in this area and the possibilities of misunderstanding inherent in any questionnaire approach, it is clear that the concept of the planning function in company B is of a totally different order to that of company A. It seems probable that differences of this order are not merely responses to different cultural patterns of the two organizations, but are likely to be related to different basic needs in the two situations. In company B, the emphasis is clearly on the need for a mechanism to coordinate a wide range of activities under conditions of substantial decentralization, an organizational structure relevant to the particular operating needs of the business.

Companies A and B represent, to a certain extent, two poles of possible organization of the planning function where different circumstances pose different critical top management needs. Most companies probably need to gain from their planning systems a more effective response both to strategic problems and coordination problems. Company C illustrates this rather more diverse pattern of organization (see Fig. 14.4). The company is a major chemical manufacturer with comparatively autonomous product divisions operating predominantly in the United Kingdom, but with important overseas activities. The company is capital intensive, exists in a situation of fairly rapid technological change and is in a growth field where there are substantial opportunities both domestically and internationally. Heavy investment is needed both in fixed assets for process operations and in research and development.

Top management of company C, therefore, faces substantial strategic problems, as well as important problems of coordination. Under these circumstances, it would be expected that the profile of responsibility of the corporate planning department would reflect these dual needs and Fig. 14.4 offers something of a compromise profile between the previous two companies. It is of interest to note that the department does have

246

Activity \ Responsibility of corporate planning department	Responsibility for initiation	Responsibility for coordination	Responsibility for detailed work	No responsibility
Economic forecasting	X		X	
Technical forecasting				X
Establishment of assumptions about the future	X		X	
Economic analysis of markets				X
Sales forecasting				X
Estimation of product life cycles				X
Determination of corporate goals	X		X	
Appraisal of top management's attitudes				
Examination of company's strengths and weaknesses	X		X	
Evaluation of top management's proposals				
Determination of markets in which to operate	X		X	
Development of new products				X
Market development				X
Manpower projections				X
Capital budgeting	X		X	
Preparation of investment proposals		X		
Planning new facilities				X
Integration of divisional plans		X		

Figure 14.4   Profile of company C: A large chemical manufacturer

247

responsibility for detailed work in the area of capital budgeting, and, given the characteristics of this business with its capital intensive, single-purpose plants, this would be a critical dimension of strategy. The other activities of the department reflect the mixture of strategic development work and the coordination needs of a complex organization.

Summary

Systematic corporate planning in large organizations is introduced in response to key needs of top managers in their particular situations. It is suggested that these needs can well be different, and can broadly be classified into strategic development needs and coordination needs. The extent to which these needs are dominant should be reflected in the organization of the planning activity.

In organizing a corporate planning process, the first step can usefully be to define the key needs and, subsequently, to adopt a systematic approach to organizing the work of the corporate planner and his department. This can be done by listing the activities necessary, by specifying the extent of responsibility which the corporate planning department should have in each activity, and allocating the remainder of the tasks to other appropriate departments or divisions. Such a framework allows reasoned consideration for organizational decisions and, once these decisions have been taken, provides both a clearer task definition for appointment of staff and the design of information flows relevant to the responsibilities allocated. A framework for analysing these responsibilities has been suggested and the framework stands the test of practice in the principal companies in the United Kingdom involved in formal, systematic long-range planning.

15. How to assure poor long-range planning for your company

George A. Steiner

A method of music-making in the Balkans is called 'singing with book'. The performer lays a book on his lap, places his hand over it, and then proceeds to sing without a single reference to the volume—which he cannot read anyway. Pleasing music is often produced this way, it is said. The analogy with planning should not be pushed too far, but it is true that too many managers are performing their planning function without reference to what is available to help them. Sometimes the 'music' is pleasing. Sometimes it is not.

In working with actual planning programs, and in combining the literature of planning for helpful hints to improve the process in practice, I have developed 25 reasons for faulty long-range planning. These are presented in this short note.

At the outset, I should like to say that these are offered for whatever help they may give a practicing manager who is having problems with his long-range planning or one who is interested in avoiding problems in the future. They are not meant for academic scholars, although some may find them useful. Discussions of the points specified can be found in the literature on planning, but not all managers have the time to study what is written to try to find these warnings of pitfalls to be avoided or signals to be heeded.

The observations are classified into three categories to help further focus the attention of managers on critical aspects of planning. Naturally, additional categories can be framed, but the three given seem to me to be appropriately comprehensive in scope. Each of the 25 points listed can, of course, be subdivided, and each can be elaborated at great length. My purpose, however, is to be brief.

The items given are not of equal importance. Failure of top management to support long-range planning (item 1) will inevitably be fatal to the process. Failure to allow adequate time and to spend sufficient money for planning (item 11) may cause poor planning, but will not necessarily be fatal. Nor are the solutions to shortcomings, when present, equally clear. In larger enterprises, for example, planning staffs are important in the process, and problems sometimes arise because their work is not sufficiently linked to those who must perform the planned tasks (item 24). The solution to this problem may be most difficult to find. On the other hand, resolution of a problem arising from failure on the part of management to decide (item 3) is not difficult—it is to decide!

The items listed in each of the three categories are not meant to be exclusive to that category. There is substantial overlapping. For example, item 8 can apply to categories I and III as well as to II. Item 24 can appropriately be included in category II. Overlap results from the fact that the planning program of a company is a mass of interlacing forces and activities that simply cannot be encompassed in a short, mutually exclusive classification.

The list is not a veiled 'how-to-do-it' prescription for long-range planning. Nor should it be considered an indirect attempt to suggest a comprehensive body of principles for long-range planning. Indirectly, of course, the list does evoke fundamental principles for sophisticated planning. Rephrasing of some items will yield acceptable principles. However, there are many more principles of effective planning than suggested by the list.

With all the shortcomings of this inventory—and there are many—the itemization may prove helpful to practicing managers as a checklist, a framework, and a stimulus to thinking. If so, the leverage of this thumbnail list can be substantial.

Twenty-five fundamental and common reasons for faulty long-range planning

I. Conceiving and understanding the process of planning

1 Lack of top management support, participation, and guidance.

2 Failure of top management to make decisions on the basis of planning.

3 Inability to clarify the role of long-range planning staff either at corporate or divisional levels, or at both levels.

4 Failure to understand that a long-range planning program cannot be introduced overnight and to expect to produce miraculous results immediately.

5 Failure to understand that long-range planning is a continuous function, not one pursued on an *ad hoc* basis.

6 Failure to recognize that planning requires change, and that the interaction of plans on people and institutions must be understood by management.

7 Failure to understand that planning is not implanted on an organization, but is part of the whole managerial process, and, as such, fits into and is subject to the principles and practices of it.

II. Developing an adequate plan and establishing realistic objectives, policies, and strategies

8 Failure to plan the plan; and, conversely, playing with planning rather than doing it and reaching conclusions.

9 Failure to develop appropriate and reasonably concrete goals for planning.

10 Failure to develop realistic strategies, policies, and operating plans to achieve goals.

11 Failure to allow adequate time and to spend sufficient money for planning.

12 Weak and ineffective staff in planning.

13 Failure to inject flexibility in planning and avoiding abandonment at the slightest deviation of actuality from anticipation.

14 Failure to assure proper review of planning documents.

15 Failure to assure proper interaction between long-range and short-range plans.

III. Organization of procedures for effective planning

16 Organization not planning-conscious.

17 Lack of understanding of organization, authority, procedures, and nomenclature of planning.

18 Failure to put plans in writing and make available for authorized personnel.

19 Failure to have director of planning (or planning staff) report to appropriate executive, and at top level.

20 Depending too much upon one man or upon committees.

21 Failure to assure participation of appropriate personnel, especially those required to implement the plan.

22 Failure to develop appropriate long-range planning staff in divisions of company.

23 Failure to provide sufficient instructions and basic data to operating divisions.

24 Separating planning from operating.

25 Failure to assure adequate machinery to implement plans.

251

PART FIVE: Corporate planning in different industries and companies

Throughout this book, attention has been concentrated on the need to develop a relevant managerial process which will help top management to do its job. While at one level of generality this job can be defined in common terms, the moment one moves to any specific industry or company different aspects of the job assume different degrees of importance and different key factors emerge as determinants of success.

Part 5 examines some aspects of corporate planning in companies with quite different critical characteristics, where the vital planning needs are essentially different. In chapter 16, on planning in technical industries, M. E. Salveson raises questions about the need to plan for the maintenance of an innovatory culture as being the most effective response to an accepted inability to predict in conditions of acute technological uncertainty. In this setting, a key planning need is the creation of a corporate culture with special characteristics that will encourage a flow of invention and innovation whose detailed specifications cannot necessarily be forecast.

In Chapter 17 N. Berg lifts up the very different problems associated with conglomerate companies, where the vital issues centre round the proportions of total resources to be employed in different business areas, and the rational allocation of funds to those areas. The problems of risk in different areas, perceptions of the company in the various fields of activity, the importance and difficulty of project selection, and the impact of different organizational reward systems are all brought out as critical areas of success or failure in the special structure of the conglomerate company. The article is equally apposite to multidivisional companies operating in a defined but broad area of technologies, such as engineering, where the common thread between divisions is tenuous.

In chapter 18, M. H. Pryor, Jr, examines certain problems associated with corporate planning in multinational companies. Even more critical than with the large multidivisional company is the question of how strategy is formulated and by whom. Where sections of the company operate in very different political and socio-economic environments, where cultural factors affect manager's behaviour in quite different ways, where measurement for control purposes is almost always bedevilled by tax and exchange considerations, very different planning concepts need to be developed. These include rational decisions on the types and amount of risk in different areas of the world, the assessment of national plans in different countries, the development and maintenance of an effective supply strategy, and planning the executive cadre in a multiple language organization.

Finally, S. Tilles and A. P. Contas examine a neglected area, the family firm. Here, in addition to the issues of product market posture, vital questions of authority, obligations, ownership, and finance provide a different framework for planning from that of the publicly owned company. In these firms, unless these issues are planned, expectations of survival or continuity at the critical moments of the family firm's life must be sharply lowered. While family firms tend to be limited in size, throughout a large part of the industrialized world they form a significant portion of business whose special problems deserve systematic consideration.

The very different planning problems in these four chapters cannot offer a comprehensive treatment of the many varieties of business firms. The sample may, however, go some way to illuminating the dissimilarities between companies, the need to isolate the key factors for planning, the importance of establishing priorities in terms of planning needs, and the importance of devising a specially designed, systematic process relevant to the needs of any one company.

(Editor)

16. Long-range planning in technical industries

Melvin E. Salveson

Long-range planning is becoming the *sine qua non* of every corporation which requires a continuing flow of profit for its survival and growth. The factors demanding increased LRP are many and impelling; the more important ones are summarized below. At the same time, the factors mitigating against effective LRP are many and impelling, and also are summarized below. Out of these countervailing forces, a broader view to LRP is suggested here. This view is concerned more with establishing the conditions for long-range 'all-weather' *viability* and *profit;* less with attempting to pinpoint specific plans, steps, and events in an amorphous, opaque future. Thus, long-range planning, as defined here, is concerned with discovering and adapting total business operations to the strong patterns and trends which underline progress and change in an industry or in the economy.

The trends which create the heaviest need for LRP are found in the technical industries. Thus, this report is orientated to those industries. In large part, it is based on studies performed by the Center For Advanced Management for an electromechanical and electronics manufacturer in a highly technical industry.

Technical industry

A 'technical' industry is defined broadly as one in which there is a high degree of scientific or technological knowledge required for performing its processes, for designing its product, or for managing its operations. Typical technical

● Reproduced with permission from *The Journal of Industrial Engineering*, September/October 1959, pp. 339-346.

industries include petrochemicals, electronic, aircraft and missile, pharmaceuticals, etc. An insistent problem in these industries requiring LRP is technological, or other 'change'. However, the change is qualitatively different from 'non-technical' industries, and this difference creates the heightened need for LRP. The women's garment industry illustrates the basic difference between change in the technical versus the non-technical industries. In that industry, for example, there is change from season to season, year to year, and period to period. A recent scientific study by psychologists indicated that these changes are motivated largely by the value of avoiding boredom in the wearer's appeal or attractiveness. Thus, different portions of the anatomy are emphasized under successive style changes; the style at one time emphasizing legs, at another the bust, at another some other portion of the anatomy. The important or significant factor here is, however, that there is no discernible change in the female anatomy. For our purposes, it has always had these components, and, happily, probably always will. The change is only in its covering apparel. Thus, new knowledge, new form, or new utility is neither created by the style change nor induces that change.

On the other hand, take the electronics industry as a counter-example. Change has been frequent in that industry, perhaps up to rate of change in the women's garment industry, but it has either been induced by or has resulted in new knowledge, new form, new utility. These, in turn, demand in that industry: new business enterprises, new equipment, new methods, differently trained personnel, etc. While some of the ideas and methods presented here may apply both to technical and non-technical industries, the emphasis in this analysis is on the changes, the underlying patterns, and the trends in the technical industries as these relate to long-range planning.

A case study

The study which is reported here was cued by a large manufacturer's loss of market position and profit. (Call it company A.) The loss could have been expected three years before it was felt, had top management been alert to the competitor's activities. But it would still have been too late to react and avoid the loss. Importantly, the whole mode of operation during these three years had been as good or better than before, so that the loss was not due to any deficiency in company A's current operations. Its difficulty arose because it was not concerned with those long-range activities necessary to keep its product and service competitive. The specific event which precipitated the problem for company A was a smaller competitor's introducing a product based on far more advanced technology, and thereby virtually obsoleting the company's leading line of products. But, the lead had been lost several years before the competitor's product appeared on the market; indeed, it had been lost in the laboratory. Company A had to adopt an inordinately expensive 'crash' program in order to regain its position.

It is to avert these kinds of reverses that long-range planning is concerned. Day to day operations also need to be efficient, of course, but unless they are carried out within the framework of broad, well-conceived LRP, they will lead only to the efficient collapse of profit, leadership, and market position. The following material resulted from analysis of the trends and patterns in the company's industry, and provided the basis for a course of action which would provide the basis for long-range planning and action.

Analysis of the evolution of the industry concerned here revealed a significant fact: *It is impossible to predict.* That is, it was agreed on presentation of the significant inventions and innovations in the industry in a chronology, that even the best informed scientists would have been unable to predict these events or even their incidence, plus or minus five years. The only predictable element was that there had been, and probably would continue to be, invention, innovation, and change, and that the relative frequency of these was roughly proportional to estimated research and development expenditures in the industry, lagged by some range of number of years.

The important company A top management conclusion and policy in response to this finding were:

1 The company should plan systematically to spawn a continuing series of these inventions and innovations as the basis for a viable, growing enterprise.

2 It should establish the mechanism for this continuing flow of inventions, innovations, and developments. This flow and the mechanism for it henceforth would be considered as important as the flow of materials, goods, and services in producing its current products and the mechanism for that flow, the factory.

At this point, the results of a study made in one of my former employments was introduced which reinforced the preceding decision. It also suggested a corroborative study of this company's different products. The purpose of the study was to determine the nature of the 'game' which management plays in the long term; the strategies available, their expected pay-offs, and the mixed or pure strategy which should be adopted in the long term.

Figure 16.1 presents the results of the first mentioned study. This graph is interpreted as follows. Those products for which that former company was both in first position in its market and had highest return on (total product) investment were also the products in which it had invested the most money in product development (on the average) prior to the original appearance of the product on the market. This is an exciting finding: to make more money, spend more on new product R and D. However, before accepting the hypothesis unequivocally, the concept was tested by a similar analysis of company A's products. The findings of this study are shown in Fig. 16.2. The results are strikingly different. The meaning of the difference is clear. In

257

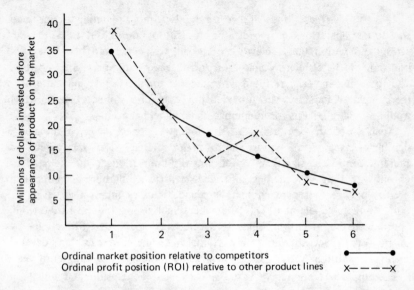

Ordinal market position relative to competitors ●————●
Ordinal profit position (ROI) relative to other product lines ✕————✕

Note: All data are disguised.

Figure 16.1   Company B: 48 products, average return on investment 23% (est.)

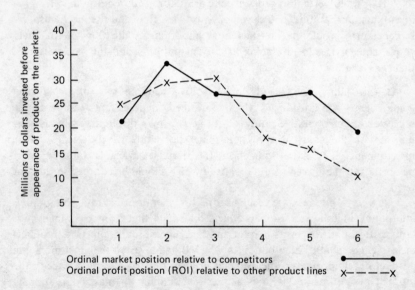

Ordinal market position relative to competitors ●————●
Ordinal profit position (ROI) relative to other product lines ✕————✕

Note: All data are disguised.

Figure 16.2   Company A: 26 products, average return on investment 17% (est.)

company A, large investment in advance of a product's first appearance did not tend to lead as strongly to first market position. Indeed, relative to some of its second-place products, some of company A's first-place products had achieved their position with less advance investment.

The study to determine the reasons for the different tendencies gave the following qualitative observations on each company. Company B maintained an aggressive research and development program, with expenditures for R and D very high as a per cent of sales, circa 6 per cent. Company A was proportionately almost as aggressive, as measured by R and D expenditures as a percent of sales. The difference here did not seem significant.

Company B, through its advertising, company slogans, etc., presented a corporate image of 'making progress', where progress included innovation and commercialization. However, it did so very conservatively. For example, one of its former chairmen of the board remarked 'Fifteen years is about the average period of probation, and during that time the inventor, the promoter, and the investor, who see a great future for an invention, generally lose their shirts. Public demand, even for a great invention is always slow in developing. That is why the wise capitalist keeps out of exploiting new inventions.'[2] While the policy at Company B subsequently has advanced, it did so only by developing systematic procedures for evaluating when and how, in detail, to develop and commercialize an invention.

On the other hand, company A, through its corporate image, slogans, and policies, better represents the pioneering inventor. There is good, though nebular, evidence that this image represents the personality and policies of the principal executives. This is a significant difference, even though it is of a qualitative character.

If the preceding difference in fact did exist, it should manifest itself in other more measurable ways. The following are some of those ways:

	Company A	Company B
1 % of R and D and engineering personnel in		
(a) central lab.	54	38
(b) product dept. lab.	46	62
(Presumably reflects relative importance of product-oriented and 'business controlled' R and D personnel.)		
2 Average number of product lines per department or business profit center.	6·4	3·1
(Presumably reflects the relative importance of any single product line to a single profit-responsible management team.)		
3 % of product lines directly traceable through evolution to original products without acquisition or merger. (See Fig. 16.3)	47	72
(Presumably reflects purposiveness and ability to commercialize on inventions and innovations arising out of R and D related to its existing businesses.)		*continued:*

	Company A	Company B
4 % of products entering directly into the major overall system produced by the company. (Presumably reflects singleness of purpose in expanding its basic business.)	39	78
5 % of engineering and R and D managers with training in management and business. (Presumably reflects commercial orientation in engineering and R and D.)	16	65 (estimated)
6 % of R and D personnel's time which may be self-directed. (Presumably this reflects relative amount of direction toward company objectives. However, Company B encouraged 'wandering' as the means for detecting commercially promising inventions discovered outside its labs.)	12½	20

Further studies

These differences cued further studies on the process of innovation, including invention, development, and commercialization. In order to disguise the companies, but yet to give concrete examples of this process, the early experience of the General Electric Company is given. Most examples and references here are taken from Passer,[4] but interestingly they form a striking parallel to the situations uncovered in this study.

The key person in the process of innovation and commercialization is the engineer-entrepreneur, the person with technical training who can see commercial possibilities in the application of scientific principles and who labors to perfect usable products and techniques. This kind of entrepreneurship has become increasingly important as the advance of science has made available new knowledge, new products new production methods, and new resources. For in the long view the most significant manner in which to increase economic welfare (and company profit) is not through better administration of existing resources or (socialistic) change in the distribution of income, but through applications of science which increase national income.

Clearly, company B is predominantly an 'engineer-entrepreneur's' enterprise. It deliberately seeks opportunity to commercialize—mindful of the dictates of its chairman, that without the test of marketability any venture would be doomed to failure. It systematically extended its business through accretions always related to its product line, and, hence, within the market and business which it knew well. Its engineering managers, as the above comparison indicates, have more training in and, presumably, understanding of the problems and methods of commercialization.

Another difference cited by the above comparison is the tendency to emphasize evolutionary entry into businesses. That is, company B tends to enter companies through expansion into related products or through enlargements of the basic system which it produces and markets. For example:

The economic orientation of Edison's inventive work in electric lighting defined his approach to the problem of subdividing the electric light (system). His goal was to invent a system which could produce light at the lowest possible cost. And his inventions were inventions primarily because he was looking for a low-cost lighting system. . . . Edison was the first inventor to realize that an incandescent lamp which could operate in a constant-voltage parallel circuit would necessarily have to be of high resistance in order to keep the cost of the copper conductors from being prohibitive. . . . Edison's work on the dynamo was also directed toward reducing costs. . . . In each case, he perceived the function of the component in the system. He then determined the characteristic of that component which would result in a *system* with the lowest production cost of light . . . the lamp, the dynamo, and the distribution network were designed to form a lighting system using the minimum amount of resources, with a meter in the system to measure it.

Through the above, we can see the evolutionary chain via which the now General Electric Company entered into its various businesses and product lines, virtually all stemming directly from Edison's original lamp, the protozoa of that company. The General Electric chain of evolution is portrayed in miniature, in Fig. 16.3.

Stage I

Edison developed the incandescent lamp which he wished to commercialize. Alone it had no future; as part of a complete system he saw it had large potential. This prepared for:

Stage II

1. The lamp business '1' required supporting businesses to make and sell a complete lighting system, including:
2. A meter business to supply meters '2' and measure energy consumed.
3. A distribution network business to provide the distribution equipment '3'.
4. An energy conversion (thermal to electrical) business, to supply electrical generation apparatus '4'.

Stage III

1. The lamp business, through research on lamps grew and spawned both indoor '1a' and outdoor lamps '1b'.

261

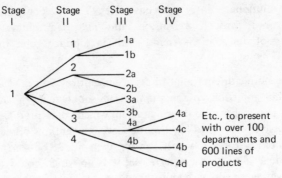

Figure 16.3

2. The meter business involved measuring '2a' and instrumentation, thus leading via knowledge of instruments into the instrument business '2b'.

3. Research and experience in distribution led to distribution hardware business '3a' through knowledge of electrical hardware, and its properties and manufacture. It also led to transformers for conserving copper losses, and thus to the transformer business '3b'.

4. The energy conversion business led naturally to knowledge and experience in both prime movers (steam engines and turbines) '4a' and to generators '4b'.

Stage IV

To abbreviate, only a small number of the evolutionary chains are shown and the remainder of the narrative is reduced. Thus, at stage IV, the prime mover business led to building the engineering and marketing knowledge and skills on which to enter both the steam turbine and gas turbine businesses (the latter of which proliferated later into aircraft gas turbines and shipboard gas turbines). The knowledge and skills in the generator business led directly to the ability to enter also the electrical motor business. While neither aircraft gas turbines nor electric motors are required in the electric incandescent lamp business, pursuit of the latter business by component engineer-entrepreneurs led to accumulating the knowledge, skill, and insight eventually necessary for entering those businesses.

The full evolution to date (1959) has led to the General Electric Company, with over 100 separate departments, producing 600 lines of products in as many markets. Some evolutionary links have been terminal ventures, however. For example, governmental action restrained the company from operating electric utilities; and, the company found that, though it was helpful to finance these utilities, there was nothing in the skills of the

262

engineer-entrepreneur which made him a good financier. Thus, General Electric withdrew early from the business of financing public utility companies, in order to sell its manufactures.

Long-range planning

Return now to long-range planning, *per se*. Could Edison have visualized that his lamp business one day would have led directly to aircraft gas turbines and thence to rocket motors? Of course not, aircraft and rocket motors were unknown at that time. Even within much shorter periods, the links have led to unpredictable new businesses. If Edison, or any other scientist, could not foresee such basic events and turnings in his enterprise, how is it possible to plan for it in the long term?

The answer to the preceding question is in planning for the *flow of invention, innovation, and new businesses* which will evolve. This requires developing a deeper skill in and understanding of the processes of entrepreneurship. Planning for specific inventions and their commercialization is short term, finite period planning. This short-range planning requires knowledge and skill in the specific problems of the business to which the planning is directed. The longer-range planning for the continuing flow of corporate life blood requires a broader set of knowledge and skills—such as:

1 The general principles of how to design business enterprises, so that whatever business evolves from invention and innovation can be profitably pursued or appropriately avoided.

2 How to recognize and develop not only required managerial talent, but more importantly, the entrepreneurial personnel to pursue new business.

3 How to set minimum, maximum, and expected rates of commercializable invention and innovation as the basis for growth and expansion.

4 How to determine criteria for branching at any node in the evolutionary chain, so as to enter only businesses which are compatible with acquired skills, knowledge, and the collective self-image and corporate image.

5 How to determine the miscibility of different product lines and businesses into operating businesses.

6 How to establish the conditions and methods for effective entrepreneurship.

7 How to design the parent corporate structure and organization for the 'flow of business' within that structure, from invention to innovation, to commercialization, and to replacement or abandonment, if appropriate.

8 How to perform the roles of chief executive and corporate staffs in a long-range plan embodying the 'flow of business'. That is, how to manage entrepreneurs, rather than how to manage other managers or individual contributors.

These areas of knowledge and skill would require many more pages to develop than are available here. However, a paragraph may be reported on each, as follows:

1 Principles of design of business enterprises–This area is amply covered by the numerous texts and papers on business organization and management, together with the literature of managing the functional components therein. However, one important lack is techniques for the integration of the various function components into a single system, in the same manner that the engineer performs the system integration and synthesis function in designing a complex system. The newly developing techniques in operations research have important application in the rational design and synthesis of business enterprises; as, for example, those being developed in the operations research and synthesis service at General Electric. Perhaps the existence of this service at General Electric reflects that company's unusual awareness of the need to bring to bear the most advanced, and powerful techniques of science and engineering in designing the many evolving businesses within its corporate structure. Toward this objective, and in a separate paper,[5] I have attempted to describe methods and techniques for designing business organizations dynamically, in the same manner that engineers must design systems to both static and dynamic criteria.

2 Development of entrepreneurial talent–The training and development programs for business are directed toward 'managers', the entrepreneur is hardly recognized. Yet, as Passer relates, '[he] is the key person in this process [of founding and growing new industries based on new technologies].' Unfortunately, the entrepreneur often may be greeted with untoward attitudes in established businesses, unless those businesses are organized to grow on the entrepreneur's labors.

For example, Maclaurin[3] writes, 'Innovations, in fact, may be becoming inherently more difficult. The current trend toward emphasizing smooth human relationships as the principle qualification for administrative responsibility tends to militate against the rise of innovators (entrepreneurs) to top positions.'

To innovate and commercialize an invention or discovery, the entrepreneur necessarily must alter many facets of his environment; change is his function, and new business his output. But, the capacity to change, or even to disagree–the first step in effecting change–is a scarce commodity.

Torrance[6] comments on the modern military entrepreneur, the Jet Ace:

Research findings indicate that certain individuals show a generalized willingness to oppose others and disagree when the situation requires it. In our studies of Jet Aces in Korea, we found that this characteristic was typical of the Ace when compared to his less successful colleagues. Asch

demonstrated a rather alarming similar picture. In 'brainwashing' susceptibility experiments, Asch generated a disagreement between individuals and
small groups on a clear and simple matter of fact in the environment. Only
one-fourth of his subjects adhered to their own correct judgements when
confronted with the different and erroneous judgements of the (experi-
mentally guided) groups.

(The experiments involved deliberate expression of erroneous opinion by the
group to determine whether the subjects would maintain their correct
opinions. *Three-quarters did not.*)

To plan in the long term requires planned cultivation of entrepreneurs—
those who can induce necessary change and who have the other moral and
intellectual qualities for business leadership. Unless this key ingredient is
provided, the best plan will remain dormant for want of the entrepreneurial
spark.

3 Rate of invention and innovation—One of the principal findings from the
study reported here is that there is a measurable rate of decay in the value of
information as contained in products, processes, or methods. This is
sometimes referred to as 'obsolescence'. However, to recognize it as a
problem in maintaining the continuous flow of new information gives the
manager and the scientist (or engineer) a better basis for planning the R and
D program, for planning the discovery and flow of new information, for
anticipating the competitive decay of previously produced information, etc.
The consequence of this insight was to study and project the trend in
information decay rates, and to estimate the magnitude of the R and D staff
and reinvestment required (a) to maintain fixed relative position, (b) to gain
relative to competitors, assuming both their continuing at current rates and
their accelerating their overall reinvestment. The general nature of the
findings on information decay rates are illustrated in Fig. 16.4, and provide
an illuminating insight on the cost of remaining competitive and progressive.

To protect proprietary information, a weapons systems example is used,
and the relative timespan is expanded. However, the same trend was observed
over short timespans, and for a number of commercial products. To illustrate,
curve 1 indicates the useful life of successive competitive weapons systems.
Curve 2 indicates the time (or, can be, cost) to develop those systems. For
example: Nelson's tiny flagship was 40 years old and still a first-rate ship of
the line at Trafalgar. Halsey's giant *Enterprize,* at three years of age, was
obsolescent before the Second World War. The B-17 took about four years to
develop and was operational for seven. The B-29 took about six years to
develop and was operational for four. The B-36 was ten years in development
and operational for only about three. The *Navaho* was in development six

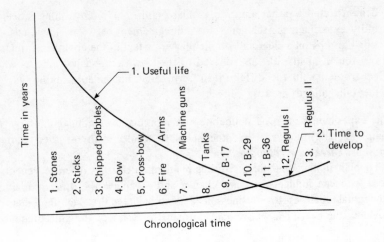

Figure 16.4

years; it was abandoned before completion because of obsolescence. *Regulus I* and *Regulus II* had similar short lives.

Obviously, the increasing cost of R and D and the decreasing lifespans of products counteract each other. The former tends to decrease a company's ability to do R and D; the latter increases the need for it. In between these, the rate of commercialization of inventions, then, needs to be controlled so as to insure an optimum program, balanced between the different phases, e.g., R and D, capital investment, advertising, market research, etc. Inasmuch as the problem of balancing and timing the various programs can be phrased in functional equations, it either becomes amenable to solution by calculus of variations, i.e., dynamic programming,[1] or these concepts greatly aid judgement solutions.

The problem is somewhat complicated by the fact that the production or discovery of inventions has elements of uncertainty. This, however, is not difficult to handle if expected, minimum, and maximum rates are used and boundaries or tolerance limits are used in the computation. For example, an upper bound(s) may be used to help delimit the number and variety of programs which can be undertaken with available resources. The lower bound(s) determine minimum innovation necessary to maintain given levels of competiveness. That is, the control of the flow of ideas is instrumental to corporate health; it must be neither too little nor too great.

4 The criteria for business branching—The General Electric Company's experience indicates that skills and knowledge are highly transferable, *vide* the branching and growth from lamps to such things as toasters, turbines, and

266

transformers. However, some branches failed. The successes and failures together provide excellent guidelines. The following are key elements in predicting the success or failure of a branch.

(a) Environmental or industrial knowledge. A working knowledge of trade practices, market characteristics, channels of distribution, and contacts with key persons may provide at least part of the basis for a successful branching. For example, National Cash Register Company has had no prior background in large-scale computers, but its very close ties to an important market via a formidable marketing organization may well permit it successfully to enter the business computer field. It offers a point of entry into that business, as the business data-processing technology expands and requires integration, at the point of initial recording, more intimately in the overall data system.

(b) Technical knowledge and skill. A prime example is General Electric's entry into the electric motor business. An electric motor is essentially a generator run in reverse. Thus, the technical knowledge and skills to design and manufacture generators, provided a strong platform for entering the motor business. The basic data involved in the industrial analysis for this kind of branching are similar to those described by Dr Igor Ansoff. The method described in his paper was used by Markowitz and Rowe as the basis for economic and military mobilization planning. The value of the analysis can be large: one company planned to branch into a business, but found that the commonality of skills was only apparent, not real. It planned to operate a far north aircraft engine repair station in the summer and a diesel repair station there during the winter while the diesel tractors were idle. Unfortunately, the skill carryover from diesel to aircraft parts was too great; the mechanics repaired diesels to aircraft specifications, and vice versa. This was, of course, too costly and inefficient, and had to be abandoned.

(c) Self-image and business flexibility. The self-image to which we refer here is a concept familiar only to those acquainted with psychoanalytic theory. For the most part, only those individuals who have been successfully analyzed will understand their self-images, and control the operation of them as the determinant of overt behavior. Others are conscious of their self-images only to the extent that they are or are not able to engage in one or another type of social, occupational, or other role, but are not conscious of the reasons for their role inflexibility. An example is cited of a manufacturer of copper hardware who successfully competed in an industrial market where one pattern of occupational role was required. The company was not successful in a commercial market, primarily because their collective self-images unconsciously made them seek defensive refuge behind the mask of being 'conservative engineers'. While they consciously rationalized their preference for this role, to the trained observer it was obvious that it was a haven of defense against the incurrence of tensions and anxieties, induced by departing from their protective role. This unconsciously imposed inflexibility caused their commercial operation to be inefficient and unprofitable, even though the company already possessed a strong platform in manufacturing skills and facilities required for that commercial business. Role inflexibility problems often are resolved by 'decentralization', so that each autonomous group within the same company can identify with the role(s) implicit in each of the several businesses which is compatible with the group's collective self-image. An alternative which was used, at least partially in this instance, is a psychoanalytically oriented training program to increase the personnel's flexibility to move between different roles. The organization, in this case, was not large enough to decentralize, hence required multiple role flexibility, through personal flexibility.

The summation of the collection of self-images is the corporate self-image. The latter is one of the most powerful determinants of corporate flexibility— both because it reigns and operates through the unconscious and, hence, cannot be reasoned and reckoned with (except in analysis), and because it is self-reinforcing. No matter what course of action is followed, or attitude projected, it tends to be self-reinforcing: the negative attitudes to be negatively reinforced and the positive, positively reinforced—precisely because one or the other attitude already existed. Hence, the results of performing any business role is to enter that role with such unconscious predilections as create the responses from the environment which tend to confirm the predilection, in favor of or against the role. Obviously, the greater the role flexibility of an individual, or of a business, the greater is its ability to capitalize on opportunities, regardless of the roles which they require. It is of little value to develop long-range plans and programs, only to find that a variety of apparently unrelated obstacles interpose themselves. These may take the form of 'that is not our line of business', 'the risk is too large', 'the economy is uncertain', or others. Alternatively, they may appear as simple inaction or delay. While it is possible to develop systematically the capacity for role flexibility, it is beyond the scope of this report to describe.

(d) Joint or byproducts. A frequent basis for branching is when the production processes yield joint or byproducts. This concept is obvious and needs no elaboration here.

The preceding are subject also to legal and moral limitations. For example, General Electric has been restrained by antitrust action from operating public utilities; the aircraft manufacturers from operating airlines, etc. However, these concepts illustrate the evolutionary chain and branches in the growth and diversification of typical, successful, large companies. To reiterate, long-range planning for such growth, requires as much the maintenance of the conditions for, and skills of, entrepreneurship as it does the development of specific action programs. Edison, in 1885, could hardly have planned for the evolutions of the GE lamp business into the toaster and aircraft gas turbine businesses. But he and his successors, by maintaining the conditions for and skills of entrepreneurship, assured that evolution.

Summary

It was mentioned earlier that there is a minimum regeneration required for maintaining a viable business. Investment in innovation (as in R and D, new markets, new products, or others) must be at least a certain minimum in order to sustain competitiveness and viability. In studying this phenomenon, the following observations were made. There is a distinct, quantifiable, and measurable input-output relationship between successive stages in an innovation cycle. It was found that the 'transfer-function' can be used in long-range planning. Graphically, it is shown in Fig. 16.5.

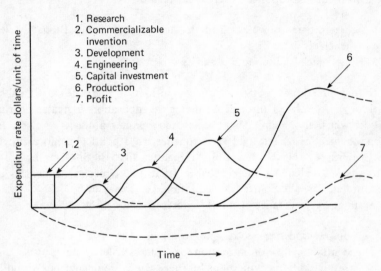

Figure 16.5 Innovation cycle: Expenditure patterns

Several important relationships can then be sought for planning purposes. Some of these are:

1 What is the average, minimum, and maximum ratio of the area under each curve to the area under the preceding curve?

2 Is there a trend in these ratios over a period of time; are they increasing or decreasing?

3 What is the characteristic lead-lag relationship between the curves?

4 Do the ratios vary from product line to product line; and, if so, how?

This study was cued by an engineering occupations remuneration study. There, for example, it was found that the higher the rate of innovation in a branch of engineering, the higher the starting and top rates of pay. Similarly, it was found that the higher the rate of innovation in an industry—up to an upper bound—the higher the return on investment. It was found that the correlation between ROI on a series of products, as a function innovation investment, was not as high as it was on an industry basis. It appeared that there was random fluctuation on a product basis, which was averaged out on an industry basis. In particular, in a whole industry there is opportunity for the operation, not only of primary breakthroughs, but also of supporting or facilitating discoveries. Thus, it appears that whole industries tend to move together, while within these broad movements, the more aggressive innovators lead. But, the leadership tends to be paced by the whole complex of limiting and facilitating innovations and advances.

In broader perspective, long-range planning must answer the question as to the division of innovational resources between:

1 Those programs which lead to lower cost (proportionately less employment).

2 Those which lead to more products.

In the broad perspective, this is important: if the rate at which the workforce is displaced through technological innovation is greater than the rate at which new employment is created on new products and services, unemployment is an inevitable consequence. In a political democracy with free enterprise, this balance can be maintained best through those free enterprises so planning their activities that the opposing tendencies are equilibrated. The alternative is social action, i.e., socialism.

In summary, long-range planning requires or achieves the following:

1 A businesswide perspective in innovation.

2 A continuing flow of innovation for business viability and profits.

3 A set of skills and conditions for successful entrepreneurship within the corporate framework.

4 Organization components for pursuing the processes of entrepreneurship.

5 Adapts the collective or business self-image to the roles implicit in foreseeable and evolving businesses; either through increasing personal flexibility or through organizational isolation of the roles (i.e., decentralization).

6 A balanced flow of resources to the phases in the innovation cycle.

7 Recognizes and plans for the gradual reduction in the direct labor force to the indirect and overhead, as the result of technological progress.

References

1. BELLMAN, RICHARD, *Dynamic Programming*. New York: McGraw-Hill, 1957.
2 MacLAURIN, W. RUPERT, *Invention and Innovation in the Radio Industry*. New York: Macmillan, 1949.

3. MacLAURIN, W. RUPERT, 'The Sequence from Invention to Innovation and Its Relation to Economic Growth.' *Quarterly Journal of Economics,* Vol. LXVII, February 1953.
4. PASSER, HAROLD C., *The Electrical Manufacturers.* Cambridge, Mass.: Harvard UP, 1953.
5. SALVESON, MELVIN E., *Dynamic Organization Planning.* New Canaan, Conn.: CAM Press, of the Center for Advanced Management, 1959.
6. TORRANCE, PAUL G., *Function of Expressed Disagreement in Small Group Processes.* Reno, Nevada: Stead Air Force Base, 1955.

271

17. Strategic planning in conglomerate companies

Norman Berg

The art and science of influencing the long-term growth of a company—call it long-range planning, strategic planning, or simply good management—has received much attention of late. There are indications, however, that this outpouring of literature, useful as it has been for a vast variety of planning problems, has as yet provided little practical help to one important group of managers: those concerned with strategic planning for the *large* and *diversified* industrial corporation. In companies of this type, the crucial question that must be answered repeatedly is: 'How much should we be spending for the future in each of our divisions?'

My discussions at a number of companies with managers interested in or responsible for long-range planning efforts, extensive field research in one large and highly diversified company, and work experience in the area of long-range planning on the staff of a large electronics company have led me to conclude that answering this deceptively simple question for the highly diversified company poses significantly different problems than does strategic planning in single-business firms, which most of the literature deals with.

These problems deserve top-level attention. Planning in large and diversified organizations is becoming increasingly important in our society, since more and more large companies follow strategies of diversification in their search for greater growth and stability and as an outlet for their retained earnings. The barriers and uncertainties presented by our antitrust laws often contribute to the trend toward diversification by making acquisitions in fields identical or closely related to the present main businesses of a large company seem unattractive.

In this article, I shall try to answer the following questions:

1 Why are the conflicts of interest and viewpoint between division managers and headquarters in diversified companies far more basic than they are in single-business firms?

2 How do these conflicts produce widely different attitudes toward risk-taking, the allocation of funds for development work, the judgement of what is an acceptable profit, and other issues?

3 Why do top executives at the corporate level typically find that they can make only limited progress toward a solution of these difficulties, even though they strive to comprehend division managements' problems, obtain unbiased information, and use the best possible data about market trends, industry conditions, and so forth?

4 What kind of view or philosophy of strategic planning will likely subject it to a deadening and uncreative bureaucracy—and what kind of perspective will contribute to a more vital, productive functioning of this important activity?

Conglomerate companies

What is a 'large and diversified' corporation? General Electric and Westinghouse, each with sales of many billions of dollars and with 50 to 100 divisions in significantly different businesses, represent the archetype of the large and diversified corporation, as we will discuss it in this article. Enterprises of this sort can appropriately be described as 'conglomerate companies'. The cut-off point for companies in this range is an organization with perhaps five or six divisions in different businesses and with total sales of a few hundred million dollars. The diversity of the company is far more important than size alone. A large mining company, airline, or integrated steel company is likely to offer significantly different, and in many respects less complex, planning problems than a smaller, but more diversified, corporation.

A conglomerate company, then, consists of a number of product divisions, which sell different products, principally to their own markets rather than to each other. In terms of a simple diagram, the various divisions of a conglomerate company could be represented as shown in the top part of Fig. 17.10. But an integrated company—a steel company, for example—could be represented as shown in the lower diagram. Conglomerate companies will, of course, have some internal sales and transfers, and integrated companies will have some external sales and purchases at various points in the process. In the main, however, the transfer of products is as shown in the diagram. The consequences of this difference are twofold:

1 The problems of simply *comprehending* the various technologies and markets the diversified company is engaged in are great much greater, in fact,

273

than the problems for a single business, even though the latter may be very large in terms of sales and assets.

2 A conglomerate company, unlike an integrated company, has the opportunity to expand its operations in any given area *virtually independently* of its plans for other areas, except that the corporate resources used to promote the expansion of one division cannot be used to promote the expansion of other divisions. An integrated company, by definition, is more constrained by the need to maintain a balance among its various activities.

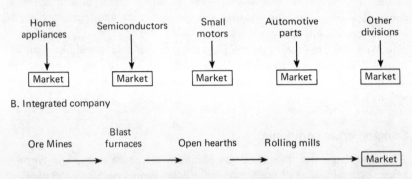

Figure 17.1   Schematic representations of two types of companies

Both of these factors are a source of considerable difficulty for the conglomerate company with regard to the rational allocation of funds for growth among the many different businesses in which it is engaged. The problem is not the simpler one which the integrated company faces of how to utilize a limited supply of chips in a single poker game. It is the much more difficult one of how to divide a limited supply of chips among perhaps 50 separate but simultaneous poker games, in which not only the rules of play and the stakes, but also the experience, ability, resources, and determination of one's own players, as well as of their opponents in the many games, vary considerably.

Allocation of funds

How is the top management of a conglomerate company to decide where it should bet its corporate chips? The problem of allocating *capital* funds has been much discussed in the literature, but these funds are only part of a company's investment in the future. Many companies spend at least as much on development in the form in which we are concerned with it in this article—that is, on *expensive* projects intended to enhance the future profits,

274

growth, or stability of the company. These development projects are, to a very considerable extent, discretionary during any given year, and they differ significantly from capital expenditures in that their cost is an expense for the year, and they tend to reduce reported current profits for the unit concerned.

With regard to the authorization of such development projects undertaken by divisions to promote division growth or profits, one highly successful and respected division manager in a conglomerate company claimed that the corporate management should have very little to say about the matter:

> If you have good division managers, 80 per cent of the say on spending money on projects for the future should be up to them. I think you have to trust the division managers to a great extent. You pay them well to know and run that part of the business for you, and you should rely on them. Presumably nobody at the corporate level knows as much about the division manager's business as he does. Things have to go from the bottom up, not from the top down; that's what a decentralized business is supposed to do. If the division manager is convinced that his division ought to spend the money for a certain project, and we have the money in the till, that should be the end of it.
>
> We have got to keep in mind what makes the corporation go. It isn't headquarters; I have never have seen a headquarters that generated income by itself. The foundation for the whole operation is the divisions; it is in the divisions that the money is spent and the money is earned. That is mainly where we have to worry about selling things for more than they cost to make. Headquarters, of course, has an important role to play, but it is too easy for them to get preoccupied with their own needs.

An offsetting argument to this division viewpoint, however, is that the corporate level is in a position to decide which game offers the best rewards to the corporation, whereas the individual division manager cannot possibly know the other 49 games in any detail. He therefore is not in a position to exercise much judgement as to where the corporation should be risking its money. It was principally for this reason that the company referred to above was engaged in efforts to move the control of the expenditure of funds for these development projects to a higher level in the company. The planning vice-president stated his position as follows:

> I suppose the simplest explanation of why we are trying to move the control of spending money on expense projects for the future up to higher levels in the corporation is that it is just not possible to set up the rules so that the self-interest of the divisions or the product groups will always coincide with the corporate interest. This presents some severe problems if you permit the divisions a great deal of freedom with regard to

determining the amount and the purpose of their expenditures for the future.

Many people, I suppose, will just say that this means the rules or the objectives have not been set correctly or carefully enough, and that they need to be refined or improved. I don't think that this is the case; we simply have to take a larger part in managing the affairs of the divisions so that they come out in the corporate interest. It is more efficient than continually refining the rules and procedures.

It is my contention that such conflicts are not merely another form of the old 'top-down vs. bottom-up' planning controversy but instead stem from (a) fundamental differences in interests and (b) difficulties in comprehending all of the activities of the conglomerate company. Let us explore the nature of, and the reasons for, the differences in interest between the divisions and the corporate level.

Conflicting interests

If significant amounts of money are spent by divisions on projects originated and evaluated by the divisions, as is likely to be true in any decentralized company, then the issue of the degree to which the interests of the divisions coincide with the interests of the corporation as a whole is crucial. Planning implies the existence of an interest and a purpose or goal; one plans *for* something. A situation in which different organizational units are spending money to attain goals that sometimes conflict with corporate goals would be a clear source of difficulty for those engaged in overall corporate planning.

Much of the writing about business planning assumes either explicitly or implicitly that the goals at various levels and in various subunits within a corporation are, for all practical purposes, identical or complementary; conflicts, if acknowledged, tend to be treated more as relatively isolated aberrations rather than as evidence of more basic and underlying factors. There are, of course, many respects in which the interests *are* identical; business *is* essentially a cooperative venture. It is also apparent, however, that there are a number of respects in which the interests of various levels and units of a large corporation are in conflict with each other. Furthermore, these differences in interest are a major source of difficulty in corporate attempts to ensure that money spent by divisions on projects for the future is expended in the *corporate* interest.

Origins of differences

The differences just mentioned stem from two broad conditions. I shall describe each of them briefly.

276

Everyday environment

The first condition is definitely the less important of the two. In any large company, the everyday environment of the divisions is significantly different from the environment at the corporate level. Managers at the division level are likely to have spent much of their working lives in their present or other divisions. Their 'real world' is the people they see and work with every day, the products they manufacture, the physical facilities of the division, and the projects that are underway in the division. Customers and customer complaints are real; the products produced for them are tangible and are probably well understood. How well the product works and how efficiently it is produced are probably the result of innumerable personal challenges, successes, and failures.

The corporation may make a great number of products, and it is somewhat difficult for the personnel in one division to feel much identification with products they do not understand very well and which are made by people they have never met in plants they have never seen. The corporate level itself may also seem to be an abstraction, a sometimes arbitrary and usually remote power which often causes the division managers trouble and worry and extra work—and which assesses a healthy overhead charge against the divisions in return for the harassment!

At the corporate level, in contrast, it is all too easy to feel that the real world consists of 'the corporation' and those quantified abstractions which show how the corporation is doing with respect to the outside world—profit and loss statements, balance sheets, the market price of the stock, and so on. *'What does it mean in earnings per share?'* is often the all-important question with regard to division proposals or problems. The real world at the corporate level becomes the external and quantitative measure of corporate performance and health; divisions can all too easily be regarded as suppliers of financial statements which merely fit into the vast corporate totals. Understanding the divisions and their products and businesses in detail, having precise knowledge and independent judgment about the many thousands of divisional development projects throughout the corporation, or being greatly concerned about the effects of decisions regarding projects on *individuals* in the divisions is simply out of the question for the corporate level. As one observer has commented: 'The central staff live in the midst of aggregates, trends, averages, and overall generalization. They are remote from the individual reality behind the words and figures that flow and jumble over their desks. They are dealing with symbols: their input is items on paper, and their output is items on paper. . . .'[1]

There is little that can be done about the problems caused by differences in the environments at different levels. Management can be encouraged to become better acquainted with operations and problems at levels other than its own, but this is likely to produce a marginal improvement only. The worlds and problems *are* different, and so the outlooks will remain different.

Compensation and Promotion

The second and by far the most important reason for the existence of different interests at different levels in the organization can be found in the workings of the compensation and promotion procedures in any large organization. Organizational rewards are more likely to come to the manager whose *own* profits and growth are noteworthy; any other contribution any single manager might make to the overall corporate profitability and growth is both minute and obscure by comparison. In addition, it is much easier in any corporation to measure the *current* performance of a manager—whether it be in terms of profits, sales growth, new product introduction, or whatever—than the provision which he makes for the future. Hence, the latter is likely to be overlooked or minimized. Indeed, the easiest measure of a manager's investment in the future is simply his current expenditures for future profits, growth, and stability—expenditures which tend to reduce his current profits. Most corporate managements find it extraordinarily difficult to decide how much any particular manager should be spending for the future and whether or not he is spending it wisely.

Executives at headquarters may wish the division manager to forgo expenditures in his own division so that other divisions with better opportunities in the future will have more to spend, to sacrifice current profits for possible greater future profits, or to take risks which are desirable from the corporate standpoint, but which have a good chance of seriously affecting his own current performance adversely. But such actions are not likely to appear as attractive to the division management as the corporate management might wish. For one thing, division managers have a different viewpoint regarding risk than do executives at the corporate level. This brings us to the next topic.

Attitudes toward risk

One of the competitive strengths of a large company is its ability to undertake large and risky projects. If £100 million are to be spent throughout the corporation on various projects for the future, some proportion of these projects can surely be of the type for which the probability of success is very low but for which the rewards of success, if it is achieved, are extremely high.

However, what might be a perfectly acceptable and even desirable level of risk for the *corporation* to undertake on a particular project, because of the averaging effect of a large number of projects undertaken throughout the company, may be much too high a level of risk to appear attractive to the particular division or individual who is striving for the current profits and who must bear responsibility for that particular project. The performance and ability of a given manager are likely to be judged on the *outcome* of the

278

project, not by whether a good job was done, even though the project failed and the risk was desirable from the corporate standpoint.

Reactions to pressure

The following comments from an experienced staff planner in a large corporation point up the possible adverse effects of pressures for current profits on the willingness of people to undertake risky projects:

> We haven't grown because there has been too much emphasis on current profit. We are, in effect, encouraging the division managers to undertake only low-risk, and as a result low-profit projects. Consequently we miss out on most of the developments that really pay off, and we seldom get into a market that is growing rapidly early enough. I think we have forgotten that business is inherently risky, and that *we have to make it possible for people at various levels in the organization to take risks.*

It is not only pressures for current profits that can encourage strong aversion to high-risk projects among division personnel. The same effect can be produced when higher-level executives check in detail on the outcome of projects, unless they do so with great care. Witness these comments from a division manager in the same large company referred to above:

> If people are going to check up on you, project by project, then it is easy to get into a pattern of looking more favorably at those projects which are more certain to come out. One way we get around this here, in this division, is to have our own kitty of project funds to work with. Nobody at the group level knows about it—they wouldn't like it, I'm sure—but I feel that we have to operate that way.
>
> Our group planning director is a smart guy, but he would have to have an auditor in here full time to prevent it. Even then, I am sure the guys out in the shop could find a way to get around it.
>
> I think this may be one of the dangers for a company as diversified as we are. We end up making things too formalized in our efforts to control the operation, and, as a result, it is the guy in a garage somewhere that takes on some of the really risky projects that may very well bankrupt him but will pay off handsomely if they work out.

With regard to the danger that such detailed checking on projects will result in the submission of low-risk projects in the future, a vice-president in the same company with extensive experience in managing a research laboratory commented as follows:

> That's always a problem, but I think we are handling it better by getting it out in the open. The danger with risk is that you won't even get to look at the projects that people turn down because they are too risky

unless you have some sort of a system for getting at them. We hope we'll be able to undertake more of the risky projects, rather than fewer, by making the process more explicit.

There are substantial advantages to some form of checking by higher levels of management on the outcome of division projects, of course, and rapid improvements in data-handling techniques are likely to make more checking increasingly common. Such information helps corporate management spot where difficulties are arising so that something can be done about the problem, and also helps it evaluate the claims for money it receives from given divisions during the next planning session. Where the selection criteria are not clear and the information on proposed projects is far from certain, past performance is undeniably useful in assessing the probability of satisfactory future performance. The problem is to find a way for higher management to retain the advantages of checking on the outcome of individual projects without unduly discouraging the undertaking of risky projects. How can this be done?

Project-failure allowance

One way to encourage more risk-taking at the division level is to establish a norm for project failures. As judged by outcome with respect to plan, *a proportion of the projects should fail.* A record of no failures is no more a sign of good performance or wise choice of projects, from a corporate viewpoint, than is a credit policy that results in no bad-debt losses. Both are unduly conservative from a corporate viewpoint.

The basic difficulty of standards of performance which equate 'good performance' with a low failure rate, as is normal in most large organizations, is that such standards may encourage behavior which is clearly not in the corporate interest. A low failure rate may be the result of truly good performance on the projects selected, but it may also be the result of:

1 Selecting only low-risk projects.
2 Expending disproportionate effort on projects which are not turning out well, when this effort might be more profitably expended on projects which are turning out better than expected and are not in trouble.
3 Showing convincing, but misleading, figures.

The time pressures on executives and the wide range of technologies encompassed by projects make it unlikely that any form of checking on projects by higher levels of management can amount to much more than seeing how many were successful.

Establishing a norm or standard which allows a manager a certain proportion of failures, then, is likely to encourage him to take on more risky projects. This obviously does not mean that, for any *specific* project, failure is preferable to success; it merely means that success on *every* project should not be weighted so highly by superiors that not enough high-risk projects will be undertaken.

Growth and profits

The varying attitudes toward risk at different levels in the corporation, which affect the choice of projects on which funds for the future are spent, are important. The influences which affect the *total* amounts of funds available to various units to be spent for the future are also important, however. The problem is not only *what* the money is spent for in each division, but also *how much* each division gets.

The basic assumption underlying the decentralization of management responsibility is that the corporate purposes will thereby be better served than they would be by a different form of organization. Along with decentralization generally goes a system of rewards, both formal and informal, which encourages a manager to seek to enlarge his *own* sales and his *own* profits. This is all done for the purpose of improving performance with respect to corporate sales and profit goals; the rationale is simply that the overall corporate goals are most likely to be achieved by a system in which the various separate businesses of which the company consists are encouraged to pursue similar goals at their own level.

Such an approach to the management of a large and diversified company has great merit; indeed, it is difficult to imagine how a large and diversified company could operate on a 'traditional' centralized basis. There is considerable evidence to show that decentralization and diversification, either product or geographical, tend to go hand in hand.[2] This approach, however, does create some particularly thorny problems with regard to the allocation of resources which are likely to affect the growth of the divisions concerned.

Money for development

The first of these problems stems from the tendency of people in a large corporation to be primarily concerned with the growth of their own unit rather than with the growth of the corporation as a whole. This is perfectly understandable and is even encouraged by the structure of rewards within the corporation. Since growth is 'good', the means by which it can be made more likely become important to the divisions. Funds to support projects intended to enhance future sales and profits are one such resource. The desire of divisions in one large company to compete for money for their own development prompted the following comment from a vice-president of planning:

One complicating factor is that *people always want to spend money for development if they are allowed to.* In our small engine division, for example, we have about 28 engineers working on product development. This is an old field, though, and about all they do is change the appearance a little once in a while and maybe move the accessories from one side to another. *We might do much better from a corporate viewpoint to put this money elsewhere.* I suppose there are lots of products like this. Some people just make dishpans; they make them well for the lowest possible price in an alley shop and don't spend a nickel for R and D. It might be we should run more of our divisions that way.

The tendency for each division to spend as much money as possible in the pursuit of its own growth objectives is tempered by the need to earn at least a minimum level of current profits as well. This immediately leads to conflict, for development projects generally reduce current profits; either can be increased at any time at the price of a reduction in the other. A division manager commented on the relationship between the level of such project expenditures and acceptable profits as follows:

The projects we do are limited by the amount we have available, but you can't separate the two that easily. The amount we have available for our projects is also influenced by the projects we have and by what an acceptable level of profit consists of. The acceptable level of profit is, of course, strongly influenced by our group vice-president. If we operate at a loss, then he has to cover it from another of his divisions or else get his profit goal reduced.

Not only, then, are the total project expenses and the level of current profits closely interrelated in any given unit; they may also be related to the profits earned and the projects undertaken at every *other* level in the corporation.

It is possible, of course, for the total corporate profits to be truly 'what is left' after 'proper provision for the future' is made at every level; it is also possible for any given level to *expand* the total funds available for either development of current profits rather than to increase one by reducing the other. In a conglomerate company studied in some detail, however, current profits and the amount of money available for development projects were felt to be closely related as a practical matter. Executives at each organizational level felt that the *balance* between these development projects and current profits at their level was relatively flexible, but that the *total amount* available to them for both of these categories was relatively fixed, since it tended to be what was left after relatively well-known price, volume, and cost factors were allowed for. In addition, division personnel acknowledged that it followed from simple logic that the corporate profit goals could only be achieved if the divisions contributed their profits.

A reduction in the profit goal for any single division in order to accommodate more of its development projects, then, would result in either (a) the reduction of the total corporate profit goal or (b) an increase in the profit goal of some other division and a likely reduction in the amount of money available for its development work.

Acceptable performance

Every division in a company is usually under pressure to produce current profits. The controller of a newly formed division in the electronics business stated the pressures quite well:

> Every division *has* to show a profit if it possibly can. That is what we are in business for. The corporation authorized a loss for us for the first two years, but that was all—and because of a cash bind for the corporation, we had to cut back even before we expected. We have been trying to run in the black ever since.

But just what *is* an acceptable profit for a particular division at a particular time? That strong profit pressures exist at all levels in almost every company is common knowledge. But is any company really in business to earn a current profit in *each* division *each* year? Is it in business to earn the same profit in each division, or 'as much profit as possible'? Surely most companies are interested in overall company profits for at least a few years into the future—not necessarily maximum individual division profits for one year in any single division at the expense of future profits in other divisions.

Influencing the long-term growth of the corporation through the planning of expenditures for future development is unavoidably related to the question of what an acceptable profit will be for a specific division. To illustrate: a newly formed electronics division might be judged to have much more favorable opportunities for growth than do many of the existing businesses in which the company is engaged. If this is so, it might be wise for the corporation to permit such a division to spend so much money for various development projects during the next five years that the division would consistently operate at a loss. This loss, of course, would have to be compensated for by the profits from other divisions if the corporate profit level is to be maintained. Presumably this could be accomplished by eliminating some of the *least desirable* projects in other divisions, thus increasing the current profits of these divisions.

To the corporate management, then, falls the role of influencing not only what the balance between current profits and development projects shall be for the *corporation as a whole,* but also what the balance shall be in *each of the divisions* of the corporation. Executives at the corporate level cannot avoid influencing this balance by asking the divisions to act either in their own best interests or in the corporate interests. Division interests are different from the corporate interests in some significant respects, and divisions are likely to spend as much for development as is made available to them. The divisions can no doubt judge what is in their own best interest better than the corporation can, but this ability is of little help to a corporate management interested more in spending the limited resources available to the corporation in *its* interest. In addition, asking the divisions to take a broad corporate viewpoint when striking a balance between their own project expenditures and current profit is asking them to do a job which men at the corporate level themselves find exceedingly difficult to do (and which the divisions are ill-equipped to attempt).

The choice for the corporation is therefore not *whether* management should influence this balance in the various divisions, but *how* it should do it. Funds for such development projects may be allocated explicitly, or, as is much more common, profit goals may be used to influence the level of project spending. Profit goals, though less precise, have the great advantage of being more 'socially acceptable'; profit needs are much easier to justify than a more explicit starving of certain divisions.

Deciding on profit goals for various divisions is done in a variety of ways. Management may set corporate-wide profit goals to be used as targets in each of the divisions; it may set goals for improvement in profits each year; it may use profits of competitors of specific divisions as goals for those divisions; it may establish an atmosphere of 'the higher the better' for profit performance; it may establish goals arrived at independently of any of the foregoing factors; it may even deemphasize or ignore current profits. But whatever the method, it affects what the divisions spend on development, which, in turn, affects the relative opportunities for divisions to shape their own future.

'Administrative' goals

The setting of profit goals for the various divisions is, of course, influenced by many factors other than the effect of the goals on project expenditures. A major factor influencing the *total* amount of profit which must be earned at the division level is the pressure on the company as a whole to earn a satisfactory current profit. Current profits are, to a considerable extent, what the management is evaluated on by the outside world. One of management's most important tasks is to translate these external pressures for satisfactory profits *today* into internal profit goals which will enable the company to earn satisfactory profits in the *future.*

284

Managements cannot, of course, do very much about the way in which they are evaluated by the external world. If this evaluation is largely in terms of current profits, they will have to learn to live with the fact. For a small company in a single business, pressures from the financial community and the stock market to earn an 'acceptable' profit affect management strongly. In a diversified company, however, these external pressures need *not* be translated directly into internal pressures for any specific division. The external profit pressures may be met by means of a variety of administratively determined, internal profit goals.

This potential flexibility in meeting external profit goals provides the large and diversified company with a competitive advantage which it should seek to exploit. There is no reason to suppose that the profit goals or the balance between development and current profits for any specific division at a certain time should bear any close relation to either the external pressures on the company or the profits earned by the competitors of a specific division. To translate such external pressures directly into internal goals is to substitute the judgement of an outside group of hundreds of thousands of investors—the 'market'—for the judgement of division and corporate managers. There may well be many cases where, because of unique opportunities to undertake projects to enhance future profits or growth, it would be in the corporate interest to permit and encourage specific divisions to show either higher or lower profits than would be indicated by external measures.

(Such 'administratively determined' profit goals have, on occasion, been criticized as being in violation of either the spirit or the letter of the antitrust laws. The absence of any illegal intent, however, such as to underprice competitors in order to drive them out of business, seems to be sufficient defense against charges of improper use of the financial resources often associated with great size.)

Division profit goals which *are* closely related to external pressures or corporatewide goals are, of course, very much easier to arrive at and to justify than are administrative profit goals. If the management at the corporate level is to influence the relative growth of the various divisions by means of the funds it makes available to them for projects to enhance future profits and growth, however, the use of administrative profit goals is essential. It is a way to shield some divisions from profit pressures while increasing the profit pressures on others.

Administrative profit goals which allow for each division's opportunities cannot be set in a formal or analytical manner. Peter Drucker, for example, has commented as follows with regard to managed expenditures, which he considers essentially as expenditures to enhance future profits: 'There are no formulas for making the decisions on managed expenditures. They must always be based on judgment and are almost always a compromise.'[3]

285

And a planning director, with staff responsibility for about 15 divisions in the large and diversified company studied, commented:

> It's tough to draw the balance between the present and the future. Division managers will always say you are milking the business, not making the proper provision for the long range, and so forth. But the long range has to arrive sometime; you just can't keep spending for the future without the future and the benefits you were supposed to get ever arriving. You have to keep asking where the benefits are from the expenditures you made several years ago. There aren't any easy answers to any of this. If there were, we would have been doing it that way a long time ago.

Can problems be avoided ?

There are some things which the corporation can do to make the interests of the divisions correspond more closely with the corporate interests. Efforts can be made to reward the manager who does a good job—but fails—on a risky project which was desirable from a corporate viewpoint (just as the manager who does a good job and succeeds on a less risky project is rewarded). And efforts can be made to reward a manager on the basis of his contribution to the long-term growth and development of the company as well as for the growth or current profit performance of his division.

It would be naïve, however, to expect that one could eliminate the difficulties caused by the existence of different interests at different levels by simply pointing out how these interests vary. Improvements, of course, are possible, but progress is likely to come slowly. Compensation and promotion practices have evolved over time and depend in part on the formal, quantitative measures of performance which often need to be relied on in large organizations. The time pressures on management personnel, the years of conditioning in a particular organizational environment, and the difficulty of accurately measuring an individual's 'good performance' from a *corporate* viewpoint make the problem of different interests a slow one to unravel.

What about moving the responsibility for making decisions which affect the relative long-run growth of the various divisions up to higher levels in the organization? How promising a solution is this? Actually, this step does not *avoid* the problems caused by different interests; it merely seeks to *constrain the actions* taken by lower units so that they will be in the corporate interest. It does not, to any significant degree, make the interests of the various levels and units any more identical than they were previously. By moving some of routine decisions which affect the long-run future of the company up to higher levels in the organization, however, many of the undesirable effects of the existence of different interests within the corporation are minimized.

286

Instead of worrying about decisions made at lower levels because they are sometimes not in the interests of a higher level, the higher levels can make some of the decisions themselves in their own interests.

There are problems and limitations to this approach also, of course. The problems fall into three main categories: (a) comprehending, at the corporate level, the many different businesses the company is in; (b) obtaining unbiased information about projects; and (c) arriving at estimates of the corporate profitability of broad courses of action drawn from broad external data. These will be discussed in turn.

Who is smart enough?

Since many of the allocation decisions at lower levels are based upon a consideration of the specific projects that are competing for the funds, it is natural to consider the problem at the corporate level as being similar. Instead of choosing among projects in a division or even in a group, the problem may seem to be simply that of choosing among projects for the entire corporation. It may appear to be a simple, logical extension of the approach which is widely used at lower levels and which has great theoretical appeal as well.

The trouble is that detailed decisions of this sort are extremely difficult to make at the corporate level in most large and diversified companies. One reason is the impossibility of finding any person or any committee at the corporate level that can comprehend in a significant sense the thousands of projects relating to the company's many different technologies and markets well enough to exercise any independent judgement about the projects. Another reason is the impossibility of obtaining objective and unbiased information at the corporate level about the costs and future benefits of the proposed projects.

The difficulty, then, is not with the manipulation of the data in order to establish a ranking of projects, but with the nature of the inputs to the analysis. Elaborate computational techniques or theories of choice are not likely to be of help, since they do not deal with the principal source of difficulty. Competition for funds to facilitate growth is likely to lead to 'optimistic' estimates which make reliance only on the figures submitted unwise; paradoxically, if men at the corporate level could know enough about the individual projects to exercise their own judgement in the matter, this very knowledge would likely result in the submission of more realistic project estimates by the divisions.

These difficulties are expressed in a statement by the vice-president of planning in the large diversified company which I studied. He was commenting on the proposal of one of his staff that a corporate approach to the allocation of funds could be based on a consideration of the divisions' individual projects on which funds would be spent—a total of perhaps 10 000 projects throughout the corporation:

Theoretically, the approach to evaluating the projects and deciding which to back is probably correct. It is based on two assumptions, however, neither of which holds in this case: (a) You need to be assured of objective data. (b) You have to have qualified people to evaluate the projects.

Those assumptions are not true for us at present, and I doubt that it is possible to make them come true. I agree that if we could get objective information from the divisions on their projects, we could probably do a better job of allocating money by dealing with the specific projects than in any other way. That's impossible, though, so I think we will just have to go from the top down. *We just can't find a common measuring stick that we can apply to all of these projects that will be reliable enough. And I don't see how we can possibly get or develop people for a corporate-level committee who would be qualified to evaluate all of these projects.*

The rubber yardstick

This vice-president's comments about the lack of a common measuring stick that is reliable enough is a key point which is not very often recognized. To quote Peter Drucker again:

In human institutions, such as a business enterprise, measurements, strictly speaking, do not and cannot exist. It is the definition of a measurement that it be impersonal and objective, that is, extraneous to the event measured. A child's growth is not dependent on the yardstick or influenced by being recorded. But any measurement in a business enterprise determines action—both on the part of the measurer and the measured—*and thereby directs, limits, and causes the behavior and performance of the enterprise.*[4]

Although in the company I have described executives at the corporate level felt that a project by project selection at their level was not feasible, most people at other levels felt that they could take such an approach at *their* level, while agreeing that the corporate level could not. This company was organized into a number of product groups, with each group made up of from five to ten divisions in somewhat related businesses. Several group-level planning personnel claimed to be able to evaluate projects from divisions in their groups, even though total group sales might be several hundred million dollars. A sample comment:

It would be completely impossible to rank projects for the whole corporation at the corporate level. You can only make such a ranking on the basis of data furnished by divisions, and the only reason we at the group level can do it is that the group vice-president that I am working with knows his divisions well enough to be able to go through the budgets project by project, on an individual basis. And I feel at home with it because I have been working with these businesses for five years.

At the division level, however, the feeling was often that moving project control even up to the group level was centralizing things too much. In response to a question as to whether it would be possible to select projects at the corporate level, for example, a division planning manager commented:

There would just be too much for any one man or committee to know. That's why we have a group organization—to help corporate management screen and interpret what is going on, and to try to help them make some choice. But I don't think that even the people at the group level can know enough about all of the projects in all their divisions to do much selection or approval of projects in detail. *I think it is a good idea to centralize the control of such projects here at the division level rather than further down in the division; we are better able to spend the funds in the division interest that way.* I also think we will get into trouble if we try to centralize by moving the control much higher. The task gets too complicated; people just can't know enough to do the job as you get to higher levels.

In short, to place control lower in the organization is seen by the higher levels as resulting in inefficiency and waste, either because the goals at the lower levels are different or because the lower levels cannot see the 'big picture' and the better opportunities for the corporation to spend money elsewhere. At the same time, moving the control to higher levels is seen by the lower levels as resulting in inefficiency and waste because the higher levels 'can't know enough about our problems'. Recognizing that such conflicts of opinion are almost certain to be expressed may lead one to avoid the temptation to keep changing the approach to planning merely in response to the comments at the various levels. As Ely Devons has commented so aptly with regard to the centralization-decentralization issue in wartime planning in England:

This conflict ... appeared at every stage in the administrative hierarchy. ... The supreme coordinators struggled for more centralization, the planners in each department for more to be left to their discretion. ... Given the limitations of the human mind and capacity, this conflict was the greatest obstacle to efficient aircraft planning. If the inevitability of this conflict is not recognized, planning becomes even more inefficient than it need be. For in such circumstances, those who influence the planning machinery oscillate between a passion for decentralization, as a

289

result of an exaggerated awareness of the inefficiencies of centralization; and a drive towards central coordination as a result of a terror of the illogicalities which emerge when important decisions are taken at the periphery. . . . The balance between the two is never found, since at each stage the evils of the existing system and the advantages of the alternative always impress most.[5]

Value of external data?

Finally, management can attempt to evaluate the desirability of spending money in various broad areas by looking at external information: size and growth of markets, price and profit trends, possible technological developments, probable strength and intentions of competitors, and so on. Reliance on this approach also has its difficulties. The principal one is simply that useful and independent estimates of long-term profitability are extremely difficult for executives at the corporate level to come by, particularly in light of the many businesses that a conglomerate company is engaged in. The vice-president of planning mentioned earlier commented as follows on the efforts of his company to use such projections as a basis for determining, in a rigorous way, levels of spending on development projects or administrative profit goals for the divisions:

> I'm afraid that future profitability is simply too difficult to evaluate when dealing with decisions of this type. The most we can do is to list a number of factors which we think are indications of future profitability, and perhaps gather some information on some of them. We don't have any analytical way of taking all of these factors into account or combining them with each other—it will simply have to be a matter of discussion and judgement. We have a lot of abstract and unquantifiable factors to deal with, and someone will just have to decide. I do think that opportunities for profits in various fields are likely to depend heavily on growing markets and on high and rapidly changing technologies, but I don't think we have a good enough way of quantifying and working with these factors yet.

Economic and social process

A major factor which permeates and complicates all aspects of any planning process, and any attempts to influence it, is that planning is an economic *and* social process. Hence, considerations other than purely economic ones must be taken into account. This observation is inescapable to anyone who has spent any significant amount of time talking with people at various levels in a large organization who are actually engaged in planning activities. For example, take the issue of why the expense funds for development projects cannot be identified and allocated as explicitly and as formally as capital funds are administered in most companies. One planning manager, responsible for a number of divisions with total sales of several hundred million dollars, summed up the general feelings very well:

This idea of allocating expense funds for development projects more explicitly is a tough one. I think it would be unwise at this point to attempt to identify these funds explicitly, in effect, put them all into a corporate kitty, then dole them out again on some basis. It would be intolerable to those who are being starved, since it would mean that their businesses are probably going to wither. It might look like the most logical thing to do, but I'll have to admit that I think a slightly devious approach lots of times works best.

What do you suppose such explicit allocation would do to the morale of the division? Also, you put yourself in a tough spot if you take the responsibility for the future away from the division manager. We, at the group level, would be in a very bad box if we cut many projects from a division and the division did poorly, and the division manager then said, 'It is because you cut out those essential projects'. If things go bad, he can always blame it on you. The same holds true for the corporate management with respect to the groups and divisions.

I definitely think we have to do this by means of profit pressures rather than by explicit allocations of project funds. We have always been able to accomplish about the same thing in effect in our groups in the past by this means. People don't take exception to this as much. The group vice-presidents know the divisions and the businesses well enough so that they can force divisions to spend more or less on development projects by the pressure they exert on profits. The main disadvantage is that you can't very well discriminate between long-range and short-range expenditures that way, but they know the divisions well enough to be able to recognize, and prevent managers from cutting out projects they think should be kept.

Of course, people kick if the profit goals are too tight, but that isn't the same as saying that someone else is going to grow at your expense. We can always say someone else is having a bad year, the corporation needs profits this year, we have cash flow problems, and so on.

The preference for using 'slightly devious' profit pressures to influence the level of project spending in the divisions, rather than explicit allocations which would unfortunately more clearly identify those divisions marked for growth and those likely to decline, is clear evidence of the need to make the planning process socially acceptable as well as economically logical and efficient. Explicit allocations might be more precise and intellectually 'neat', but it is much easier to justify difficult profit goals than an equivalent decision to starve certain divisions at the expense of others.

Another important consequence of the fact that the planning process is not just an economic one is that the corporate management can *influence* but not *direct* what happens in the divisions. As corporate executives adopt a strategy to deal with the problems arising from the different interests of the divisions, for example, the divisions will change their own strategy to further their own interests. A corporate staff man with considerable experience in planning commented as follows on the efforts of the corporate level to find some basis for allocating development funds among the divisions:

> You know, if we set up some formal and analytical system for splitting up the money among the divisions, we're likely to have trouble with the people trying to beat the system as soon as they figure out how it works. The proposals would probably be inflated a little bit at first anyway, and I suppose if we discount the proposals, they will inflate them even more the next time. *That might make the second year of this more difficult than the first, rather than easier.*

Inescapable realities

Viewing the process as closed and deterministic and similar to an engineering design problem leads the manager to seek further and further refinements in procedures and in definitions, always hoping that each successive step will lead one closer to the goal of ensuring that all decisions will be made in the corporate interest. A point of diminishing returns is soon reached, not because the new procedures do not in fact improve upon specific present shortcomings of the system, but rather because the situation keeps changing as people find some other way to further their own interests, and because the procedures themselves may entail other and more serious costs.

Compensation and promotion policies have a strong and unavoidable effect on how any planning system works. If the organization tends to reward current profit performance, or sales growth, or success on projects, or stability of earnings, or conformance to plan or to corporatewide 'guidelines', any planning system will be hard-pressed to direct the attention and efforts of division management to areas in which, from a corporate long-range viewpoint, they 'should' be doing more or 'should' be acting differently. This is a limitation affecting any planning system. It is an outgrowth of the basic organizational environment in which any planning process operates. Efforts to 'tie people down' will all too soon result in a deadening and uncreative bureaucracy, responsive neither to the market nor to competitors.

Conclusion

In perspective, I believe four main ideas stand out in my study of strategic planning in large and diversified companies.

1 *An essential prerequisite to understanding and prescribing for strategic planning in a conglomerate company is to view the process as a multilevel activity.* The corporate level, units at the group level, and units at the division level, *each* exist in an environment which is in some respects unique. At each level, considerations of stability, profits, or growth *at that particular level* are better understood and of more immediate concern than are similar considerations for other levels. Executives at each level tend to view the process and the problems from the standpoint of their own interests and environment. Planning activities at each level are not simply a part of an overall corporate activity in which each part contributes only to the corporate interests. Each unit is engaged in planning activities which at least partially reflect the unique environment and interests of that particular unit. To the extent that the interests of the divisions and the corporation conflict with each other in significant respects, so will the goals to which each unit directs its planning efforts.

2 *The strategic planning process in a conglomerate company involves non-economic as well as economic goals at each organizational level.* Assuming that the process is not—or asserting that it should not be—influenced by non-economic goals is unlikely to result in realistic suggestions for the practicing administrator. These non-economic or social goals of the planning process may include, for example, efforts to ensure the stability, or perhaps promote the growth in size or importance, of any number of social systems or groups within the company, as well as efforts to maintain or create, in these many social systems, an environment satisfactory and rewarding to its members. The opportunity for creative and worthwhile contributions, and the degree of responsibility retained at one's *own* level for some of the important and significant decisions and actions affecting one's own future, are clearly influenced by the nature and operation of the planning process. As a result, it would be foolish to expect that such non-economic goals will not have an important effect on the planning process.

3 *Viewing strategic or long-range planning as an activity separate from and independent of short-range planning and current profit goals is both misleading and dangerous.* Strategic planning does not affect only the future, and current operations are not concerned only with the present. Every company is faced with the problems of surviving and maintaining stability today as well as making provision to ensure survival and stability tomorrow. Providing for the future very often detracts from current performance; for instance, it may mean reducing current profits to undertake development projects which may enhance future profits or stability. It is the planning system which makes possible the continuous balancing of the need to show satisfactory performance this year with the desire to be in a position to show satisfactory performance in the future as well.

293

4 *Planning cannot be neatly formularized.* To quote once more an experienced and able corporate planner: 'If there were any easy answers to any of this, we would have been doing it that way a long time ago.' Corporate strategy in any conglomerate company is the result of a complex planning process. Executives are not likely to get much help from simple 'how-to-do-it' prescriptions based on the assumption that strategic planning is a single, vertical, and largely economic process which can be broken up into distinct divisional tasks, each of which contributes solely to the corporate planning task, and each of which is no different in principle from the corporate planning task. Complex problems seldom have simple solutions.

References

1. MORGAN, THEODORE, 'The Theory of Error in Centrally Directed Economic Systems.' *Quarterly Journal Economics,* August 1964, p. 398.
2. See CHANDLER, A. D. JR, *Strategy and Structure.* Cambridge, Mass.: Institute of Technology Press, 1962, especially pp. 14-17.
3. DRUCKER, PETER, *The Practice of Management.* New York: Harper, 1960, p. 85
4. DRUCKER, PETER, 'Long-Range Planning Means Risk-Taking.' Reprinted from *Management Science,* April 1959, in *Long-Range Planning for Management,* ed. D. W. Ewing. New York: Harper & Row, 1964, p. 18.
5. DEVONS, ELY, *Planning in Practice.* London: Cambridge UP, 1950, pp. 14-15.

18. Planning in a worldwide business

Millard H. Pryor Jr

The term 'worldwide business' conjures up images of a caravan of llamas transporting Winchester rifles through the Andes, the ubiquitous Coca Cola sign in New Guinea, and a host of other enterprising firms successfully exploiting global opportunities for their products. By now, almost every significant industrial organization in the United States has moved into international markets. In many cases, however, the carefully laid plans of some of the most successful domestic firms have missed their mark so widely that these companies have been unable to take advantage of opportunities in even the most promising foreign markets.

Global problems

The failure of many international planning programs cannot be attributed solely to inexperience. Above and beyond the fundamental dilemmas imposed by nationalism, several aspects of the international organization's mode of business operation present planning problems which do not face companies operating principally in one country.

From the planning standpoint, the most important characteristic of the international firm is not the dispersion of its assets in a variety of geographic locations, but its operation in many different political and socioeconomic environments. This is not to suggest logistic problems do not occur. The complexity of managing farflung activities and numerous organizations speaking a variety of languages makes two-way communication between headquarters managers and the field infinitely more difficult than it is within an organization located in a single country. The physical problems of transmitting and receiving instructions and information alone make it clear that blanket application of domestic planning methods to international business operations will present major technical problems. Moreover, if domestic methods are blindly followed, many factors critical to success in the international field will inevitably be overlooked.

This article points out the most common mistakes made in planning worldwide operations, and discusses some of the steps which can be taken to assure the effective planning of the major business functions of a worldwide organization.

Common mistakes

Business planners, especially those in organizations that have been successful in developing long-range plans for domestically-oriented operations, tend to make three mistakes in planning their worldwide business.

1 *The detailed development of long-range strategic plans is often overcentralized.*

A realistic recognition of the complexities of international activities suggests that the corporate planners, unlike their counterparts in solely domestic organizations, are quite restricted as to the amount of detailed programming which they can *profitably* undertake. (The development of individual goals and strategies for an international company's entire overseas operations is a gigantic task which, if formulated solely at the corporate headquarters level, would require a planning department staffed with personnel paralleling all the company's key overseas managers.) Furthermore, as discussed at a later point, there are certain major activities which *cannot* be properly planned outside the local environment. Thus, a company's international planning staff, if organized separately, will inevitably tend to be a good deal smaller and more compact than planning staffs dealing with comparable-size domestic operations.

2 *In an attempt to telescope the process, international long-range planning is often conducted on a regional basis, rather than in terms of individual countries.*

While superficially a good deal of similarity may exist between countries in the same geographic region, more often than not there are significant differences in each nation's political and social environment. As a result, plans made in terms of regional groups often fail to take into account the factors that will determine whether or not such strategies will be successful. Specific examples are easy to come by:

(a) For many years, the Singer Company had no separate organization in Canada, treating its operations there as an extension of its US activities.

Ultimately, the blanket application of strategy developed primarily for the United States caused a serious decline in Canadian profits. After a separate Canadian division was organized, the trend was almost immediately reversed.

(b) Although Bolivia and Argentina have essentially the same cultural heritage, their political environments and levels of sophistication differ substantially, and very different marketing and supply strategies are required in these countries.

(c) Australia and Canada, while in different hemispheres and almost always managed in different divisions of international companies, are much more similar politically and culturally than are Japan and Korea or Mexico and British Honduras.

In order to derive any benefits from worldwide, long-range strategic planning, programs must be developed on a country-by-country basis first, and only then expanded into regional or worldwide plans.

3 *The implications of local politics are often not sufficiently stressed in long-range business planning.*

While corporate planners devote considerable attention to quantifying the effects of economic changes in the US environment, domestic business plans rarely take into consideration the effect of major political shifts in the United States. In many areas of the world, however, the effect of various political changes on business plans is dramatic. Corporate executives, accustomed to dealing with domestic plans which have been condensed to one or two pages of statistical data, often cannot see the need to take the time to plow through the voluminous reports that are required to spell out the effects of overseas political trends or to 'waste' time reviewing local politics with the key managers of their international operations. Yet, in many cases, the soundness of overseas long-term plans hinges to a great extent on the accuracy of assumptions based on local political trends.

Major functions

Many of the problems underlying the establishment of a formal international business planning system are familiar to domestic planners. These include the interdependence of objectives and plans, pressures to reduce paper work without eliminating necessary information, and the need to reconcile short-run flexibility with long-term strategy.

Like domestic planning, global planning requires a comprehensive information system that will provide top management with a continuing picture of significant events. Because of the decentralization of many planning activities in international companies, information systems for such organizations must fulfill the additional role of providing top management with an accurate picture of the long-range plans of the units which have done their own planning.

297

Utilizing the information available at headquarters, corporate planners in an international company should assume responsibility for three major activities:

1 The establishment of financial objectives and goals for every country in which the company is active.

2 The development of companywide supply strategies for use in worldwide manufacturing and purchasing.

3 The creation of plans on a centralized basis for hiring and training key managers throughout the world.

Additionally, there are other major areas of business, such as research, taxes and administration, that can greatly benefit from corporate planning on a worldwide basis. However, when all the major functions have been properly planned, the specialized planning which these other functions require will tend to fall into place and should not, as a rule, present any insuperable problems.

The one major function which *cannot* be planned on a highly centralized basis is marketing. Also, the extent to which a corporate headquarters can plan the introduction of specific products into various national markets depends on the degree of technical sophistication and the end use of the product line overseas.

Information flows

Typically, a company's information system follows the same pattern as its accounting system, which inevitably is constructed in terms of the organization structure. Over the last 20 years, many international companies have evolved from functional to geographic organizations, initially tending to group their international operations under one administration. It has been persuasively suggested that many international organizations may ultimately find it desirable to form large regional divisions of equal weight, coordinating products through the use of product managers at the corporate level.[1]

Comparing performance

While the regional management of activities within a group of different countries can be justified on an operating basis, the diverse character of each region usually makes it difficult for corporate headquarters to obtain comparable information which will permit top management to evaluate the performance of one overseas area with another. However, corporate planners, by gathering information on a country by country basis and classifying it into appropriate groups, can provide top management with a new perspective on overseas operations. In many instances, this method of gathering information permits analysis of the various strategies employed in those countries having similar economic and cultural characteristics and leads to very pertinent insights. Thus, it may be more meaningful to compare a company's operations in Thailand with those it has in Nigeria than to compare its Thailand activities with those in Japan or, in the same vein, Nigeria's with South Africa's.

The manner in which countries are to be grouped will depend, to a large extent, on the nature of a company's product or product lines. Companies marketing *capital* goods may find that Rostow's classification of countries into five economic stages is the most effective way to view operations.[2] On the other hand, companies in the *consumer durable* goods field may find that grouping countries by personal consumption expenditures is a more meaningful way to study worldwide activities. A series of composite indicators developed for each group may prove to be of substantial help in evaluating overseas division and area performance, and in applying the lessons learned in one market in the formulation of plans and strategies for other areas.

Measuring results

One of the most difficult tasks in creating a worldwide flow of information is to develop and apply a consistently valid method of measuring the results of the company's global operations. The constant shifting of the relationships of world currencies often reduces the study of overseas financial reports, constructed 'according to generally accepted principles', to a somewhat meaningless comparison of apples and oranges.

At attempt to use the concept of 'return on investment' provides a good example of the difficulty of finding a frame of reference which will yield meaningful information. What is meant by return? Is it local currency return or dollar return? If dollar return is implied, and the local currency is devaluating rapidly, what exchange rate should be used? Should it be the exchange rate at the end of the month in which the profit was earned, or the latest quoted exchange rate as applied to profits earned during the period up to that point? Perhaps, to be more conservative, the exchange rate used should be the one which it is anticipated will be quoted at the time profits are remitted or, at least, when they are invested in assets not subject to devaluation.

Even if a definition for 'return' is agreed on, it is still necessary to determine what constitutes 'investment' under these circumstances. Is it the original dollar investment, the current dollar value of the investment, or the remittance value of the investment?

Reporting data

The most appropriate form for reporting overseas operating results depends, to a large extent, on the goals against which the results are being measured In evaluating how well a company's overseas organization compares with similar local operations, it obviously is not necessary to make allowance for certain home office expenses or to compensate for currency remittance losses. On the other hand, where overseas information is sought for use in determining the advisability of planning further investments in a particular country, the local operating data and balance sheet figures should be adjusted, not only for exchange rate and expropriation losses, but for any potential losses as well.

Unfortunately, in all too many instances, foreign financial data are reported in a manner designed to facilitate consolidation with domestic figures rather than in a form that can be used for making necessary strategic decisions.

Costs of information

Another major problem facing management is the reconciliation of the need for sound information in many overseas areas with the economic reality that the markets in those areas may not be large enough to justify the expense of obtaining the data. This dilemma is particularly acute in the emerging countries of Africa and the Far East which show exceptional promise for many companies that have never before participated in those markets.

Many international companies obtain information concerning local economies from their overseas employees who, more often than not, have not had any formal training in this activity. Not surprisingly, much of the data collected by such personnel is not useful in pinpointing current and potential economic trends. In order for the global planners to monitor the key changes occurring in such areas, it is often desirable to supplement these overseas reports with headquarters-sponsored studies which are periodically issued to top management, summarizing significant trends and recommending, whenever necessary, the modification of previous assumptions.

Financial objectives

While financial goals vary from company to company, most US corporations attempt to earn a return on investment and enjoy a growth in earnings per share equal to or exceeding that of other comparable American companies. The use of similar American organizations as a standard reflects the fact that, by and large, stockholders of publicly owned corporations in the United States choose between alternative investments in common stock of comparable US companies. The objective of earnings and growth, however, must be modified when setting financial goals for the overseas operations of an international company. There are several reasons why this is necessary:

1 Political risks are much greater abroad than in the United States. The danger that either war losses or expropriation will result in partial or complete loss of investment is far from remote. The Singer Company's experience in operating in every area of the world open to it provides an excellent example of the basic risks inherent in international business. In the last 60 years, Singer had gross earnings from overseas operations of approximately $670 million. However, over the same period, total assets in 39 countries, with a book value of more than $145 million—and actual fair market value considerably higher—were either confiscated, nationalized, or destroyed because of war action. Furthermore, the figure does not include many losses due to riots and civil commotion. To compensate for such risks, the return in any foreign country should be greater than the return in the United States by an amount at least equal to the cost of war risk and confiscation insurance.

2 Loss of investment and earnings due to currency inflation represents a significant risk in many areas of the world. While most companies utilize local borrowing to hedge against such losses, it is often impractical or impossible to completely eliminate risks, and any return on investment should include a factor to compensate for potential currency loss. Normally, such a factor is based on the cost of local overseas bank financing.

3 The costs of managing an international operation are usually greater than those in a comparable domestic business. Such additional expenses relate to transportation, communication, and various additional salary allowances for non-nationals, and vary substantially from country to country. In certain instances, however, the cost of absentee administration will be more than offset by the reduction in cost of necessary headquarters office services required by the overseas operation. This is particularly true when the product lines are less complicated than in the United States and thus require less technical assistance from headquarters.

'Compensatory' goals

As a result of the potential risks in international operation, it is desirable to establish what can be called long-range, 'compensatory' financial goals for operations outside the United States. Such goals are constructed by adding to the basic financial goals established for domestic operations factors which quantify the long-range overseas political and monetary risks and the extra costs of absentee management. For example, if an appropriate long-range goal for activities in the United States is a 12 per cent return on invested capital, long-range compensatory goals for an international company's activities in

301

three different countries could be established in the manner shown in Fig. 18.1.

While compensatory goals provide an indication of the minimum level of return which a company should look for over the long run when making an investment commitment overseas, it is unrealistic to use such goals to evaluate the effectiveness of local management. That is because this approach does not take into consideration how profits compare with the return which local investors are earning. For example: in Mexico—a country with an excellent investment climate, a sound currency, and a reasonably low cost of absentee administration—local investors ordinarily receive a greater return on their investments than a compensatory goal structure would indicate is appropriate. This is due not only to a chronic capital shortage, but to the historical attitude of Mexican capitalists and local competitive practices.

	US Operations	Country A operations	Country B operations	Country C operations
US, financial goal	12	12	12	12
Compensation for political risk	—	—	2	5
Compensation for currency risk	—	1	2	25
Absentee management factor	—	1	—	2
Compensatory financial goal	12	14	16	44

Figure 18.1 Hypothetical international long-range 'compensatory' goals in terms of % return on investment

Consequently, while an original decision to invest in an international market should be based on the assumption that long-range compensatory goals can be met, overseas managers should be expected to take advantage of the local business climate and meet what might be termed 'comparative' financial goals, i.e., a return on investment close to the return enjoyed by comparable local businessmen. As a general rule, most foreign operations will rarely achieve local comparative goals since certain practices, particularly those relating to taxes, considered perfectly appropriate by the most respectable overseas businessmen, are usually not followed by the larger international organizations.

A comparison of compensatory and comparative financial goals with operating results in the three hypothetical countries cited in Fig. 18.1 might portray the pattern of returns shown in Fig. 18.2. Note that:

1 Operations in country A, while achieving the compensatory goal, are not earning a return in line with similar investments within the country. This suggests that the local overseas managers are not taking advantage of the profit opportunities in their markets.

2 Local managers in country B deserve applause, both because their organization is earning a return in excess of the compensatory goals and

	Country A	Country B	Country C
Compensatory financial goal	14	16	44
Local comparative goal	20	25	35
Actual results	14	22	32

Figure 18.2   Hypothetical comparison of international financial goals and results in terms of % return on investment

because it appears to be operating on a basis comparable to that of similar local companies.

3 While the managers in country C are also earning an appropriate return on investment when compared with local investors, the long-term risks in that country are such that the organization should earn a much higher return than that of local competitors, in order to justify its investment. The obvious difficulty of achieving a significant increase in return on investment suggests that consideration should be given to reducing or eliminating the investment in that country.

The determination of local comparative goals is quite difficult. Published information is rarely of much value, since accounting practices in most countries do not indicate true profit levels. Currently, one of the large international accounting companies is completing a survey designed to develop such data, based upon the experience of its overseas personnel. In the future, as more companies become interested in determining local expectation returns for comparable overseas businesses, more data should become available.

'Recovery' funds

Another basic financial objective of almost all international companies is to generate sufficient funds to assure the payment of adequate dividends to shareholders. Although in 1920 and 1921 Singer paid its French shareholders several dividends directly in francs, which its French organization had accumulated, the payment of a global organization's dividends almost always requires the remittance of profits to the country in which the company is headquartered. But such remittances have the well-established result of adversely affecting the balance of payments of remitting countries.

Where this occurs, the goals of the international organization and the objectives of other countries often come into direct conflict. This is not a critical problem in the mature countries, which have a long history of multilateral foreign trade and strong reserve positions. However, it is a problem of paramount importance in the emerging countries, where the need for imports is significant and exchange reserves are low.

The assurance of an adequate flow of funds from overseas operations into corporate treasuries requires a specialized type of planning, which can be termed 'recovery' planning, and should be carried out for each country in which the company operates. Recovery planning involves four elements:

1 *Maintenance of corporate records that will readily indicate the inflow and outflow of funds, whether in the form of merchandise, direct investment, remittances, or other types of payments in goods or services.* The accounting practices of many large companies make such a determination almost impossible unless the accounting system has been specifically designed to provide such information.

2 *Evaluation of the future political climate in each country, with conclusions concerning the short- and long-range potential for remitting profits and capital, devaluation of currency, and risk of war loss or expropriation.*

3 *Establishment and continual revision of recovery goals, stated in terms of target payback periods for the company's investments in every country in which it operates.*

4 *Coordination of overseas marketing, supply, and financial plans, in such a manner as to assure the proper implementation of recovery programs.* While such an activity is generally considered part of the chief financial officer's function, recovery programs often involve barter transactions and various marketing tactics which are usually outside the traditional scope of his office and which may require assistance from other corporate staff members.

It should be emphasized that although many recovery plans are short-range, such corporate planning does not imply the need or desirability of taking a short-range view toward business opportunities in any overseas market. Recovery planning, however, can provide an additional insight into the desirability of making an initial global investment and, once the commitment is made, continuously furnishes a scale against which the cash flow implications of various strategies can be evaluated.

Supply strategy

Efficient planning of manufacturing and purchasing strategy offers international companies a greater opportunity to reduce costs than does any other single planning activity. The problems involved are, not surprisingly, among the most complex facing corporate planners. Every country in the world has created numerous institutional constraints of varying severity in an attempt to keep for its citizens the wages and profits of local investment production. Traditionally, tariff policy is used to force local manufacture, initially by inflicting high duties and ultimately by closing the borders to imports.

For example: before the Second World War, one international organization supplied all of its Latin American, Far Eastern, and African markets from three plants located in North America and in the United Kingdom. By the end of 1963, the pressure from local politicians for on-site manufacturing facilities had forced the company to supplement its original three sources of supply with more than 20 additional plants erected during the postwar period within those marketing areas.

The formulation of global supply programs is an intensely pragmatic matter, which demands not only the most sophisticated evaluation of future overseas political trends, but the use of all the traditional tools of quantitative analysis as well. The projection of the future costs of investment operations in the emerging countries, however, is extremely difficult. It often hinges on currency revaluations, future social legislation, and other factors which can only be anticipated by the most thorough analysis—coupled with a generous helping of good luck.

Restrictive elements

Overseas national marketing organizations often evidence a good deal of chauvinism concerning the superiority of locally manufactured products in the well-developed areas of the world, particularly in Europe. Country of origin legislation makes it mandatory to disclose where products are manufactured. Therefore, supply programs have to be planned so as to take into consideration the long period of adjustment which national marketing organizations often require to reconcile local pride with commercial reality.

Other considerations bear on global supply planning. Once manufacturing and purchasing strategies have been formulated, the assumptions on which they have been based must be continually monitored. A small change in a country's tariff structure can eliminate the need for a plant; a border dispute between two nations can necessitate a complete shift in source of supply.

Further, even after a company has made the decision to establish manufacturing facilities within certain countries, it is becoming more and more necessary that it take into consideration the national plans of the country regarding the location of factories and the determination of what goods to produce. As these local plans change, it may be necessary for corporate executives to reverse many of their original make-or-buy decisions and increase or curtail estimated production levels.

While comprehensive peacetime planning of national production and resources was, at one time, almost exclusively practised by the Communist countries, a significant number of nations have recently formed national planning organizations in an attempt to develop overall plans for their economies. The extent of this activity was revealed by a recent questionnaire circulated to businessmen in 67 countries (see Fig. 18.3).

305

	Near East & Africa	Latin America	Europe	Far East	Total All areas
A. How active?					
Countries with active national planning organizations	12	11	12	9	44
Countries with no national planning organizations at this time	2	6	5	3	16
Countries whose policy is unknown	6	1	0	0	7
Total responses	20	18	17	12	67
B. How useful?					
National plans very useful in planning local operations	0	0	2	1	3
National plans of some use in planning local operations	3	2	3	7	15
National plans of no use in planning local operations	9	9	7	1	26
Total responses	12	11	12	9	44

Figure 18.3   National planning organizations

According to this survey, two-thirds of the countries polled have national planning organizations. On the other hand, few of these have produced plans that are of any assistance to international businessmen whose companies have local facilities.

In spite of the limited amount of influence which national planning has had on international business activities in the past, the success of France and other European countries in utilizing this technique,[3] coupled with the proliferation of new planning groups, suggests that the concept will gain more and more acceptance and that, in the near future, national plans will become a significant factor in developing international business strategy.

Management mobilization

The ability to mobilize and shift management personnel from country to country accounts for one of the major economies contributing to the success of many large international companies. Long-term corporate manpower and personnel planning has been practised by international companies for many years. Although fundamentally similar to the planning carried out in domestic operations, worldwide planning has to take into consideration many more factors, such as:

1 The probability that in some countries restrictions will be imposed on the rotation of non-national managers into key local positions.

2 The multiple-language skills which will be required by future overseas managers.

306

3 The necessity of integrating the various compensation programs dictated by national laws into a companywide system that will permit rotation of key personnel into different countries.

Rotation factors

Since the end of the Second World War, many of the local business traditions in the emerging countries have been replaced by the same practices that are followed in the United States and Western Europe. As a result, key personnel who are rotated through one or more international positions can usually function quite effectively in many new overseas assignments after a very short adjustment period. However, while the amount of initial indoctrination required for them to function in many emerging countries has diminished, the increase in contacts with local government officials and the need to keep constantly abreast of local news developments make it more important than ever for such personnel to be able to speak the local language.

Furthermore, because of nationalistic pressures, it is becoming increasingly difficult in certain emerging countries to rotate non-local managers routinely into middle and upper management posts. In certain instances, citizens of one country have become totally unacceptable to the governments of other countries. Thus, some of the flexibility which used to characterize international manpower planning has begun to disappear. All of these factors are making it more necessary than ever for corporate international manpower planning to be carried out on a long-range basis.

Marketing strategy

Marketing is conspicuous by its absence from the functions which can be planned at the corporate headquarters level. It is in this phase of overseas business activity that the variations in social patterns and the subtlety of local conditions have the most pronounced effect on basic business strategy and tactics. For this reason, the responsibility of marketing planning must be carried out by those overseas executives who are most familiar with the local environment. Also, the modest amount of quantitative information concerning customer motivations and attitudes, such as is normally available concerning markets outside the United States, must often be augmented with rather extensive sampling and surveys at the local level. The conversion of this information into future marketing strategy is a highly subjective task which also is best carried out by personnel completely conversant with local consumer needs and trends.

The operating experience of many international firms appears to confirm the desirability of assigning long-range planning of marketing activities to local managers. Most companies have found relatively few advantages in intensively coordinating their various overseas distribution and sales networks, and even the most product-oriented organizations usually administer these functions on a national or regional basis, with only a modest amount of intercompany coordination of local advertising and promotion.

The *sine qua non* of a well-prepared, domestic long-range plan is its relating of all operations to each other and the careful tracing and optimizing of the activities of one function or department with all the others. In contrast, the differences in the markets and sociopolitical environments of each country in which a global company operates restrict, to a large extent, the alternative uses which can be made of most of an international organization's intangible resources, and a host of legal and logistical obstacles reduce the ability of the worldwide firm to easily shift about its physical resources. As a result, there is often relatively little value in completely integrating corporate long-range plans for international activities into a single, comprehensive, and interrelated system.

Personal presentations

Since the local marketing plan is usually the basic document on which most of the other plans of the company are developed, it is extremely important that these plans be fully understood at the corporate headquarters level. To some extent, this can be accomplished by developing standard definitions of terms and by imposing standard formats of presentation.

It is impossible, however, to anticipate all of the factors that may be considered critical in each country. For this reason, it is almost always desirable to supplement local marketing plans with additional detailed descriptions of the strategies to be employed. Preferably, this is best covered through personal presentations made by overseas management.

Person to person contact of this sort is also beneficial through the contribution that corporate planners can make to the development of local marketing plans. In many instances, global planners can play a significant role in supplying local management with important information concerning current and potential competition from outside sources. Also, in the case of companies marketing products such as oil or chemicals, which are subject to worldwide price fluctuations, corporate planners are often in a much better position to provide accurate assumptions concerning future local price trends.

Product specifications

Cultural differences within individual countries have also, up to the present, seriously limited the value of corporate headquarters product planning. As a rule of thumb, the closer a product or product line is to the ultimate consumer, and the less technologically advanced it is, the less practical it is to attempt to determine detailed product specifications outside the actual market in which the product is to be sold. Thus, for example, while it may be possible at the corporate level to plan a line of laboratory instruments on a worldwide basis, it is less feasible to forecast the demand for specific washing machine models within various global markets. It would be completely impractical for headquarters management to attempt to plan what styles of household furniture should be marketed in various overseas areas.

The difficulties of introducing a new product or product line into overseas markets also seriously limit the use of corporate product planning. Pressure from local trade groups and government agencies has resulted in a bewildering maze of laws and regulations which greatly lengthen the odds against successfully marketing any new product or product line overseas. The US Department of Commerce lists 27 such non-tariff barriers—including special marking, labeling, and packaging. In addition, there are numerous regulations requiring the local production of advertising and promotion materials, as well as excessive specifications, standards, and safety requirements, and various restrictions on the display of goods at overseas trade fairs and exhibitions.

Headquarters role

While the responsibility for planning future products or product lines must ultimately lie with the overseas managers, headquarters planners can perform a coordinating role. By drawing on the planning information system, they are able to provide top management with a picture of local product requirements which can be used to standardize some product lines. Also, by collecting data on similar economies and reviewing the results of the organization's activities in countries with comparable economic levels, global planners can isolate areas where potential local markets may exist for products currently being sold in other areas of the world.

This analysis of market potential is particularly useful in matching technical products or product lines to particular markets. One well-known manufacturer of high-precision instruments, for example, pursues a global program of systematically reintroducing products which have become obsolete in one market into new, less technically sophisticated areas.

Conclusion

While the US government's concern with domestic poverty serves to emphasize the lack of a uniform standard of living throughout the nation, the differences between *per capita* income in the United States and most of the countries of the world are many times greater than those which exist domestically.

In addition to the variety of economic levels encountered overseas, the implications of the vast differences in cultural patterns cannot be over-emphasized. While there is some evidence to support the theory that many cultural contrasts are tending to disappear, it is probable that many years, and perhaps even centuries, will elapse before cultures and tastes of the rest of the world become as uniform as they are in the United States.

The wide variation in living patterns throughout the world makes it necessary to develop multiple strategies for almost all of the major functions carried out by worldwide organizations. However, in contrast to the domestic manager, who typically is a product of the same environment in which he functions, even the most experienced international businessman can only hope to gain insight into a few of the multitude of cultures in which his company may operate.

Thus, in spite of cultural, conceptual, intellectual, and physical obstacles, the importance of designing and maintaining a formal, comprehensive planning system assumes special significance.

Alternative possibilities are so numerous, mistakes so costly, and the need to move boldly so vital, that only by using sound global planning tactics now, to trace out the future implications of various strategies, can organizations take the affirmative steps necessary to continue profitable participation in the worldwide opportunities of the future.

References

1. CLEE, GILBERT H. and SACHTJEN, WILBUR M. 'Organizing a Worldwide Business.' *Harvard Bsns Rev.*, November/December 1964, p. 55.
2. ROSTOW, W. W. *The Stages of Economic Growth.* London: Cambridge UP, 1960.
3. See BASS, W. P. 'Economic Planning, European Style.' *Harvard Bsns Rev.*, September/October 1963, p. 109.

19. Planning in the family firm

Seymour Tilles and Arthur P. Contas

The evolution of the family firm

The family firm has two sets of aspirations: one with respect to its own economic future, and one with respect to the family's relationship to it. Both determine its long-term evolution.

Companies generally choose to express their economic aspirations in such terms as growth, profitability, addition of new products, geographic expansion, or competitive advantage. In the family firm, there is an additional set of aspirations. These may be stated in such terms as: whether the next president must be a family member; whether the family wishes to retain absolute control; or whether the firm must retain its traditional affiliation with a particular craft or community.

Family firms might be ranked on a scale whose major dimension would be the degree of congruence between the family's aspirations and the firm's aspirations. At one end of the scale are the companies that are still essentially projections of the individuals who founded and still run them. At the other end of the spectrum are those companies where the management can be characterized as professional, in the sense of being devoid of family influence. Between these ends of the spectrum—from the total dominance of the founding father to the disappearance of the family influence—most family firms can be identified at some point of evolution.

In successive generations of ownership, family members may continue to occupy management positions. Many companies have successfully preserved a relationship of joint association between the family and the firm for a number of succeeding generations. DuPont is probably the most well known, but there are numerous others.

Later stages in the evolution of the family firm are often characterized by

• Reproduced by permission of The Boston Consulting Group.

periods of growth and diversification. When a major opportunity for rapid growth arises, or a major program of diversification is undertaken, the controlling family must face the issue of whether it will dilute its ownership interest in order to accomplish these goals. This is necessarily a very personal decision, but it has important implications for the future relationship between the family and the firm.

An understanding of this spectrum of evolution ranging from 'the firm as me' through 'the firm as our family' to 'the firm as itself' is an essential perspective for those concerned with planning the company's future.

The distribution of authority

The most fundamental variable affecting the planning process of any company is the distribution of authority within it. In any company, there are two well-established bases of influence. One is the organizational hierarchy. The other is ownership. In the family firm, there is always present, to some degree, a third basis of authority, as basic as the other two: blood relationship. It is the existence of this relationship, as a variable in the planning process, which distinguishes family firms from others.

Blood relationship is often a much more deeply rooted basis for authority than either ownership or executive position. The relationship of father to son, of older brother to younger, or uncle to nephew are such deeply embedded bases for behavior that in most companies, where several members of an immediate family are simultaneously active, they behave essentially as family members and only incidentally as fellow executives or stockholders.

By and large, our ideas about corporate management have come down from the study of non-family situations. In the family firm, these are generally of limited relevance, for the relationships between family members in management, and the relationships between other family members and the firm, pose problems outside of conventional management concepts. Consider, for example, the following cases:

1 One chief executive of a closely held company was very much concerned with his widowed mother's insistence on larger dividend payments. He felt these funds were needed for reinvestment to realize major opportunities for growth.

2 Another large family company is a major factor in its industry in sales, but shows less than ordinary profit performance—its return on investment is, in fact, quite low. The company is little more than a loose confederation of autonomous units. The family executives in charge of them prize their autonomy more than enhanced performance. As a result, they never exploit their combined resources.

312

3 A third family company is not doing as well as it might because the patriarch refuses to accept the fact that the division which is his first love is a drain on the corporate treasury. The sons would like to close it down, but do not want to force a confrontation with their father over this issue.

As situations such as these suggest, the family firm is *both* a family and a firm, and it acts so as to optimize its satisfactions along both dimensions.

One of the most useful ways of thinking about a family firm is in terms of the overlap between the three basic dimensions of authority. These are the family tree, the organization chart, and the stock distribution. The way in which they are related is a useful means of identifying the essential planning problems of a particular family firm.

Early in its evolution, the family firm is characterized by a high degree of overlap between these bases of authority. If the firm has been founded by a single individual, he usually represents, for most of his executive tenure, all three bases in one. The future of the company is what *he* chooses to make it. He will pursue *his* interests, and he will gamble on promising products with *his* money.

After the reign of the founding father, the firm often becomes a coalition rather than a monarchy. As such, it is subject to both the advantages and disadvantages of dispersion of power. On the one hand, there is a more active discussion of future direction on the part of members of the coalition. But, on the other hand, it is far more difficult to generate the degree of consensus that is the necessary prelude to action. This represents a difficult period in the management of many family companies. Non-family executives may hesitate to differ openly with members of the family. And within the family, differences of opinion concerning future strategy may arise. Some of these may crystallize around different generations, where the conservatism of age appears to be arrayed against the rashness of youth.

As the firm continues to evolve—through succession from generation to generation—the growth of the firm and the use of non-family management are likely to increase the dispersion of the three bases of authority. Consequently, one valid way of viewing the essential planning problems of the family firm is in terms of preparation for, and management of, these transitions in the distribution of authority.

There are two major expressions of this authority. One is the determination of the future course of action of the firm. The second is the distribution of the prerogatives of ownership. The major constraint on the exercise of this authority is the network of obligations which characteristically evolve around the family firm. The major planning problem is the achievement of consensus with respect to a course of action which satisfies both contributors to the firm's future success and claimants to its benefits.

Obligations—to whom and for what

Our study revealed that an important characteristic which vitally affects planning in the family firm is the network of obligations which it accumulates. There are obligations to the stockholders, to the younger generation of family members, to the non-family executives, to the employees, and to the community in which the firm is located. It is rare that all such obligations are made explicit; but their existence is nonetheless real and has a direct effect on actions which determine the future of the firm.

The stockholders

In a recent discussion of alternative dividend policies which might enhance the liquidity of his company, one chief executive exclaimed, 'I couldn't do that—Aunt Jessie would kill me!' His remark touches on one of the most critical planning issues for the family firm—how to satisfy the requirements of the claimants to the income of the firm. Basically, what any company owes its stockholders is (a) a return on investment (capital appreciation or current income or both); (b) an equitable transfer arrangement if the holder should decide to dispose of his stock; and (c) some assurance, if he retains his holdings, that the firm is being managed with due regard for the future.

What makes this issue less than objective in the family firm is that family living standards and aspirations are usually formed at a time when most of the income to the owner-manager is in the form of salary. When the founder passes away, his widow or children are likely to become major stockholders, desiring the same income level, but now in the form of dividends. As the children acquire separate families, the dividend pressures on the firm are intensified, particularly as the dispersion of ownership reduces the amount of each heir's holdings. The double taxation imposed on dividend income further magnifies these problems.

One of the important ratios affecting the liquidity of the family firm is the rate of growth in number of family claimants compared with the rate of growth of earnings after taxes. If it is an increasing ratio, a serious family problem is in the making. If it is not resolved, it can become a problem for the firm as well.

The younger generation

Another difficult issue for a family firm to resolve is what is it, precisely, that it owes the younger generation? Is it an assured income whether they work or not? Is it an opportunity on a priority basis to be a part of the management team—or even a clear shot at the chief executive's job, whatever their qualifications?

The desire of chief executives to have their sons succeed them is often one

314

of the most deeply rooted aspects of family firms. There are many companies who have shed all other attributes of family companies except that one. Many of them have long since gone public, with the family having sold off all but a minority of outstanding shares, and representing only a small proportion of the executive team. And yet, the family name of the chief executive continues to be the same.

Still, in considering obligations to the younger generation, the other side of the question must also be faced—whether members of the younger generation should be permitted to disassociate themselves from the firm if they wish. And even for those who do wish to affiliate with the company, positions must be found for them which are commensurate with their ability.

Family companies differ greatly in the personnel policies they adopt for family members. Some make it clear to younger members of the family that they are expected to pursue their careers within the firm. Others permit the young men of the family to make their career choice on a completely unrestricted basis. And still others discourage family members from beginning their work career within the firm, but welcome them in executive positions once they have proved their capabilities elsewhere.

Not everyone realizes the degree of emotional stress that younger family executives may be subjected to. If they do not succeed, they suffer from painful comparison with the family's successful members. If they do rise to the top, they may still be deprived of the satisfaction of knowing whether they could have made it 'on their own'. Sometimes, when a younger chief executive takes over the leadership of the firm, he may prematurely launch a vigorous change in direction to 'prove what he can do'.

One of the objectives in planning for the executive development of the younger generation who will be active in the firm is to provide them with opportunities to demonstrate their capabilities before the time comes for them to assume the tasks of leadership.

Non-family executives

The family business must enact—by decree of tradition—relationships to non-family executives which in other business organizations would be determined by more impartial organization policies. In the family firm, the non-family executive may or may not have (a) the opportunity to advance to the position of chief executive; (b) the opportunity to participate in equity ownership. and (c) the opportunity to participate in the board of directors.

The opportunity to become chief executive—The position of chief executive has particularly powerful symbolism in the family firm. It is to the firm what the monarchy is to national aspirations—an extension of the paternal image on a much greater scale.

The desire to have the family's leadership perpetuated is so prevalent that it has resulted in some unusual patterns of succession. In a number of cases, relatives who had made their careers in other companies were asked to join the family firm in order to assure that succession would remain within the family for an additional generation. Again, a non-family executive may be appointed as president to fulfill a role analogous to that of regent until the family heir is ready to exercise power in his own right. This occurrence is so common that perhaps the valid criterion for assessing the opportunities for non-family executives might be two successive presidents outside the family rather than a single such instance.

The opportunity for equity ownership—In our interviews with executives of family companies, we found many who are opposed to equity participation on the part of non-family executives. Their opposition did not stem from any apprehension concerning undue influence or a desire to keep ownership within the family. It was motivated by a sincere desire to act in the best interests of those associated with the firm.

There are some worthwhile arguments for this position. The value of the company stock may very well decline, leaving the non-family executive who acquired equity in an awkward financial position. Moreover, where a company is closely held, a minority interest is an asset of such uncertain value that it may raise more problems than it solves. And finally, it might simply be in the best interest of the non-family executive to discourage his total dependence on the fortunes of a single company for his financial future.

Despite the admitted risks of stock options, they may hold attractions for non-family executives. One reason in particular for this is that in case the company is sold, employees who are stockholders exert a much greater degree of influence over the conditions of sale than those who are not. Since selling out is not an uncommon occurrence, equity participation can be a very realistic advantage for non-family executives.

The opportunity to participate on the board of directors—Election to the board of directors usually designates a non-family executive as one of the inner circle. It is his admission into the confidential councils of the clan. As a director, he will have access to much confidential data about the company—a particular mark of acceptance in family firms.

Whether the non-family executive perceives membership on the board as a privilege or a pain may well depend on what transpires at its meetings. Where the boardroom is simply an arena within which family feuds are fought and refought, non-family executives may view membership as a painful privilege.

In all of the companies studies in the course of our research, however, the election of non-family executives to the board was a significant ingredient in the process of professionalizing the company's management practices.

The employees

Family firms are frequently characterized by an unusual degree of personal loyalty on the part of their employees. It begins with the long-standing association between the owner-manager and his employees, and it usually continues through successive generations of family executives. It is a traditional attribute of which many family firms are deservedly proud, and one which can be a definite advantage.

Still, family firms do not face easy managerial decisions in addressing their obligations to their employees. One pitfall is the temptation to place too great an emphasis on employee loyalty as a measure of family leadership; this, in turn, can lead to costly excesses in paternalism.

There are other sensitive areas in the relationships between the family firm and its employees. One issue which must be decided is how much information about the company's performance shall be given to them. While one of the advantages of the family firm is privacy, the converse side of the picture is that the sharing of information is one means of motivating members of the organization.

Another sensitive aspect of employee relationships is the influence of retired executives, who may willingly seek—or allow themselves to be drawn into—involvement in the daily affairs of the firm because of the attachments which long-standing employees continue to hold for them. While such attachments may be a source of great emotional satisfaction for the retired family members, they can short-circuit or diminish necessary channels of communication between their successors and the employees.

And finally, obligations to employees may even become a significant factor in the selection of a new chief executive. In dealing with management succession, the family firm must decide to what extent obligations to employees dictate that the new chief executive must represent a continuation of the past relationship between the members of the family and the members of the firm.

The community

As a group, family firms demonstrate an unusual sense of obligation to the communities in which they are located. This is particularly true of the firms located outside metropolitan areas. In fact, it appears to be a direct function of the relationship between the size of the company and the size of the town. Where the firm is large and the town is small, there will be a particularly strong sense of civic responsibility.

Even in cases where outside ownership has diminished family influence over the policies of the firm, a community will often continue to expect the firm to be responsible for the economic welfare of the local area. As one executive said, 'We have to live in this town, and I can't afford to disregard the attitude of the townspeople toward what we do in our company.' Giving legitimate expression to this sense of obligation is an issue of some concern to many companies. The issue is world-wide—Eindhoven, Ivrea, Dearborn, and Fitchburg have all shared this concern.

As family firms grow and eventually acquire a significant stake in other parts of the world, community obligations may come into conflict with desirable competitive moves. For example, more than one New England company has decided against importing some of its overseas product made at lower cost because this would jeopardize local employment. In such instances, the family firm may face serious competitive disadvantages.

Financial issues

The financial issues related to planning in the family firm can be stated essentially as the three classical problems of funds flows: putting money into the business, keeping it there, and taking it out. But again, these issues must be approached from the dual context of the needs of the family and the needs of the firm.

Raising capital

The continuing demands of a growing company for capital—particularly in the current business environment of rapid change and prosperous times—place particular stress on the management of a family firm. Up to a point, a family enterprise has strong financial resources as a well known member of its local business community. (In fact, one financial counsellor has deplored the tendency of local bankers to extend far too much credit to local family firms.)

In spite of the fact that the family resources can be made available to guarantee or supplement borrowings, they are still not unlimited. Increasingly, funds tied up in the business limit the personal liquidity of family stockholders and may not be available for estate settlement taxes and expenses just at the time they are most needed.

A further matter of concern in financial planning is that the business usually represents an overwhelming proportion of the family's total assets. This presents the family with two kinds of problems. One is that of finding additional funds to finance the company's growth. The other is the converse problem of not putting all of its eggs in one basket.

Raising equity capital by recourse to the public equity market involves dilution of family control and earnings from the enterprise. The whole decision on raising permanent capital by public issues is such a major choice that it implies a great deal more to a family firm than merely raising capital. Going public is, in effect, a major change in management style for the firm.

Retaining capital

The two major obstacles to retaining capital for the family firm are the dependency of family members on dividend income and Section 531 of the Internal Revenue Code (excessive retained earnings). Of the two, the expectations of family stockholders are more difficult to deal with.

In the early phase of family firms, the mechanism by which the owner shares in the success of the company is largely through his salary. When he retires, the company must face for the first time an additional level of expense to continue to afford him the benefits of ownership. Succeeding generations of his heirs, many of whom will make no contribution to the firm and draw no salary, will represent an important set of claimants on the company's liquid resources.

A growing firm, with a demonstrable need for accumulated earnings, has a good chance of successively withstanding a challenge by the Internal Revenue Service with respect to Section 531. A growing firm, with a proliferation of second, third, and fourth generation stockholders, has a much more difficult problem in setting dividend policies which take into account its own growth needs.

Liquidity needs

Financial planning for the firm and estate planning for the family must be considered jointly in planning for liquidity requirements. Many family firms that are able to cope with their financial obligations toward the stockholders and their dependents find their ability to do so seriously threatened by the obligations incurred towards the federal government through estate taxation. One experienced trust officer has commented that many heads of family firms think they can use the same dollar twice—once as working capital to continue to operate the business, and once as estate taxes so that they can continue to own it.

Key-man insurance policies and buy-out agreements are only some of the methods which can be considered for proper estate planning which will insure the needed liquidity upon a change in ownership management. Once again, the problem of company-sponsored liquidity versus individual stockholder liquidity must be faced and planned for in advance.

Management succession

The dynamics of management succession in the family firm are different from the non-family firm—a change in chief executives often represents a change in generation. Thus, it comes at less frequent intervals, but it can cause major problems in adjustment and direction each time it occurs.

Then, too, there are unforeseen variables which can affect the line of succession. Personal occurrences within the family—the career choice of a son or the marriage of a daughter—can have major implications in determining the candidacy of the future chief executive. And the merits and aspirations of able non-family executives must also be considered.

Thus, a change in chief executive represents one of the most sensitive and potentially disruptive periods for the family firm. In addition to the expected organizational adjustments caused by such occasions in non-family businesses, a change in leadership in the family firm is a deeply felt emotional experience both for members of the family and members of the firm.

Under these circumstances, the elevation of a younger man to take charge of executives many years his senior can create a host of delicate personal problems, even where there is a strong sense of loyalty towards the family. It is not uncommon in such cases for some of the senior non-family executives to leave the company, just when their experience is most needed.

The most serious problem of all, of course, is that caused by the unexpected death of the chief executive. This precipitates both the sudden need to designate a successor and also a major upheaval in the pattern of authority and ownership distribution. The avoidance of such a crisis can only be accomplished by the establishment of contingency plans for management succession which protect the firm just as various forms of insurance and estate planning protect the family.

In any case, the selection of a successor is the most important aspect of planning for management succession. It is unfortunately postponed all too often either because it poses painful problems of choice or because on some occasions the incumbent chief executive wishes to postpone or avoid thoughts of his own retirement. But experience indicates that little is gained, and many options of sound planning for the future are lost, by avoiding the issue of management succession.

Like all of the other planning issues in the family firm, those related to management succession are best dealt with if they are perceived as being of a long-term character. Executive development is inherently a long-range process; and the organization itself must also be prepared for these critical periods of transition. One of the most important elements of planning in the family firm, therefore, is making provisions for continuity of leadership, so that the values of tradition can be combined with the flexibility which the future requires.

Laying the foundation for effective planning

Corporate goals and personal aspirations

The problem of maintaining objectivity in planning the corporate future exists with particular sharpness in the family firm, because the concentration of power often precludes the expression of a broad range of opinion.

In the non-family firm, the separation of authority between management and ownership provides a degree of built-in objectivity. Management must justify itself to ownership, and there are mechanisms for reporting on performance and discussing the future—the annual report, the stockholders meeting, and the board of directors. The family firm need observe no such measures of accountability. However, it has an even more critical need for insuring that the organization's future is being charted objectively.

In spite of the founding father's intuitive genius for sensing the needs of the market place, sooner or later—often in his own lifetime—the family firm becomes prone to becoming internally focused. The company becomes preoccupied with internal problems—with relationships between individuals, or a pet project or department—rather than with the more valid issues of what is going on in the world around it. When this happens, the firm runs the risk of becoming enamored of a particular way of doing business and losing sight of the fact that its basic direction is becoming less and less appropriate. The early history of the Ford Motor Company is perhaps the best known example of this pitfall.

The family firm must make a special effort to create mechanisms for insuring objectivity. The key step which makes effective planning possible is for the chief executive to ask his executive group, 'What should *we* try to become?' instead of merely asking himself, 'What do *I* want to do?' The challenge to the family firm, and particularly to its chief executive, is to make its aspirations shared aspirations, so that there is genuine commitment on the part of others besides the patriarch to what the company should be.

Building executive teamwork

Reconciling the points of view of the various executives who comprise the management team can be particularly difficult in the family firm. Where one or more of these executives are members of the family, there may be both a functional imbalance and a communications gap. In such cases, the other members of management may be reluctant to share their thoughts frankly or press for consideration of important problems. And even the second level of management may be inhibited from developing an interest in corporate policies, viewing such matters as the prerogative of family members, and an objective evaluation of the company's performance is seriously jeopardized.

For whatever reason, coordination of major functions within the family firm must be worked at with particular diligence if coordinated corporate plans are to be developed. One of the most effective means of accomplishing this broadening of perspective is by freeing up the channels of communication and involving the executive team in a frank exploration of issues and a discussion of significant future projects.

The sharing of ideas, especially in the early phases of their development, is

321

one of the major prerequisites for getting marketing, engineering, production, and other functions of the management organization, to pull together in the interest of integrated future action. In this way, important implications for the company can be identified and dealt with before ideas have hardened and feelings have jelled with respect to alternatives.

One president of a New England firm has invested four hours weekly for several years in meetings with his executive team for general discussions about the company's activities and future plans. The result, he believes, is improved current performance and a shared perspective about where the company is heading.

Achieving executive teamwork and involvement in the family firm is admittedly no small task. For family executives, it may require sensitive guidance in achieving more objectivity about their contribution to the firm. For non-family executives, it may require more encouragement in expressing their frank opinions about what they believe to be the best interests of the organization. These aspects of interpersonal relationships among the executive team must be worked out if individual points of view are to be expanded into corporate wide perspectives.

The executive group must work together smoothly as a team, rather than as a group of talented individuals, each of whom is an extension of the chief executive. They may need help and assistance in developing the managerial skills which will enable them to participate in this dimension of management. But such education and assistance is available from numerous sources. Making provision for their use can strengthen executive teamwork in the planning effort.

Using the board of directors

As a group of counsellors having a wide range of experience and mature insights, an active and interested board of directors can provide valuable assistance to the chief executive and thus add still another dimension to the planning effort. In all too many family firms, unfortunately, the board is either conspicuous by its absence or serves merely as a rubber stamp. Yet the creation of an active, viable board has been found to be a most effective mechanism for objectively evaluating the company's situation and planning for its future.

There is no hard and fast rule on what the composition of the board should be. Some chief executives may prefer purely outside representation because they believe this assures complete objectivity. Others may feel that some representation from key members of the management group affords equal advantage. In either case, it is clearly desirable to have the most effective outside representation possible. In selecting criteria for membership on the board, executive experience (especially other chief executives) and

322

industry knowledge (perhaps customers or suppliers) should take precedence over community position or amount of stock-ownership. Some members of the family may well derive more benefit from selecting a qualified outsider to represent them on the board than by insisting on sitting themselves.

Interesting capable outsiders in membership on the board need not necessarily be a difficult or costly activity. Assurance by both word and deed that the contribution of the board will be a valued one is often a sufficient motivation for acceptance, and financial remuneration can be modest.

In the family firm, the board of directors performs a purely advisory service; it cannot 'manage' the business, and it should not be used to second guess the decisions of operating management. But it can become thoroughly familiar with the aspirations and capabilities of the company. And by developing experience in working together as a team, it can serve as a valuable sounding board for the discussion of the strategic problems of the firm. A board which fulfills such a function is clearly a valuable source of help to the chief executive in all of the major aspects of planning the firm's future.

Financial planning: dealing with the obligations of ownership

For the family firm, corporate financial planning and individual estate planning must be carried on simultaneously if the long-term financial needs of both the company and family are to be dealt with comprehensively.

Within this dual context of the needs of the family and the firm, the financial issues that must be dealt with are (a) making proper provision for the allocation of ownership; (b) dealing with the problems raised by the family's investment concentration; and (c) preserving the firm's liquidity.

Making proper provision for the allocation of ownership

From a financial point of view, it is not always easy to make explicit exactly what the arrangements for future ownership should be. However, one approach that may be helpful in dealing with this issue is to consider the overall aspects of ownership as comprising several distinct elements:

1 Control (management direction).
2 Present worth.
3 Current income.
4 Future earnings.

Viewing the ownership of the firm in these component parts can be quite helpful in building an estate plan which comes to grips with the need for an appropriate allocation of various benefits and responsibilities. For example, a plan which aims at securing current income for the widow (via preferred stock dividends), future earnings to the son presently active in the business (via a non-voting common), and present control to the senior family member (via a voting common stock) is one illustration of the allocation of ownership.

Within a given category, such as future earnings, the use of arrangements which include gifts, voting trusts, testamentary trusts, and foundations can provide for flexibility in the subdivision of specific obligations. In addition, it can help minimize both current taxation and future legal costs and complications.

The separation and allocation of the benefits of ownership need not be confined to the securities of the firm. It may also be done with respect to the firm's assets. For example, real estate, buildings, raw material reserves, trade marks, and patents may be allocated to specific beneficiaries if it serves the purposes of both financial planning in the firm and estate planning in the family.

The division of the overall aspects of ownership has very direct implications for the problems of management in the future. It presents successor management with a significant set of new obligations, and also imposes some important constraints on the flexibility of response to new strategic challenges. Consequently, whatever the eventual goals, the proper disposition and management of the assets bound up in the family firm can only be methodically worked out within the framework of both an estate plan for the principal stockholders and a financial plan for the firm.

Dealing with the problems raised by the family's investment concentration

Sooner or later, the family business faces a fundamental choice between diversifying its own activities and earnings sources—as a means of broadening the family's investment concentration—and permitting the firm's stockholders to diversify their own holdings through the reinvestment of dividends or capital distributions.

While business diversification may eventually be a prudent course from a corporate point of view, it is not particularly wise to undertake it solely as an answer to the family's need for diversified holdings. For one thing, diversification from within demands capital and technical skills which may well have to be assembled from outside the firm, and which may require additional investment of family resources. For another, acquisition and diversification bring a whole new range of managerial responsibilities to the firm.

There is some historical evidence which indicates that as family generations disperse, the viewpoints and needs of individual stockholders will diverge. The longer the issue of individual versus corporate diversification is postponed, the more serious it becomes. For some companies, especially those with a proliferation of heirs who are not associated with the business, it makes a great deal of sense to encourage stockholders to plan their own diversification program. One New England company which did not do this is currently not in a position to meet the dividend pressures of the 60 heirs of the founder, almost all of whom have remained dependent on the earnings of the firm. It is now facing raids from outside bidders, as the stockholders are seeking income for personal diversification from outright sale of their holdings. On the other hand, where the family is committed to the firm as a vehicle for diversification, this *can* be an appropriate course. Perhaps the most successful illustration is that of the Chandler family of Los Angeles and the Times Mirror Company which they control. Mr Norman Chandler decided that the company should not depend solely on its newspaper but should build up income from other sources. The objective was to double the size of *Times Mirror* in six years. Today, the Chandlers own a smaller proportion of the stock, but in a larger, more diversified company.

Assuring corporate liquidity

In a sense, the major issue underlying all of the obligations and opportunities which face the family firm is the need for preserving the liquidity of the firm's financial resources. Growth, diversification, dividend pressures, and the claims of estate taxation—all of these represent threats to corporate liquidity.

To be sure, growth and diversification may represent significant opportunities for the firm. But for them to be realized, both family and firm must be committed to this corporate aspiration, and stockholder dividend pressures accordingly eased. In any case, stockholder dividend policies should be carefully adjusted to the present and future financial needs of the firm. This is, in the long run, a far wiser course of action than permitting the family to dictate to the firm what the dividend policy will be purely in terms of individual self-interest.

All too often, stockholders of the closely held firm are not given the opportunity to realize what they might gain by deferring present income (i.e., by accepting reasonable rather than excessive dividends). Vague and abstract talk about the corporation's growth requirements may sound unconvincing or insufficiently specific. One of the important advantages, therefore, of articulating a specific plan of action is to enable stockholders to better appreciate the opportunities that can be pursued if retained earnings are put to work within the corporation.

In the case of the family firm, such an articulated long-term plan should include provision for meeting the company's liquidity needs in the event of the death of a major stockholder, as well as provisions for planned growth. The claims of estate taxation can be a serious threat to the firm's resources. All too often the heirs of major stockholders have no liquid assets of their own to cover the taxes which inevitably accompany the transfer of the stock-ownership. To retain control of the stock, the firm must see that funds are found to pay the estate taxes. This particular contingency is one of the most serious that can arise for the family firm; and it is the one which makes personal estate planning for the major stockholders such a vital matter of corporate concern. For the estate plan not only deals with the allocation of ownership; it is also the principal means of making provision for protecting the liquidity of both family and firm.

On going public

One major step which a number of firms have taken in recent years to address these very financial issues is that of 'going public'. Since going public is a major transition away from being a family firm, it merits some separate discussion as a particular option available to the family firm.

One aspect of going public which is frequently mentioned by managers of family firms is that it makes both explicit and limited the obligations of the firm to members of the family. In fact, one president of a family firm insisted on making it a public company because this was the only way both he and his relatives could emotionally accept a limitation on their mutual financial obligation

According to a survey of closely held firms which went public during 1959-61,[1] the reasons given were the following:

1 To raise capital (64 per cent).

2 To facilitate estate settlement (27 per cent).

3 To realize capital gains (16 per cent).

4 To establish a market for family and management stockholders (8 per cent).

5 To prepare for a merger or acquisition (10 per cent).

For all practical purposes, the decision to go public is almost irrevocable. (A recent and single exception was the George A. Fuller Co., which reversed the process and 'went private' by selling the firm's assets to an inside group of management and redeeming the outstanding publicly held shares for cash.)

According to the results reported by the Corplan Associates study, only 51 per cent of the firms felt that going public had been a beneficial experience. This should perhaps not be construed as strongly as to make it seem an argument against going public. Some of the dissatisfactions were perhaps a result of poor planning in specific cases. There is a little doubt, however, that this option should be carefully evaluated and that there are particular difficulties to be anticipated. Perhaps one of the most important is the high cost of raising capital by this method—some 35 per cent of the firms in the study felt that the underwriting costs were excessive. Then, too, premature underwriting at high prices can aggravate the problems of subsequent issues.

Indeed, the aftermarket for the initial equity is one of the most critical aspects of going public. If the stock price drifts down, future efforts at equity financing may be jeopardized. On the other hand, a thin but active market can overprice the stock, complicating estate settlement problems for family stockholders. Supporting the market price with corporate funds is a rather costly stopgap measure, and a further drain on capital resources.

As a one-time experience, about which there is only limited information available from which to learn, going public will undoubtedly bring mixed satisfactions to the family firm—achieving some advantages and removing some personal satisfactions and conveniences. Undoubtedly, the best possible professional counsel should be secured before taking this step. The key issue to be decided is whether the financial interests of the family and those of the firm are so divergent as to be better off separated; a decision which can only be made from inside the organization.

Making provision for continuity of leadership

Since the dynamics of succession in family firms do make periods of management transition potentially stressful to the organization, there is all the more reason to prepare for them carefully. Both the mechanisms for choosing a successor and the mechanisms for preserving continuity within the organization have an important bearing on this issue.

Choosing a successor

How the next chief executive will be selected involves both who will choose him, and the criteria which will be used as a basis for choice. Here, the current chief executive has a major decision to face concerning the extent to which he himself wishes to determine who will come after him. If he does not wish to do this alone, he must create the mechanisms which can make that choice, or assist him in his decision.

A major issue which must be faced explicitly is what criteria will be used in the selection process and, particularly, what weight will be given to family affiliation. But in any case, planning for management succession should be carried out as early as possible in the development of the people who are serious contenders for the position of future chief executive. Viewing executive development as a process to be planned for on a continuing basis will do much toward preserving the options of the firm in selecting the most appropriate successor when the time comes for his actual designation.

Once a future chief executive has been selected, there remains the sensitive problem of timing the announcement of the decision and preparing him for his future responsibilities. It is sometimes useful to consider a division of authority which will elevate the younger man to the presidency while the senior executive assumes for a time the titles of chairman of the board and chief executive officer. This permits the younger man to grow into his eventual responsibilities gradually while the guidance and counsel of his predecessor are still available. It does, however, require sensitivity on the part of the older generation in timing an appropriate and graceful withdrawal from the forefront of executive action. (In at least one company examined in the course of our research, the retired chief executive's continued efforts to exert his influence on current management issues provoked a contest of factions which strained relationships within the management group severely for a time.)

Providing for the orderly transfer of authority

The essential elements in the orderly transfer of authority during management transition in the family firm are the chief executive himself, the executive team, and the board of directors.

The chief executive has the critical role in involving these groups in planning the company's future, so that they will have a commitment to its goals. Change and continuity require the sharing of perceptions, values, and insights. If effective foundations for planning have been laid, periods of management transition need not shake the organization's continuity of purpose. Especially in family firms, a great deal of executive time should be explicitly devoted to discussing the organization's future. This is so because the issues are complex, the communications problems often difficult, and the personal relationships delicate. Only a substantial amount of dialogue can generate an objective consideration of the issues. But out of such dialogue can come not only constructive contributions on current planning issues from members of the executive team and the board, but stronger organizational relationships and shared perspectives which reinforce continuity of purpose.

In most companies, the necessary first step is simply that of making the time to learn to discuss planning issues effectively.

Getting the planning job done: the role of the chief executive

Effective planning for the future in the family firm depends essentially on the leadership of the chief executive. It is he who determines the way the firm resolves the various interlocking relationships which it faces: the relationship of past to future, of family to non-family, of stockholder to management, and of generation to generation. The chief executive stands at the confluence of these relationships and by his behavior—both implicit and explicit—

determines what the future will be. However, it should be emphasized that such responsibilities for leadership are by no means limited to the family firm. But the role of the chief executive in the family firm is a special one, for it combines two powerful roles—that of head of the family and that of head of the economic unit. As such, there are in many family firms far fewer constraints on the personal inclinations of the president than in non-family firms. And many of the constraints that do exist stem from the configuration of family relationships, rather than from the economic interests of the firm.

As a result, the chief executive of the family firm largely determines what its future aspirations will be. He does this in many ways, some of which he may not even be aware of himself. If he thinks or speaks of the future in terms of 'being a $20 million company', or 'earning $2.00 a share', or 'a fourth generation Jones as president', that will become a guideline for the company's development. If he is not careful, his associates may even attribute to him some aspirations which he does not really hold. He can only avoid this by making a concerted effort to make his aspirations explicit, in a context within which they can be objectively examined.

In addition, the chief executive is the only one in a family firm who can create mechanisms for insuring some degree of continuity. If he creates an active and effective board, there will be one. If he creates an active and effective executive team, the company will have one. If he chooses to do neither, no one else can.

Further, the chief executive influences the future of the firm enormously by the manner in which he disposes of his personal assets. By drawing his will, creating trust arrangements, and making explicit plans for the business as well as for the family, he vitally affects what will subsequently become of the organization he heads.

And finally, the chief executive affects the future of the firm by the willingness with which he seeks assistance in his tasks. The chief executive who feels that he must unilaterally decide on the future of the organization closes off one of the major resources available to the company: the combined capabilities of those to whom he has ready access, especially his own executive team and board. Accepting assistance is not synonymous with sacrificing leadership. In fact, creating the mechanisms for assistance is one of the critical challenges which face the chief executive of a family firm. Not only will such mechanisms extend the effectiveness of his own leadership, but they will continue to serve the organization under the leadership of his successor.

Reference

1. 'Going Public', Corplan Associates, an affiliate of IIT Research Institute, Chicago, Illinois.

PART SIX : Case histories of existing corporate planning systems

The final part of the book offers three examples of planning systems in different situations, International Business Machines, International Minerals and Chemical Corporation, and Pilkington Brothers Ltd. The danger of offering examples is that readers may feel that the examples are to be followed. Since the underlying argument in the book is the need for a planning process to be tailormade for the specific needs of the firm, the offering of examples with that expectation would be a total contradiction.

In reading these examples of planning systems, I suggest that it may be more helpful if the reader approaches them with a series of questions which have been raised earlier in the book. Some of these are:

1 What are the critical top management problems in this company?

2 Does the process described appear to help top management to cope with these problems? Specifically, how does it do so?

3 Is the timespan over which planning takes place relevant to top management's time horizon?

4 How would a chief executive make his own inputs into this planning system?

5 Has responsibility for different parts of the planning work been sensibly allocated?

6 What knowledge, aptitudes, and skills would the 'director of corporate planning' need to have?

7 How should I judge the performance of the 'director of corporate planning'?

8 Does it appear that plans are made on an appropriate information base?

9 Is there an effective linking mechanism between strategy, projects, and operations?

10 Are there any aspects of these examples which would profit my company if they were introduced? What benefits would I expect if they were introduced?

Finally, it may be useful to examine these examples against the 25 fundamental and common reasons for faulty long-range planning advanced by G. A. Steiner in his article 'How to assure poor long-range planning for your company'. (See page 251.) How do these three examples measure up?

(Editor)

20. Corporate planning: The keystone of the management system

W. W. Simmons

The objective of this article is to examine corporate planning and its position in a management system of the future. I believe a properly established planning process can become the keystone of corporate planning in a management system. First, it will be helpful to review some current trends in this area.

Figure 20.1 shows a typical management system in its simplest form. The organizational structure is at the top of the system and the divisional or subsidiary unit at the bottom. The linkages are four major areas:

1 The planning process.
2 The operating guidelines.
3 The control system.
4 The management development programme.

These linkages interact, as indicated by the arrows, between the structural organization and the operating groups, as well as between themselves.

Figure 20.2 is a detailed diagram of the processes of a typical management system, and Fig. 20.3 shows the trends prevalent in these processes.

In the planning process, emphasis has been swinging from operations to markets and business areas. Several years ago, Theodore Levitt, in his now-classic article 'Marketing Myopia', made a simple, but far-reaching,

● Reproduced with permission from *Long-Range Planning*, Vol. I, No. 3, December 1968, pp. 2-9.

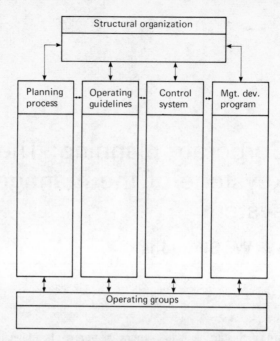

Figure 20.1   A management system: General

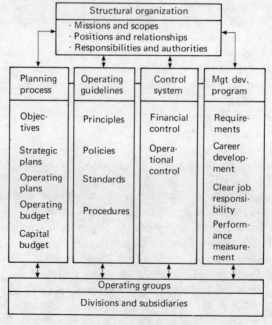

Figure 20.2   A management system: Detail

334

| Structural organization |
| · Missions and scopes |
| · Positions and relationships |
| · Responsibilities and authorities |

Planning process	Operating guidelines	Control system	Mgt dev. program
Operations	Fixed	Budgets	Action
+	+	+	+
Markets & businesses	Open to change	Plans	Goal-oriented

| Operating groups |
| Divisions and subsidiaries |

Figure 20.3   A management system: Trends

observation. He said businesses must examine the needs of the markets they serve, and then develop products to serve these needs. The word 'myopia' refers to the traditional practice of developing products in search of a market: certainly, there is always the temptation to market every product as it emerges from the engineering laboratories. However, there may not always be a market for something with a given set of specifications, even though good development money is in it. If sensitivity to changing market definition and business needs is developed and also made the basis of product development decisions, then businesses can experience controlled and efficient growth.

In operating guidelines, there has been a movement from fixed policies and procedures to an attitude of 'open to change'. Today's management encourages every member of its organization to challenge each fixed policy when it appears to constrain the organization unnecessarily in its pursuit of goals and objectives.

In the area of control systems, control to plans has been added to budget control. It is no longer satisfactory to say we have met the budget. It is equally important to be able to answer the question: have we implemented the plan successfully for which the money we spent was intended?

Management development programmes have been moving from straight action requirements to the establishment of goals to guide these actions. This trend is analogous to the fans not appreciating the football-player who runs a hundred yards in the wrong direction.

Planning process

It is my contention, and others agree, that the role of planning in the management system should provide corporate management with flexibility and continuity. Planning is the essential ingredient to continued growth and success. Maximizing operational efficiency is not enough. It is also not sufficient to only develop well-thought-out ideas about where the corporation should be and what it should be doing in the future. One must be able to implement, in an orderly fashion, these ideas. Many schemes now exist for structured problem-solving and analysis. Some of these schemes have been put into practice, most notably through work by the Rand Corporation and the American Department of Defense. This vigour has not, however, permeated industrial management to a significant extent at this time.

Analysis, for analysis sake, accomplishes little. Analysis must serve as a basis for action. It is the simple step of reducing thoughts to actions, or proposed actions, which is as important an element of planning as analysis. To implement a plan, there must be a close association between the planner and the implementer. In fact, he should ideally be the same person.

Many multidivisional corporations, of the non-holding company orientation, are run on a decentralized basis with operating responsibility delegated to divisional management. These divisions, however, are not operated as isolated entities, but are knitted together by a corporate management team applying a synergistic effect: the two-plus-two-equals-five phenomenon. This overview and integration of the total operation helps direct the future of the corporation in the right directions.

When there are independent divisions, usually there is no hierarchy of plans. With corporate strategic planning, however, there is a corporate plan at the peak. A strategic plan for a corporation should be more than just a tabulation; it should range beyond the confines of the current organizational structure, and should seek to define the best courses of action for the future. It should be based on matching opportunities against available resources, as well as on realistically available future resources.

Most corporations have a corporate plan built around the ideas and actions of top management. However, few corporations have taken the step of developing an explicit document of guidance, updating it when the need arises, and including in it the most current information. Divisional plans, however, do enter actively into the total direction of the corporate plan.

Strategic planning

The value added which distinguishes a corporate plan from the sum of the division's plans, and similarly divisional strategic plans from the sum of its departmental or functional plans, can be described by three processes fundamental to strategic planning:

1 Environmental analysis.
2 Objective setting.
3 Strategy formulation.

Looking briefly at these processes (Fig. 20.4), it is apparent that there are several separate and important steps in each of these areas.

The top section of Fig. 20.4 describes the steps involved in environmental analysis, principally balancing external opportunities against internal capabilities. The next process, objective setting, is shown in the middle area. With preliminary objectives in mind, one can then move on to the third process, strategy formulation. In addition, there are reciprocal processes which act to

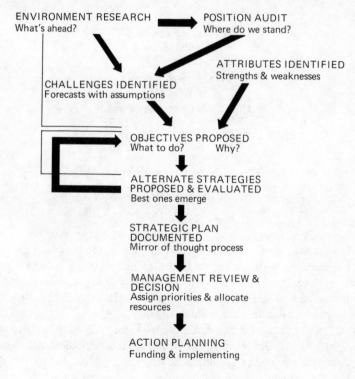

Figure 20.4   Strategic planning process

refine both objectives and strategies, as the alternatives are played against one another.

A simplified form of the strategic planning process is shown in Fig. 20.5. It illustrates the thought process behind the work flow. These questions are asked for any task, whether it be a major mission of a division, or simply a plan for tomorrow's office activity.

During the development of IBM planning system, we instituted eight major changes which modified our operation to reflect the strategic planning processes just described.

First, we lengthened the planning period. (A standard planning joke in our organization is the definition of planning: 'What's for lunch?') We used to limit our long-range look to five years, but, since the plans were reviewed in the middle of the first year, it really covered only four and a half years. This is a short timespan in the computer business, and it was all too easy to project rather than plan, and did not give us a long enough look at what new products were needed to enter our markets. We extended the period to seven years.

ENVIRONMENT—Backdrop
    What really is my business?
    Where is it going?
    What are my key assumptions?

OBJECTIVES—Quantities
    Why not more or less?

STRATEGY—Clear course of action
    What will it do for my division?
    Why this one?
    What risks?
    What dependencies?

Figure 20.5   A strategy: The thought process

If the plan represents a seven year projection of known products, it must fall below management's desire for growth based on the product's life cycle. Thus, management must participate in the change necessary to meet its own and external expectations for the corporation. The timespan differs, but there is a time for each business left and right of the dotted line in Fig. 20.6. Only top management can affect the curve to the right.

Second, we changed the name of the plan from 'long-range' to 'strategic': this helped to make the planning effort more real by not allowing a manager to feel that it was long range, out of touch, and could be put on the shelf. The plan is documentation for a departmental manager's strategy to cause action today, based on a long-term look and a set of objectives. The

338

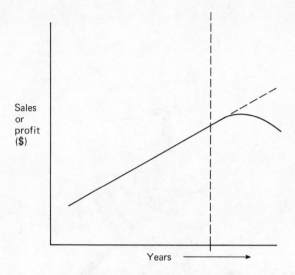

Figure 20.6   Planning versus projection

manager's annual operating plan (the two year look) now becomes the implementation of his strategic plan.

Third, we stressed the hierarchical nature of planning with the strategic plan at the top of the divisional hierarchy (Fig. 20.7). Planning documents should include only information vital to helping top management of a division or the corporation to guide current and future actions. When discussing this subject with divisional management, the following example helps to illustrate what we are looking for.

Consider the hypothetical case of a manager who has been in charge of his division for several years. He is given a special task, for example, a year's assignment with the Federal Government with the understanding that he will return to his former position in the division after that time. The question: What document should this man leave with his division to ensure continuity of direction? We believe it should be a strategic plan. Obviously, it should not detail all things of ongoing significance, because these would be overseen by his existing staff and his assistants. It should transmit overall strategies and objectives, so that decision-making, during the year he is away, continues to move the division in the directions he has established, based on experience and success. The plan should contain, in essence, the guidance that a general manager gives to a division. It should include narrative and quantitative information. It should be meaningful both as a stand-alone document, and for transmitting basic information about the division to a division's management team and to corporate management.

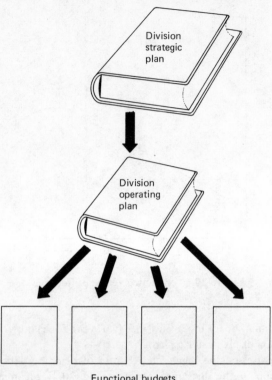

Figure 20.7 Hierarchy of plans

Fourth, we determined that strategic plans should be kept current by updating them annually. Essentially, we extend the plan an additional year during a review early each following year. Traditionally, we had started a new long-range planning cycle each year. With the new approach, the plan is maintained continuously throughout the year, with a single set of objectives spanning from year to year. To provide for changes several times a year, with the necessity for revising pages, all plans are in looseleaf form. Change is basic to planning. Consequently, while planning for change, we have recognized that our strategic plans themselves will change.

Fifth, we worked towards a documented corporate plan, in addition to divisional strategic plans. The corporate plan would not be a sum of the divisional plans, but would represent the actions the corporation proposed to take beyond the traditional domains of the divisions.

The corporate office is the company's top management group. It is composed of the four senior officers: the chairman, the president, the vice-chairman, and the chairman of the executive committee. Previously, their

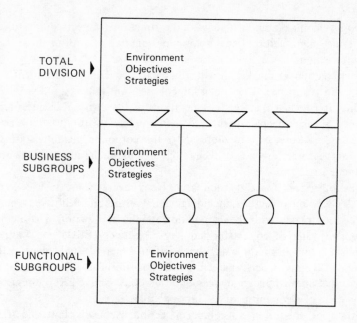

TOTAL
DIVISION ▶

Environment
Objectives
Strategies

BUSINESS
SUBGROUPS ▶

Environment
Objectives
Strategies

FUNCTIONAL
SUBGROUPS ▶

Environment
Objectives
Strategies

Figure 20.8   Division strategic plan

role was an annual review of long-range plans. Today, they are spending far more time on the future of the company; on the strategic aspects of today's problems. In 1967, the corporate office established a management committee composed of four senior executives who have had experience in all aspects of the business. One of their primary responsibilities involves planning for the corporation. This committee reviews divisional plans and synthesizes them so that the corporate office can better relate the operations of the various businesses to the corporate plan.

Sixth, the corporate staff role, which was primarily one of auditing the operations of the divisions, changed to one of relating divisional plans to future environment, and evaluating the feasibility of strategies. It now provides a different slant on problems of corporate significance by providing better syntheses of divisional plans which can be merged into a total corporate picture. Key staff areas, including marketing, engineering and technology, manufacturing, service, finance, and planning, prepare documented critiques of each plan for review by the management committee.

Seventh, we changed the content and format of the divisional strategic plan. This is one of the most significant changes in the system (Fig. 20.8). As indicated earlier, the plan expresses, in three major sections, what is important to a division over the next seven years. The first section is an overview of the total divisional operation. The second section addresses the various business areas of the division. The third section, the focus of our previous planning approach, covers the functional aspects of the division: marketing, manufacturing, technology, personnnel, etc. All of these sections are interrelated.

Each section is divided into distinct parts covering environment, objectives, and strategies. The environment section indicates those external conditions which will affect the operations of the division, business area, or function during the plan period. Elements of the environment, for example the economic forecast, are supplied by the corporate planning staff. Other elements, such as forecasts of technology in a particular industry, are evolved by the division.

The objectives for a division arise from several sources. The division's overall economic objectives, including annual results and profit, are a contract the division makes with the corporation for the plan period. These contract agreements are called established key objectives (**EKO**) and have been established by corporate management after a period of dialogue with the division. Divisional management then obtains subsidiary objectives for itself, by product lines, application areas, and functions. Unlike EKOs, these are not in the form of a commitment to corporate management.

Strategies are the broad courses of action which divisions undertake to meet their objectives. They are stated in both narrative and quantitative form. If the environment describes a new market which is to be developed, and specific assumptions have been made in analyzing this market, the strategy then states explicitly what courses of action must be taken to meet the objectives.

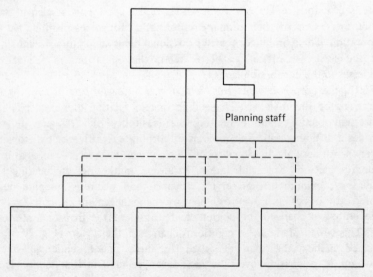

Figure 20.9   Organization for planning

The detailed action plans, which fulfil the broad courses of action, are not included in the strategic plan, but are the focal point of the two year operating plan.

In every plan, emphasis is on the new and different things which will change the direction of the corporation. Ongoing activities require mention for budget entry, to make sure that adequate resources exist to carry out their mission. Because most functional decisions are concerned with product lines, and most market and other environmental changes occur in this context, planning emphasis is on business areas. In the office products division, for example, the plan discusses electric typewriter plans in one section, dictating equipment plans in another section, and composing equipment plans in a third section.

With the emphasis on change, the specific qualifications of the change must be indicated, otherwise the plan is meaningless. Verbs like 'improve', 'increase', 'enlarge' are undesirable unless modified by quantitative measurements indicating how much will be accomplished in a given time period. This is difficult to accomplish, for most people prefer to remain ambiguous. One humorous suggestion for solving this problem is to assign quantitative values to each verb: improve = 5 per cent, increase = 10 per cent, and enlarge = 15 per cent.

Top management guidance on the overall question is provided through the established key objectives. If too many objectives are set, top guidance becomes a halter rather than a guide, and divisional management can no longer operate in an entrepreneurial fashion. But without leadership, controlling the direction of growth is impossible.

Good strategic divisional plans serve two purposes. They provide important tools for divisional management to communicate to its own management and to measure its progress in attaining its objectives; and they also provide corporate management with a picture, at all times, of a division's ability to meet its objectives, thus assuring divisional management continuous operational freedom. The latter is the most difficult part of implementation of the new planning operation. It is difficult to assure divisional management that the more carefully they plan and detail their actions, the less interference they will have from top management. There is a built-in feeling that the more divisional management describes its broad courses of action, the more susceptible it will become to corporate interference or second-guessing. The key, of course, is to ensure that top management attacks only major problems, and delegates as much as possible to divisional management.

Eighth, we changed our planning organization (Fig. 20.9). We have always believed that planning is a catalyst, and that it should be done by operating management. Planning has a dotted-line relationship: this approach was upheld in a Stanford Research Institute survey. It was shown that when planning units do the actual job, the corporations had experienced little

343

enthusiasm for planning. However, in those corporations where the planning group had concentrated on weaving planning into the fabric of the management system, executives contacted felt that greater headway had been made in preparing their companies to meet the challenges of the future. We have attempted to observe this latter approach.

Our corporate planning function includes an environment group, an objective determination group, a strategy group, and a management science group: these are guidance groups. The actual planning work is done by divisional management and by corporate staff functional groups.

The objective-setting group, for example, does not make market forecasts, nor attempt to perform work the divisions must do in forecasting their operations. This group reviews the data the division generates, for credibility, reproducibility, and consistency; it relates the data to the total goals of the business, and its findings become the basis for a continued dialogue with the divisions and corporate management.

---

1. Planning period
2. What do we call it?
3. Hierarchial nature of planning
4. Continuous updating
5. Documented corporate plan
6. Role of staff
7. Content of plans
8. Organization for planning

Figure 20.10   Key changes

Similarly, the environment group prepares an environment statement for the total corporation, but spends most of its time working with the divisions, making sure management understands the way to approach its environment.

The strategy group spends as much time with divisions working on their strategies as it spends on corporate strategies which will become part of the corporate plan.

In summary, Fig. 20.10 restates the eight major changes to the planning system.

A typical year

Now let us look at how they all fit together. Figure 20.11 represents a typical year of operation of the system.

The frame, from left to right, is a calendar. The functional activities are shown to the left in the form of the various levels of management involved: first, corporate management (called at IBM the 'management review committee' and the 'management committee'); second, the corporate staff;

344

third, the divisions and subsidiaries. The documents of planning which pass between these management levels are also shown in the diagram.

At the top level is the continuing corporate planning process. During the first half of a year, the strategic plans are being reviewed and updated, and an additional year is added to them. The objectives are reviewed as early as possible, and the planning targets are assigned to divisions and subsidiaries. The divisions revise their plans in the light of possible changes, rethinking the entire process, and developing a current strategic plan. This is reviewed at the divisional headquarters before being submitted to the corporate staffs. When

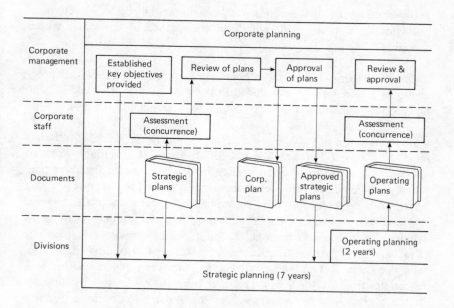

Figure 20.11   A planning system (Time shown: 1 year)

these reviews of strategic plans are completed by the management committee, the corporate office meets, approves the divisions' strategic plans and the corporate plan, and merges them to provide the best possible overall planning for the corporation.

These approved plans are the basis for the regular operating plan which is prepared during the second half of the year. This plan is approved at the end of the year and ensures that the overall strategies are implemented in the operations that ensue during the next year. The operating plan is a byproduct of the strategic plan. It represents not only the ongoing operations of the business, but also the new and revised operations which must be implemented to make the strategic plan a meaningful one.

345

With the new strategic planning approach, several principles had to be observed to make the new system work satisfactorily. These included:

1 **Top management participation**—Understanding and direction from top management was necessary not only in operating the system, but in designing it. Many sessions were held with the corporate office and the management committee to make sure the system reflected their needs and desires. Meetings were held with all divisional managements to make sure they also supported the system.

2 **Objective setting**—It was confined to a minimum number of objectives, to maintain the benefits of decentralized entrepreneurial operations within divisions.

3 **Divisional plans**—They concentrate only on important matters. If every divisional undertaking were included in the strategic plan, it would become burdensome, rather than a management aid to understanding the future.

4 **Computerization**—A system was used to provide a viable quantitative method to permit frequent updating of data. Called a 'business planning system', it is not a sophisticated business model, but a simple planning report generator which creates from basic inputs the standard reports of a planning system. Among these reports are an income and expense statement, a source and application of funds sheet, a summary of manpower requirements, and a summary of facility requirements. The inputs for these reports are: volume of sales, basic cost factors, marketing costs, development costs, production rates, rates per square feet per person or function, etc. The computer mathematically relates this data for the final reports. The relationships are, of course, up to the planner, and he fits them into the system. The business planning system assures that all aspects built into the system are considered, and that each change in input data is looked at in terms of its effect on other parameters.

The business planning system provides conveniently for eight years of projections—one year of actual and seven years of future; any combination of years can be arranged. It also provides for subsetting, or designing the plan into major *classes* of products. This is usually the case in IBM, but it could be subsetted to cover *individual* products when the necessary inputs are available concerning the product. The computer program for the system is written in a language which we developed: PSG—planning systems generator. This language eliminates the need for special programmers to determine the inputs, factors, and displays. All housekeeping—the format and dimension statements—are performed internally by the computer through macro-instructions.

This computerized planning system provides another important asset,

346

which may be one of the greatest benefits for this approach to strategic planning. As all planners know, regardless of how carefully a plan is devised, it cannot eliminate surprises resulting from unanticipated external or internal events. Consequently, decisions are often made because of unforeseen occurrences, and some of these decisions could be quite signficant. With a computerized method of continuously updating the plan, these decisions can be immediately tested by trying various inputs to determine their effect in future years. In short, the plan becomes a simulator for those decisions which must be made without the benefit of long-range study.

To make sure all parts of the corporation understand the intent of the system and its usefulness, seminars are conducted regularly in all divisions and with all corporate groups, to review in detail each of the subjects discussed in the planning document. In addition, documentation of the procedures involved are included in a planning handbook.

In short, planning can now serve its full purpose: identifying business opportunities available to the corporation; assuring pursuit of these opportunities; and assuring continuous improvement in operating performance over the long term. The last ingredient is the attitude and ability of the people within the organization to understand and use the system. This, as well as the continuing refinement of the system itself, will determine its ultimate success.

21. Anatomy of a long-range plan

Donald J. Smalter

Since truly successful planning results in a growth pattern for earnings, let us examine first the characteristics of a growth company. A growth company is differentiated by these criteria: it tends to be technically advanced; risk-takers are among the management group; they are return on investment conscious. Growth companies are organized for development, not merely organized for ongoing operations, but also for the entrepreneurial aspects of management.

Growth companies do certain things in a different way. They deliberately stimulate innovation, initiative, and vigour. They deliberately research their environment. They create advantageous change in that environment, not waiting for change to adversely affect them. Finally, they sustain high earnings per share growth, and set targets for achievement. The other noteworthy aspect of growth companies is that they tend to operate in growth segments of the world's economy, or at least they pick products within their own segment that tend to have excellent growth rates. And finally, growth companies are full of good planners, not just at the top, but 'in-depth', throughout the organization.

My intention in this article is to write about 'The Anatomy of a Long Range Plan'. I will relate a description of IMC's plan, not the substance of it, but the structure of that plan. The reader may then relate it to his own company and his own problems and particular needs. I am not advocating that each plan should be exactly the same, because every company is structured differently and their problem focus is different. But hopefully, after reading this article, a senior manager will be better able to design his own planning processes. Note my emphasis on the planning 'process'.

● Reproduced with permission from *Long-Range Planning*, Vol. I, No. 3, March 1969, pp. 2-8.

The five year plan

We now assemble a *five year plan* in two volumes. It is the process of pulling the *plan* together that counts, not this final document. IMC had initially conducted long-range planning on an intuitively identified project basis at the corporate level. In changing the system, my first thought was this: What would be in a binder representing our long-range plan if I had it on the shelf? I asked a number of supposedly knowledgeable experts and received rather nebulous answers. Nobody seemed to know!

I began to think it through myself, with the objective in mind that if I could determine the structure, i.e., what had to be in the binder, I would then have a better grasp of the process of assembly. Also, we would then know better how to organize the corporation effort or, to use my favorite term, 'mobilize' executive involvement. Volume 1 of the plan has an outline as illustrated in Fig. 21.1. There is a section on overall objectives, which breaks

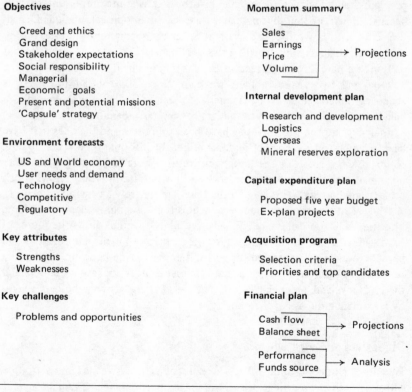

Objectives

Creed and ethics
Grand design
Stakeholder expectations
Social responsibility
Managerial
Economic goals
Present and potential missions
'Capsule' strategy

Environment forecasts

US and World economy
User needs and demand
Technology
Competitive
Regulatory

Key attributes

Strengths
Weaknesses

Key challenges

Problems and opportunities

Momentum summary

Sales
Earnings
Price → Projections
Volume

Internal development plan

Research and development
Logistics
Overseas
Mineral reserves exploration

Capital expenditure plan

Proposed five year budget
Ex-plan projects

Acquisition program

Selection criteria
Priorities and top candidates

Financial plan

Cash flow
Balance sheet → Projections

Performance
Funds source → Analysis

Figure 21.1 IMC five year plan. Outline of contents: Volume 1

down into: a creed, a 'grand-design' statement of the corporate purpose, statements on stakeholder expectations, social responsibility objectives, managerial objectives, i.e., how we are going to manage the business, economic mission goals, i.e., specific targets of achievement by a certain time, identification of the present and potential missions in which IMC would be involved; and, finally, a capsule statement of corporate strategy.

The second section is fairly short; it covers the whole corporate business environment, but not only of the US. Since IMC makes nearly one-half of its profits from foreign sales, we are concerned with the world, and we try to identify a forecast of key changes and trends that will be occurring in our environment in the broadest sense. Next, there is a section which identifies corporate strengths and weaknesses, followed by a section on the key issues or challenges, problems, and opportunities that we see ahead of us in the next five years. Next, there is a section, primarily financial tables, which lists the dollar sales and earnings targets, the price realizations expected, the sales volumes, and a profit and loss statement complete through the five years. The sixth section is an internal development plan for research and development programs, and logistics (economic distribution is quite important to IMC because much of our business is in heavy commodities). Included is an overseas plan, as we visualize overseas areas as sizeable opportunities and in our prime business, the growth rates are higher. Last, but not least in that section, we have a minerals reserve and exploration plan. In this case, we plan well beyond five years. In fact, we plan 25 to 30 years ahead, as far as acquiring mineral reserves. Next, there is a section on the capital expenditure plan, i.e., the proposed five year budget for capital expenditures.

Included are the projects that have been proposed, and the ones that have been rejected for a variety of reasons: either the information was inadequate, or the risk too great, or the investment returns were too low. Now this does not mean that these projects are necessarily dead, but it clearly shows which projects are 'in-plan'. This is not a rigid plan, but merely a provisional plan.

The eighth section contains an acquisition program, selection criteria, priorities, and top candidates. Finally, a financial section shows the source of funds and the use of funds. Because we visualize a lot of opportunities and because we have generated opportunities by planning, our debt as a percentage of capital structure is about 50 per cent. We believe we understand the risks involved, and believe, too, that we are doing the shareholders a favor by maximizing the use of their equity.

Objectives and strategy

The first section of volume 1 pertains to objectives. We had more trouble with these than anything else in the planning discipline. There is a great amount of confusion in the literature, and this is my concise resolution from my study. There are objectives related to creed or ethics. There should be objectives related to stockholder relations, investors, lenders, employees. There are objectives related to social responsibility, and managerial objectives related to how we are going to manage the business. Are we going to pay our employees a little extra? How far down in the ranks are we going to communicate our planning information and objectives? Next there are the broad objectives related to economic purpose in the world economy. These broad objectives, once established, tend to be rather stable and unchanging. They must be reviewed, but not very frequently.

Finally, there are the objectives that planners grapple with most of the time, economic mission goals. These goals are dynamic and ever-changing. These goals relate to profitability performance, market standing, productivity, efficiency, and resource position.

When we survey the corporate stakeholders, there are quite a few people that have a stake in the typical corporation. If the investor benefits can be maximized, all others will benefit. The key challenge is to continue earnings per share growth upward in a steady trend to maximize the price-earnings

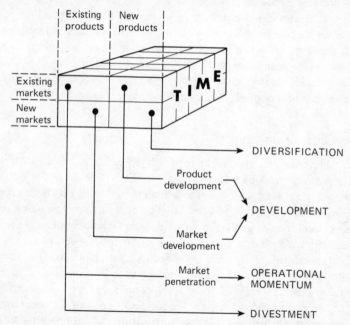

Figure 21.2   Developing a strategy for growth. Management must attempt to establish a rational 'balance' or 'mix' of these fundamental growth strategies, based on their needs and opportunities through time, grappling with the resource trade-offs, e.g., short-term profits versus long-term gains, further market penetration versus new-market development.

351

ratio. IMC's P/E ratio over the last decade has crept up from 11-12 to 18-20. Our observations of the stock market reveal that if we can grow at 15 per cent per year, with a significant amount of growth history behind us, we will deserve a price-earnings ratio in the 20-25 range.

The trick of achieving a high earnings per share growth, of course, is finding and selecting the right projects. Our calculations indicate that to achieve that earnings per share growth target of 15 per cent would require an average in investment returns of about 12-15 per cent per year. A 10 per cent earnings per share growth will require an average 10 per cent return. This has been clearly placed in front of every manager of any importance in the corporation, to make him realize the 'name of the game'.

Another section in volume 1 is titled the 'Environment'. There are many facets to the environment that we have to consider—eight in number: the investment community, government regulatory, social and cultural environment (and this is becoming more important to us as we invest overseas), the political environment (especially again overseas where this is a problem), the technological environment, product demand or customer needs, the competitive environment, and the economy.

Another key aspect of the planning job from the corporate standpoint is to attempt to establish some balance in growth strategy based on present products versus possible new products and present markets and possible new markets (see Fig. 21.2). We have some sizeable ambitions regarding the lower right box, i.e., acquisitions with related diversification objectives. Around that chart we have designed a system of plans, including a program-plan for each of the business or product lines in which we are involved.

Product lines or missions

The second volume of the *five year plan* is divided into numerous sections, covering various product lines or missions. Each section has a charter, a position audit showing where profits are made, how well we utilize capacity, an environment audit and forecast, a statement of strategies and related programs, specific sales goals and profit goals, resource requirements to carry the program out, a plan performance analysis, indicating return on sales and return on investment, and, finally, a sequenced action plan outline. Since we have an interest in over a dozen product lines of potential corporation interest, we compare each of these to be certain that we are allocating our funds to the most productive area. We make this analysis to be certain that the best lines, with the most attractive opportunities, are provided with our limited funds.

On the right of Fig. 21.3, the sections are related to specific corporate functions, e.g., information systems, purchasing, mining and exploration, research and development, marketing services, and manpower and organiz-

Product line or mission	**Corporate function programs**
Program packages (condensed)	
	For: Information systems
Charter	Procurement
Position audit and attributes	Mining and exploration
Environment forecast	Research and development
Strategies and programs	Marketing services
Goals—sales and profit	Manpower and organization
Resource requirements	
Performance analysis	Contains:
Acquisition candidates	Challenges
Action plan outline	Objectives
	Programs and projects
	Capital requirements
Mission performance	Expenditure budget
comparison	Effort allocation analysis

Figure 21.3   IMC five year plan. Outline of contents: Volume 2

ation. Each of these sections contains a statement of the functional environment, the problems or issues, the objectives, programs, capital requirements, facility expenditures, and expense budgets, and finally, an effort allocation analysis, e.g., in *what* directions for *what* purposes? *How* much money will be spent toward each objective, returning *what* benefits?

The process we ask line management to go through is illustrated in Fig. 21.4.[1] On the upper left, first, completely understand your position, audit your position for the resources that you have at your disposal, the capacity utilization, the profit sources, how much investment is involved, the market share. Next, on the lower left, undertake environment research which establishes what is ahead. From this, prepare forecast with clearly stated premises. Out of such an analysis, problems or issues can be identified that must be responded to. The next step pertains to the process of establishing goals, identifying and evaluating alternative strategies, i.e., the means of achieving these goals. Finally, all this must be assembled in a package plan as shown in the third box, followed by a management review and 'go' or 'no-go' decision to commit the resources. Management must look at various proposals versus other possible uses of those funds. If the resources are committed, action must then be planned in sequence, or programmed, and scheduled. A thorough understanding of this simple process is important for everyone involved. This step is probably the most difficult one because it requires a perceptive, imaginative person, someone who can recognize some of the subtle, as well as the obvious, problems. We ask these fundamental questions: What problems exist? What market needs might be profitably filled? What opportunities are perceived? What threats and constraints must be overcome? What conditions are satisfactory now which could change? What issues

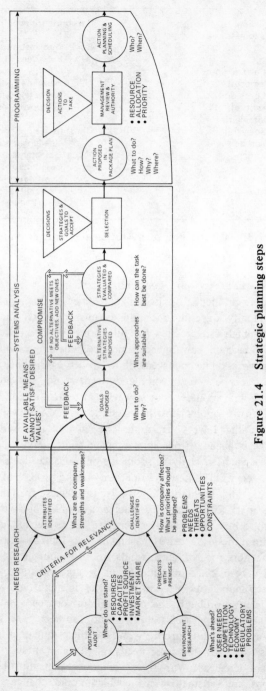

Figure 21.4 Strategic planning steps

354

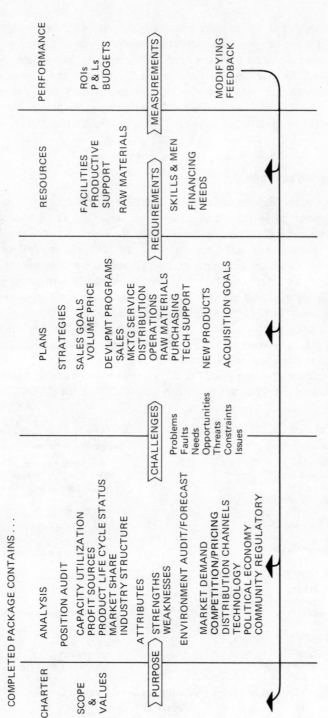

Figure 21.5 Product line package

deserve extended study, perhaps even extensive mathematical, quantitative analysis, in order to resolve an appropriate course of action? This first phase of the process is termed 'Needs research'. This involves the establishment of the problems, by searching for these problems, and then trying to establish which problems are most important to devote attention to. Some of the problems can be answered or solved very simply. Other problems or challenges (in this positive sense) require intensive analysis and study.

The program package

For each product line or mission, we assemble a package which has the contents shown in Fig. 21.5: an analysis section, plans which state goals, development programs, and acquisition goals; the resource requirements for facilities, raw materials, skills, and financing; the total package analyzed for performance via return on investment, profit and loss statements, expense budgets, and, wherever possible, with a cost—benefit analysis of the proposed expense. When a general manager 'comes forward' with such a package, it does not mean that the whole total package will be accepted without alteration, because this package must be systematically and thoroughly reviewed, then compared with other resource requirements, and allocations resolved in a complex, iterative, and imperfect process.

In the program package plan, the environment must be analyzed carefully (see Fig. 21.6). We look at the industry that each of these product lines is

Industry structure	Technological trends
Source of earnings	User needs research
Channels and costs	Technological forecast
Transport costs	Opportunities and threats
Innovative opportunities	
	Market trends
Regulatory constraints	
	Geographical outlook
Macro-economic factors	Product mix changes
	Demand expectations
Competitive situation	
	Momentum share
Position audit	
Attributes and strategies	Potential
Likely new activity	(for more effective participation)
	Penetration
Customer profile	Development
	Integration
Position audit	Innovation
Present sales strategy	

Figure 21.6   Environment audit-forecast

involved in, and attempt to clearly understand where the earnings are made in that industry, what the channels of distribution are, the transport costs, the possibilities for opportunity. We look at regulatory constraints, the macro-economy, the competitive situation, customer profit, technological trends, market trends, our momentum share of the market; we ask the analyst to identify where the potential lies for more effective participation.

In a multidivision company like IMC, or in a multiproduct company, the product line planning must be well coordinated with the staff planning. The manager who heads a given product line must coordinate his objectives and projects for raw materials procurement with the staff mining and exploration group at headquarters. Simultaneously, the staff plans, of course, must support each product line.

The planning schedule

This total process of corporate wide planning must be assembled in some form of schedule, as it is an involved process. There is a lot of recycling or iterative steps, a sizeable readjustment effort, and it is very difficult, if not impossible,

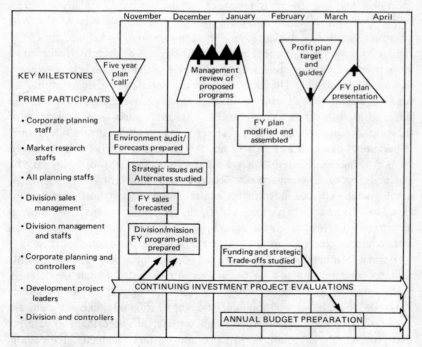

Figure 21.7   Planning-programming-budgeting sequence

357

to neatly schedule, although we have attempted to sequence it on a critical path chart. In simplified form, it is only three major steps, i.e., planning, programming, budgeting, as illustrated in Fig. 21.7. That process involves seeking and identifying all the problems, studying them for a course-of-action, trying to resolve a strategy framework, establishing the specific goals across the five years, assembling the *five year plan,* reviewing each program package, and finally, resolution of a total five year plan which is published in the aforementioned two volumes. The third and final step is the one-year budget which we often call the 'one year slice'. At first, we had difficulty coordinating and integrating the five year plan with the one year plan. Each year, we have achieved a greater degree of integration, so that this year our capital plan for the first year of the five years will be almost identical to the capital plan that finally results.

Project evaluation

There are other types of planning that require the attention of the corporate planner, e.g., the resource requirements planning. Initially, my attention was directed to program planning, being deeply involved in the creation of programs. My task today is reversed, because we have so many programs being proposed. The key problem now is the sorting out of the best proposals. It involves this question: Where are we going to bet our chips? The capital budgeting task is concerned with ranking the projects by their relative attractiveness. Another aspect of the resource planning task is how expense monies are allocated. The cash flow from operations provides a 'pool' of funds available for allocation. Of course, taxes must first be paid, and dividend levels must be determined in a trade-off study versus retention of these funds for internal growth. The US tax structure favors retention *if* reinvestment can earn in excess of about 7 per cent. Funds can be increased by borrowing, with careful analysis of the risks. This pool of funds may be allocated between competing short-term and long-term uses, e.g., sales development expenses, advertising, capital investment, venture development expenses, exploration expenses, and finally, R and D expenses. We have to understand the relative cost-benefit impact of these expenses on more than just an intuitive basis, in order to make rational judgements on allocation.

Formal planning should not produce overconfidence. The documents volumes 1 and 2 are not, in themselves, important, although they have a useful purpose in communicating our plans throughout the organization. Everyone, then, has a common understanding of what our goals are. They are also useful for accountability, although we have not used them to date for that purpose. My key point is this: It is not the final documents that counts. It is a dynamic planning capability, the *process* that really counts.

Implementation

A system of plans is an essential device to bring order to the long-term decision-making process. I believe it is desirable to identify the model system, and then seek to make it operational. The system we have created is uniquely designed for IMC. I hope its exposure here will prove of some value to the reader.

Effective corporate planning, however, does not consist simply of a system. The success of corporate planning is not measured by the production of impressive-looking books titled *Five year plan: Company confidential.* Any aspiring plan will not happen merely because it is neatly documented. It is still very necessary to *make it happen.* What planning can do for a corporation depends *not* on creating rigid, standing plans, but rather on creating a dynamic planning capability. Success stems from a top management that:

Is determined to grow.
Inspires an atmosphere of growth in the company.
Fosters an awareness of environmental change.
Sets high goals.
Develops formal strategies and a budgeted growth plan.
Reshapes the organization to fulfill new objectives.
Encourages entrepreneurial talents.
Stimulates interdependence and collaboration.
Develops suitable incentives, and, most notably,
obtains broad executive involvement.

These things are being done by many companies. Good management accomplishes growth and development through efficient, planned utilization of all available resources. The well-managed organization does not meekly economize and avoid new ventures. Instead, it recognizes opportunity and accepts the entrepreneurial challenge of deploying its resources profitably to capitalize on these opportunities for its own good and for the good of society.

Reference

1. SMALTER, D. J. and RUGGLES, R. 'Six Lessons from the Pentagon.' *Harvard Bsns. Rev.,* March/April 1966.

22. The development of long-term corporate planning at Pilkington

L. B. Pinnell

The Pilkington group of companies makes and sells flat glass, safety glass, fibreglass, pressed glass (including television glassware and high-voltage insulators), and optical glass. It has works in the UK, Canada, the Argentine, South Africa, Rhodesia, Nigeria, India, Australia, New Zealand, Sweden, and Eire, and interests in associated companies. It the last 10 years sales have more than doubled to over £100 million annually and the group now employs 33 000 people. Growth has taken place through the expansion of its major customers in the building and motor industries, through the spread of manufacture to new territories, through the development of new processes and products, and through acquisitions. The invention of float glass has given the group the technical lead in the world's flat glass industry, most of which uses or will use the process under licence.

Introduction of formal corporate planning

The explosive growth of the Pilkington Group after the Second World War naturally reflected considerable planning throughout the organization for many years, but, by 1964, the size of the group and the complexity of the choices facing it led to the decision to develop the group's long-term thinking along more formal lines. A planning advisory committee (PAC) was set up under the group chairman, and included the senior group directors among its members.

• Reproduced with permission from *Long-Range Planning*, Vol. I, No. 4, June 1969, pp. 14-19.

The purposes of this committee were to consider the economic, political, and competitive position of territories and products, and the best means of development of the group's interests and resources in money, technology, and management skill over the following 10 years. It was to coordinate the planning policies of the various parts of the group, to ensure that all necessary information for such plans and their execution was collected and made available, to consider priorities and programmes, and to make recommendations to the general board.

In parallel with the PAC, other committees were established, then or subsequently, to deal with particular types of plans which would have a major impact on the final corporate plans considered by the PAC. A chairman's consultative committee was to consider, in principle, important new proposals of a strategic nature; a technical policy advisory committee would direct and consider the plan for research and development, and a coordinating committee would supply the plans of the other central service departments.

The formation of the planning advisory committee was followed by the appointment of a group planning adviser, from outside the Pilkington Group, who had some experience of corporate planning, but no knowledge of the glass industry.

Some principles

First, it had been obvious from the beginning that overall direction to the group's formal corporate planning activities had to come from the centre. The planning advisory committee had the task of formulating group objectives, assumptions and policies, which after approval by the group general board would be for the guidance of the individual management committees and subsidiary boards. Some of these objectives would be positive directions to plan for the achievement of particular results, while others would have to impose some limitations so that developments proposed by the management committees and subsidiary boards would not greatly exceed the group's resources. It was recognized that this overall guidance needed to be agreed, written down, and communicated.

Second, it was felt that detailed planning had to be made the responsibility of management generally. The group was to establish a decentralized planning system, operating within the group objectives and policies already referred to, but placing the planning responsibility firmly with the management of the operating units and central service departments.

Formal long-term corporate planning was unlikely to be fully accepted throughout the group unless it was seen as a tool to be used by operating management, and the resulting plans were more likely to be achieved if they were prepared by those who would be held responsible for carrying them out. A central planning department could certainly have undertaken a variety of useful investigations, working in conjunction with the appropriate units, but confining the activity to this would have delayed the time when management throughout the group fully exercised its own planning responsibilities.

Third, it was seen that if planning by the operating units was to be effective, it ought to be organized on prearranged and comprehensive lines. The operating units needed a framework to help them collect the necessary data and assemble their ideas systematically. This framework should ensure that all functions in the management structure made their contribution to the detailed planning work.

Fourth, although the likely benefits of the planning activity as such were recognized, it was not felt that it should be an end in itself. A system was needed which would make clear to the management of each operating unit whether the objectives, policies, and actions they proposed were accepted. Having gained this acceptance, the system should ensure that the appropriate action was initiated to implement the action called for in the early years of the plans. There would then need to be a method of measuring progress against the plans and revising them at intervals to take account of any subsequent major changes.

Fifth, it was recognized that much had to be learnt about formal long-term corporate planning in practice. Much knowledge could be gained from other organizations, but it was felt wrong to make elaborate inquiries and preparations spread over a year or two in an attempt to create, on paper, a theoretically ideal planning procedure. The best way to learn was to make a start and gain experience as quickly as possible.

Guidelines for planning

Experts on formal corporate planning sometimes suggest that objectives laid down in the early stages should be extensive, detailed, and quantified, and that these should apply, for example, to the volume of sales, shares of markets, productivity targets, profit margins and so forth for each company involved. While it would have been possible for the centre to conduct exhaustive researches into desirable objectives for many of the group companies, product by product, market by market, process by process, and so forth, it was felt this would delay for too long the introduction of the formal planning procedures throughout the organization. Initially, much of the work in each business would involve the gathering of facts, the clarification of ideas and the study of the implications of particular assumptions and alternative courses of action. That would take time. It was believed that many precise ideas about detailed objectives could only emerge gradually as the formal planning work proceeded throughout the organization. While plans required agreement on objectives, this agreement was to some extent likely to be a byproduct of the planning process itself.

Objectives

Instead of laying down many detailed objectives at group level, it was decided to establish a few objectives of major importance, which it was hoped would influence management thinking in all their plans. These took the form, first of certain development projects which the group wished to pursue; second, a blanket objective for return on capital was fixed at a level well above the current achievement of nearly all the operating units in the group. No dates were set for the achievement for this objective and no separate profit objectives were set for each operating unit. All that was required was that each plan should provide for progress towards the common objective, the local management being given the task of devising ways and means within established group policy. Third, a further financial discipline was imposed which required that each plan should provide for a positive cash flow over a defined period of time.

Statement of policy

Little detailed policy guidance was provided from the centre initially, but it was seen during the preparation of the first long-term plans that questions arose in the minds of management which needed answering in a broad statement of policy. Examination of the completed plans showed that, in addition to the policies that were already being pursued by the general board, others appeared to be not only highly desirable, but essential throughout the group if the financial objectives were to be achieved and the plans successfully implemented.

Thus, between the completion of most of the first cycle of plans in 1967 and the start of work on the second cycle in 1968, the group chairman prepared and the planning advisory committee recommended to the general board a 'statement of group policy' which was subsequently distributed to other directors and to senior managers. The statement of policy referred to fields of activity in which the group wished to be involved, relationships it desired with other organizations, areas of strength on which it wished to build, certain vulnerabilities which it wanted to overcome, and certain key policies which it wished to follow in financial, research, personnel, and other fields.

Assumptions

The first written assumptions which were provided from the centre consisted of general statements, e.g., that the planners should assume no general war and no worldwide economic depression during the period of their plan. Subsequently, the emphasis switched to the provision of common economic

363

assumptions for the United Kingdom operating units. These now cover such matters as the probable overall growth rate of the UK economy, future exchange rates, the rates of inflation to be assumed for the various elements of cost, future tax rates, and the question of UK entry into the European Common Market. Assumptions about customer growth rates are left to be forecast by each operating unit.

The most difficult of the assumptions provided from the centre concerned future rates of cost inflation. Not all companies allow for inflation in their planning since to do so adds considerably to the task of financial evaluation of the plans. It also compels consideration of future selling price policy which some organizations may regard as superfluous on the grounds that cost inflation will eventually work itself out into price inflation also. However, the planning advisory committee took the view that this would be an unrealistic assumption. The group was faced with rising costs in all markets, but selling prices could often not be adjusted in step because of competition or government controls. It seemed important to allow for the impact of cost inflation in the plans so as to foresee any resulting squeeze on profits and thus encourage managers to devise remedies.

The guidelines as to objectives, policies, and assumptions emanating from group level have been supplemented by others laid down by management in the operating units. In 1967, the operating parts of the organization were reorganized and grouped under the supervision of five divisional boards each having worldwide responsibility for a product group. Each divisional board accepted a responsibility for determining divisional objectives and policies, reviewing and approving divisional plans, transmitting them via the planning advisory committee to the general board, and subsequently, monitoring progress. In addition, the group committed itself to the development of 'management by objectives', emphasizing the need for written objectives at all levels of management.

In setting objectives, the board of a worldwide product division will wish to ensure coordination of planning by its operating units, particularly where one product division is a major supplier to another or where there is an important product flow within the division or where export markets could be supplied by several of its operating units. Guidance may be given as to worldwide trends in customer requirements affecting the mix of future product sales, and technical objectives covering new or improved products and processes may also be laid down.

The planning instructions

Detailed planning instructions were devised covering corporate plans to be prepared by each operating unit, plans to be prepared by the central service departments, and plans concerned solely with research and development.

The following questions are designed to help explain the plan for each of the main functional activities (marketing, technical, production, distribution, manpower and financial) in terms of the following:

    (a) Objectives
    (b) Assumptions
    (c) Policy and action to be taken
    (d) Help needed from elsewhere in the Group

1. Marketing

    (a) *Objectives*

        For the following items, where do we stand now, what do we aim to achieve by 1972/73 and what might we achieve by 1977/78?

            Local market share—Exports—New products sold (not already sold by 1968)—Sales volume—Selling prices—Revenue—Productivity of manpower—Trading profit as percentage of revenue—from existing products—from new products.

    (b) *Assumptions*

        On what assumptions (in regard to possible important future developments largely outside our control) is our plan based?

           Examples: The broad economic outlook

                    Growth, or otherwise, of the user industries

                    Changing requirements of existing customers

                    New types of customer and new uses we hope to supply

                    Effects of: government policy

                              import duties and controls and developments of Free

                                  Trade Areas

                              price controls

                              regulations connected with safety, health, building

                                  standards, etc., favouring or hindering our sales

                              competition—from our type of product

                                      —from other products

    (c) *Policy and action proposed to achieve the objectives*

        What broad policy does the plan envisage to achieve the results in (a) above? What action do we plan to take during the next five years to carry out this policy? When will this action be taken?

            Examples: Marketing organization

                    Distribution channels

                    Changes in the product range

                    Changes in the mix of products

                    Standardization of the product

                    Pricing and/or terms of payment

                    What action do we propose for any unprofitable products?

    (d) *Help needed*

        What particular help will be needed from the rest of the division or group if the marketing plan is to be achieved? When?

            Examples: Manpower

                    Services—such as market research

                    Product development

Figure 22.1   Extract from the questions to be answered

For the corporate plans a 10 year period was fixed as standard. As the flat glass industry is capital intensive and the minimum economic unit of production requires an investment of several million pounds, any major capital projects resulting from the plans were thought unlikely to be in operation before the fourth or fifth year, and their full financial consequences could not be effectively calculated unless the analysis covered several more years. All product divisions at present adhere to the 10 year period, but further thought may be given to this.

Where a board is considering the desirability of a particular time scale for detailed quantitative planning, e.g., five years, it will need to ask itself certain questions. Does it wish to see in its plan the achievement of a specific objective which cannot be attained in five years? Does the plan include an important project which cannot be properly evaluated in the five year period? Does it provide for a major programme of action involving a series of steps continuing beyond the five year period? Is any major change in the external environment expected, the nature and effect of which cannot be shown in the data for the five years? As the answers will vary from one division to another, the companies may eventually adopt several different timescales for detailed planning purposes, and somewhat longer ones for expressing their broader strategic aims.

Since the main purpose of the plans is to explain the action to be taken to achieve the objectives, their core is considered to lie in an explanatory text rather than in the figures which quantify the plan. It was felt that this text must answer prearranged questions and that these questions must be so designed so as to aid managers in stating the objectives, assumptions, policy, and action to be taken, and the anticipated results. In the absence of such questions, there could be avoidable gaps in management thinking, and, perhaps, a tendency to 'forecast' possible future events, rather than state a plan of action. Extracts from the questions to be answered in the second cycle of corporate plans are given as Fig. 22.1.

The quantitative information required by the planning instructions for the corporate plans is designed to ensure a logical step by step approach which brings together the calculations of the various functional managers to form a coherent statement. These were devised in discussion with each product division so as to ensure a common overall framework. Details naturally vary from one product division to another, but are standardized within each division. Plans for manpower requirements and financial results are expressed in standard form by all product divisions. Figure 22.2 lists some of the data which is required in the corporate plans.

The separate planning instructions for the central service departments relate to functions, such as personnel, management services, marketing services, purchasing, secretarial, legal and financial departments. The purpose of the questionnaire designed for them is to encourage cost-benefit thinking

366

(a) Marketing	The overall market volume (forecast)
	Our intended share
	Our sales volume
	Product mix
	Sales prices
	Revenue
	Marketing manpower and expenses
	Measurements of productivity
	Contribution to profit
(b) Production	Volume of output required
	Yields and losses
	Capacity required
	% utilization of capacity
	Additions to production facilities
	Materials, fuel and manpower required
	Production costs
	Measurements of productivity
	Contribution to profit
(c) Technical	Planned improvements in production efficiencies
	throughput rates
	yields
	qualities
(d) Distribution	Volumes to be shipped by alternative methods
	Distribution facilities required
	Manpower required
	Distribution costs
	Measurement of productivity
	Contribution to profit
(e) Administration (including headquarters departments)	Timetable for services to be developed
	Manpower
	Expenditure
	Measurements of productivity
	Contribution to profit
(f) Manpower	Overall manpower strength
	Overall productivity measurements
	Management requirements
(g) Financial results	Sales values
	Costs
	Profits and profit margins
	Capital employed
	Sales and profits on capital employed
	Cash flow

Figure 22.2   Minimum quantitative data required in a corporate plan

and to try to assess the long-term consequences of their short-term proposals. Each department is asked what are the objectives of its activities, how its resources of personnel and money are allocated between each activity, how the achievement of its objectives can be measured, and how effectively its activities are being used by the group. Having established these facts about the present position, the department must then consider whether its objectives should be changed, whether they could be better met by increasing or decreasing its activities or by relinquishing or taking over activities currently performed elsewhere. It is asked what opportunities it sees for achieving its agreed activities more efficiently and economically. Finally, it is asked to show for each future year what resources it will require in terms of numbers of employees and expenditure, distinguishing between the resources it will need to carry on its present range of activities and those extra resources or reductions in resources which result from changing its range of activities.

The presentation of the research and development plans makes use of a visual network which displays the detailed technical objectives for new and improved products and processes in relation to the overall corporate objectives. Within this display the emphasis is again on cost-benefit analysis showing the likely expenditure to achieve the desired objective, the likely return on the probability of success.

Planning organization

It had been generally recognized that, while the overall responsibility for long-term plans in each company rested with its executive chairman or management director, he and his line managers were entitled to have assistance in their preparation. It was seen that a coordinator should be appointed in each operating unit responsible to the chief executive so as to provide this help. The coordinator's job would not be to plan, but to ensure that planning was done by the line managers. Ideally, he would need to be involved at all stages of the work, obtaining agreement on timetables for the completion of successive sections, arranging for questions to be answered and facts to be collected, arranging meetings at which progress was reviewed, analysing the quality of the work done and assembling the work of several functions into a corporate plan.

For the most part the men appointed were temporarily assigned to the work, either transferring their normal responsibilities to others or, alternatively, having a range of non-routine functions to perform which enabled them to concentrate attention on planning coordination for a reasonable period of time. All these men were found from within the business. Most had a background in production or accounting and most had no prior experience of formal long-term corporate planning. By the start of the second cycle of

368

Job title: Manager, Divisional Planning
Responsible to: Managing Director

Objective

1. To improve the profitability of the division by organizing and coordinating the preparation of appropriate plans covering all operations of the division for approval by the divisional board followed by submission to the planning advisory committee and the general board, and subsequently to monitor the implementation of the plans within the division.

Main activities

2. Assists the managing director in setting divisional objectives, assumptions and policies for use as a basis for divisional plans.
3. Organizes the preparation and presentation of divisional plans to meet the objectives set by the general board and the divisional board for long-term growth and profitability.
4. Produces and provides a format and instructions for planning within the division, including the overseas companies, and a timetable to meet the dates set by the divisional board and the planning advisory committee.
5. Advises and assists in the preparation and presentation of plans for all UK operations and overseas companies.
6. Provides liaison and coordination to ensure the proper interaction of plans between:
   (a) individual functions of the division
   (b) other divisions and the division
   (c) group functions and the division
   (d) overseas companies and the division
7. Monitors the preparation to timetable of all divisional planning activities.
8. Advises the managing director as to the effectiveness of the division's UK operating plans for each of the division's functions in relation to group and divisional objectives.
9. Consolidates all the division's UK plans and produces a complete plan document approved by the managing director for presentation to the divisional board and, after amendment if required, to the planning advisory committee.
10. Receives, examines and comments on all overseas companies' plans to the managing director prior to presentation to the divisional board and the planning advisory committee.
11. Ensures, in conjunction with the managing director, that adequate procedures are drawn up and applied for the effective implementation of the plans.
12. Collaborates in all planning matters with group planning department.
13. Keeps abreast of developments in planning procedures and techniques, and ensures that, where appropriate, they are introduced and used.

Figure 22.3   Job description

plans, ideas as to their precise functions began to crystallize, and Fig. 22.3 gives the job description of one of the present divisional planning managers.

Review and approval procedures

At the outset, it was known that a timetable was needed to stimulate completion of the work on the long-term plans, but it was less clear how much time should be allowed. In practice, this was usually underestimated and the first corporate plan was presented to the planning advisory

369

committee eight months after agreement had been reached on the first planning instructions.

It would have been possible to have all corporate plans presented to headquarters at about the same time and therefore equally up to date, but imposing a common completion date would have ignored the varying degrees of readiness in the operating units, their very different sizes and the different complexities of their problems. Moreover, if all plans were to be presented by a common date, it might be impossible for the head office organization to consider them adequately and without delay. Consequently, each operating unit was asked what completion date would be most suitable for it, and this resulted in a timetable for presentation of the first plans spread over 15 months from September 1966 to January 1968. The system of staggered completion dates has continued in use for the second cycle of plans.

Between completion of a corporate plan by the operating unit and its discussion at the planning advisory committee, a process of analysis at the centre is necessary because the committee members to whom the plan is presented cannot have time for prolonged study of all its details. Ideally, this process of analysis should concentrate on the adequacy of the objectives as revealed by the plan, and the appropriateness of the policies and actions proposed to achieve them. The validity of any apparent underlying assumptions also needs checking. Such analysis has become more effective since the second cycle of plans has been received because it has been possible to compare them in detail with their predecessors. There are, of course, certain to be variations between the two, but the examination of any major changes can bring to light any controllable factors which may be having an adverse effect on the achievement of the long-term objectives of the organization. Discussion with the operating unit can then focus attention on those aspects of management where performance is disappointing. Completion of the plan document can then be followed by immediate action to put right certain weaknesses exposed, either by a change of policy or by the setting of personal managerial objectives to achieve changes in future, or by appointment of working parties to find solutions to the situations revealed.

Following its discussion of the long-term plans with the company concerned, the planning advisory committee is not in a position to give formal approval to them, but can indicate either broad agreement or advice that particular objectives or policies should usefully be followed or reconsidered. Subject to any major qualifications of that kind, the operating unit is expected to go ahead and implement its plan, and obtain approval for any capital projects via the normal board channels.

370

The group plan

The planning advisory committee obtains approval of the overall plans of the companies and group service departments by means of a consolidation for the general board. Responsibility for drafting this group plan for consideration by the PAC rests with the group planning adviser.

This document is partly analytical, and seeks to answer the questions: What do the plans mean in total? What would the group become if they are all achieved? Would the group achieve its overall objectives? What major policies would be necessary in the operating units, over and above any laid down at group level? What resources would be required? How would these compare with those likely to be available? Having analysed the position which would result from the plans of the operating units, the planning advisory committee considers any other major projects which it wishes the group to pursue. The addition of these 'strategic' projects provides a group picture in terms of available financial resources and their proposed utilization, both for the development of the existing businesses and for ventures into new fields, and the group plan is then ready for general board discussion.

From plans to action

The literature on formal long-term corporate planning puts great emphasis on the activity of planning and relatively little on the conversion of plans into action. Yet this requires as much, if not more, effort from the management of an organization.

No standard procedure has been laid down in the Pilkington Group to help bring this about, but one approach sees it as a five step process. The first step, the establishment of group and divisional objectives, is followed, as a second step, by the establishment of compatible functional objectives (marketing, production, technical, distribution, personnel, and financial) within each corporate plan. In the third step, each functional objective is broken down and apportioned among each manager reporting directly to the functional head. For example, a functional objective to reduce costs by x per cent of revenue to a lower percentage resolves itself into subsidiary objectives for cost improvement by each of the managers concerned. Fourth, each manager then has the task of devising an action programme designed to achieve his objective, agreeing this with his superior. This process is repeated down through the management hierarchy, seeking agreement of action programmes at each step. The fifth step involves the creation of financial budgets.

In this concept, the corporate plan sets out the functional objectives which, in total, are designed to achieve the corporate objectives. The feasibility of achieving the functional objectives will have been determined when compiling the plan, but the detailed programme of action remains to be

371

stated in terms of targets to be achieved by individuals. Those, in turn, can be expressed as lists of personal objectives defining the actions to be taken at specified dates in the future and the results anticipated. The annual departmental budget becomes an end-product showing in financial terms the resources required to achieve the manager's agreed objectives and the benefits expected to accrue from their achievement. Thus, the budget becomes the financial expression of the first year of the long-term plan.

Translating this concept of budgeting into a regular management activity is not easy, and in some organizations it may be thought best if preparation of the long-term plan and the budget are viewed as independent activities undertaken for different reasons. However, this very easily results in confusion, since it may not be clear to managers whether they are expected to implement the budget or the first year of the long-term plan. Worse still, the budget may simply represent the financial *status quo* and be unrelated to any programme of action, thus inhibiting progress towards the longer-term objectives.

In an attempt to avoid the budget 'floating unattached', one solution is to merge the two, so that the budget is the same as the financial data in the first year of the long-term plan. This eliminates confusion and avoids some duplication of effort, but has its own disadvantages. It requires that all long-term plans should be completed at the same date close to the start of the financial year. This does not necessarily result in good planning. Moreover, the system may stultify the planning effort because attention may be concentrated on writing down money figures which are almost certain to be achieved in the coming year rather than agreeing on longer-term objectives and programmes of action to achieve them.

In Pilkington, the tendency is to find a compromise solution whereby annual budgets are not abolished as a separate exercise, but neither are they divorced from the long-term plans. Budgets must be in line with the short-term objectives of the organization, but since they are prepared at a time of year different from the preparation of the long-term plan, unforeseen events outside our control will have occurred in the meantime. Thus, there are certain to be differences between the two sets of data for the coming year. However, before a budget can be approved, these differences must be identified and justified. If the variance from the first year of the long-term plan cannot be justified, the budget will have to be amended before it is finally approved.

From that stage onwards, the regular financial reporting system relative to the budget will serve as a vital check on performance. But this alone will not be adequate to help translate plans into action. There must also be, under the procedure for 'management by objectives', a regular review of the actions which managers have taken compared with those which they have previously agreed to take in support of the corporate plans.

372

In conclusion

As is well known, the benefits of formal long-term corporate planning are not easily measured because the exact situation in the absence of formal planning can only be guessed at. Nevertheless, during a three year period one needs to take one or two hard looks at the effectiveness of the system. One such 'look' was taken at the end of 1967, at which the planning personnel from all the divisions, at home and abroad, discussed the lessons learnt from the first planning procedures and broadly agreed on improvements needed in the second cycle. This year the opportunity is being taken to sound out the opinions of all the top management of the group companies as to the value of their planning efforts, and ways in which the system can be made more effective.

There will be differing views as to the best ways of approaching this, but some key questions suggest themselves. Do the operating companies receive adequate guidance on objectives and policies? Do the detailed planning instructions help managers to work together in devising their plans? Do the plan documents effectively communicate to the group what managers want to do? Is it clear to managers whether their plans are agreed? If they are agreed, can the long-term plans be used as a basis for decisions and action in the short term? And so on. Whatever the exact approach, those responsible for developing the system have a duty to be continuously critical of its workings, and ready to reshape it at intervals so that it becomes a more effective instrument of management.

Printed by William Clowes & Sons Limited, London, Colchester and Beccles